ROUTES OF
CHURCHILL'S WARTIME JOURNEYS

Moscow

Yalta

Teheran

Adana

Athens

CYPRUS

Alexandria

Cairo

CHURCHILL
as Warlord

1 *Churchill crosses the Rhine : behind him is Alanbrooke, with Montgomery on the right and Simpson on the left*

CHURCHILL

as Warlord

Ronald Lewin

'The great man of his age is the one who can put into words the will of his age, tell his age what its will is, and accomplish it. What he does is the heart and essence of his age; he actualises his age.'

Hegel

'I am perhaps the only man who passed through both the supreme cataclysms of recorded history in high executive office. Whereas however in the First World War I filled responsible but subordinate posts, I was in the second struggle with Germany for more than five years the head of His Majesty's Government.'

Winston Churchill, Preface to *The Second World War*

𝕊𝔇 STEIN AND DAY/*Publishers*/New York

First published in the United States of America in 1973
by Stein and Day/*Publishers*
Copyright © 1973 by Ronald Lewin
Library of Congress Catalog Card No. 72-96544

All rights reserved
Printed in Great Britain
Stein and Day/*Publishers*/7 East 48 Street, New York, N.Y. 10017
ISBN 0-8128-1560-2

For Sylvia
'I married and lived happily ever afterwards.'
Winston Churchill, *My Early Life*

Contents

List of Illustrations

Acknowledgments

'As for errors due to inaccuracy or ignorance, he hopes that they
are not so many as to lessen the delight of reading, or cause him
to be suspected of negligence. But he knows that they are likely to
be so numerous that he is afraid to make more than a general
acknowledgement of the assistance which many friends have
readily given him, lest they should be involved in the discredit of
his blunders.'

Robert Bridges, *The Spirit of Man*

Nevertheless, I must record my gratitude to Lieutenant-General Sir Ian Jacob
for his generous assistance over a long period, and for permission to quote from
his diary. Lady Liddell Hart kindly gave me access to the papers of her husband,
the late Captain Sir Basil Liddell Hart, and Lord Keyes to those of his father, the
late Admiral of the Fleet. To General Sir James Marshall-Cornwall, Major-
General Douglas Wimberley and Group Captain F. W. Winterbotham I owe
the benefit of their (as yet) unpublished autobiographies.

For further information, advice, insights and encouragement I am indebted
to Field Marshal Sir Claude Auchinleck, Brigadier R. G. S. Bidwell, Lord Blake,
Brigadier Michael Calvert, the late General Sir Miles Dempsey, Captain Charles
Drake, R.N., Major-General Sir Charles Dunphie, General Sir Richard Gale,
Dr Hugh L'Etang, the late Captain Sir Basil Liddell Hart, Major K. J. Macksey,
Sir John Masterman, Brigadier C. J. C. Molony, Vice-Admiral Sir Ian McGeoch,
Field Marshal the Viscount Montgomery, Admiral of the Fleet the Earl Mount-
batten, General Sir Richard O'Connor, Captain S W. Roskill, R.N., Marshal of
the R.A.F. Sir John Slessor, the Viscountess Slim, Lieutenant-General Sir
Arthur Smith, General Sir James Steele, Major-General John Strawson, the
Warden of Rhodes House, Oxford (Sir Trevor Williams) and Dr Gerald
Woolfson.

R.L.

The Author and Publisher would like to thank the Imperial War Museum for
their kind permission to use the photographs appearing in this book. The original
of the portrait of Churchill by Frank O. Salisbury, reproduced on the jacket, is
at Chartwell. The Author and Publishers are most grateful for permission to
reproduce it. Acknowledgment is made to the authors and publishers of the books
quoted in the text and listed in the Bibliography. Churchill's *The Second World
War* is published by Cassell & Co. and the British *Official Histories* by
H. M. Stationery Office.

The Stretching of a Bow

'Is not the way of heaven like the stretching of a bow? It is the way of heaven to take from what is in excess in order to make good what is deficient. . . . Who is there that can take what he himself has in excess and offer this to the empire?'

Lao Tzu

'I could not be reproached either for making the war or with want of making preparation for it. I thought I knew a good deal about it all, and I was sure I should not fail.'

Winston Churchill

In his essay on Churchill Lord Snow records an extraordinary observation by Lord Hankey. 'Once—I think it was in that same summer of 1943— he startled a group of us by remarking that whoever had been in power, Chamberlain, Churchill, Eden, anyone you liked to mention, the military position would now be *exactly the same*. Wars had their own rules, politicians didn't alter them, the armies would be in the same position to a mile.' In 1943 Hankey had good reasons for feeling dubious about Churchill, with whom his relationship, ever since Gallipoli, had been ambivalent. After doing the state outstanding service for many years, as Secretary of the Cabinet, he became a member of Chamberlain's wartime administration. But under Churchill his stature diminished—Chancellor of the Duchy of Lancaster, Paymaster-General, and then . . . the sack. Those who stress Churchill's magnanimity should read the letter from the Prime Minister in which Churchill gave Hankey his *congé*: it is peremptory, brief, brutal and uncompromising.* Still, Hankey was a man of strong principles and strong ideas, ideas deeply rooted in experience, and what he said in 1943 was probably based less on pique than on his profound and first-hand knowledge of what had happened in the First World War. So the question stands: is his Tolstoyan summary correct?

Surely not. The most cursory consideration of Chamberlain's conduct of the war from September 1939 to May 1940 reveals that he lacked the aptitudes essential both for the higher direction of his country's military effort and for the effective manipulation of those great alliances, with

* The original is in the Hankey Papers in the archives of Churchill College, Cambridge.

Russia and the U.S.A., in which good luck enmeshed Great Britain from 1941 onwards. It is, in fact, inconceivable that, had Chamberlain remained Prime Minister, the military position in 1943 would have been, as Hankey asserted, *exactly the same*. And had Halifax succeeded Chamberlain, instead of Churchill, it is indisputable that the war would have taken a different course. The availability of the Cabinet Papers for the latter 'thirties and the crucial year of 1940 has confirmed what was already evident, that Halifax also lacked qualities necessary for a leader in a final confrontation with Hitler and the *Reich*, even though, after Hitler occupied Czechoslovakia in March 1939, his mood changed from appeasement to something more militant.* Hankey was wrong. The shape and character of the war were radically affected by the way Churchill handled its direction—in matters both large and small. Its pattern bears his personal stamp.

But at 6 p.m. on 10 May 1940 when, as the Germans were flooding into Holland and Belgium, Churchill kissed hands and became Prime Minister he was already 65. His character was set, immutably, and his previous life-experience was vast. In politics his record begins with his unsuccessful contest of the Oldham by-election in July 1899. Thereafter he became Unionist M.P. for Oldham in October 1900; crossed, in 1904, to the Liberal benches; became Parliamentary Under-Secretary of State at the Colonial Office in 1905, President of the Board of Trade in 1908, Home Secretary in 1910, First Lord of the Admiralty from October 1911 to May 1915 and, until November, Chancellor of the Duchy of Lancaster. He returned as Minister of Munitions in 1917, Secretary of State for War and Air in 1919, Secretary of State for Air and the Colonies from February to April 1921 and, for the Colonies only, till October 1922. In 1924 he was Chancellor of the Exchequer under Baldwin, having crossed the floor of the House once more. At the outbreak of war, on 3 September 1939, he was again appointed First Lord of the Admiralty. And in the field of military affairs, as in the political, his experience was far-ranging and first-hand. Apart from all that he learned as a Service Minister he had observed and engaged in war in many theatres—as a spectator of the Cuban civil war in 1895; as an officer at the front with the Malakand Field Force on the N.W. Frontier of India in 1897 and during the Sudan campaign of 1898—when he rode with the 21st Lancers in their dramatic charge at Omdurman; as a war-correspondent and prisoner in the Boer War and in

* Yet he might so easily have followed Chamberlain: the majority of the Conservative party wanted him, Churchill declared that he would serve 'with or under anyone', and Attlee believed that Labour preferred Halifax, though the party would accept Churchill as an alternative.

1915–16, after the Gallipoli *débâcle*, as a battalion commander on the Western Front. Since his contribution to the higher conduct of the Second World War was so idiosyncratic it is therefore necessary to ask a preliminary question. What temperamental characteristics and what established attitudes of mind—deriving from this unique experience—were brought to bear by Churchill in May 1940 on his unenviable task? Both habit and personality affected the way he handled the war: what followed his appointment as Prime Minister cannot be properly understood without some comprehension of all that preceded it.

Churchill was a man of excess: indeed it may rightly be said of him, in Lao Tzu's terms, that between 1940 and 1945 he emerged as one able to 'take what he has in excess and offer this to the empire . . . in order to make good what is deficient'. He was excessive in emotion; in egocentricity; in physical and mental energy: excessive in his single-minded concentration on selected objectives. ('Excessive' is here used not in a pejorative sense, but to mean 'far above the average'). For a war leader these traits were at once a strength and a weakness, but they had been evident in Churchill's character since his earliest days and by 1940 nothing could change him. He remained what he then was. It is true that in his 66th year he had outgrown the haunting fears of his first manhood which led him to suppose that he was doomed, like his father, to a premature death, and that a lifetime's effort and achievement must be crammed into a niggardly span of time—a fantasy which accounts for much of that thrusting egoism noted by friends and enemies alike in the Churchill who made his way to the front bench at an early age and coruscated under Asquith's mantle. But it is also true that 1940 marked a re-emergence, for throughout the 'thirties he wandered in the political wilderness. De Gaulle described his own period out of office, from 1946 to 1958, as 'the crossing of the desert'. Churchill, when he acquired supreme power, was determined never to return to the desert, and also to prove beyond question that his belief in himself was justified and that he was eminently fitted for the highest office. During the Second World War, therefore, his egomania was far from being diminished: if anything it was intensified. The strength he drew from it was obvious: allied to his innate courage and pugnacity,*

* Glowering ferocity in the face of opposition, almost animal in its instinctive hostility, was a constant throughout Churchill's life. Colonel Richard Meinertzhagen was a schoolboy contemporary of Churchill's at Harrow. 'One day their paths crossed on the street. It was customary, under such conditions, for Harrow boys to contest the right of way, so Richard tried to cannon into Churchill, trying to force him into the gutter. He hit a body hard as iron and as he bounced off was treated to a glance from Churchill's deep-set eyes that he never forgot. It was neither victorious nor amused, merely a warning to keep off, but of a menacing intensity that Richard recognised later in the eyes of a wild boar about to charge him.'
John Lord, *Duty, Honour, Empire*, Hutchinson 1971

it sustained him—and enabled him to sustain others—in the darkest hour, and provided that confidence and dynamism which forced the war effort forward.

He believed, no less than Hitler, that he was one of Providence's chosen few: a man set apart, selected to rise above the ruck of humanity for the consummation of a pre-destined purpose. This was a note he often struck. In 1908 the Liberal Charles Masterman wrote to his wife:—'Winston swept me off to his cousin's house and I lay on his bed while he dressed and marched about the room, gesticulating and impetuous, pouring out all his hopes and plans and ambitions. He is full of the poor whom he has just discovered. He thinks he is called by Providence to do something for them. "Why have I always been kept safe within a hair's breadth of death," he asked, "except to do something like this?" ' And at midnight on 28 July 1914, as the lights were going out over Europe, Churchill wrote to his wife in a mood of introspection:—'Everything tends towards catastrophe and collapse. I am interested, geared up and happy. Is it not horrible to be built like this?' He felt precisely the same in 1940:—'I thought I knew a good deal about it all, and I was sure I should not fail.' Thirty years later, in fact, he was still that performer in a perpetual drama about whom A. G. Gardiner observed in 1908:—'He is always unconsciously playing a part— an heroic part. And he himself is his most astonished spectator. He sees himself moving through the smoke of battle—triumphant, terrible, his brow clothed with thunder, his legions looking to him for victory, and not looking in vain. He thinks of Napoleon*; he thinks of his great ancestor. Thus did they bear themselves; thus in this awful and rugged crisis will he bear himself. It is not make-believe, it is not insincerity; it is that in this fervid and picturesque imagination there are always great deeds afoot, with himself cast by destiny in the Agamemnon role.' Destiny, Providence: these are the recurrent themes.

But this strength of inner conviction was matched by a weakness. The sheer intensity of his self-absorption sometimes caused him to fail to notice a wood because he was utterly committed to a single tree. Over and over again, in his strategic appreciations during the Second World War, this flaw can be noticed. 'Sensible men concentrate on the essential', remarked Frederick the Great. It is no disparagement of Churchill's outstanding capacity to penetrate to the heart of a matter to say that sometimes his excessive concentration on the inessential led him, and his country, astray. Charles Masterman put the point well. 'In nearly every

---

* He had a large collection of Napoleana: 200 expensively bound volumes are now in the Bevin Library, Churchill College, Cambridge.

case an idea enters his head from the outside. It then rolls round the hollow of his brain, collecting strength like a snowball. Then, after whirling winds of *rhetoric*, he becomes convinced that he is *right*; and denounces everyone who criticises it. He is in the Greek sense a Rhetorician, the slave of words which his mind forms about ideas. He sets ideas to Rhetoric as musicians set theirs to music. And he can convince himself of almost every truth if it is once allowed thus to start on its wild career through his rhetorical machinery.' When Churchill was certain that he was right, *ruat coelum*, nothing could shake or distract him: an inflexibility which marred his war leadership as it did that of Hitler, and which his wife had in mind when she observed, in 1945, that 'Winston has always seen things in blinkers'.

This egocentric self-assurance was qualified and undermined by physical and psychological limitations. There was, for example, the well-attested fact of his intermittent phases of depression. Churchill appears to have been one of those mental types known as cyclothymic—oscillating periodically from a state of *angst*, gloom and uncertainty to one of an exhilaration sometimes euphoric. At its worst the depression could be desperate, inducing those moods which Churchill himself christened 'Black Dog'. And though Churchill's physical and moral courage could never be impugned, it was, as Lord Snow puts it, 'the highest kind of courage, the kind that exists superimposed on an active and anxious imagination.' 'When I read Moran's book,' Snow remarks, 'I found him noting that Churchill, though so brave, was also apprehensive—deliberately taking risky wartime airtrips, and then worrying about the chances of fire: anxious about all kinds of danger, and then running into them'. Moreover, his physical structure was wrong. Pudgy and Pickwickian, he had an almost epicene softness of skin and a notable economy of hair—though these frailties were counter-balanced by an iron constitution. (The young subaltern who steered his regimental team to victory in an important polo Cup Final with his right arm strapped to his side lived on in an elder statesman who endured more taxing and dangerous wartime flights than either his allies, Roosevelt and Stalin, or the dictators of Germany, Italy and Japan.)* It has, indeed, been suggested that because he had the wrong body for a Great Man the mental struggle to overcome his physical deficiencies was yet another factor intensifying his self-absorption. However that may be, it is clear that any assessment of Churchill as a war leader must take such imponderables into account—without exaggerating them; for has it not been observed that 'since 1908 eleven

* See endpaper map, 'Churchill's wartime journeys'.

out of thirteen British Premiers and six out of ten American Presidents have had illnesses while in office which have incapacitated them to some degree'?*

'Churchill is preoccupied by his own vivid world, and it is doubtful how far he has ever been aware of what actually goes on in the heads or hearts of others. He does not react, he acts; he does not mirror, he affects others and alters them to his own powerful measure.' Sir Isaiah Berlin, in his *Mr Churchill in 1940*, was drawing attention to another of Churchill's characteristic traits which, deriving directly from his self-absorption, was evident throughout the whole course of his career and perhaps particularly during the Second World War: his *remoteness*, his lack of empathy for others, his detachment from ordinary human affairs and his inability to grasp an alternative point of view. This took many forms. Sometimes it was expressed as an absolute lack of consideration: his staff at 10 Downing Street and in the Defence Office, for example, have more than once put on record the way he used them (aided, it must be said, by their ready connivance), with a total disregard for their personal convenience. Occasionally it was revealed as an ignorance of the facts of life. His Private Secretary John Colville says 'he was horrified when I told him I was going off to South Africa to train, starting in the ranks as an Aircraftman, 2nd Class. "You mustn't", he said, "you won't be able to take your man." It had not crossed his mind that one of his junior Private Secretaries, earning £350 per annum, might not have his own valet.' And long ago his close friend and acute observer the late Lady Asquith (Lady Violet Bonham Carter) noticed how, during the Indian summer of Edward VII's reign, 'At balls as elsewhere he was impervious to his surroundings, blind and deaf to the gyrating couples, the band, the jostling, sparkling throng. I remember once in a momentary lull directing his attention to the appearance of a friend of his who crossed our line of vision looking her very best. "Look—there goes X. Isn't she looking lovely tonight?" He looked at her, appraised her beauty and replied, "Yes—there goes X—a great woman—sagacious—chaste." This choice of epithets took my breath away. There were a hundred different adjectives which could with truth have been applied to X. But if one had scoured the dictionary with a tooth-comb it would have been impossible to discover three which less described her. She was neither "sagacious," "chaste" nor "great". Did he, I wondered, know any more about the human content of these people who belonged to his own world than about that of the Liberal rank and file?'

The imperviousness of a pachyderm was, of course, a considerable

* Hugh L'Etang, *The Pathology of Leadership.*

2 *1940. Warden of Britain*

3 *1943. Convalescing at Marrakesh*

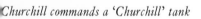

Churchill commands a 'Churchill' tank

5 *1942. Flying home from Bermuda*

asset. War is a hard master, as Thucydides declared, and the master in war must himself be hard. In the appointment and dismissal of subordinates, for example (political as well as military), Churchill was frequently to act with a cold objectivity which could seem to be callous but was often essential. And though he appears to have felt little malice towards the people of Germany (his initial acceptance of the Morgenthau plan for 'pastoralisation' can now be seen to have been a temporary aberration); though his acceptance of area bombing, with its predictable consequences of huge civilian casualties, was due more to his craving for offensive action than to crude motives of revenge; nevertheless his temperament was such that over the years he gradually shifted, in this respect, into a sort of disengaged inhumanity. In January 1941 he was much concerned about the probable fate of the Italian settlers in Abyssinia when 'those savage warriors who have been burned with poison gas get among them', but by 1943 he contemplated without reservation a policy of indiscriminate bombing of Italian cities, as an alternative to invasion of the peninsula. In March 1941 he said 'he was unmoved by bloodthirsty demands for the destruction of Germany. He would never condone atrocities against the German civilian population. The ancient Greeks, he remembered, once spared a city not because its inhabitants were men but because of the nature of man'. All the same, John Colville (whose words these are, and who speaks with the intimate awareness of a Private Secretary) confessed that 'it may be that as time went on, and the accumulated horrors of the war hardened all our hearts, he grew indifferent to the sufferings of the German cities'. 'I remember,' Colville has written, 'being surprised by the apparent equanimity with which he received an account of what befell Dresden in 1945'. In the great debate before D Day about the Interdiction Programme which was planned, by the bombing of appropriate centres, to disrupt decisively the road and rail communications feeding the Normandy front, it is doubtful whether Churchill's distaste for the project was wholly the result of his sympathy for the inevitable damage to the French civilian population. A more subtle fear was that the British, taking the larger part in the Interdiction Programme, might cause more resentment among the French people than the Americans, and that in the balance of influence which would have to be established after the liberation of France this might weigh heavily in the Americans' favour. Such pragmatism is the lot of the leader in total war.

Yet here, as so often, Churchill presents a paradox. The hard heart was soft at its core. Within definite limits the Prime Minister, like the Churchill of previous decades, could display warmth, consideration, loyalty

6 *Battle of Britain, 1940. Churchill in the mess of 615 Fighter Squadron, of which he was honorary Air Commodore*

and magnanimity in his dealings not only with individuals but also with larger groups, and even nations. The limits can easily be plotted. First there was his family: for those at the centre and indeed those on the fringe of this nexus of relationships he felt an unqualified affection and would spring instinctively, like the protective leader of a pack, to the defence of any threatened member. Then there was the 'Secret Circle', that small, hand-picked *élite* of Private Secretaries and other staff who provided the cocoon within which he nestled: unscrupulously though he used them, they were the first to recall his many acts of imaginative and unexpected kindness on their behalf. And when he bestowed his friendship—as he did but rarely—it was an absolute gift: none of the egregious errors of the first Earl of Birkenhead, for example, could budge Churchill from his commitment. For Eden he had almost a paternal regard. Such disparate characters as Beaverbrook and Lord Cherwell retained his firm support. These subjective loyalties, nevertheless, were sometimes the Achilles heel of the war leader: he was prone to make appointments rather because of long association with a man than because of the individual's aptitude for the job. He could not conceive that those whose gallantry and ability had impressed him in earlier wars might have retained their gallantry but not kept pace with his astonishing self. It was only the militant opposition of the Chiefs of Staff, for example, which prevented him in 1940 from elevating Admiral Sir Roger Keyes, the legendary hero of Zeebrugge, to the vital post of Chairman of the Chiefs of Staff Committee.* Alexander was a special case. For Churchill this was the *chevalier sans peur et sans reproche*: he could do no wrong. But it was a fantastic mis-judgement on Churchill's part, after the war, to withdraw Alexander from the Governor-generalship of Canada, where he was reasonably well placed, and to make him Minister of Defence, where he was utterly at sea. By contrast, if Churchill could not understand or feel affinity for a man he was doomed—this is well exemplified, for example, in his treatment of Wavell and Auchinleck, whose merits he never fully grasped: to a substantial degree, of course, because they themselves failed in a prime requirement—that of the Commander-in-Chief in the field to be articulate in his communications with his political master.

Yet in other spheres his antennae were far-reaching. Running through the famous minutes which are quoted in the appendices of *The Second*

---

* Even more astonishing was his offer, on 23 May 1940, of the post of General Officer Commanding, 'in control of all land, sea and air forces at home in the event of invasion', to Marshal of the R.A.F. Lord Trenchard. Trenchard, who had retired as Chief of Air Staff in 1929, was 67. He refused the offer on the grounds that the job could only be done properly by a Deputy Prime Minister—which infuriated Churchill.

World War is an unwavering theme—his compassion for the ordinary people of England, bombed, rationed, puzzled, vulnerable. This compassion—and his courage—are poignantly reflected in a passage in Ismay's *Memoirs.* In September 1940, after the first major air raid, Ismay conducted Churchill on a tour of inspection of the London docks.

Our first stop was at an air-raid shelter in which about forty persons had been killed and many more wounded by a direct hit, and we found a big crowd, male and female, young and old, but all seemingly very poor. One might have expected them to be resentful against the authorities responsible for their protection; but, as Churchill got out of his car, they literally mobbed him. 'Good old Winnie,' they cried, 'We thought you'd come and see us. We can take it. Give it 'em back.' Churchill broke down, and as I was struggling to get him through the crowd, I heard an old woman say, 'You see, he really cares; he's crying' . . . Ismay continues 'On and on we went until darkness began to fall. The dock authorities were anxious that Churchill should leave for home at once, but he was in one of his most obstinate moods and insisted that he wanted to see everything. Consequently, we were still within the brightly-lit target when the Luftwaffe arrived on the scene and the fireworks started. It was difficult to get a large car out of the area, owing to many of the streets being completely blocked by fallen houses, and as we were trying to turn in a very narrow space, a shower of incendiary bombs fell just in front of us. Churchill, feigning innocence, asked what they were. I replied that they were incendiaries, and that we were evidently in the middle of the bull's-eye!'

He had no knowledge of what it was like to be a man in the street, but his imagination could reach out to his countrymen *en masse.* Similarly, as has been seen, he could think of the German people without malice, however much, at times, he might appear unresponsive to their sufferings. Indeed, maliciousness was foreign to his nature. The tender and assiduous attention he paid to Chamberlain between the latter's resignation and his death must always be held in Churchill's honour. He found it difficult to kick a man when he was down, and he loathed witch-hunts. One of the very few recorded instances of an extreme acerbity is his vindictive snarl at General Monro who, dispatched to Gallipoli to replace Ian Hamilton, after a brief investigation sent back the telegram recommending evacuation. 'I should like him to starve,' said Churchill, 'to starve without a pension in a suburban hovel facing a red-brick wall.' 'You don't *mean* that,' said Lady Violet Bonham Carter. 'Yes I do mean it—that is how I want him to live to the end of his days—staring into a blank wall.'

Because Churchill led his country out of the fiery furnace of 1940 to the apparent triumphs of the VE and VJ days, and because, during those years, he marshalled his people in a firm phalanx behind him, there is a prevalent tendency to remember the period when his exercise of absolute power was universally accepted, and to overlook the fact that, when he grasped the reins of that power, in May 1940, he was operating from a very weak base. But this received idea is a fallacy. Few national leaders can have undertaken so daunting a responsibility with, at the outset, so tenuous and uncertain a support. His King and the majority of his party would have preferred Halifax. (When Churchill first entered the House of Commons as Prime Minister it was observed that Chamberlain was more loudly applauded by the Conservatives, and that it was the Labour benches which rose more readily to Churchill.) *The Times* could not stomach him. The country as a whole was prepared to accept him on trust, feeling instinctively that here was the man for a crisis, a man with Clemenceau's spirit: a confidence soon to be justified by the great fighting speeches of that summer and autumn. But in May 1940 Great Britain was not *sure* about Churchill. Why was this?

The British parliamentary system has generally required that a successful leader should be able to rely on a strong and loyal body of supporters—either because he has a vigorous backing in Parliament or because he represents some dominating 'interest' in the country, territorial, industrial, financial. Churchill was short on both counts. His trenchant criticism of Appeasement and, in longer term, his variegated political record had estranged him from the main *bloc* of Conservative opinion. He was still under his father's shadow, and there were too many other memories—the savage Edwardian assailant of the Naval Estimates who, as First Lord of the Admiralty, became overnight the chief exponent of naval expansion; the man who had twice changed his party; the sin-eater for the Gallipoli catastrophe; the intemperate and ineffectual opponent of Bolshevik Russia who also, in 1922, had appeared, by the part he played in the Chanak affair, to have brought Country and Empire to the verge of another world war; the controversial Chancellor of the Exchequer; the mordant censor of the Government of India Act; the lonely Cassandra of the 'thirties. 'Instability' was still the cry, echoing voices which had been heard at the beginning of the century—Alfred Lyttelton saying 'he trims his sails to every passing wind', Leo Maxse describing him as 'half alien and wholly undesirable', Bonar Law writing him off as a turn-coat. To instability was added the suggestion of senility. Already, in 1931, Harold Nicolson was entering in his diary 'A great round face like a blister. Incredibly aged. Looks like pictures of Lord Holland. An elder statesman. His spirits also have declined and he sighs that he has lost his old fighting power'. Palpably inexact, such comments nevertheless reflect a real mood. In any event the henchmen in the House of Commons on whom Churchill could rely were singularly few—Duncan Sandys, Brendan Bracken, and who else?—for although there were other critics of Chamberlain within the party they were loosely organised in two separate and distinct groupings under the banners of Eden and Amery. And even Churchill's backing within the Labour party was diminished by memory and suspicion. 'Troops at Tonypandy', however unjustified a myth, was still remembered, while his sustained partiality for Franco's side in the Spanish Civil War, not revoked until December 1938, hardly commended him to the many Socialists in Great Britain for whom this had been a traumatic experience.

Outside Westminster, moreover, Churchill had no roots. Of course he had a constituency: but during his long political career he had held several, he was not a true constituency M.P., and in any event a constituency is no firm base for a Premier. He had no broad territorial connections in the country, no cohort of squirearchy or block of trade unions behind him; and if he could be said to represent an 'interest' it was presumably that of 'men of good will' (a combination always amorphous and usually ill-organised), and of 'Imperialism'. Furthermore, on the eve of his appointment an episode occurred which called into question the stability and accuracy of his judgement: the Norwegian campaign. Chamberlain bore the brunt of criticism for this miscarriage—and rightly so: for as a Prime Minister who should have retained a firm grip on affairs he failed, over Norway, to set up that proper arrangement for the conduct of a Combined Operation which might have kept Churchill under control. But it was already obvious at the time, and has been conclusively proved since, that many of the major errors—errors in strategy and tactics, simple avoidable errors of organisation—were Churchill's fault. Hot-headed, muddled and interfering, the First Lord of the Admiralty seemed to have made a mess of things. And in Whitehall, as in Westminster, there were at first grave doubts about his reliability. Ismay, soon to become his faithful supporter, has registered in his autobiography the feeling of dismay which pervaded the Service staffs when Churchill's appointment was announced, and Colville is blunt about it. 'In May 1940 the mere thought of Churchill as Prime Minister sent a cold chill down the spines of the staff at 10 Downing Street. ... Our feelings at 10 Downing Street were widely shared in the Cabinet Offices, the Treasury and Whitehall.'

All these considerations deeply pre-occupied Churchill during his conduct of the war. They go far to explain the attention he devoted to the House of Commons, the meticulous fashion in which he sought to explain his actions and policies to his fellow M.P.s, and the nervousness he felt (for example during the summer of 1942) when it seemed that his command of Parliament was slipping. His procedural requirements—all his orders and instructions must be formally recorded *on paper*—and his continual emphasis on the correctness of his relationship with the Chiefs of Staff were part and parcel of a determination never to be found, unprotected, far out on a limb. He had fought his Wilderness Campaign in the 'thirties: never again. His activities must be covered in the eyes of his contemporaries and of posterity by a façade of propriety. This was less difficult for him because he so deeply revered the traditions of British democracy, and particularly of Parliament. He had no inclination, like Cromwell, to remove its bauble and send it packing. On the contrary, as another of his Private Secretaries, Sir John Martin, has written: 'throughout the war he was careful to preserve the authority of Parliament. At no time was Parliament's right of criticism restricted, and, if anything, he seemed oversensitive to parliamentary opinion, insisting on debates and votes of confidence even when it was clear that he enjoyed the support of the overwhelming majority.' Behind all this, of course, lay the wound of Gallipoli. Churchill learned much from, and never forgot, his rejection in 1915. In 1940 and thereafter he had no wish to become an Ishmael once again.

To mention Gallipoli is to remember that Churchill had more direct experience of warfare than any previous Prime Minister. Eden and Macmillan served with distinction as infantry officers on the Western Front, and Attlee at Gallipoli, but none of them compared with Churchill: nor did Hitler—for his military career, which earned him the Iron Cross Second Class in 1914 and the Iron Cross First Class in 1918, was restricted to the somewhat limited scope of a lance-corporal *Meldegänger*, or battalion runner, carrying messages from Company to Regimental Headquarters in the List Regiment. Churchill's battle experience was far more varied, and in it he always displayed a mixture of bravery and bravado. On 18 September 1897 he wrote from the North-West Frontier of India 'I rode on my grey pony all along the skirmish line where everyone else was lying down in cover. Foolish perhaps, but I play for high stakes and given an audience there is no act too daring or noble. Without a gallery, things are different'. This yearning for an audience could easily lead him to overplay his hand—as in his attempt to save Antwerp in October 1914, when he appeared on the scene in the uniform of Trinity House, reminded one witness of 'a scene in a melodrama where the hero dashes up bare-headed on a foam-flecked horse, and saves the heroine, or the old homestead, or the family fortune, as the case may be', and reduced the Cabinet to roars of laughter when Asquith read out to them his signal proposing that he should resign as First Lord of the Admiralty and take over the local command.

It was such indiscretions, too often repeated, which perpetuated the legend of his instability. Yet he was a true man at arms. After his resignation from the Government in November 1915 he departed immediately for France, where Sir John French offered him a Brigade. Churchill asked that he might first have some practical experience of the trenches. Frostily received by the Guards battalion to whom he was attached, he rapidly won their respect and was even offered by its Colonel the post of Second-in-Command: when he later took over a battalion of the Royal Scots Fusiliers his impact was vitalising. He had a genuine flair for soldiering, and an informed awareness of the working of the military mind. During both his periods of office at the Admiralty, moreover, he identified himself closely with the Navy, and was exceptional in his efforts to meet the serving officer. His interest in aviation was continuous. This reservoir of experience, knowledge and personal interest was invaluable to him as a war leader, perhaps the greatest benefit being that there never occurred, during the Second World War, that disastrous schism between politicians (the 'Frocks' of '14–18), and Service chiefs which hampered Britain's efficiency in the earlier conflict.

In certain important respects, however, Churchill was a prisoner of his own past. Though he was happily at home in a world of vast armies and air-fleets, and though he understood more percipiently than Hitler the nature and requirements of global warfare, he nevertheless had definite limitations of vision and attitude—the limitations of a cavalry officer educated in a series of campaigns which were the fag-end of the British imperial tradition. His military ethos was to a considerable degree that of pre-1914.* Though he had been one of the foster-parents of the tank, for example, he never fully comprehended the nature of modern armoured warfare or the technical restrictions within which an armoured commander had to operate. There were times when he truly seemed to be thinking of the tank as a horse. He was incapable, for example, of grasping that one could not disembark a Valentine or a Crusader or a Sherman at Suez and fling it straight into the battle-line: that mechanisms had to be adjusted to meet the special conditions of the desert, that tank-com-

---

* 'I found that Winston's tactical ideas had to some extent crystallised at the South African War, just as his ideas on India's political problems, as I discovered later, had not advanced much from his impressions as a subaltern in the nineties.' Note by Field Marshal Lord Wavell, quoted in John Connell, *Wavell, Scholar and Soldier*, p. 256.

manders had to assimilate new tactics, that navigation in a featureless landscape was an art to be patiently acquired—and that all this took time. His natural desire for action, in fact, sometimes ignored the military necessities. This certainly affected his relations with the Americans. As Kent Roberts Greenfield, Chief Historian of the Army, pointed out in the lectures on 'American Strategy in World War Two' which he delivered at Memphis State University in 1962, 'given our highly sub-divided system of mass-producing the complex and varied implements of modern warfare, it can be argued that the American military chiefs, far from being rigid theorists, were guided by practical sense in insisting on steadfast adherence to large and definitely scheduled objectives . . . when Mr. Churchill characterises our undeviating adherence to a cross-Channel attack on a given date in the spring of 1944 as typical of American mass-production thinking, this amounts to accusing the Americans of having a mass-production economy. The corollary of the British concept was elasticity, the seizure of opportunities as they arose, to take advantage of the enemy's weakness. The experience of TORCH should have been enough to show that this was no easy matter once a large force was committed and its massive structure of overseas bases and communications established. This was a fact that Mr. Churchill's restless imagination seems never to have grasped.'

Actually, Churchill did grasp the fact. He knew quite well that when anything like TORCH (the Anglo-American invasion of N.W. Africa) had started it could not be put into reverse: he rebelled, however, against being rushed into a major operation if there were good grounds for doubting its viability. Nevertheless, in spite of his intimate acquaintance with the Western Front in the First World War, where the zones behind the firing line were crammed with bases, stock-piles and every other kind of rearward installation, he pestered his commanders with complaints about the ratio of troops at the front to troops on the lines of communication, and he was always eager to demonstrate how what he considered to be a plethora of supply lorries could be cut down to provide more operational transport in the forward areas. On the very eve of D Day in 1944 Montgomery had an awkward confrontation with him about the proportion of administrative troops and vehicles to be carried over to France in the first waves of the invasion. Ismay also endured many lectures on the size of the 'tail' in the various theatres of war: but once, at least, he was able to hoist Churchill with his own petard, when in 1942 the latter was protesting about the huge quantity of vehicles being shipped to the Middle East. Ismay quietly reminded the Prime Minister of what he himself had written long ago, in *The River War*:—'Victory is the beautiful bright-coloured flower: transport is the stem without which it would never have blossomed.'

These blind spots were due far more to Churchill's cast of mind than to any lack of information or the opportunity to acquire it. During the 'thirties, when he was preaching about the resurgence of Nazi Germany and the imminent danger of war, he was certainly given access to some though not all relevant Government papers. The intermediary was his old friend the late Sir Desmond Morton, whose function on the staff of the Committee of Imperial Defence, from 1929 onwards, was to service it with facts about foreign re-armament. He was head of the Industrial Intelligence Centre, whose brief was 'to discover and report the plans for the manufacture of armaments and war stores in foreign countries'. Three Prime Ministers—Macdonald, Baldwin and Chamberlain—allowed him to feed Churchill with confidential matter. Another of Churchill's informants was the millionaire Canadian industrialist William Stephenson who, as head of the intelligence organisation in the U.S.A. known as B.S.C. (British Security Co-ordination), played an invaluable part, from 1940, in the integration of the Anglo-American war effort. But he drew on many other sources: there were plenty of people, at home and abroad, who were ready to aid and advise. And the Government itself (even if this was only an attempt to stifle the critic by enlisting him), was not unwilling to find a place for him in its cautious preparations for war—his membership of the Air Defence Research Committee is an instance. Yet in spite of his untiring efforts to equip himself with knowledge about his country's, and its potential enemy's, military preparations and plans, there were gaps. His ideas about the employment of armour are a particular case in point.

From the early 'twenties Churchill was in regular touch with Liddell Hart who, with General Fuller, was the foremost exponent of the armoured concept. The Churchill file in the Liddell Hart papers reveals that they exchanged correspondence from time to time; Liddell Hart would often send Churchill a copy of his latest book; and in 1938 Liddell Hart was appointed by Churchill as military adviser to the 'Focus' group, an occasional assembly of 'Mr. Winston Churchill and ten or twelve important people from various sides of national life', men and women of good will who met to discuss the developing crisis. Another pioneer of armour was General Hobart, who formed and trained the famous 7 Armoured Division and during the war (owing to Churchill's intervention on his behalf after the military establishment had discarded him), raised from scratch 11 Armoured Division, and 79 Armoured Division whose specialised armour made D Day possible. At some point during the 'thirties Hobart (who was Inspector of the Royal Tank Corps and commander of the only Tank Brigade) 'arranged what must be considered a clandestine meeting with Mr. Winston Churchill, as the latter endured his spell in the political wilderness. During a lengthy discussion Hobart put the facts of the deteriorating balance of tank power before Churchill, but it seems with only partial effect, for of the German breach of the Allied Front in 1940 Churchill later wrote: "I had seen a good deal of this sort of thing in the previous war, and the idea of the line being broken, even on a broad front, did not convey to my mind the appalling consequences that now flowed from it . . . I did not comprehend the violence of the revolution effected . . . I knew about it but it had not altered my inward convictions as it should have done." '*

Of those 'inward convictions' it must be clearly stated that no amount of criticism can diminish their ultimate and beneficial power. Churchill was, indeed, like Bunyan's Mr. Standfast who, as he passed through the waters to the Celestial City at the end of his pilgrim's journey, observed to his companions 'This river has been a terror to many, yea, the thoughts of it have often frightened me. But now methinks I stand easy, my foot is fixed upon that upon which the feet of the priests that bare the Ark of the Covenant stood, while Israel went over this Jordan'. It was precisely because Churchill was firmly anchored to his faith in Britain's destiny, utterly unshakeable in his inner certainties, that, at a time of terror to many, he himself was not frightened. Yet the very force of his convictions could sometimes sweep him into dangerous channels of thought.

Certainly he was suffering, when the war began, from many self-generated delusions. For all his intense efforts to understand he had mis-read the European panorama. His emotional aversion from the Republican Government's cause in the Spanish Civil War was an error. His romantic regard for *la gloire* of France blinded him to the fact that the country was rotten at heart, and its army commanded by men of straw. (Stalin was equally mistaken: but not Hitler.) And in his way (until the truth began to dawn as the war proceeded), he was as naive as Roosevelt in his failure to comprehend the true nature of the purposes of the Soviet Union. It was already becoming clear to some in the latter 'thirties—though not to Churchill—that the possibility of Stalin's *effective* co-operation during 1938/39, in a league to defeat Hitler, was a will-o'-the-wisp.

Deep among the 'inward convictions' lay his sense and interpretation of history. In a penetrating assessment of Churchill-the-historian Professor

* Kenneth Macksey, *Armoured Crusader*, p. 118.

Plumb has written* that 'History was the heart of his faith; it permeated everything which he touched, and it was the mainspring of his politics and the secret of his immense mastery. ... He is, perhaps, the last great practitioner of the historic theme of England's providential destiny'. (Here the theme of Providence emerges again: but it was not for nothing that as war approached Churchill advised that other *aficionado* of Providence, Hitler, to study English history and contemplate his doom.) Throughout the 'thirties Churchill had been immersed in history. He had published *My Early Life*, *The Eastern Front*, the four-volume *Life of Marlborough*; and he had written the greater part of *The History of the English-Speaking Peoples*, though the proofs had not been corrected when the war began and it was not, in fact, launched on its money-spinning career until 1956.

A study of these books tells one much about Churchill's conduct of the war. His concept of history was a fantasy. It was Whig. His *Marlborough* is prejudiced, inexact, inadequate in its reference to available sources: his *English-Speaking Peoples* is a fairy tale. No professional historian would turn to either as a text-book. And misinterpretation or ignorance of other historical facts could warp his judgement of military truths. 'For Churchill, the core of English history lay in the struggle of its gentlemen against the Crown for their liberties, and then, when these had been won, in the harmony with it on their forward march to wealth and Empire.' But this taught him nothing, for example, about the Far East, to whose realities he was almost as blind as Hitler about the U.S.A.: he never, until disaster struck, understood the importance of proper defensive arrangements for Singapore, though these were regularly on the *tapis* between the wars, and there was no reason why he should not have been alert.† And yet, in an important if imponderable sense, his intuitive *rapport* with the destinies of the Island Race, fortified by his amateur pre-occupation with its history, paid many dividends. Lacking both the limitations of the Little Englander and of the man with the short term view, Churchill could place the worst in a proper perspective. As Professor Plumb puts it: 'A less historically based statesman might easily have been unnerved by the collapse of France

---

* J. H. Plumb, 'The Historian', in *Churchill, Four Faces and the Man.*

† Churchill had considered the matter as far back as 1924. In the *Baldwin Papers* there is a long letter from Churchill to Baldwin in which he declared 'I do not believe there is the slightest chance of it' (war with Japan) 'in our lifetime. ... She cannot menace our vital security in any way.' This, dated 15/12/24, reflects the conventional wisdom of the day. But as Chancellor of the Exchequer he was fully abreast of the prolonged and impassioned debate in the Chiefs of Staff Committee over Singapore in 1925/1926, at the end of which Trenchard surrendered to Beatty and Cavan on the issue of fixed coastal guns as against defence by air power. See Andrew Boyle, *Trenchard*, p. 550 foll.

and the deep penetration of the German armies into Russia; but Churchill well knew that an encircling alliance had only temporarily failed in the previous three hundred years of European history and, short of a qualitative change in the balance of weapons, was unlikely to fail in 1941 or 1942.' Moreover, his unravelling of the politico-military web in which Marlborough was entangled stood him in good stead when he too had to manipulate a Grand Alliance. Indeed, had one to select a single paragraph as representing the quintessence of what Churchill derived from history, one could not do better than to quote this from his *Marlborough*:—a declaration of faith which was nobly echoed in his post-Dunkirk broadcasts and speeches. 'No dreamer, however romantic, however remote his dreams from reason, could have foreseen a surely approaching day when, by the formation of mighty coalitions and across the struggles of a generation, the noble colossus of France would lie prostrate in the dust, while the small island, beginning to gather to itself the empires of India and America, stripping France and Holland of their colonial possessions, would emerge victorious, mistress of the Mediterranean, the Narrow Seas, and the oceans. Aye, and carry forward with her, intact and enshrined, all that peculiar structure of law and liberty, all her own inheritance of learning and letters, which are today the treasure of the most powerful family in the human race.'

That quotation, so relevant in 1940, sharply underlines something central in Churchill's idea of history which, though he never formulated it in theoretical terms, had a most practical impact on his conduct of affairs: the notion that *what has happened once can happen again*. It is not by anything Churchill wrote in this connection that his interpretation of history can be gauged: it is by how he behaved. In the exciting days of his collaboration with Lord Fisher, for example, when Churchill was First Lord of the Admiralty at the beginning of the First World War, he, like Fisher, was deeply committed to the dubious project of a British naval penetration into the Baltic. As First Lord of the Admiralty in the Second World War, Admiral Sir Peter Gretton notes in his study of Churchill and the Royal Navy, *Former Naval Person*, 'His mind returned to the First War; and his first scheme, which he pursued with great determination, was for a sortie into the Baltic. . . . ' (Operation CATHERINE, as it was called, was hopelessly impractical.) Again, though it is no longer possible to believe in the *canard* that during the Second World War Churchill was determined to achieve a massive military intrusion into the Balkans, there is no doubt that his great concern with that area, his pressure for the seizure of islands in the Eastern Mediterranean, and his perennial conviction that Turkey must and could be drawn into the war all represented, at a conscious or sub-conscious level, a desire to see Gallipoli re-enacted. From this same source, also, from his feeling that history can be repeated, flowed frequent objurgations to his field commanders to remember former British successes which were the analogue of their own missions.

There is another important area of Churchill's mind which is illuminated by his historical writings. The *English-Speaking Peoples* eloquently describes the advance of the small island to imperial power, but it has little to say about the strongest roots of that power. The former President of the Board of Trade had neither a true understanding of, nor any kind of sympathy for, the industrial and technological bases of England's predominance. In his history military prowess is prominent: but where are the dark satanic mills? The Industrial Revolution might hardly have happened. Nor, compared with the soldiers and statesmen, do the scientists receive honourable mention. Newton, Faraday, Rutherford and their peers are either passed by in silence or thrown a few desultory words.

With such an outlook—romantic, aristocratic, philistine and unsophisticated—the astonishing thing is that in a war which was a *materialenschlacht*, sustained by mass production and scientific invention, Churchill found himself so much at home. Here, as elsewhere, he had his limitations. As Professor Greenfield has pointed out, he never fully grasped the correlation between strategy and industrial planning. Like Hitler he was fascinated by the by-products of science, but he never penetrated the scientific mentality. (This was cruelly revealed when in May 1944 the great physicist Niels Bohr came to see him to try to warn him about the implications of the atom bomb. There was a complete failure of inter-communication: Bohr said afterwards that 'we did not speak the same language', and Churchill even went so far as to write to Lord Cherwell 'What is all this about? It seems to me Bohr ought to be confined or at any rate made to see that he is very near the edge of mortal crimes'. This was one of the rare occasions when Churchill verged on Hitler's paranoia.) There were indeed times—particularly during the autumn of 1940—when many leading personalities were gravely concerned about the direction of the nation's scientific war effort. But, when all is said, it was under Churchill's aegis, and to a considerable degree because of his grasp of what was necessary, that Great Britain was outstanding in scientific research and in the effective application of discoveries to military purposes—outstanding far beyond the achievement of Germany.

The study of history and his enormous experience of affairs taught Churchill another truth: the leader must be decisive. He once said that to govern is to choose. It was a lesson easy to learn, since his whole nature, energetic, imperious, self-assured, responded instinctively to the challenge of command. Lord Balfour once heard him observe of his service on the Western Front that it gave 'opportunity for calm reflection'—a characteristic paradox—and remarked that Churchill was 'like the Duke of Marlborough—most master of himself amid the din of battle'. Without this ability to accept the responsibility of decision, life-or-death decision, he would never have been able to fulfil so triumphantly the function of a War Lord. Yet like Churchill's other great gifts this one also was qualified by a weakness: he interfered too much. He must impose his will. Whatever the level of subordination—Chiefs of Staff, Commanders-in-Chief in the field, executives on a lower grade—they all felt his probing finger and heard his hectoring voice. Often this relentless urge to supervise and intrude was of the greatest value, but there were times when he was wrong: times when those affected were driven to fury. One of the most powerful factors contributing to Churchill's fall over the Gallipoli issue was the feeling in the Navy that his interference had been disastrous. During his second period as First Lord he displayed the same tendencies—most noticeably over Norway. The habit would continue until the end. Its dimensions, however, can only be adequately assessed if it is seen in a true perspective. Churchill harried, interfered, over-ruled, dictated: persistently and unashamedly. But in his lectures on 'American Strategy in World War Two' Professor Greenfield lists over twenty *major* occasions when Roosevelt took decisions 'against the advice, or over the protests, of his military advisers'. The record of Hitler and Stalin in this respect is notorious—and at least none of Churchill's commanders was imprisoned or executed. Nor did Churchill commit Hitler's error of taking over direct command of armies in action, with the consequence that the Head of State was personally associated with the fortunes of his troops and stigmatised for military disasters which otherwise would have been attributed to his senior commanders.

Churchill's disqualifications as a war lord were manifold—disqualifications both intellectual and temperamental. It is only sensible to acknowledge and list them before attempting an assessment of his performance in that rôle, for he succeeded in spite of them. Hitler's defects of character were of fundamental significance: Churchill's peripheral. The flaws did not penetrate to the central core of his strength. And he had other considerable assets. When he took up his task as Prime Minister he came to it with clean hands: even in the eyes of his critics he was free from the taint of appeasement. Moreover, by comparison with Roosevelt or the dictators he enjoyed another huge advantage. The world was his oyster. He could travel freely within it, moving, as he magisterially required, wherever he thought necessary. Because of his special position the President of the United States was never able, like Churchill, to dart about continents in impromptu efforts to untie Gordian knots. (Hitler, of course, clung more and more to his command posts, while Stalin was immured in Moscow.) And there was another benefit for Churchill the War Lord. His constitutional rôle did not prevent him from visiting the scene of action.* In the fighter control rooms in 1940, in the Egyptian desert, at the triumphal march past at Tripoli, on the Normandy beaches, off the coast of southern France and at the crossing of the Rhine his visible presence was an inspiration to the man at the front. Hitler controlled his war by *mystique* and, like Stalin, by fear: Churchill, by affection.

His performance passed an acid test. His Chiefs of Staff were professionals of exceptional calibre. None was puny or pusillanimous. Yet Pound only left his post because of death and Dill because of exhaustion: Alanbrooke, Portal and Cunningham remained steadfast to the end. They may have disagreed with many of Churchill's ideas; they may have been infuriated by his quirks; and each was capable of resigning over a principle. None did. Churchill was a man they could live with, a man to serve. Whatever their differences he retained their admiration and, more importantly, their respect. They were a different team from Hitler's entourage—the subservient lackeys, Keitel, Halder, Jodl, Zeitzler, and the transient subordinates, their opinions disregarded, uncertain of their tenure, their very lives dependent on a master's whim. And there is an even simpler test: Britain survived. To achieve this was Churchill's unwritten mandate in May 1940. Perhaps Stalin won the peace: but that was beyond Churchill's power, or Britain's, to prevent.

The theme of this opening chapter is vividly summarised in the words with which Lord Normanbrook, who served in the Cabinet Secretariat from 1941 to 1946 and as Secretary to the Cabinet from 1947 to 1962, prefaced his essay on the Prime Minister.† 'Walter Bagehot, in contrasting the British constitution with that of the United States, said of the former that it has this advantage that in a sudden emergency the British people can choose a ruler for the occasion. "It is quite possible," he wrote, "and even likely that he would not be ruler before the occasion. The great

---

* 'Unfortunately as the war went on Hitler visited the front less and less frequently, and in the final stages not at all. By so doing he lost contact with the feelings of the troops and was no longer able to understand their feelings and sufferings.'

Guderian, *Panzer Leader*

† In *Action This Day*.

qualities, the imperious will, the rapid energy, the eager nature fit for a great crisis are not required—are impediments in common times. . . . But by the structure of the world we often want, at the sudden occurrence of a grave tempest, to change the helmsman—to replace the pilot of the calm by the pilot of the storm." '

2

An Iron Peg 1940

'Who knoweth not of the great preparations our potent and
malicious adversaries did make (nay do make) against us, in-
tending the bloody conquest of our country, the servile thraldom
of our people, a rooting out of our name and nation . . . when all
our neighbour countries round about us have been infested with
bloody wars and massacres, blood streaming in their streets, with
civil dissensions and foreign invasions?'

Sir John Croke, 1598

'The impression I had of Tudor was of an iron peg hammered
into the frozen ground, immovable. And so indeed it proved.'
Winston Churchill in *The World Crisis*,
describing General Tudor, commander of the 9th Division, on
the eve of the great German offensive of 21 March 1918. The 9th
Division held fast: so, in 1940, during the Battle for Britain, did
Churchill.

Churchill's most laudable victory in 1940 was the conquest of himself. No
previous Prime Minister in British history attained so complete an ascendancy not only over people and Parliament, not only over the armed
services of the Crown, but also over the means of communication which, in
modern societies, had already proved to be the key to supreme power.
Hitler, Stalin and Mussolini were the exemplars. As the months dragged
by, as crisis followed crisis, and as Churchill's charisma persuaded the
sceptical military chiefs, the cynical Civil Service, the uncertain House of
Commons and the baffled man in the street that he, and he alone, was
capable of extracting the country from disaster, there seemed little to
prevent the emergence of a latter-day Cromwell. Churchill's personal
position, certainly by the winter, was even more secure than that of
Hitler during the 'thirties, for it was based on firmer foundations. And yet,
as Sir Isaiah Berlin rightly observed in his *Mr. Churchill in 1940*, 'This is
the kind of means by which dictators and demagogues transform peaceful
populations into marching armies; it was Mr. Churchill's unique and
unforgettable achievement that he created this necessary illusion within
the framework of a free system without destroying it or even twisting it.'
When on 19 August 1945 the three Chiefs of Staff drove together 'in a
landau pulled by four bays in the King's procession to St. Paul's', to attend

the Thanksgiving Service for Victory, their journey in a single carriage symbolised a unity-in-trinity, a brotherhood within the High Command which Churchill had fostered rather than fragmented: and when, in July of that year, the voters rejected Churchill in favour of Attlee, the election symbolised the working of a democratic process which, during the war years, Churchill had not only defended but preserved.

From the start he was fully aware of the inherent advantages of his office. 'Power in a national crisis, when a man believes he knows what orders should be given, is a blessing. . . . The loyalties which centre upon number one are enormous. If he trips he must be sustained. If he makes mistakes they must be covered. If he sleeps he must not be wantonly disturbed. If he is no good he must be pole-axed.' Churchill was sure he knew what should be done: and if one takes the first phase of his administration, from 10 May to 15 September (the climacteric of the Battle of Britain), it may be said that more orders were issued from the top than in any comparable period of intensive direction by a single man—and more effective orders. Neither Lloyd George's elevation to the premiership in December 1915 nor Roosevelt's declaration of a New Deal was followed by a sequence of *diktats*, appointments, reorganisations, exhortations and inventions so varied, so confident, and so well-judged. Kennedy's 'Hundred Days' are not of the same order. In a similar period of crisis neither Stalin after BARBAROSSA nor the French Government after the initial disasters of 1914 acted with an equivalent energy or relevance.

Of the many tasks which immediately faced Churchill five had priority —to keep France in the fight; to form a government; to instruct and inspire the British people, and by so doing to assure Hitler and the world of Britain's determination; to create an effective system for High Command in war; and to inveigle the United States more deeply into the conflict by the exercise of example and persuasion. Of these the first was beyond his power, the second presented few difficulties, and the third was managed triumphantly: in the long term, it was Churchill's dexterous and far-sighted handling of the fourth and fifth of his problems which proved the most constructive. His efforts to overcome them must now be examined in this sequence of priority, for it was at this time that he established his predominance and laid the foundations of his war direction.

During the first days of his premiership Churchill continued to work from his old rooms in the Admiralty—courteously allowing Chamberlain a month for his departure from No. 10 Downing Street. From the first, therefore, he was surrounded by memories of decision and action, of making war: for was it not in this same building that he and Fisher had plotted the combinations which led to victory at the Falklands? Was it not here that the great drama of the Dardanelles campaign had been contrived? And here, too, in recent weeks, he had been brooding on another invasion in a longer perspective: for during his reign as First Lord he was accustomed, from time to time, to work over the chapters of his *English-speaking Peoples*. F. W. Deakin (the Oxford historian who assisted him in his researches, and was later to serve with distinction as British representative with Tito), recalls how, in the midst of the Norwegian affair, 'Naval signals waited attention, admirals tapped impatiently on the door of the First Lord's room, while on one occasion talk inside ranged round the spreading shadows of the Norman invasion and the figure of Edward the Confessor . . . I can still see the map on the wall, with the disposition of the British Fleet off Norway, and hear the voice of the First Lord as he grasped with his usual insight the strategic position in 1066.'* Then, as throughout the war, the shadow of history was close to Churchill's shoulder: it is impossible to appreciate his military concepts and conduct without realising that this was always so and that, for him, contact with the past had an organic relationship far different from Hitler's brooding over Frederick the Great, or Stalin's extempore re-vivification of Russia's ancient heroes.

The Battle of France was lost before it began. As he faced it on 10 May Churchill might well have quoted to himself Foch's remark at the Doullens conference of 26 March 1918, when in the midst of another catastrophic German breakthrough he was appointed Supreme Commander. 'It is a hard task you offer me now: a compromised situation, a crumbling front, an adverse battle in full progress.' The situation was compromised by many factors, of which the immediate and salient one was the French insistence on, and British acceptance of, Plan D. (It is clear that, while in retrospect Churchill criticised the Chamberlain government and its military advisers for accepting the Plan, in spite of grave doubts as to its viability, he too was ignorant about its real implications, just as he was powerless to influence its implementation or, in the event, to avert its consequences. 'At the moment in the evening of May 10 when I became responsible no fresh decision about meeting the German invasion of the Low Countries was required from me or from my colleagues in the new and still unformed Administration.') Once Plan D became operative: once the Allied Northern Group of Armies dashed forward into Belgium, and

* F. W. Deakin. *Churchill the Historian*, the third Winston Churchill memorial lecture, given in the University of Basel, 10 January 1969.

once the irresistible German armoured assault through the Ardennes penetrated and destroyed General Corap's Ninth French Army, the situation was irrecoverable—irrecoverable in the sense that it might conceivably have been countered by the devotion of the fighting man and the generalship of Joffre which, in 1914, prevented disaster, but could not possibly be restored by the disheartened troops and nerveless commanders who represented, in 1940, the French inheritance from two decades of decay. The dykes had burst, and Churchill could only endeavour to resist the inevitable.

Nevertheless, like Foch in 1918 he replied to the offer of a hard task with 'I accept'. His endeavours may be summarised as an attempt, at the military level, to grapple with the consequences of a German capability and a French incompetence which he himself had failed to foresee: at the political, an unremitting effort to inject his own will to survive into the minds of the French government. A political collapse must, of course, involve military defeat, and to that extent Churchill's effort was pragmatic. But there was a larger issue, not always understood by those who criticise his military interventions. Churchill was seeking to sustain not only France the ally, France whose armies could alone provide a mass to block the German thrusts, but also the France of the centuries, France the flower of civilisation. His actions during the weeks of May and June 1940 must be interpreted with an awareness that he was tortured by intolerable dilemmas: by the brutal demands of military necessity on the one hand and, on the other, by deeper compulsions. When on 16 May he signalled from the Quai d' Orsay to the Cabinet in London, with reference to French appeals for more fighter support. 'It would not be good historically if their requests were denied and their ruin resulted,' he was speaking as a statesman, conscious of far more than fell within the narrower ambit of a Minister of Defence.

Churchill made five flights to France, sometimes at considerable risk. On 16 May he visited Paris, having been told by Reynaud of the breakthrough at Sedan and that already 'the battle was lost'; on 22 May he was at the H.Q. of the French Supreme Commander in the Château de Vincennes; on 31 May he was back in Paris; on 11 June the Supreme War Council met at Briare on the Loire; and finally, on 12 June, at a conference in Tours, it became clear to him that the French capitulation, announced on the 17th, was imminent. The misery and the pathos of these ventures are vividly described in the memoirs of Churchill himself, of Ismay (who accompanied him), and of General Spears (his personal representative with the French Prime Minister). He pulled out every stop: inspired oratory, bad French,* offers of British aid, signals to President Roosevelt, even the famous offer of a 'Declaration of Union' between the two countries (which was not, as is sometimes supposed, Churchill's own brainchild: nor had it his wholehearted support). But this single-handed effort to preserve the integrity of France was, and was bound to be, fruitless.

The *fainéant* Gamelin, the shrivelled husk of Weygand, Pétain (whose pessimistic chauvinism, so evident in the dark hours of 1918, had only intensified with the years), and Reynaud himself, resilient, patriotic, but eroded by the defeatism of his entourage and his importunate mistress— these were not, like Churchill, men to match the hour. Even General de Gaulle, it is now clear, had not yet attained this stature in Churchill's eyes: for though he recalled addressing him at the conclusion of the Tours conference as *l'homme du destin* the record is definite that when de Gaulle finally escaped to England Churchill was deeply disappointed at not receiving a figure-head of more evident authority. It was characteristic, however, that during this intense crisis he could not restrain that *penchant* for the minute particulars of military operations which would sometimes amaze, and more often infuriate, his advisers and commanders throughout the war. His message to Reynaud of 21 May, for example, must be one of the most remarkable communications ever dispatched from one Prime Minister to another. 'It is not possible to stop columns of tanks from piercing thin lines and penetrating deeply. All ideas of stopping holes and hemming in these intruders are vicious. Principle should be, on the contrary, to punch holes. Undue importance should not be attached to the arrival of a few tanks at any particular point. What can they do if they enter a town? Towns should be held with riflemen, and tank personnel should be fired upon should they attempt to leave vehicles. If they cannot get food or drink or petrol, they can only make a mess and depart. Where possible, buildings should be blown down upon them. . . . ' In retrospect this seems ridiculous, and *c'est rigolo* must certainly have been Reynaud's reaction: but such a judgement is superficial. It was his over-mastering passion to get things right, his probing down to the finest detail, his refusal to be prevented by protocol, personalities or the fear of appearing foolish which enabled Churchill the War Lord to keep his fingers on the

---

* This was no novelty. When Churchill made his controversial visit to Antwerp in October 1914 his purpose was to prevent the Belgian command from removing their troops from the city. On 3 October Asquith wrote to his *confidante*, Venetia Stanley: '. . . the intrepid Winston set off at midnight and ought to have reached Antwerp by about 9 this morning. He will go straightway and beard the King and his Ministers, and try to infuse into their backbones the necessary quantity of starch . . . I don't know how fluent he is in French, but if he was able to do himself justice in a foreign tongue, the Belges will have listened to a discourse the like to which they have never heard before.'

pulses. The benefits of a constant surveillance far out-weighed the many occasions when his queries or exhortations were childish, petulant or ill-considered; the stimulus for his subordinates counted for far more than his intemperate browbeating and not infrequent injustice.

As for the military situation, Churchill realised the rot in his inheritance at his very first meeting with the French High Command, in the Quai d'Orsay at 5.30 p.m. on 16 May. It was here that he saw the true significance of a *Blitzkrieg*. Gamelin, the Commander-in-Chief, reported.

> The General talked perhaps five minutes without anyone saying a word. When he stopped there was a considerable silence. I then asked: 'Where is the strategic reserve?' and, breaking into French, which I used indifferently (in every sense): '*Ou est la masse de manoeuvre?*' General Gamelin turned to me and, with a shake of the head and a shrug, said: '*Aucune*'.

> There was another long pause. Outside in the garden of the Quai d'Orsay clouds of smoke arose from large bonfires, and I saw from the window venerable officials pushing wheelbarrows of archives on to them. Already therefore the evacuation of Paris was being prepared.

> Past experience carries with its advantages the drawback that things never happen the same way again. Otherwise I suppose life would be too easy. After all, we had often had our fronts broken before; always we had been able to pull things together and wear down the momentum of the assault. But here were two new factors that I had never expected to have to face. First, the overrunning of the whole of the communications and countryside by an irresistible incursion of armoured vehicles, and secondly NO STRATEGIC RESERVE. '*Aucune*.' . . . What was the Maginot Line for? It should have economised troops upon a large sector of the frontier, not only offering many sally-ports for local counter-strokes, but also enabling large forces to be held in reserve; and this is the only way these things can be done. But now there was no reserve. I admit this was one of the greatest surprises I have had in my life.

Remembering the Marne, Cambrai, the spring offensive of 1918, he thought it obvious that the correct response to the Germans' irruption on a relatively narrow front should be a counter-attack on its flanks. One of his first questions to Gamelin was: 'When and where are you going to counter-attack the flanks of the Bulge? From the north or from the south?' But such ideas were otiose. Gamelin's Order No. 12 (issued on 19 May, instructing the Northern Armies to drive southwards through the Panzers endangering their communications), was never executed, and Gamelin was sacked. His replacement, Weygand, was equally dilatory and equally ineffective. No significant counter-moves occurred. During these vital days, however, Churchill in London brought immense pressure to bear on Gort in France, as he sought to compel the C.-in-C. to switch the B.E.F.

into a southward attack which might cut off the Germans by meeting the northward-moving French. The French of course, never performed their part in Churchill's dream. It cannot be denied, however, that the Prime Minister's pressure on Gort was ill-advised and might even have been disastrous. If Gort had loyally attempted the 'attack in the south', which he knew to be impossible, the fighting troops of the B.E.F. might never have reached Dunkirk. At one point Churchill even intended to visit France himself to force Gort on: luckily he was unable to leave London, and Ironside, whom he sent in his place, was compelled to face the realities.

The military moves which Churchill tried to impose by his interference were ill-judged. Before that interference is absolutely condemned, however, it should be remembered not only that he was frantic to keep the fight alive but also that until a few weeks ago he had been accustomed, as First Lord of the Admiralty, to the issuing of operational orders *direct* to the Fleet at sea—a questionable but hallowed Admiralty practice. Moreover, at this stage of the war he was not yet reined in by a trusted or indeed a competent C.I.G.S.

The truth was that neither Churchill nor anyone else in London appreciated the extent of the French collapse. A perfect example of how they were blinded occurred on the 23rd. 'Weygand came on the line with the totally false information that a re-formed French 7th Army under General Priére had started its northward assault and had already captured Amiens, Albert and Péronne. There was no reason to doubt Weygand's report and gloom gave way to elation. The Germans must have shot their bolt; perhaps the Miracle of the Marne, that historical parallel of which everybody had been day-dreaming, was really going to be repeated.'* Yet Churchill was not without information and wise advice. He had sent his old and trusted friend Admiral Sir Roger Keyes to act as his personal representative with King Leopold, the Commander-in-Chief of the Belgian forces in the field. A detailed contemporary record exists in the Keyes archives of how Sir Roger, in signals and direct conversations with Churchill on the cross-channel telephone, strove to enlighten him about the true situation on the northern front and the grave danger of the southward offensive about which he was so passionate.

Churchill struggled hard to make Reynaud energise his armies: the best that the British could do, however, was to take the strain against the German thrust and launch their minor armoured attack at Arras. The Belgian capitulation, following the sudden, complete and unexpected

---

* J. R. Colville, *Man of Valour : the life of Field Marshal the Viscount Gort*, p. 213. Colville was Churchill's private secretary at the time.

collapse of the French, produced its inevitable consequences, and Churchill could only endorse the War Office telegram dispatched to Gort on 27 May which ordered him 'to evacuate the maximum force possible'. This was one of the occasions when his magnanimity was found wanting. In a broadcast Reynaud made the Belgian King Leopold the scapegoat for France's failure. Churchill's connivance, under French pressure, in this sorry act of character-destruction can only be excused by his readiness to do anything to keep France (and Britain) in the fight.

After the decision to 'Dunkirk' had been taken, a further question had to be answered. Should the British abandon the French, and withdraw behind the moat of the Channel? Churchill's decision, supported by his Chiefs of Staff, to send back to western France such troops as could be scratched together and, as he bravely put it in a minute to Ismay on 2 June, to 'reconstitute the B.E.F.', was criticised at the time and has been subsequently condemned. It was certainly not welcomed by Alan Brooke* who, having brilliantly commanded a Corps until Dunkirk, was now appointed to rally the British rump in western France, and knew that, militarily speaking, his mission was hopeless. But Churchill was correct. The French had been defeated, but they were not *absolutely* finished. The French fleet must, if possible, be preserved. And there were larger, long-term issues. Had Britain then washed her hands of France, would Roosevelt's difficult task not have been rendered impossible? Would Lend-Lease, for example, have been contrived so soon? France in June 1940 was even more important than Greece in 1941. Dogged loyalty to an ally was at that moment as necessary a symbol of Britain's determination to fight tooth and nail as was her readiness, a little later, to undertake the ruthless neutralisation of the French fleet.

But when the Battle of Britain followed it was evident that what had happened in France was not so vital as what had not happened. The metropolitan fighter squadrons of the R.A.F. had been employed generously; their strength had been pared to the bone; but enough had been held back to make possible the hair's-breadth defeat of the *Luftwaffe* in the autumn of 1940. Yet the myth about the part Churchill played which has been propagated in books, newspaper articles and broadcasts is inaccurate and unjust. It has called into question both the reliability of his judgement and his sense of responsibility as a Prime Minister.

The controversy revolves around the events at 10 Downing Street on 15 May. The received idea is that at a Cabinet meeting Dowding, the Commander-in-Chief, Fighter Command, made an impassioned plea that

---

* Hereafter referred to by his later title of Alanbrooke, by which he is more generally known.

not a single further Hurricane should be sent to France and, in the face of an angry Prime Minister determined to squander his precious squadrons beyond the Channel, won the day, even though he lacked the support of the Air Staff and the Secretary of State for Air.* As A. J. P. Taylor puts it in a dramatic footnote to his *English History 1914–1945*: 'When argument failed, Dowding laid down his pencil on the cabinet table. This gentle gesture was a warning of immeasurable significance. The war cabinet cringed, and Dowding's pencil won the battle of Britain.'† The facts are different: they are founded on the carefully checked recollections of Lieut.-General Sir Ian Jacob, one of the few people alive who was present at No. 10 that day,‡ and on the Cabinet Papers for 1940.

The Air Staff was fully alert to the dangers of running down the metropolitan fighter force. Already, on 13 May, both the Secretary of State for Air and the Chief of Air Staff had urged that no more fighters should be sent to France. Churchill was not seeking to squander Fighter Command, or playing fast and loose, as a Prime Minister, with the vital interests of his country: he was feeling for an acceptable number of aircraft which might fit his dual responsibility both to France and to Britain—and never succumbed thereafter to French clamour for further support. Only ten extra squadrons were committed, on that and the next day, and of these six only operated from airfields in southern England. The argument continued, in fact, until as late as 4 June, but at no time was Churchill seeking to destroy Fighter Command. Indeed, on 3 June he asked the Chiefs of Staff to review the situation, but particularly specified that there should be no drain on Fighter Command which would be harmful to the air defence of Great Britain. The unresolved mystery in this episode is Churchill's conviction, re-iterated in his memoirs, that Dowding had told him that Britain's minimum requirement for home defence was only 25 squadrons. Nothing supports this mis-conception, whereas there is abundant evidence to show that both Dowding and the Air Staff had tabled a much larger figure. Still, neither Churchill nor his Cabinet cringed. (Nor was any cringing implicit in the decision on 15 May to send 99 aircraft that night to bomb the Ruhr—the first act in the Strategic Bomber Offensive.)

---

* See Robert Wright, *Dowding and the Battle of Britain*, for an extreme expression of this idea.
† A. J. P. Taylor, *English History 1915–1945*, p. 485.
‡ Private communication. Sir Ian is also certain that Dowding's *démarche* occurred not at the meeting of the War Cabinet, which started at 11.30 a.m., but at the preliminary meeting of the Chiefs of Staff (with Churchill in the chair), which began at 10.15. He heard Dowding's statement. He was present at the meeting of the Chiefs of Staff, but absent from the session of the War Cabinet.

'My experiences in those first days were peculiar,' Churchill recalled. 'One lived with the battle, upon which all thoughts were centred, and about which nothing could be done. All the time there was the Government to form and the gentlemen to see and the party balances to be adjusted.' But no time was wasted in assembling the Coalition. By 15 May the 34 members of the War Cabinet, and Ministers of Cabinet rank, had all been appointed. Only the War Cabinet had overall responsibility, the other Ministers simply answering for their own departments. By restricting its membership to five—himself, the Lord President of the Council (Chamberlain), the Lord Privy Seal (Attlee), the Foreign Secretary (Halifax), and the Minister without Portfolio (Greenwood)—and by excluding the Service ministers Churchill took a first step towards the centralisation of authority on himself. He well understood the comment of Lord Acton in his famous *Inaugural Lecture*: 'great and salutary things are done for mankind by power concentrated, not by power balanced and cancelled and dispersed.' But it was his second step which was the more important. With the King's blessing, but with no written charter or mandate from Parliament, he nominated himself Minister of Defence. His guiding principle was Napoleon's maxim, that 'A Constitution should be short and obscure'. As the war years passed—and notably in 1942—the Prime Minister would be openly criticised for over-burdening himself with responsibilities too great, it was felt, for a single man. But in total war all power is centripetal, as Hitler, Stalin, and Roosevelt were fully aware. In the circumstances of 1940, and considering the qualities and capacities of his subordinate ministers, Churchill's decision to make himself a War Lord (as neither Asquith nor Lloyd George had attempted to do in 1914–18), was not only defensible: it was a duty. He was *capax imperii*.

The embodiment in Churchill of both political and military authority provided the keystone for a new High Command structure which proved to be the most efficient central system for running a war ever evolved, either by Great Britain or any other country. Ismay, rather than Churchill, was its architect: but those inclined to dismiss him as 'only a politician', swayed by emotion and prone to opportunism, should examine its articulation carefully, for its economy and logic are impressive, and it was Churchill who both readily adopted Ismay's creation and subtly adapted it to suit his own way of working. His emotions, nevertheless—always at their most dangerous when they caused him to react instinctively under pressure—very nearly wrecked the structure's foundations while they were still being moved into place.

Under Chamberlain arrangements for managing a war had been loose and ill-considered. Responsibilities were left undefined, or lodged in the wrong hands. The Norwegian campaign, in fact, revealed a state of chaos in the regions of policy control and staff planning as grave as that which ruined the Gallipoli operation. The Chiefs of Staff reported to a 'Standing Ministerial Committee on Military Co-ordination' (consisting of the Minister for the Co-ordination of Defence, Lord Chatfield; the three Service Ministers; and the Minister of Supply). This committee in its turn made 'recommendations from time to time to the War Cabinet as to the general conduct of the war'. The Chiefs of Staff, moreover, instead of acting in a corporate capacity were prone to issue orders independently to their three separate services. When Chatfield resigned, on 3 April 1940, Chamberlain sought to strengthen a chain containing so many weak links by the absurd but desperate remedy of appointing Churchill, still First Lord of the Admiralty, as Chairman of the Co-ordinating Committee; *primus*, as it were, *inter pares*. At the end of April he went further, remitting to Churchill the responsibility, on behalf of that Committee, for guiding and directing the Chiefs of Staff. This improvisation could not have lasted long in practice and was terminated, of course, by Chamberlain's fall. However, when Churchill assumed his larger function at the end of April he was supplied with a staff officer, General Ismay, who was also to be a member of the Chiefs of Staff Committee: in addition, he was to be given 'a suitable Central Staff'. It was here that Churchill saw his opportunity and here that his instincts came most dangerously into play. His weakness for the well-known face caused him to insist on an *ad hoc* staff, composed of his familiars—Oliver Lyttelton, Desmond Morton, Professor Lindemann and others. This was Lloyd George's notorious 'Garden Suburb' in Churchillian guise. Providentially Ismay dug in his heels, seeing immediately both the inadequacy and the menace of such a device. Somehow he contrived to prevent any irreversible decisions until the German invasion of France put all into the melting-pot. There can be no doubt, however, that had Churchill possessed such a staff *in being* when he became Prime Minister, its existence would have prevented, or seriously delayed, the infinitely better alternative which was now introduced.*

Churchill required what he called a handling machine. Ismay was its pivot, becoming Chief Staff Officer to the Prime Minister as Minister of Defence and retaining, at the same time, his place on the Chiefs of Staff

---

* The day after Churchill became Prime Minister Sir Alexander Cadogan, Permanent Under-Secretary of State for Foreign Affairs, noted in his diary 'I'm afraid Winston will build up a "Garden City" at No. 10, of the most awful people. . . .'

Committee. Instead of the conglomerate of court favourites who might have been employed, the well-established Military Wing of the War Cabinet Secretariat (a group, initially, of some dozen skilled officers, Jacob, Hollis and others), was given the second function, under Ismay, of forming the Office of the Minister of Defence. The Chiefs of Staff, moreover, now began to operate in their proper rôle as a 'combined Battle Headquarters, "a superchief of a War Staff in Commission" '. Churchill presided at many of their meetings, and they always attended the Defence Committee (Operations). Apart from Churchill himself, the latter was the focal point at which the military and political elements in the High Command were fused.

What Churchill did, in effect, was to destroy the old Committee for Military Co-ordination. Retaining a small War Cabinet, he introduced under it the Defence Committee (Operations) consisting of the Deputy Prime Minister, the three Service Ministers, and at a later stage the Foreign Secretary. Other Ministers attended as required, and the Chiefs of Staff were always present. Another sub-unit, the Defence Committee (Supply), conveniently freed those concerned with policy and operations from many distracting problems. Directly under the Chiefs of Staff* worked the Joint Planning Staff (headed by the Directors of Plans of the three services, and supported by an inter-service team), and the Joint Intelligence Sub-Committee which, chaired by Cavendish–Bentinck of the Foreign Office, consisted of the Directors of Intelligence of the three services plus a representative of the Ministry of Economic Warfare, and was also supported by an inter-service staff. Such was the bone-structure, and of it Churchill could rightly claim that 'one lived in a stream of coherent thought capable of being translated with great rapidity into executive action'. Even under Lloyd George, in the first war, there had been wide gaps between the service directorate and the central political dynamo. Now all was brought within a unified and organic relationship: lines of responsibility were clarified: nobody relevant was out in the cold. And Churchill's intimate relationship with the Chiefs of Staff was invaluable: it is not only the resultant pressures and frustrations which can be gauged from the Alanbrooke Diaries, but also the sense of a unique and day-to-day combination. Nothing like this emerged on the Axis side: and even Roosevelt's Chief of Staff, George Marshall, though he was trusted and respected by the President, never enjoyed the ready access and

---

* Chamberlain had created three Vice-Chiefs, to 'double-bank'. Their meetings had the status of the Chiefs of Staff Committee. The first session was on 27 April 1940, and the Vice-Chiefs continued in commission thereafter.

camaraderie which Churchill so abundantly offered to his advisers.* Moreover, when the United States entered the war, and the Allies established their Combined Chiefs of Staff Committee, it was on British foundations that this powerful instrument was modelled.

The United States were an ally *de facto* long before becoming one *de jure*: but during the months between Dunkirk and Pearl Harbour the special relationship was always delicate and often imperilled. Full alliance only intensified the strain. It was in this area that Churchill as War Lord made a major contribution to the military success and survival of the British, for his manipulation of the fragile lines of communication was feline, adroit, and far-sighted. De Gaulle has written that to resist the British machine 'when it set itself in motion to achieve something, was a severe test. Without having experienced it oneself, it is impossible to imagine what a concentration of effort, what a variety of procedures, what insistence, by turns gracious, pressing and threatening, the English were capable of deploying in order to obtain satisfaction'.† This well describes Churchill's Protean method of negotiating with the Americans: but what has to be remembered is that it was usually negotiation conducted from a position of weakness. Fundamentally, British self-interest was matched by American self-interest, and fundamentally Churchill was suppliant rather than dominant. The French say of a love-affair that *il y a toujours l'un qui aime et l'une qui se laisse aimer*. Such was Churchill's situation *vis à vis* Roosevelt.‡

Both the President and his military advisers were convinced that in the defeat of German aggression lay the prime American interest: Japan, even in the event of hostilities, must take second place. But effective American support for the British after Dunkirk was impeded by many doubts and difficulties. On the one hand, in 1940 the strength and equipment of the

---

* It was typical of Churchill's policy of integration that in 1941 he should minute to Ismay that he was 'anxious that Commanders-in-Chief should be kept fully informed of the situation, but reluctant to increase the circulation list of highly secret papers.' Ismay was therefore to 'organise a special secret information centre in the Office of the Minister of Defence which Commanders-in-Chief could visit whenever they came to London. No trouble should be spared in organising this centre. . . .' The Special Information Centre was set up near Ismay's Private Office, equipped with topical Top Secret files, and regularly used by visiting Commanders-in-Chief, from at home and abroad, to brief themselves on forward planning which might otherwise not have come within their purview. See *The Inner Circle*, by Joan Bright Astley (who set up and ran this invaluable port of call).

† General de Gaulle, *The Call to Honour*, p. 167.

‡ At the Chiefs of Staff meeting on the day after Pearl Harbour, 'someone continued to advocate the same cautious approach to America that had seemed politic when her intervention was in doubt. (Churchill) answered with a wicked leer in his eye, "Oh! that is the way we talked to her while we were wooing her; now that she is in the harem, we talk to her quite differently!"'
Arthur Bryant, *The Turn of the Tide*, p. 282.

American armed forces was at a nadir, so that Marshall and his staff, knowing that Germany would sooner or later have to be tackled, were nevertheless gravely concerned about the good sense of robbing themselves of scarce and precious *matériel* to re-equip British forces which, in the event, might be too weak or ill-led to use them profitably. Then there was the American navy which, however much it might pay lip service to 'Germany first', normally acted in a way which put the Pacific first. And many dissentient voices could be heard. German, Italian and Irish communities and sympathisers in the United States were a powerful counter-balance to the Jews, the Poles, and the representatives of other occupied or oppressed nations. There was also the special, and perennial, problem of American elections. Such was the confused and delicate situation with which Churchill was presented. It has often been described: perhaps nowhere more accurately and more vividly than in the diaries of General Lee.* Raymond Lee was sent over in 1940 to work under the cover of American Military Attaché in London. His real function was to file for Washington constant and informed estimates of Britian's military situation, and simultaneously to act as a high-level liaison officer for the various vital contacts and meetings which were secretly established between the British and American services before the United States entered the war. He was shrewd but detached, Anglophile but objective. His diaries mirror Churchill's dilemma—the gnawing doubts at the centre of the American command complex, the disastrous effects of Ambassador Joseph Kennedy's Anglophobia, and Roosevelt's own attitudes, essentially aimed at supporting Britain with America's 'arsenal of democracy', but, as always, shrouded, wavering, and incalculable.

15 May was symbolic. During that day not only were the decisions taken which reserved a minimum strength of fighters for the Battle of Britain and started the Strategic Bomber Offensive: in the afternoon Churchill also drafted the first of those private messages to Roosevelt which, signed 'Former Naval Person',† provided him with a characteristic, unique, and astonishingly effective channel of communication. Occasional meetings, telephone talks, and the intimate link of Harry Hopkins would later strengthen it and extend its range, but it was essentially by this means that Churchill fostered and developed a mutual confidence. In his very first letter he presented a shopping-list—40 or 50 older destroyers, several

---

* *The London Observer : The Journal of General Raymond E. Lee, 1940–1941.*
† The use of this pseudonym had a purpose. A shared interest in naval affairs was a strong bond between a Prime Minister who had twice been First Lord of the Admiralty and a President who recalled with nostalgia his appointment as Assistant Secretary of the Navy.

hundred of the latest types of aircraft, anti-aircraft equipment, steel, and so on. The rapidity of reaction was extraordinary. On 3 June Marshall demanded a survey of 'the entire list of the American reserve ordnance and munition stocks'. Within a week 600 laden freight cars were in transit to the New Jersey docks, and on 11 June British ships were already loading. Half a million rifles and 900 75 mm. field guns, although aged, were a useful import. And though the question of destroyers was more difficult, a formula (the provision of facilities at West Indian and other bases), was devised to give Roosevelt the necessary political room for manoeuvre. These American subventions culminated at the end of the year in Lend-Lease, 'the most unsordid act in the history of any nation'—or perhaps the most enlightened act of self-interest. It was the direct consequence of Churchill's long and masterly letter to Roosevelt of 8 December, 'one of the most important I ever wrote'.*

American self-interest was certainly promoted, continuously, from 1940 until the end of the war. The 'special relationship' was no fiction, as many acts of generosity and forbearance by Roosevelt and his administration were to prove. But it was something less romantic, something less idealistic than Churchill made it out to be, for the façade concealed ugly realities. The ethos of the United States is commercial, and it must never be forgotten, as the story of the alliance unfolds, that time and again the Americans contrived to extract from their military aid advantages in their world-wide commercial rivalry with Great Britain. Lend-Lease provides a perfect example. The British were compelled to agree to sell nothing abroad containing Lend-Lease material, which was reasonable: but also not to sell anything similar to items received under Lend-Lease, *even if it was of British manufacture*. Moreover, American representatives in Great Britain maintained a constant surveillance to ensure that these draconic requirements were observed. The effect on Britain's export trade was profound. And there were other manifestations. For instance, when in 1941 and 1942 Pan American Airways began to function on the trans-African routes, to provide extra military transport, they openly attempted to use this as a lever for advancing their long-term commercial interests, and to establish themselves as competitors with B.O.A.C. for the civilian passenger and freight traffic to the Far East.†

Yet what alternative had Churchill, either in 1940 or later? He has been accused of sacrificing Britain's tomorrow for the sake of Britain's today:

* Reproduced in *The Second World War*, Vol. II, pp. 494–501.
† See Lord Tedder, *With Prejudice*, pp. 218 foll., for a detailed account of this unsavoury episode.

but he had no option. The truth was that Britain was bankrupt. In August 1940 the Chancellor of the Exchequer estimated that over the next twelve months expenditure in North America would be at the rate of some 3,200 million dollars: at the time, British holdings of foreign exchange and American securities were worth only £490 million, and by April 1941 the reserves of gold and dollars were down to twelve million dollars. (All gold in British banks, incidentally, and all foreign securities—tied up by seventy miles of tape—were secretly shipped across the Atlantic during 1940 and lodged in vaults in Montreal.) In effect, therefore, Churchill had to bargain for the means of survival as best he could.

Nothing, however, could more conclusively convince a potential ally than the spectacle of a Great Britain not only determined to survive but actually surviving. As to determination there was no question: Churchill had made this crystal clear in his negotiations with the French, had confirmed it in the secret conferences of the Cabinet, and had displayed it to the world by his lion's roar on the radio and in Parliament. The end was undoubted: but the means? Men had returned from France, but little *matériel*. By mid-July, as the Army sorted itself out, it was evident that of some 25 miscellaneous divisions available for home defence only one was fully equipped with field artillery: most had only a handful, or nil.* Anti-tank guns hardly existed. Hundred of tanks had been lost, and of the residue most were thin-skinned or light. Between 10 May and 20 June 944 R.A.F. aircraft had gone, of which 386 were Hurricanes and 67 Spitfires. On 15 June Dowding had only 1094 pilots. Moreover, by an extraordinary historical anomaly, no ready-made plans existed for meeting an invasion. Racial memory had failed. Always, in the past, the possibility of an assault from overseas had been taken into account. When a French invasion seemed likely in 1798 the Keeper of the State Papers was told to 'discover what arrangements were made, for the internal defence of these kingdoms, when Spain, by its Armada, projected the invasion and conquest of England; and how far these wise proceedings of our ancestors may be applicable to the present crisis of public safety'. During the First World War, in spite of pressure from the Western Front a minimum of one cavalry and four infantry divisions was always retained for Home Defence. But in the 'thirties the only threat that was seriously contemplated was from the air. In 1940 the equivalent of the 100 Martello towers erected between 1804 and 1812, to guard the coasts from Essex to Sussex, was the

---

* 'The whole of the army equipment available at home on the morrow of Dunkirk was barely sufficient to equip two divisions', M. M. Postan, D. Hay and J. D. Scott, *Design and Development of Weapons*, p. 117. (*History of the Second World War, United Kingdom Civil Series.*)

necklace of lattice masts which marked the radar stations of *Chain Home*. Churchill and his commanders had to start virtually from scratch.

Certainly the initial defence plan was elementary. It was produced by the Commander-in-Chief Home Forces, Ironside, at the end of June, and endorsed by Churchill himself. But it contained grave flaws. The front line consisted of static troops on the invasion beaches, intended to fight where they stood. Further inland, a line of anti-tank defences, running across S.E. England and then northwards, was to protect London and the midland industrial centres. Finally, a main reserve for a final counter-attack was to be held back under the Commander-in-Chief. Fortunately on 19 July 'Tiny' Ironside, a mammoth of a man who had been promoted above his capacities, was replaced by Alanbrooke. The latter's incisive mind, supported by recent experience of fighting a modern war in France, swiftly discerned the plan's weakness. The general responsible for Eastern Command, for example, was overseer of the whole coast and hinterland from Sussex to the Wash, the area most exposed to an invasion but one dangerously split by the Thames. Alanbrooke immediately divided it into two commands. He stopped, so far as possible, the enthusiastic construction of anti-tank ditches and concrete pillboxes (sometimes in very odd places), as a linear defence behind the coast. He checked the jamming of entries to towns and villages by huge roadblocks. The beaches were now to be held only by light forces, and stress was laid on the assembly and training of aggressive and highly mobile reserves which, grouped inland, could move speedily to eliminate enemy beach-heads before they had been consolidated. Though at first all this was represented by not much more than a blue-print, Brooke worked with frenetic energy, seeking to re-arrange not only the locations but also the mentality of the Army, to fit it for a wiser form of defence whose virtues Churchill had already grasped for himself: though he had also grasped, from first-hand experience, the difficulty of implementing it. After a visit to Montgomery's 3rd Division (perhaps the best equipped, best trained, and best led division then in the country) he minuted:

(*Action this Day*)
Prime Minister to Secretary of State for War   *3 July 40*

I was disturbed to find the 3rd Division spread along thirty miles of coast, instead of being, as I had imagined, held back concentrated in reserve, ready to move against any serious head of invasion. But much more astonishing was the fact that the infantry of this division, which is otherwise fully mobile, are not provided with the buses necessary to move them to the point of action. This provision of buses, waiting always ready and close at hand, is essential to all mobile units, and to none more than the 3rd Division while spread about the coast.

I heard the same complaint from Portsmouth that the troops there had not got their transport ready and close at hand. Considering the great masses of transport, both buses and lorries, which there are in this country, and the large numbers of drivers brought back from the B.E.F., it should be possible to remedy these defects at once. I hope, at any rate, that the G.O.C. 3rd Division will be told today to take up, as he would like to do, the large number of buses which are even now plying for pleasure traffic up and down the sea front at Brighton.

Alanbrooke's appointment did not, therefore, occur by chance. Churchill had already seen the light. When, shortly after the Brighton visit, Eden, the Secretary of State for War, proposed that Ironside should be put out to grass, Churchill made a point of inspecting Alanbrooke's Southern Command and testing his mind during four careful hours. 'We seemed to be in agreement on the methods of Home Defence.' Two days later Alanbrooke became C.-in-C. Home Forces.

This decision displays Churchill at his best. He knew of Alanbrooke's magnificent leadership of 2 Corps before Dunkirk. He knew that after Dunkirk, when Alanbrooke went back to France, he had stood up to his Prime Minister and demonstrated to him the folly of his interventions. (Churchill preferred the commander who *really* stood up to him: it was those who temporised, failed to press their arguments home, or broke under the strain of his own pressure* who most displeased him.) He respected Eden's judgement. Alanbrooke's brother Victor had been a fellow cavalry officer in the 'nineties, and with another brother, Ronnie, he had been at Spion Kop and galloped into Ladysmith on the first night of its relief. Nevertheless, amid his multitudinous other preoccupations he was at pains to satisfy himself personally as to Alanbrooke's fitness for the supreme post before ratifying his appointment. Churchill's choice of commanders cannot be treated summarily: it deserves detailed study. But though it was sometimes wrong—as wrong in his wanting to impose Keyes on the Chiefs of Staff as he was wrong in selecting Gott to command 8 Army in August 1942†—his deeper instincts were often right: right, for example, in his rough dismissals of Wavell and Auchinleck. His choice of

---

* Of his argument with Lord Fisher at the time of the Dardanelles Churchill wrote in *The World Crisis*, 'War is a business of terrible pressures and persons who take part in it must fail if they are not strong enough to withstand them'.

† See p. 157.

7 *In 'Flying Bomb Alley', 1944. The Prime Minister with his wife and daughter, Subaltern Mary Churchill of Anti-Aircraft Command*

8 *Bombs on Ramsgate: Ismay in the doorway*

BATTLE OF BRITAIN, 1940

9 *Coventry Cathedral*

Alanbrooke—like Roosevelt's of Marshall—as his main prop throughout the war can only be described as inspired.

In 1940 his faculties were at their highest pitch. He was in the state ascribed by Falstaff to the influence of sherris sack, 'apprehensive, quick, forgetive, full of nimble, fiery and delectable shapes', as those unique minutes reveal. What progress is being made with rockets and sensitive fuses, with automatic bomb sights and radio direction finding? Can the Navy transfer pilots to Fighter Command? Can Turin and Milan be bombed? What about more felling of timber, to reduce imports and save shipping? Can't more regular troops be brought from India, and a better reserve be built up in the Middle East—'Our weakness, slowness, lack of grip and drive are very apparent on the background of what was being done twenty-five years ago?' To Ismay: 'I should like to be informed upon (1) the coastal watch and coastal batteries; (2) the gorging of the harbours and defended inlets (i.e., the making of the landward defences); (3) the troops held in immediate support of the foregoing; (4) the mobile columns and brigade groups; (5) the General Reserve.' When Eden proposes the Local Defence Volunteers, it is Churchill who seizes on the seminal idea, and in a creative moment writes to the Secretary of State for War 'I don't think much of the name "Local Defence Volunteers" for your very large new force. The word "local" is uninspiring. Mr. Herbert Morrison suggested to me today the title "Civic Guard", but I think "Home Guard" would be better. Don't hesitate to change on account of already having made armlets, etc., if it is thought the title of Home Guard would be more compulsive.' Who is responsible for making the 'sticky' bomb? 'Any chortling by officials who have been slothful in pushing this bomb over the fact that at present it has not succeeded will be viewed with great disfavour by me.' What is happening about the repatriation of evacuated French forces? And their wounded? Why can't civilians be employed on defence works, to release more troops for active defence? The Press must handle air raids 'in a cool way'. 'Everyone should learn to take air raids and air-raid alarms as if they were no more than thunderstorms.'

This is but a selection from minutes by Churchill dashed off *in the month of June alone*. Of course some were unnecessary, some were undeserved irritants and some produced delay or confusion. But what is most striking about them is the range, the relevance, and the commonsense of the Prime Minister's concerns: the least pause for reflection is enough to make plain that had Chamberlain survived as Prime Minister, or Halifax been chosen to replace him, something both vibrant and constructive would have been lacking in the higher direction of Britain's defence. Lord Normanbrook made the point, as an observer in the Cabinet Office at the time. 'This stream of messages, covering so wide a range of subjects, was like the beam of a searchlight ceaselessly swinging round and penetrating into the remote recesses of the administration so that everyone, however humble his range or his function, felt that one day the beam might rest on him and light up what he was doing. In Whitehall the effect of this influence was immediate and dramatic. The machine responded at once to his leadership. It quickened the pace and improved the tone of administration. A new sense of purpose and urgency was created as it came to be realised that a firm hand, guided by a strong will, was on the wheel.'*

There were, nevertheless, two dangers latent in the centralised control which Churchill established with such speed and such manifest competence. The first was never more than a possibility. Alanbrooke described it bluntly, as he looked back in his *Notes on My Life*†: 'There was no form of Combined Command over the three Services. . . . There were far too many commanders. The Navy had the C.-in-C., the Home Fleet, C.-in-C., Nore, C.-in-C., Portsmouth, C.-in-C., Plymouth, C.-in-C., Western Approaches. The Army had the C.-in-C., Home Forces; and the Air Force had the A.O.C.-in-C., Fighter Command; the A.O.C.-in-C., Bomber Command, and the A.O.C.-in-C., Coastal Command. There was no co-ordinating head to this mass of commanders beyond the Chiefs of Staff Committee and the Admiralty, Air Ministry and War Office. It was a highly dangerous organisation. Had an invasion developed, I fear that Churchill would have attempted as Defence Minister to co-ordinate the action of these various Commands. This would have been wrong and highly perilous, with his impulsive nature and tendency to arrive at decisions through a process of intuition as opposed to "logical" approach.' Alanbrooke was undoubtedly correct. Churchill was himself aware of the need for a Supremo, as his offer to Trenchard on 23 May indicates. But when Trenchard rejected the post of General Officer Commanding, 'in control of all land, sea and air forces at home in the event of invasion', on the grounds that only a Deputy Prime Minister could have tackled the job effectively, he was a realist. Churchill would never have stomached a Deputy with such powers: nor, indeed, is it easy, on a survey of possible candidates, to name any individual capable, *at that time*, of undertaking the task. The risk was unavoidable.

The other danger, also unavoidable (since it stemmed from Churchill's temperament), was less sinister. In his perpetual search for the offensive,

---

* Lord Normanbrook, in *Action This Day*, p. 22.
† Alanbrooke in Sir Arthur Bryant, *The Turn of the Tide*, p. 201.

and his passion for tangential enterprises from which it was difficult to detach him, he was prone to concentrate the energies of his commanders and planners, and even the actual strength of his forces, on secondary and irrelevant objectives. How often this was to happen! The Baltic, Pantelleria, Norway, Turkey, the Dodecanese, Sumatra did not always do credit to his judgement: and there are other examples, less notorious, which lie buried in the files of the Joint Planners and the Chiefs of Staff. General Sir James Marshall-Cornwall witnessed the birth and the death of one of these fantasies. He was commanding III Corps on the Welsh Marches. On 26 July he was summoned to dine at Chequers, and closely interrogated by the Prime Minister.

He continued: 'I assume, then, that your Corps is now ready to take the field?' 'Very far from it, Sir,' I replied. 'Our re-equipment is not nearly complete, and when it is we shall require another month or two of intensive training.' The P.M. looked at me incredulously and drew a sheaf of papers from the pocket of his dinner-jacket. 'Which are your two divisions?' he demanded. 'The 53rd (Welsh) and the 2nd London,' I replied. He pushed a podgy finger on the graph tables and said: 'There you are; one hundred per cent complete in personnel, rifles and mortars; fifty per cent complete in field artillery, anti-tank rifles and machine-guns.' 'I beg your pardon, Sir,' I rejoined; 'That state may refer to the weapons which the ordnance depots are preparing to issue to my units, but they have not yet reached the troops in anything like those quantities.' The P.M.'s brow contracted; almost speechless with rage he hurled the graphs across the dinner-table to Dill, saying: 'C.I.G.S.! Have those papers checked and returned to me tomorrow.'

An awkward silence ensued; a diversion seemed called for. The P.M. leant across me and addressed my neighbour on the other side: 'Prof.! What have *you* got to tell me today?' The other civilians present were wearing dinner-jackets, but Professor Lindemann was attired in a morning-coat and striped trousers. He now slowly pushed his right hand into his tail-pocket and, like a conjuror, drew forth a Mills hand-grenade. An uneasy look appeared on the faces of his fellow-guests and the P.M. shouted: 'What's that you've got, Prof., what's that?' 'This, Prime Minister, is the inefficient Mills bomb, issued to the British infantry. It is made of twelve different components which have to be machined in separate processes. Now *I* have designed an improved grenade, which has fewer machined parts and contains a fifty per cent greater bursting charge.' 'Splendid, Prof., splendid! That's what I like to hear. C.I.G.S.! Have the Mills bomb scrapped at once and the Lindemann grenade introduced.' The unfortunate Dill was completely taken aback; he tried to explain that contracts had been placed in England and America for millions of the Mills bombs, and that it would be impracticable to alter the design now, but the Prime Minister would not listen. . . .'

After dinner Churchill said, 'I want the Generals to come with me', and stumped off into the billiard-room with Dill, Ismay and Marshall-Cornwall.

On the billiard-table was a rolled-up map, which the P.M. proceeded to spread out. It was a large-scale map of the Red Sea. The P.M. placed his finger on the Italian port of Massawa. 'Now, Marshall-Cornwall,' he said, 'we have command of the sea and the air; it is essential for us to capture that port; how would you do it?' I was in no way prepared to answer a snap conundrum of this kind, and indeed had no qualifications for doing so. I saw Dill and Ismay watching me anxiously and I felt I was being drawn into some trap. I looked hard at the map for a minute and then answered: 'Well, Sir, I have never been to Massawa; I have only passed out of sight of it, going down the Red Sea. It is a defended port, protected by coast defence and anti-aircraft batteries. It must be a good 500 miles from Aden, and therefore beyond the cover of our fighters. The harbour has a very narrow entrance channel, protected by coral reefs, and is certain to be mined, making an opposed landing impracticable. I should prefer to wait until General Wavell's offensive against Eritrea develops; he will capture it more easily from the land side.' The P.M. gave me a withering look, rolled up the map and muttered peevishly: 'You soldiers are all alike; you have no imagination.'*

In that vignette Churchill is displayed at his infantile worst, and it is right that he should be so displayed, for such performances were a part of the whole. Yet an assessment of Churchill's overall achievement must contain as its *leit-motiv* the truism that the whole is greater than its parts, and the critic must bear in mind continually that Churchill's lapses, even the most lamentable, were cancelled out by his positive contributions. This is the universal verdict of all those who, working most closely to him at the time, had most reason to be discommoded by his follies.

The presence at a Chequers dinner-table of Professor Lindemann (created Lord Cherwell in 1941), is a reminder that in the eyes of many he was the *éminence noire*, the Svengali responsible for many of Churchill's wilder aberrations. But Cherwell was like his master: if he had not existed in 1940 it would have been necessary to invent him. When Churchill took into his Private Office at 10 Downing Street this old friend,† to run a statistical section and act as his scientific and economic adviser, he did so because he realised that, since both science and economics would play a

---

* From the unpublished memoirs of Sir James Marshall-Cornwall. Massawa surrendered to a Free French unit, under General Platt's command, on 8 April 1941. In Churchill's defence it must be remembered that in 1940 the air and submarine base of Massawa seemed a serious threat to the Red Sea convoys. He had simply got his priorities wrong.

† It is often forgotten that the Churchill/Cherwell connection was not a latter-day manifestation. They first met as far back as 1921, and their interplay in the military field was early. When, for example, the Anti-Aircraft Defence Sub-Committee was instituted in 1925, and the then Professor Lindemann was invited to serve on it, the invitation was 'almost certainly issued on Churchill's initiative'. See S. W. Roskill, *Hankey : Man of Secrets*, Vol. II, p. 406.

crucial part in his direction of the war effort, he must have at his side a man on whom he could rely to present to him the significant facts and issues in their essence. Cherwell alone possessed Churchill's confidence and the intellectual ability to comprehend and to clarify, in these special spheres. This arrogant vegetarian, snobbish and self-certain, the antithesis of all that normally inspired Churchill's affection, foreign by birth and alien in his way of life, made huge mistakes in the advice he proffered: but, like Churchill, he was one whose positive qualities outweighed the errors which, from time to time, vanity or miscalculation caused him to perpetrate. It was a tragedy that his great rival, Sir Henry Tizard, whose genius enabled Fighter Command to face the Battle of Britain with a properly functioning radar system, failed to win the Prime Minister's trust and was remote from his friendship: but it was a fact. For better or worse, Cherwell was inevitable.

Whether Churchill himself believed, in his secret heart, that an invasion would occur now appears unlikely. On 10 July, indeed, he composed for the Cabinet a closely reasoned minute in which he argued that it would be impossible for the Germans to invade because 'it would be a most hazardous and even suicidal operation to commit a large army to the accidents of the sea in the teeth of our very numerous armed patrolling forces'. Nevertheless he had to act as if he believed, and for Churchill action was tantamount to conviction. As his old friend Admiral Fisher would have said, he prepared to receive boarders *totus porcus*. And of course he could not know, at first, that Hitler, surprised by the speed at which he had reached the Channel, had no immediate plan for, nor even any intention of invading: his original idea was to preserve Britain and the Empire, in some conveniently neutralised form. It was not until 2 July that Keitel issued the preliminary O.K.W. order, entitled *The War Against England*, which began 'The Führer and Supreme Commander has decided ... that a landing in England is possible, provided that air superiority can be attained and certain other necessary conditions fulfilled'. And it was a fortnight later before Hitler endorsed and extended this document by his still tentative Directive No. 16, whose opening words, 'I have decided to begin to prepare for, and if necessary carry out, an invasion of England ... ', were uncharacteristically indecisive. Churchill did know something, though not all, of how German preparations were being ruined by inadequate intelligence,* inadequate planning, and internecine rivalry and

---

* During the summer of 1940 six German agents reached Eire: between September and November 25 landed in Britain, mainly by parachute or boat. All were apprehended. Some were executed, some 'turned' and used as double agents. See Sir John Masterman, *The Double-Cross System*.

suspicion within the Army, the Navy, and the *Luftwaffe*. And he knew that suggestions for a peaceful settlement were being floated in many quarters —by Von Papen in Turkey, and by the German Chargé d'Affaires to the British Ambassador in Washington; by well-meaning civilians like Mr. Plesman, the general manager of the Dutch airline K.L.M., who operated through the Dutch Ambassador in London; by Prince Hohenlohe, by the Spanish King and the King of Sweden. These overtures left Churchill cold. His reaction is best expressed by a note to the Foreign Secretary which can now be read in the Cabinet Papers for 1940: 'I might add that the intrusion of the ignominious King of Sweden, as a peace-maker, after his desertion of Finland and Norway, and while he is absolutely in the German grip, though not without its encouraging aspects, is singularly distasteful'. And he was equally frigid about pacific fellow-countrymen, who were described in a minatory minute by the Chief Diplomatic Adviser to the Foreign Office, Sir Robert Vansittart: 'It is now probable that we are about to be the object of an American peace-feeler, perhaps even of a peace offensive; and all our own loose-thinkers are on the scent. These people range from bishops and Quakers to cowards and cranks, from capitalists to communists, from peers to ordinary dyspeptics. . . . '

All dubieties, however, dissolved as, during latter July and early August, *it seemed certain*, in Churchill's words, *that the man was going to try*. There were many converging strands. Intelligence sources revealed that Operation SEA LION was now in hand, and in the first week of August Alanbrooke reported that a definite invasion threat was developing along the south coast as well as the east, which at first had seemed more vulnerable. The nightly flow of barges and other craft from the Low Countries to French Channel ports; the increasing evidence of military and *Luftwaffe* concentrations, and the swift re-construction in London of the Germany 'order of battle' from intercepted radio signals; the presence of two mountain divisions near Boulogne (for the Folkestone cliffs?); the multiplication of long-range batteries . . . these and other manifestations were 'hard' enough, and they were supported by less ponderable communications from the Continent. A chaplain in the Belgian army, for example, managed to send over a carrier pigeon with a 5000-word message together with 14 maps.* This menacing situation was reviewed at a special meeting of the Chiefs of Staff on 26 July, at which it was agreed that 'until Germany had defeated our fighter force, invasion by sea was not a practical operation of war'. A correct deduction followed: the preliminary to such

* 'This message gave us much valuable information on invasion preparations.' Major-General Sir Kenneth Strong, *Intelligence at the Top*, p. 68. The priest was later executed by the Germans.

an invasion must be a large scale offensive against the whole complex of our air-defence system.

During the consequent Battle of Britain, as in the Battle for France, Churchill's role was essentially hortatory rather than executive. Action lay in the hands of the squadrons, the radar operators, the Observer Corps: with Keith Park at No. 11 Group and Dowding at Fighter Command. By remaining in London the Prime Minister could share the bombs—he had several narrow escapes. His broadcasts diffused sanity and defiance. Frequent visits to the fighter stations (culminating in the visit to II Group H.Q. on the day of victory, 15 September, of which there is a magnificent set-piece account in *The Second World War*), and to the areas of 'incidents' stiffened morale. Moreover, whatever views may be held about the manic performance of Lord Beaverbrook at the Ministry of Aircraft Production (a controversial matter, too technical to be handled here), Churchill did his utmost to stimulate him and all others concerned in the nightmare task of maintaining an output of fighters, so successfully that when the Battle ended there were more aircraft available than at the beginning.* But inevitably his post was *hors de combat*, and his supreme function was to find the words which warned his country and the world that

> Comfort, content, delight,
> The ages' slow-bought gain,
> They shrivelled in a night.
> Only ourselves remain
> To face the naked days
> In silent fortitude,
> Through perils and dismays
> Renewed and re-renewed.†

Nevertheless, though it was unknown to more than a very small circle at the time, there were two executive decisions, taken by Churchill on his own responsibility, which were to have the most profound long-term effect in what he called 'the Wizard War'—the scientific struggle for air power. The decisions were made separately and for different purposes, but they were linked in a chain of cause and effect, and although the causes were manifold one was predominant—the tragic *apartheid* of Cherwell and Sir Henry Tizard.

Since the outbreak of hostilities in September 1939 Tizard had acted as

---

* Between 10 July and 31 October the R.A.F. lost, from all causes, 915 planes. On 10 July 656 were ready for operations; on 25 September, 665. Loss of pilots mattered more than loss of planes.

† Rudyard Kipling, '*1914*'.

unofficial Scientific Adviser to the Chief of Air Staff. It was not to Tizard, however, but to Lindemann, the Scientific Adviser to the Prime Minister, that on 12 June in the following year a young scientist in Air Intelligence, R. V. Jones,* broke the news that he had just received a critical message: 'Knickebein Cleves established fifty-three, twenty-four north, one degree west'. The significance of this cryptogram derived from the fact that in the spring documents had been found on a German bomber, referring to the operation of a 'Knickebein beacon'; that a similar reference had been discovered on a second aircraft; and that on 23 May Jones had put forward the thesis that the *Luftwaffe* might be capable of bombing under the guidance of a radio-navigational system. These hints had been reinforced by further evidence, and now an actual source for such a beam had been identified at Cleves, one of the nearest points in Germany to Great Britain. Lindemann immediately informed Churchill, whose energetic reaction resulted in the formation of a unit to 'investigate signals of a suspected frequency both from a specially fitted van and from an Anson aircraft'. In all this Tizard played no constructive part: his attitude was one of open scepticism, and his normally sane judgement was undoubtedly unbalanced by Lindemann's involvement.

When, therefore, Churchill decided that the issue was so grave as to warrant his personal supervision, Tizard was on the wrong side of the fence, as became plain at a summit conference assembled by the Prime Minister in the Cabinet room on the morning of 21 June. This was attended by Churchill, Lindemann, Beaverbrook, Sinclair (the Secretary of State for Air), Newall (the Chief of Air Staff), Portal (A.O.C.-in-C. Bomber Command), Dowding (A.O.C.-in-C. Fighter Command), Watson-Watt (the radar pioneer), Tizard and R. V. Jones.† Its consequence was an initiative on Churchill's part whose value can hardly be estimated. 'Being master, and not having to argue too much, once I was convinced about the principles of this queer and deadly game I gave all the necessary orders that very day in June for the existence of the beam to be assumed, and for all counter-measures to receive absolute priority. The slightest reluctance or deviation in carrying out this policy was to be reported to me. With so much going on I did not trouble the Cabinet, or

---

* It was at Tizard's suggestion that Jones (now Professor of Natural Philosophy, Aberdeen University), was transferred from Oxford to provide the Air Ministry with information about German scientific progress.

† Here is a reminder that throughout his memoirs Churchill constantly and unscrupulously employed the dubious arts of *suggestio falsi* and *suppressio veri*. In his description of this meeting he sought to magnify his own significance. He therefore wrote that 'about fifteen persons were present, including Sir Henry Tizard and various Air Force commanders'. See *The Second World War*, Vol. II, p. 339.

even the Chiefs of Staff. If I had encountered any serious obstruction I should of course have appealed and told a long story to those friendly tribunals.' By the time German night-bombing began in earnest, during August, sufficient progress had been made for the Knickebein beams to be profitably jammed, and though successors were introduced, *X-Gerät* later in 1940, *Wotan* in 1941, the impetus provided by *Knickebein*, and by Churchill's personal intervention (which culminated in the formation of a permanent interservice counter-measures committee), meant that the British were never effectively out-manoeuvred in this vital area of the Wizard War. But Tizard, by his unfortunate miscalculation, had man-oeuvred himself out of a job. Immediately after the meeting on the 21st he went to the Athenaeum, where he wrote a letter of resignation from his posts as adviser to the Air Staff and Chairman of the Scientific Advisory Committee.

Churchill's second executive act in this field, however, was to dispatch the unseated Tizard on an errand as delicate and as momentous as any British Ambassador has undertaken. For many months the possibility had been ventilated of sending to the United States a mission 'to negotiate with the U.S. Army and Naval Authorities and men of science, and in-dustrial firms, on the free exchange of information about matters to be put forward by the Admiralty, War Office and Air Ministry, and to arrange for manufacture in the U.S.A. of the required equipment . . .'. The critical sentence in the inter-service recommendation, which was written on 9 July, read: 'In exchange for facilities afforded to us by the Americans, to provide full information on certain subjects which the Departments con-sider may be released to the American authorities.' On 1 August, in the midst of the Battle of Britain, Tizard was summoned by Churchill and confirmed as leader of the mission. 'I asked if he would give me a free hand,' Tizard noted in his diary, 'and would rely on my discretion. He said "of course"—and would I write down exactly what I wanted. So I said I would go, and wrote out a paper which I left with his secretary'. Tizard's self-drafted brief, which began 'To tell them what they want to know', was the start of one of the most secret and most important acts recorded in history of collaboration between a belligerent and a non-combatant nation. When Tizard and his mission departed for the States on 14 August they took with them confidential information (and in some cases specimens, or films of equipment in action), which covered Britain's most forward thinking on radar, on jet engines, on gun turrets, on rocket-defence of ships, multiple pompoms, chemical warfare, and explosives.*

* See Ronald W. Clark, *Tizard*, Ch. Eleven, 'The Mission to the United States'.

Most important of all was a commonplace black metal box from the Army and Navy Stores, in which was transported the cavity magnetron, described in the history of the U.S. Office of Scientific Research and Development as 'the most valuable cargo ever brought to our shores'. From the exploitation of this new valve, whose disclosure opened up unexpected vistas from the Americans, there flowed incalculable benefits for the Allied cause; in many other fields the Tizard Mission unleashed Anglo-American co-operation at an unexampled level of trust and fertility. But the Mission would never have left England had Churchill not been prepared to shoulder the enormous responsibility, *which he alone could carry*, and if his wooing of Roosevelt had not been so pertinacious and so well-calculated.* And yet it is an example of another aspect of Churchill's complex character, of something harsh and unforgiving, that it was not until March 1941, some five months after his return, that Lindemann's enemy learned indirectly, from America, of the value the Prime Minister placed on his Mission. 'I was glad to hear this', Tizard commented in his diary, 'as the P.M., who sent me there, had not found time to see me since my return, and had not even acknowledged a preliminary report that I sent him; nor had I been brought into any of the discussions on co-operation with America that had taken place since I came back.' There are many strange things, Euripides wrote, but nothing is stranger than man: and of none is this more true than of Churchill.

These two dramatic episodes illustrate vividly the schizophrenic atmosphere of 1940, in which Churchill had simultaneously to grasp whatever might be useful in the short term while setting in motion projects whose results could only emerge in the later stages of a long war. When the Russian Ambassador, Maisky, called on him on 3 July he asked, 'What will be your general strategy now, after the fall of France?', and Churchill, drawing on his cigar, replied with a smile, 'My general strategy at present is to last out the next three months'. That was indeed the case: if England could endure until the September solstice rough winter weather in the Channel might at least defer invasion until the following spring. The immediate requirement, therefore, was for what might be made available immediately: but though this short-term impera-

---

* A special case was Churchill's careful fostering of Colonel (later Major-General) William Donovan, who became head of O.S.S. (Office of Strategic Services), and thus in charge of American secret intelligence and special operations overseas. In 1940 he functioned as a roving and fact-finding personal representative for Roosevelt in Britain and the Mediterranean, and was instrumental, for example, over the transfer of the Sperry bomb sight, and the 50 destroyers. His reports to Roosevelt strengthened the President's hand, and Churchill prudently exploited the connection.

tive sometimes produced valuable and unexpected dividends in the long term, there were other cases where the present was demonstrably the enemy of the future. Aircraft and armour are examples.* Beaverbrook, with Churchill's authority, gave an over-riding priority to fighters: but inevitable though this decision was, it had a serious effect on the heavy bomber programme—which, nevertheless, soon came to be seen as the main source for a counter-offensive. 'The conditions in the Ministry of Aircraft Production under Lord Beaverbrook and his immediate successors were unpropitious to long-term programmes.'† Three heavy bombers, the Stirling, the Manchester and the Halifax, had been ordered during the spring of 1937, and these were expected to be in production by 1940, while by April 1942 3500 should have been delivered. In fact, no operational planes became available until 1941, and it was not until the spring of 1943 that the target of 3500 deliveries was attained. In the case of tanks the results were—at least potentially—even more disastrous. On 11 June Churchill called for a plan which would provide 500 or 600 tanks by March 1941—a crash project: they were to be 'over and above the existing programme and were not to interfere with it'. All was concentrated on model A22, later known as the 'Churchill', which was virtually ordered off the drawing-board. But the consequence of impetuous and emergency action was such that of the first 1200 produced 1000 had to be 're-worked', while even in November 1941 the War Office reported that 'Churchills' would be useless for the Middle East, or for sustained operations in the United Kingdom, without no less than 16 modifications.

There were, however, substantial credits. Arnhem and D Day were far distant, but it was Churchill's insistence, against opposition, on the recruiting and training during the invasion months of a few thousand paratroopers which led to the 1st and 6th Airborne Divisions. It was Churchill who, also against opposition, fought through the formation of the first Commando-type units—'Leopards', as he liked to call them‡ —for use both against an invader and as invaders themselves. And so ambivalent was the conventional military establishment about the

---

* And even here there was schizophrenia. 'If it came to a choice between hampering air production or tank production, I would sacrifice the tank. . . .' Minute of Churchill to Beaverbrook, 9 August 1940.

† Postan, *op. cit.*, p. 125.

‡ Churchill's prehensile memory was at work. When he was commanding his battalion of the Royal Scots Fusiliers on the Western Front he watched a demonstration of a trench raid by the Canadian battalion which had evolved the technique—the first Commando-type operation in the First World War. He wrote to his wife on 16 January 1916, 'The splinters flew all over the place. It was like a skirmish: but no one was hurt. The Canadians grinned from ear to ear to see me. Wonderful fellows: like leopards.'

activities of an inventive Major in the Royal Engineers, Millis Jefferis (later Major-General Sir M. R. Jefferis), that Churchill had to place him, for safety, under the wing of Professor Lindemann. Even so, he had to keep up the pressure.

Prime Minister to General Ismay   *24.8.40*

Report to me on the position of Major Jefferis. By whom is he employed? Who is he under? I regard this officer as a singularly capable and forceful man, who should be brought forward to a higher position. He ought certainly to be promoted Lieutenant-Colonel, as it will give him more authority.

Jefferis' unorthodox section for the swift development of special weapons, named MD 1, was essentially a by-product of Churchill's short-term needs in the summer of 1940. Yet from it came the Limpet magnetic mine, which could be planted on the underwater side of an enemy ship: over half a million were made. Of the Clam, a smaller version, two and a half million were manufactured—nearly 1,000,000 going to the Russians. The 'L' delay-action fuse was invaluable for sabotage and other purposes: 5,000,000 of these went all over the world. One invention, the Jefferis Shoulder Gun (more generally known as the P.I.A.T., or Projector Infantry Anti-Tank), became a standard equipment of immeasurable value. It was Churchill, too, who personally rescued General Hobart from the oblivion of the Home Guard,* to which the Establishment had consigned this pioneer of armour.

The date at which a short-term menace of defeat was converted into the long-term possibility of survival can now be defined as 15 September. This, the beginning of BARBAROSSA, the attack on Pearl Harbour and the 1943 victory in the Battle of the Atlantic represent four decisive steps towards V.E. Day: the Normandy landings and OVERLORD, though of enormous significance, were not *vital*. 10 July, the day on which attacks on Channel shipping began, is conventionally accepted as the start of the Battle of Britain; 15 August, when in 1786 sorties the *Luftwaffe* made its greatest effort of the campaign, in an attempt to eliminate Fighter Command, may be taken as its peak; but 15 September decisively marked its conclusion. Churchill, it will be recalled, spent that day at the H.Q. of the Fighter Group chiefly involved: his relief informs his recollections.

It was 4.30 p.m. before I got back to Chequers, and I immediately went to bed for my afternoon sleep. I must have been tired by the drama of No. II

* See Chapter 1, p. 15.

Group, for I did not wake till eight. When I rang, John Martin, my Principal Private Secretary, came in with the evening budget of news from all over the world. This had gone wrong here; that had been delayed there; an unsatisfactory answer had been received from so-and-so; there had been bad sinkings in the Atlantic. 'However,' said Martin, as he finished this account, 'all is redeemed by the air. We have shot down one hundred and eighty-three for a loss of under forty.'

In fact, not 185 German aircraft were destroyed (as was immediately claimed), but 60, for a loss of 26 planes and 13 pilots from Fighter Command. But this was enough: Churchill's instinctive relief was fully justified, for on 17 September Hitler postponed SEA LION until further notice— and exact intelligence sources made this immediately clear to Churchill and the Chiefs of Staff. In effect this meant cancellation, for the next favourable period of moon and tide was not due until the second week in October, and on 12 October Hitler called the invasion off.

Though the worst horrors of the *Blitz* and the Battle of London lay ahead an essential breathing-space had been secured. The Russo-German Pact had been confirmed, the Japanese New Order proclaimed, and 27 September saw the forging of the alliance between Germany, Italy, and Japan. But Churchill's stewardship had prevailed, and with the passing of the years it becomes more and more evident that the stewardship was Churchill's. His aberrations had been on a minor scale: his achievements gigantic and beyond expectation—even, perhaps, beyond his own. Many of his actions, intuitions, inspirations, were off-the-cuff, immediate responses to urgent challenges. But, viewed from a distance, the arabesque of the impromptu can be seen to contain a recognisable design. This War Lord was *capax imperii*.

3

The Year of the Locusts 1941

'The old wars were decided by their episodes rather than their tendencies. In this war the tendencies are far more important than the episodes.'

Winston Churchill, Resignation speech in the House of Commons,
15 November 1915

At the time of the Agadir crisis in 1911 Churchill composed a visionary memorandum, entitled *Military Aspects of the Continental Problem*, in which he analysed the probable opening phases of a war with Germany. In the first twenty days, he calculated, the Germans would drive the French back on Paris. Each successive day would weaken their armies, as losses increased, lines of communication were stretched, and, from the thirtieth day, Russian pressure began to tell. 'By the fortieth day Germany should be extended at full strain both internally and on her war fronts, and this strain will become daily more severe and ultimately overwhelming.' This is precisely what happened in 1914: by the twentieth day the French were in full retreat, on the thirty-third day the Allies turned and started to move forward across the Marne, and by the thirty-ninth day it was the Germans who were withdrawing. If this pattern is applied to the Second World War it will be seen that 1941 represents the intermediate phase—a period when, at a superficial level, everything appeared to be going wrong, on every front. Yet by the overstretching which produced their spurious successes the Germans laid themselves open to counter-attacks, and when initiative returned to the Allies, in the autumn of 1942, these continued remorselessly until the end of the war. In 1941 every crop of hopes seemed to be consumed by locusts before it could be harvested: but the future was safe underground.

Apart from final victory, the strategic aim most cherished by Churchill during the Second World War was to convert the Mediterranean into Mare Nostrum. Two decisions, taken by him on his own responsibility and at great risk, laid essential foundations for the consummation of his purpose which occurred in 1943 and 1944: but during 1941 the very bed-rock appeared to be dissolving. His first, and fundamental, initiative followed the fall of France. 'So formidable did the situation appear at the end of June,' he recalled, 'that Admiralty first thoughts contemplated the abandonment of the Eastern Mediterranean and concentration at Gibraltar'. Such was the defeatist attitude of the First Sea Lord, Admiral Pound: but, fortified by the more positive reaction of Admiral Cunningham, the Commander-in-Chief on the spot, Churchill firmly and decisively vetoed the proposal, carrying with him the Chiefs of Staff, who on 3 July informed all Commanders-in-Chief that the fleet was to remain in the Eastern Mediterranean. Thereafter, in spite of many disasters, the British were never driven from these vital sea-lanes in any absolute sense. But when Churchill took his decision, in the summer of 1940, before experience had proved that the Italians' use of their predominant air and sea-power would be craven and inept, he was committing an impressive act of faith.

In the circumstances of the time his second decision was even more courageous. While the Battle of Britain was still being fought he agreed that virtually half of the best armour in the country should be urgently dispatched to the Middle East. 'It is odd,' he noted, 'that while at the time everyone concerned was quite calm and cheerful, writing about it afterward makes one shiver'. And indeed the proposition came from the War Office. On 10 August Dill, the C.I.G.S., informed Churchill that it was intended to send immediately to Egypt one cruiser tank battalion, one light tank regiment, and one infantry tank battalion—154 tanks in all, together with precious stocks of field and anti-tank artillery. But it was Churchill the Prime Minister, and only Churchill, who could endorse the proposition: his ready approval was one of those strokes in the field of High Strategy which rarely fall within the scope of a commander, and are even more rarely essayed. It should be weighed in the same scale as his order, on 28 July 1914, for the Battle Fleet to leave its Channel station and, sailing by night, without lights, to pass through the Straits of Dover and move by the dangerous North Sea route to a haven of safety at Scapa Flow. Moreover, it was Churchill who pressed for the tanks to be sent direct to Egypt, through the Mediterranean, and not *via* the Cape as the Admiralty desired. He accepted the advice of the professionals, although in the light of events it appears that his daring had more justification than their caution. Even so, the convoy arrived in sufficient time to make possible the destruction of the Italian army in North Africa, in which the Matildas of the infantry tank battalion had a crucial role.

These dispositions, together with Churchill's relentless pressure on the War Office and Wavell to bring to the highest pitch the Army of the Nile, and the massive reinforcement of the Mediterranean fleet which was effected by Operation HATS in September, bore early but deceptive fruits. A growing sense of superiority over the Italian fleet culminated in the attack by Cunningham's torpedo-bombers at Taranto on 11 November, in which *Littorio* and two older battle-ships were sunk at their moorings for the loss of two aircraft. And soon the great foray along the African shores, master-minded by Wavell and executed by General O'Connor, would reach its climax at Beda Fomm—an operation well summarised in Wavell's Special Order of the Day of 14 February 1941

> The Army of the Nile, as our Prime Minister has called us, has in two months advanced over 400 miles, has destroyed the large army that had gathered to invade Egypt, taking some 125,000 prisoners and well over 1000 guns besides innumerable quantities of weapons and material of all kinds.

The results of decisions taken *ad hoc* seemed to be coalescing in a recognisable design: but the locusts were already gathering. And during the process which led to these results there also gathered signs that, on his lower level of performance, Churchill was proving—as he would continue—unable to shed habits of irrelevant action or prejudiced judgement which marred and sometimes nearly destroyed, his previous career. He still had not learned, and he would never learn, the truth embodied in a note Asquith made in his diary in 1916: 'There are two fatal things in war. One is to push blindly against a stone wall, the other to scatter and divide forces in a number of separate and disconnected operations.' Thus in November he was obsessively seized by the idea put forward by his old friend Roger Keyes, then directing Combined Operations, for capturing and holding the rocky little island of Pantelleria (some 150 miles N.W. of Malta) Cunningham's argument, that enemy possession of Sicily would neutralise Pantelleria, and that to sustain Malta was already an almost intolerable burden for his fleet, overcame the Prime Minister's ardour—for the time being—but much energy was consumed by his hard-pressed advisers in distracting him from a project which was patently ill-conceived.*

In regard to Wavell, moreover, prejudice had begun to warp his judgement in a sinister and dangerous fashion which contributed directly to the disasters of 1941. Wavell had been summoned back to London in August

---

* In justice to Churchill, it should be noted that the Chiefs of Staff at first supported this project: their enthusiasm, however, waned, while his persisted in the face of facts. On 13 January he wrote to the Chiefs of Staff, 'I remain completely of opinion that WORKSHOP' (the code-name for Pantelleria) 'is cardinal.' And so incensed was he by Wavell's opposition that he made the extraordinary suggestion recorded in Eden's diary for 5 December: 'Winston unhappy at (Pantelleria) plan being turned down . . . and proposed that I should go out to command in Middle East'.

10 *With the battalion of the Royal Scots Fusiliers Churchill commanded in France in 1915*

COMRADES IN ARMS

11 *Egypt, 1942. Churchill visits the 4th Hussars, whom he joined in 1895*

12 *Lunch in London's docks*

BATTLE OF BRITAIN

13 *Rivetting a Spitfire*

1940 for a series of summit conferences on the Middle Eastern situation. Out of these emerged, on the credit side, the concept of 'armour for Egypt'. But there was an immense debit. Wavell's taciturnity* generated in Churchill's mind those waves of suspicion and distrust by which his Commander-in-Chief Middle East was ultimately engulfed. Even the apparently miraculous abolition of an Italian army did little to allay his doubts. This became evident while O'Connor was still waiting with his troops for permission to exploit his victory and advance to Tripoli. There was an imminent German threat to Greece. At a War Cabinet meeting on 11 February the danger was discussed, and it was decided that maximum forces should be diverted to meet the menace. After the meeting Dill told his Director of Military Operations, Major-General Kennedy, that: 'I gave it as my view that all the troops in Middle East are fully employed and that none are available for Greece. The Prime Minister lost his temper with me. I could see the blood coming up his great neck and his eyes began to flash. He said: "What you need out there is a Court Martial and a firing squad. Wavell has 300,000 men, etc. etc." I should have said, "Whom do you want to shoot exactly?", but I did not think of it till afterwards.'† This was four days after Beda Fomm. Lord Butler heard him observe of Wavell, some months later, 'I do not understand his intellect. It may be my own fault, but I always feel as if in the presence of the chairman of a golf club.' Here was a tragic myopia.

Hitler's drive to the south during 1941 was the direct consequence of Churchill's Mediterranean policy, which had resulted in the collapse of Italy as a credible military power. The first steps in Mussolini's suicide as a war leader were his ill-considered, and worse organised, invasion of Greece, and his failure to extract from his admirals and generals those victories which enormous superiority at sea and in Africa should have swiftly achieved. But it was the British reaction which decisively impelled Hitler to intervene in the Balkans and the Mediterranean, committing his forces in far greater strength and for far longer than he had ever intended. When he invaded Russia his rear must be secure: nor could he allow his prestige to be tarnished by the defeat of his ally. He acted accordingly. As early as 20 November 1940 he wrote to the Duce to explain an all-embracing strategic plan. He would endeavour to get Spain into the war, thus blocking the gates of the Mediterranean. German divisions would

---

* 'I well remember one of the meetings at No. 10 when Wavell was quite unable to explain what his situation was and what he intended to do. I thought at the time that he would be replaced then.' Sir Ian Jacob, private communication.

† Major-General Sir John Kennedy, *The Business of War*, p. 75.

move through Bulgaria into Greece, and *Luftwaffe* bombers would be transferred southwards to destroy the British fleet. Yugoslavia and Turkey would be neutralised. Now, in 1941, this masterplan was set in motion, and it is essential to see it as a whole when assessing Churchill's contemporary decisions. All its dimensions and implications were in the forefront of his mind: they were the inescapable parameters. When Harry Hopkins arrived in London at the beginning of January, as Roosevelt's personal representative, he observed of Churchill in his first report to the President on 10 January that 'he believes Hitler will permit Mussolini to go only so far downhill—and is now preparing for the attack which must bring its inevitable result. He knows this will be a blow to British prestige and is obviously considering ways and means of preparing the British public for it'.

Meanwhile the winter *Blitz* raged over the cities of Britain—London, incessantly; Coventry, and the great industrial centres; then, after a relative lull in January and February, the '*Luftwaffe's* tour of the ports'. From the beginning of March Portsmouth, Merseyside and the Clyde were heavily attacked. But after one of the worst assaults on London (10 May, when the House of Commons was ravaged), the raids diminished, and were not substantially renewed until 1944. The reason was simple: BARBAROSSA. The *Luftwaffe* moved east. Churchill's duties as Prime Minister, and his quick empathy* kept him keenly aware of the human consequences of the bombing, by which, between June 1940 and June 1941, 43, 381 civilians were killed and 50,856 wounded. As in the Battle of Britain there was no major executive action open to him, but a steady flow of minutes and directives impressed their responsibilities on his ministers. He studied closely the performance of Anti-Aircraft Command, instituting what were known as the night air defence or N.A.D. meetings which were held at least twice weekly and often in his presence. He constantly examined the expenditure of A.A. ammunition in relation to the number of aircraft destroyed, and peremptorily grilled General Pile (C.-in-C. A.A. Command), about the implications of the statistics. And the man who, as a battalion commander on the Western Front, paid close and expert attention to the *minutiae* of trench engineering, can be observed advising his Home Secretary on the correct technique for draining Anderson air-raid shelters. 'Bricks on edge placed loosely together without mortar, covered with a piece of linoleum, would be quite good, but there must be a drain and a sump. I am prepared to help you in a comprehensive scheme to

* A remarkable example of his humanity was his initiation of the scheme for compensation for War Damage—against Treasury advice.

tackle this.' By broadcasts, by tours of inspection, by sharing the common man's dangers, he notably sustained morale. But as Minister of Defence he could take a more pragmatic view, since the effect of the *Blitz* on the British capacity to wage war, though intermittently damaging, was never, as Göring had hoped, lethal. After eight months' bombing the aircraft factories and heavy industry emerged scarred but still productive; oil stocks and storage facilities were not gravely affected; ports and railways continued to function; and though food reserves had in some respects been heavily reduced, enough remained in hand for disaster to be avoided —so long as further replenishment could be assured.

This was the crux. Just as, during the First World War, the U-boats almost succeeded where Zeppelins and Gothas failed, so in 1941 the danger appeared to be that, while Göring had been contained, Dönitz and Raeder might win a decisive victory. The *guerre de course* of auxiliary armed surface-raiders continued. In Atlantic sorties the battle cruisers *Scharnhorst* and *Gneisenau* eliminated 115,622 tons of shipping between 22 January and 22 March, and during the first fortnight of February the *Admiral Hipper* accounted for 34,000 tons. The graph of loss from attacks by aircraft—particularly the long-range Focke-Wulfs—rose steadily: 78,517 tons in January; 89,305 in February; 113,314 in March. But it was the submarine which continued to offer the most daunting threat. During the last six months of 1940 U-boats disposed of 471 ships of 2,186,158 tons: and though in January the monthly rate of loss fell notably, to 126,782 tons, it increased thereafter, every month, until in June the peak figure was reached of 310,143 tons. The full dimensions of the situation may be gauged from the fact that in March, April and May the total losses from all causes rose in each month to over half a million tons: they should be set against the figures for the two worst months of 1917 when, before the convoy system brought relief, the Admiralty and the Government were reduced to despair. (In May of that year the total of British losses was 593,206 tons: in June 683,325.) As they added up their sums in these dark days Churchill and his advisers had few grounds for anticipating that with the sinking of the *Bismarck* on 27 May interference with Atlantic convoys by the German battlefleet would cease; that the armed raiders would wither away; that attacks by aircraft would soon be mainly limited to the Mediterranean and the Russian convoys; and that new methods, new equipment and intensive training would cause the losses from U-boats to diminish dramatically during the second half of the year. It is, in fact, all too easy to understand the emotional pressures behind this outburst in *The Second World War*: 'Indeed, it was to me almost a relief to turn from these deadly under-tides to the ill-starred but spirited enter-prises in the military sphere. How willingly would I have exchanged a full-scale attempt at invasion for this shapeless, measureless peril, ex-pressed in charts, curves and statistics!'

The lament was uncharacteristic, because it was Churchill's prime quality as a war leader that he was always at his best when things were at their worst—'most master of himself amid the din of battle'. Preparing for invasion in 1940; facing an implacable Stalin, eyeball to eyeball, to inform him that a Second Front was deferred; persuading the Americans not to give the Pacific priority over Europe; marshalling counters to the menace of the V weapons—these were the times when his experience, his energy, his statesmanship and his massive common sense seemed to fuse together in the white heat of danger. The dross was purged. Indeed it was precisely at times when the heat was off, when his imagination could roam freely, unshackled by the practical needs of the insistent present, that he was most prone to indulge his weakness for the tangential, the idiotic, the unattain-able. And so, in the spring of 1941, he applied himself with supreme concentration to the supreme issue—survival. For this, he saw, was what was at stake in the Atlantic. 'Battles might be won or lost, enterprises might succeed or miscarry, territories might be gained or quitted, but dominating all our power to carry on the war, or even keep ourselves alive, lay our mastery of the ocean routes and the free approach and entry to our ports.'

The problem, as in 1917, was to bring cohesion, energetic management, imagination, and a concentration of all available resources to bear upon this vital sector of the war. In January the Import Executive, under the Minister of Supply, and the Production Executive, under the Minister of Labour, were established to co-ordinate and promote all that could be done at home by way of rationalising the use of merchant ships and effectively administering dock labour and port facilities. 'I shall myself,' Churchill wrote to the Minister of Shipping on 4 January, 'keep in the closest touch with the Import Executive, and will endeavour to give the necessary directions'. But this, it might be said, was basically a defensive move: attack was the more important issue. Already, in August 1940, Churchill had minuted to the First Sea Lord, 'The repeated severe losses in the North-western Approaches are most grievous, and I wish to feel assured that they are being grappled with the same intense energy that marked the Admiralty treatment of the magnetic mine. There seems to have been a great falling off in the control of these Approaches.' His proposal, however, that the centre of control should be shifted from

Plymouth to further north had not been immediately acceptable to the Admiralty. In February all was changed. The Western Approaches Command was moved to Liverpool: and here the C.-in-C., working closely with Coastal Command, was able to grasp the situation from a central point where, as the *Official History* puts it, 'under the direction of a highly skilled staff from both services, the naval and air sides of the Atlantic battle were fully integrated, and a constant watch was maintained over the whole vast battlefield and over the hundreds of warships, merchantmen and aircraft involved in the unremitting prosecution of the campaign'. Henceforth, and until the end of the war, Liverpool was to be the nerve-centre for an ultimate and absolute victory.

But it is the function of the true war leader not simply to administer and dictate: he must also inspire, and one of his arts is to find simple but dramatic combinations of words in which the essence of a situation becomes significant and intelligible. Roosevelt knew this. Hitler had his own verbose methods. But it was Churchill—Churchill the artist as much as the demagogue—who had the most profound sense of the value of the right word as a battlecry. His scrupulous attention to the choice of effective code-names for important military operations was no mere pedantry. And how subtle, for example, was the shift from 'Local Defence Volunteers' to 'Home Guard'! Now, once again, the lion roared. 'This mortal danger to our life-lines gnawed at my bowels. Early in March exceptionally heavy sinkings were reported by Admiral Pound to the War Cabinet. I had already seen the figures, and after our meeting, which was in the Prime Minister's room at the House of Commons, I said to Pound, "We have got to lift this business to the highest plane, over everything else. I am going to proclaim 'the Battle of the Atlantic'." This, like featuring "the Battle of Britain" nine months earlier, was a signal intended to concentrate all minds and all departments concerned upon the U-boat war.'

It was not barren nominalism—the employment of verbal abstractions without any corresponding reality. A 'Battle of the Atlantic Committee' was immediately instituted. The first meeting was held on 18 March, with Churchill in the chair, and during the critical period, until 8 May, long sessions occurred every week. It was composed of the War Cabinet and other relevant Ministers, the Chiefs of the Naval and Air Staffs, and a number of scientists. Here, at the highest level, all the important factors could be held in focus. It was the executive instrument for the overall plan of campaign issued by Churchill on 6 March under the title 'The Battle of the Atlantic. Directive by the Minister of Defence'. The thirteen paragraphs of this magisterial document, simple, clear and comprehensive, described in unequivocal terms what must be done and how it should be effected. It was Churchill's habit to publish in full, in *The Second World War*, only those of his papers of which he was most proud or which he considered most important. This is one of them,* and rightly so. Certainly neither Chamberlain nor Halifax could have written it.

But even a hagiographer could hardly ascribe to the Prime Minister alone Britain's temporary emergence, during the latter half of the year, from the crisis at sea. This was the fruit of hard and constructive effort at many levels in many departments and Commands, and no doubt that effort was, from time to time, impeded or misdirected by Churchill's own enthusiasm. Yet he would have been inhuman if he had been master of every detail, or never chased a will-o'-the-wisp. As a fragment of the Greek poet Archilochus observes: 'The fox knows many things, but the hedgehog knows one big thing.' Churchill in this crisis knew what the one big thing was, and did it: co-ordinate, decentralise, supervise, and refuse to take 'No' for an answer. And there was good reason for him to claim, subsequently, that 'it was a great advantage that the whole process of our many decisions could be passed continuously through a single mind'. Before Halder, the Chief of the German Army Staff, was dismissed in September 1942 as a result of disagreement over Hitler's conduct of the Russian campaign, he noted in his diary, 'Feverish reactions to momentary impressions and a complete failure to understand the command machinery and what can be done with it are the hall-mark of this so-called "Leadership".' Whatever his critics may allege, and frequent though his minor aberrations may have been, such a charge cannot be justly laid against Churchill's conduct as a War Lord. In the big things he rarely went astray.

In his Directive on the Battle of the Atlantic one factor, of central importance in the conduct of the battle, was omitted. This was the steadily increasing co-operation of the United States. Behind a façade of non-involvement Roosevelt deviously continued to enmesh his country by interpreting with daring liberality the concept of 'all acts short of war'. And in January two significant events occurred, premises from which, in retrospect, the mounting American contribution seems to flow with the inevitability of a logical process. But nothing was inevitable *at the time*. America had, indeed, a self-interest in the preservation of Britain as a bulwark. Yet the many restrictive pressures on Roosevelt might well have imposed far greater caution if, as he took Churchill's measure, he had been

---

* *The Second World War*, Vol. III, p. 107: also at Appendix O of Roskill, *The War at Sea*, Vol. I.

unable to decide that Britain could, and would, survive, and that Churchill was not only capable but also trustworthy.

The first event was the arrival in London on 9 January of 'Roosevelt's Man Friday', Harry Hopkins. His mission was remarkable. The official letter of authorisation from the President simply observed: 'Reposing special faith and confidence in you, I am asking you to proceed at your early convenience to Great Britain, there to act as my personal representative. . . .' He had no other status. But in fact his task was to assess the validity of the British war effort and, in particular, the British Prime Minister, and to send the President frank and secret reports of his findings. Churchill knew nothing of Hopkins, and had to be briefed by Brendan Bracken: Hopkins had grave reservations about Churchill. Nevertheless he came, he saw—and he was conquered. In his first report to Roosevelt, written on the notepaper of Claridge's hotel, he confessed his conversion. In the thirty pages of his final report he wrote:

> In the two weeks since my arrival in England I have spent twelve evenings with Mr. Churchill and I have explored every aspect of our mutual problems with him. I have also had extended conferences with all the Cabinet Ministers and most of the Undersecretaries. I have had long and detailed conferences with the Chief of the Imperial General Staff, Sir John Dill, and with the First Sea Lord, Admiral Pound, and with the Chief of the Air Staff, Sir Charles Portal, and with the Chiefs of the Fighter and Bomber Commands. I have visited Scapa Flow and the Coast Defences at Dover and various cities and towns and airfields. They have given me complete access to all confidential information which is concerned with my mission here. I believe insofar as it is possible to get a picture here in a short time, I have got a reasonably clear perception not only of the physical defences of Britain, but of the opinions of the men who are directing the forces of this nation. Your 'former Navy person' is not only the Prime Minister, he is the directing force behind the strategy and conduct of the war in all its essentials. . . . The spirit of this people and their determination to resist invasion is beyond praise. No matter how fierce the attack may be you can be sure that they will resist it, and effectively.

From this faith Hopkins never budged. It was an enormous achievement on Churchill's part to have convinced this shrewd and sceptical spy, nor was it done without conscious and dexterous diplomacy. But the dividends were inestimable. Roosevelt's policy was confirmed and fortified: for Britain, in the short term, it was a tremendous benefit that on his return Hopkins became the effective executant of, and driving power behind, Lend-Lease. Moreover 'there was started at this time correspondence without precedent: an informal, off-the-record but none-the-less official correspondence between the heads of two Governments through a third party, Hopkins, in whose discretion and judgement each had complete confidence'.* In other words, Churchill was able to use Hopkins as a stalking-horse about matters which he felt unable to raise directly with Roosevelt in the 'Former Naval Person' exchanges.

The second event, as unique, in its way, as the Hopkins mission, was the conference which began in Washington at the end of January, continued until the end of March, and produced the plan, or rather the set of conclusions, known as ABC-1. Nothing illustrates better the fruitful but Alice-in-Wonderland relationship which Churchill had established with the United States than these staff talks, in which Rear-Admiral Danckwerts, Major-General E. L. Morris, and Air Commodore Slessor, with Rear-Admiral Bellairs to lead them, reviewed with their opposite numbers the whole field of common Anglo-American military interests, and produced a report which was endorsed by the Chiefs of Staff of both countries. The talks were conducted in the greatest possible secrecy. The British were supposed to be 'technical advisers to the British Purchasing Commission', and always wore civilian clothes. (Slessor, however, recalled that 'perhaps the only criticism of the selectors of the team was that it would have been difficult for the least suspicious enemy agent in Washington to take us for anything but British officers; Ted Morris and Dancks in particular were almost caricatures of the popular idea of what a British general and admiral ought to look like.') The dominating theme of the report was that, should Britain and the United States become jointly involved in a war with Germany and Japan, their concentration of effort would be on *Germany first*; a British Joint Staff Mission was established in Washington (to provide, later, the basis for the Combined Chiefs of Staff organisation); and many other arrangements were proposed and accepted for Anglo-American co-operation.

Until Pearl Harbour turned into a formal alliance what has been called a common-law marriage these two acts of engagement between a belligerent and a non-belligerent, no more than peaks in a continuing process, were followed by a stream of others, immensely valuable in every sphere of the war, but in none more so than in the Atlantic battle. Apart from the Tizard mission (see p. 49) pooling of intelligence proceeded at many levels. The F.B.I. joined with 'the quiet Canadian', William Stephenson, in checking espionage and sabotage by the agents of Germany, Italy,

* Robert Sherwood, *The White House Papers of Harry L. Hopkins.*

Japan, Vichy France, Spain, and (until BARBAROSSA), Soviet Russia.*
American military and technical specialists visited Britain for study and
instruction, and British aircrews were trained in the U.S.A. As to the
Battle of the Atlantic, the steps taken during 1941 read like a calculated
escalation, though each, from the President's view-point, was politically
hazardous, and from Churchill's manna from heaven rather than an
automatic provision. Nevertheless, the ladder ascended: 1 February, U.S.
Atlantic Fleet formed; March, U.S. mission in the U.K. selects naval and
air bases; 3 April, Roosevelt orders transfer of 10 coastguard cutters; 4
April, refitting of British warships in American dockyards agreed; 7 April,
U.S. naval and air bases open in Bermuda; 11 April, American Defence
Zone advanced to all waters west of 26° West . . . and so on, until on 1
September the U.S. Navy is authorised to escort any nation's shipping in
the Atlantic, and on the 11th Roosevelt announces 'From now on if German or Italian vessels of war enter these waters they do so at their own
peril'. Churchill's declaration of 'the Battle of the Atlantic' had indeed
been no mere exercise in nominalism.

It is, however, an index of his burdens that on the eve of the day his
Directive was issued, 6 March, he wrote a long letter to Eden in Cairo,
stating that circumstances 'make it difficult for Cabinet to believe that we
now have any power to avert fate of Greece unless Turkey and/or
Yugoslavia come in, which seems most improbable. We have done our
best to promote Balkan combination against Germany. . . . We do not see
any reason for expecting success . . . rapid German advance will probably
prevent any appreciable British Imperial forces from being engaged'.

When the restoration of the Greeks after the First World War was under
consideration, Hankey recorded in his diary an observation of Lloyd
George: 'with their geographical position and control of their islands, their
friendship in case of war may be valuable to a maritime power whose communications in the eastern Mediterranean are peculiarly open to attack
from submarines lurking in the islands. As he puts it "You never know
when this little mouse may not serve to gnaw the rope that binds the
British Empire".' Now, as Hitler set in motion the strategy which he had
described to Mussolini in November, Churchill was faced not simply by a
nibbling mouse but by a *tiger-sprung*, the leap of a ferocious killer. Wavell
had foreseen this in a remarkably accurate appreciation of the task of

---

* See H. Montgomery Hyde, *The Quiet Canadian*, for details of the extensive and fruitful
collaboration between Stephenson's 'British Security Co-ordination' and U.S. agencies like the
F.B.I. and O.S.S. The collaboration was continuous from 1940 to 1945. It was at Churchill's
personal request that Stephenson undertook his transatlantic mission.

Middle East Command which he had sent to the C.I.G.S. as early as 31 July 1940. '. . . whether Italy is openly hostile or nominally neutral, our only possible counter to the German intention to bring S.E. Europe under her power is by a domination of the Mediterranean at least as complete as in the Great War *as early as possible*. If not within the first month or two of war, it may be too late. . . .' In the winter of 1940/41 the signs were abundant that it was probably already too late. In October Hitler had virtually given the Duce a free hand in Greece, but by November he confessed to a 'regrettable blunder', and in mid-December he issued an order for an invasion of Greece, MARITA, which might, if necessary, be extended to an occupation of the whole country. By mid-February the Defence Committee was weighing, at its meetings on the 10th and 11th, a War Office estimate that the Germans were assembling in Roumania some 30 divisions (including five armoured), whose spearheads might reach the Greek frontier, via Bulgaria, on 12 March and be in Salonika a week later. Moreover, the transfer of *Fliegerkorps X*, with its 150 bombers, from Norway to the Mediterranean instantly abolished Britain's growing maritime ascendancy. On 10 January the aircraft carrier *Illustrious* was almost destroyed: on the 11th the cruiser *Gloucester* was hit, and the *Southampton* sunk. Aircraft working from Benghazi, and from bases on Rhodes and the Dodecanese, began to block the Suez Canal with magnetic mines so effectively that on several occasions in February the Canal was closed, with serious delays to traffic. It seemed that from every quarter a net was closing round Mare Nostrum before it was even ours.

Years later Churchill complained (in a conversation in 1948), that 'they now say that I went to Greece for the wrong reasons. How do they know? The point is that it was worth it'.* His policy may have been

'begotten by Despair
Upon Impossibility'

but it was the only statesmanlike course. For the British the Balkans have always been remote countries of which they have known nothing: but to Churchill they were a vivid presence. His experience of the Great War had taught him what it meant when they crumbled—and how easily they could crumble. The nightmare of Germany in occupation of the northern shores of the Mediterranean; of a *putsch* through Turkey towards the Canal, and the vital oilfields (which Hitler and his High Command actually considered that winter, and only rejected after careful examination); of the British fleet driven from the sea; of Malta, Gibraltar, Alexandria aban-

* Lord Boothby, *My Yesterday, Your Tomorrow*.

doned; of the great gains in North Africa dissipated—all this now seemed imminent. If the Führer had had his will, most of it would indeed have happened: much of it did. Churchill's decision to reinforce Greece was not, therefore, as is often suggested, the romantic gamble of an amateur: it was the best that could be done by him, or by anyone else in charge of Britain's affairs, in a situation of extreme weakness. For what was the alternative? Hindsight is a delusive guide, since hindsight is sharpened by the knowledge that within a few months Hitler would invade Russia, and so engage vast armies elsewhere. But *at the time*, although Churchill had reason to suspect the Führer's intentions in the east, he had no certain grounds for knowing how and when they would be implemented. Was there any sense, therefore, in abandoning Greece, ignominiously, and allowing Wavell to advance to Tripoli? To maintain the Army of the Nile so far to the west would, in any circumstances, have presented a formidable administrative problem: with the Germans swarming over the Balkans, in Greece, in Sicily, in the Dodecanese, and with *Fliegerkorps X* (almost certainly reinforced), in command of the skies, it would have been impossible. 1941 was not 1943. Moreover, the decision to support Greece with all available aid was *not that of Churchill alone*. It should be remembered that it was only taken with the agreement of, and after lengthy consultation with, the Chiefs of Staff and the interested governments of Australia and New Zealand. It was not taken before Eden and Dill, the C.I.G.S., had been sent to the Middle East to examine the situation with the Commanders-in-Chief on the spot, or before Churchill had specifically ordered them to reject the proposal if they doubted its viability. Wavell went into Greece without protest, on the basis that there was a reasonable prospect of success: the documents in the case are indisputable.*

Nothing could be done about Spain: but nothing needed to be done, for Franco gave Hitler his *congé*. Yugoslavia was inaccessible politically and militarily: militarily, because armed intervention on a significant scale was obviously impossible, and politically because German agents and agencies pullulated in Belgrade and the royal faction was more concerned with self-interest than with taking risks. For months beforehand London knew of the mounting opposition against capitulation to the Nazis, which

---

* After years of reflection Ismay wrote to General Sir Richard O'Connor, on 19 January 1949: 'H.M.G. were perfectly prepared to drop the Greek adventure when it was reported that Papagos was blowing hot and cold. But we got a very strong united protest from the authorities then in Cairo, namely Eden, Dill, Wavell, Cunningham and Tedder, suggesting that we were duck-hearted and that the Greek campaign was not only essential from the political point of view, but also advisable from the military point of view. ... I might add that I was also pessimistic about the Greek adventure, but I must admit that having regard to the advice of the men on the spot we had no option.' (private communication.)

culminated in the *coup* of 27 March when the pro-Axis government was displaced by General Simovitch. Had the *coup* occurred earlier, it might have been marginally more difficult for the Germans to over-run Yugoslavia, but there is no indication that Churchill contemplated the possibility. Turkey, however, seemed a better prospect. But Turkey knew only too well that the bleating of the lamb excites the tiger: it was precisely because her government saw that they were open to German assault that they refused to do anything to stimulate it—and they were, as they would remain, equally fearful of Russia's intentions. This soon became clear to General Sir James Marshall-Cornwall who, on Churchill's orders, was sent to Ankara in December with a small mission to endeavour to bring the Turks into the war. (He was the only senior officer qualified as a first-class interpreter in Turkish, and in the previous year had signed the Anglo-Turkish Military Agreement.) 'My tour of Turkish military units and establishments convinced me that they would stand no chance against German invasion; far from being a worth-while ally, Turkey as a co-belligerent would prove a most expensive drain on our resources. German panzer divisions could have quickly over-run Thrace—an ideal terrain for tanks; Istanbul could be reduced to ashes in a few hours by German bombers. The Turks were very backward in tank warfare and A.A. defence. Their field artillery was entirely horse-drawn. They had, in fact, a bow-and-arrow army.'* Wavell foresaw an inevitable wastage if he was instructed to push some of his small forces into Anatolia: Cunningham envisaged grave problems for the Navy. In any case, when on 31 January Churchill appealed personally to the Turkish President, offering him ten squadrons of aircraft and 100 A.A. guns as the price of his co-operation, he was politely snubbed, in spite of his rhetorical claim that 'the victories we have gained in Libya will enable us to give a far more direct and immediate measure of aid to Turkey in the event of our two countries becoming allied in war, and we will make common cause with you and use our growing strength to aid your valiant armies'. The Turks knew better, and when, early in April, Rommel counter-attacked in North Africa the British case was destroyed. On 9 April, as the Germans poured into Greece, Marshall-Cornwall obtained an interview with Inönü and, in Churchill's name, invited him to enter the war: but the President, whose suspicion of British pretensions was now confirmed, merely roared with laughter.

It thus appears, in retrospect, that any attempt to consolidate an effective alliance of the Balkan powers in 1941 could have produced no more than a house of cards. But a scrutiny of Churchill's contemporary

* Private communication.

signals and directives does not suggest that in his heart he believed much more than this was possible. Nevertheless, he was convinced that the effort must be made and, like Lord Hermiston in Stevenson's novel, 'on he went up the great, bare staircase of his duty, uncheered and undepressed'. His case must rest on the argument that there was no satisfactory alternative to an unsatisfactory policy: his critics should not evade asking themselves whether the expulsion of the British from Greece and Crete had worse consequences for Anglo-American relations than any other course of action which Churchill might conceivably have followed. Roosevelt's telegram to Churchill after the evacuation is relevant. It began: 'You have done not only heroic but very useful work in Greece, and the territorial loss is more than compensated for by the necessity for an enormous German concentration and resulting enormous German losses in men and material. Having sent all men and equipment to Greece you could possibly spare, you have fought a wholly justified delaying action. . . .' And equally relevant is Churchill's telegram to Wavell of 3 June. In this he announced that some 74 ships were coming across the Atlantic, at President Roosevelt's order, bringing to the Middle East 200 light tanks and many other important items. Would such succour have been sent to a country which had just abandoned an ally?

Certainly the result was expulsion. This was in part because when, at the beginning of March, the Greeks were finally persuaded to accept an Imperial Expeditionary Force, the bases of a possible defence immediately dissolved. General Papagos refused to withdraw his troops from their advanced positions, in Macedonia and Albania, to what the British rightly considered to be the more tenable Aliakmon Line. But it was the Belgrade *coup d'état* which was crucial. This caused Hitler to reshape radically his operation MARITA which, initially, had only been aimed at Greece. Now he decided that Yugoslavia must also be not only assaulted, but annihilated. He therefore reacted violently. Ten divisions were hurled south, and of these five, including three armoured, engaged the scattered and ill-equipped Imperial force. All fronts collapsed, and Papagos requested that the British should re-embark to avoid the devastation of his country. Of the 62,000 who were sent to Greece about 50,000 were in the end recovered by the Navy: but their guns, tanks and transport remained. In his signal to Wavell of 17 April, in which he gave the orders for evacuation, Churchill added, 'Crete must be held in force': but even this would shortly prove to be impossible. Nothing was now left of the house of cards except, somewhere among the ruins, the embers of resistance. But it would be long before a Tito would emerge. In the meantime, it can be seen that there is not even any truth in the old argument that British intervention in Greece fatally delayed Hitler's invasion of Russia and perhaps saved Moscow. The insurgents in Belgrade were a stronger reason for deferment. Until the day of the *coup*, 27 March, the notional date for BARBAROSSA was 15 May. On 27 March this was put back a month, and on 7 April Brauchitsch issued a warning that D Day would be 22 June. This was confirmed at the end of April. Brauchitsch gave the Yugoslav situation as the reason for postponement.

Along the southern shores of the Mediterranean, moreover, the locusts were already at work. In 1940 Hitler had seen the need for, but had not activated, his own expeditionary force to come to the aid of the Duce's incompetent African army. But on 14 February a reconnaissance and an anti-tank battalion, the forerunners of the *Afrika Korps*, disembarked at Tripoli with Rommel in command. This was an overture to two years of conflict, in which it appeared at times that Churchill's Mediterranean ambitions would be shattered: a conflict bringing the Germans closer to the Nile Delta and the Suez Canal than that great drive through the Caucasus so feared in 1941, so imminent in the summer of 1942, which never in fact materialised. Wavell completely mis-judged Rommel's potentiality. But so did Hitler. On the available evidence, and bearing in mind the logistic difficulties, Wavell appreciated that the Axis in Africa had neither the strength nor the ability to achieve and sustain an easterly advance. 'I do not think,' he reported, 'that with this force he will attempt to recover Benghazi'. Nor was this the Führer's intention. It was Rommel who noted the weakness of the Western Desert Force, and Rommel's unpredictable mastery of desert manoeuvre which, by 11 April, drove the British back to the Egyptian frontier, leaving a frail garrison invested in Tobruk. Rommel was frank about what he was doing. 'There'll be consternation amongst our masters in Tripoli, and Rome, and perhaps in Berlin too,' he wrote on 3 April. 'I took the risk against all orders and instructions because the opportunity seemed favourable. . . .'

But between the beginning of April and the middle of June, when the situation in the desert was temporarily stabilised after the failure of Wavell's BATTLEAXE offensive, it was Churchill who continued to feel consternation—not because his commanders were attacking but because, in his view, they were insufficiently aggressive. He diagnosed three necessities: to cut off Rommel's supplies, to reinforce Wavell with armour, and then to destroy the Axis in North Africa. Amid all his other preoccupations —the *Blitz*, the Atlantic, and disintegration of the Balkans—he erupted with the passionate energy of a wounded animal: with a rage so ferocious that at times it blinded him to the facts. He was always prone to upbraid his commanders for failing to go up to the front and take charge of the fighting: now *he* would command. So much, he saw, depended upon ruthless concentration of effort at the key point—the desert. The requirements for success were not too large, the opposition not too daunting, if only the will to act could be elicited. At times it seemed to him that he was carrying everything on his own back—cautious Chiefs of Staff, an exhausted fleet, generals in the field who flagged or failed. Passion made him unjust to others: but it was a justifiable passion. Nor did he lose his poise. Alanbrooke, who was not yet so closely involved with Churchill that a detached view was impossible, noted on 27 May: 'It is surprising how he maintains a light-hearted exterior in spite of the vast burden he is bearing. He is quite the most wonderful man I have ever met, and it is a source of never-ending interest, studying him and getting to realise that occasionally such human beings make their appearance on this earth— human beings who stand out head and shoulders above all others'. But frustration growls in the minutes.

Prime Minister to General Ismay, for Chiefs of Staff　　　　*20.4.41*

. . . The fate of the war in the Middle East, the loss of the Suez Canal, the frustration or confusion of the enormous forces we have built up in Egypt, the closing of all the prospects of American co-operation through the Red Sea—all may turn on a few hundred armoured vehicles. They must if possible be carried there at all costs. . . .

Prime Minister to C.I.G.S.　　　　*22.4.41*

We must not forget [about Tobruk] that the besieged are four or five times as strong as the besiegers. There is no objection to their making themselves comfortable, but they must be very careful not to let themselves be ringed in by a smaller force, and consequently lose their offensive power upon the enemy's communications. Twenty-five thousand men with 100 guns and ample supplies are expected to be able to hold a highly fortified zone against 4,500 men at the end of 700 miles of communications, even though these men be Germans; in this case some of them are not. . . .

But Churchill was unable to command from the front, and what was obvious to him in his map room in Whitehall could seem entirely different to the man on the spot. In his first essay, therefore, he was grossly at fault. Rommel could only survive if he was supplied. What more logical than to deny him his main port—Tripoli? In his memoirs Churchill ascribes to

Pound and the Admiralty the proposal signalled to Cunningham on 15 April: '. . . an attempt must be made to carry out a combined blocking and bombardment, the latter being carried out by the blocking ships at point-blank range as they approach the harbour. After carefully considering the types of ships which can be used it has been decided that *Barham* and a "C" class cruiser should be used for the purpose.' There can be no doubt, however, that this was a Churchillian *diktat*, and that Churchill was wrong—as Cunningham robustly maintained, pointing out that it was ten to one against an effective sealing of the harbour by a sunken battleship, and that in any case the price would be the certain loss of some 1000 highly trained officers and men. Cunningham won: but still, against his better judgement, was compelled to bombard Tripoli with his battle fleet. The enterprise was unexpectedly successful, no ship being hit, but the Admiral signalled to the Admiralty that 'it has taken the whole Mediter-ranean Fleet five days to accomplish what a heavy flight squadron working from Egypt could probably carry out in a few hours'. Here Cunningham slipped, for he had laid himself open to a crushing counter from his Prime Minister. 'About your air support: you should obtain accurate information, because no judgement can be formed without it. The Chief of the Air staff tells me that the same weight of bombs as you fired of shells into Tripoli in 42 minutes, viz., 530 tons, might have been dropped

(a) by one Wellington squadron from Malta in 10½ weeks, or

(b) by one Stirling squadron from Egypt in about 30 weeks'.

It is an interesting point, however, that Churchill's signal to Cunning-ham of 24 April, of which this is the third paragraph, is emollient and explanatory. It concludes with flatteringly secret information about Roosevelt's intentions in the Atlantic, and ends: 'I have taken the pains to give you this full account out of my admiration for the successes you have achieved, your many cares, my sympathy for you in the many risks your fleet has to run, and because of the commanding importance of the duty you have to discharge'. The Former Naval Person was not always so douce with his Admirals. (Tovey, C.-in-C. of the Home Fleet at the time of the P.Q.17 disaster in July 1942, provides a different example.* The

---

* As do others. After the French squadron escaped from the Mediterranean and reached Dakar, at the time of the abortive expedition in September 1940, the Flag Officer commanding the North Atlantic Station, Admiral North, was summarily dismissed and, in spite of the doubts felt about his punishment, was never allowed 'to vindicate myself before whatever board or tribunal their Lordships may see fit to appoint'. After 8th Army reached Tripoli in January 1943, Montgomery trenchantly criticised the Navy's efforts in clearing the blocked harbour. The Commander-in-Chief Mediterranean, Admiral Harwood (who at the River Plate had been responsible for the sinking of the *Graf Spee*), was relieved of his command, with Churchill's knowledge and approval.

Times obituary observed that 'Tovey, who was never a man to pull his punches or mince his words, made it plain that he regarded the Admiralty's constant interference in the conduct of his operations as the chief cause of the calamity. There is no doubt that at this time Churchill wished to have Tovey, whom he once described as "a stubborn and obstinate man", relieved of his command'.) But Wavell had also achieved many successes, in spite of many cares and in the face of many risks; he, too, discharged a duty of commanding importance; in East Africa, that spring, his small army either killed or captured a quarter of a million Italians, and overran a million square miles: yet he was to be accorded neither explanations nor sympathy.

In a second round, his advisers were at fault and Churchill triumphantly right. On the morning of Sunday 20 April he was in the country working in bed, as usual, when a signal arrived from Wavell describing his shortage of tanks and adding 'Stop press. I have just received disquieting intelligence'. The German division recently disembarked at Tripoli had been identified as armoured—it was, in fact, 15 Panzer. Churchill's reaction was instantaneous. Ismay was summoned, and within hours the Chiefs of Staff in London received a peremptory order to detach at Gibraltar the tank-transports of the fast convoy W.S.7, about to leave Cape-about for the Middle East, and send them, accepting all risks, straight through the Mediterranean. There was strong opposition from the Admiralty. Dill and Alanbrooke resisted a reduction of the dangerously few tanks available in Home Forces to meet invasion. At the Defence Committee next day, however, Pound agreed to run the ships through, and on 10 May the *Tiger* convoy, having lost one transport, delivered at Alexandria 234 tanks and 43 Hurricanes. Churchill signalled to Wavell: 'I have been working hard for you in the last few days. . . . If this consignment gets through the hazards of the passage . . . *no Germans should remain in Cyrenaica by the end of the month of June.*'* The message was Wavell's sentence of execution.

But the episode has another significance. How often one reads, in wartime diaries and post-war analyses, those absolute condemnations of Churchill for acting against the advice of his professional advisers, as though this was in some sense sacrosanct! Yet Chiefs of Staff have never been endowed with Papal Infallibility. If he himself, only too often, was misguided and obdurate, the heads of all three of the armed services, at different times and in different ways, were equally aberrant in the policies they proposed. To their credit, and to his, there was never a disastrous

* Author's italics.

schism: but with a war to wage it is understandable if, on occasion, Churchill summoned all his pugnacity, his eloquence, and his fertility of contrivance to master them when judgement or instinct convinced him that they were wrong. Understandable, too, that sometimes his response was acid. On the day the *Tiger* convoy passed Gibraltar and entered the Mediterranean, 6 May, Dill addressed to the Prime Minister, and circulated to his colleagues, a memorandum entitled 'The Relation of the Middle East to the Security of the United Kingdom'.* The good sense of much of this paper is overlaid by a pervasive defeatism: as is now known, Dill was approaching the end of his tether. But this time there was nothing emollient in Churchill's reply. 'I thoroughly agree with you in para 8,' he wrote, 'that our military advisers under-rated the Germans in Norway, in Belgium, and in Libya. Of these Belgium is the most remarkable. Yet I never remember hearing a single British soldier point to the weakness of the Sub-Maginot Line or deprecate our occupation of Belgium. I only mention this to show that even the most expert professional opinion may sometimes err amid the many uncertainties of war'. And then he added, 'I wonder whether the German action in the Balkans can be cited as an example of "their capacity for overcoming the most formidable of difficulties". As a mere exercise in historical perspective, I should have thought the opposite was true . . .'.

Error was not exclusively his: if, for example, he was hectic and impetuous over the question of tank-production, was he not struggling with the consequences of one of the most lamentable episodes in British military history, that combination, before and after 1939, of lethargy, myopia, order, counter-order and disorder exhibited by a sequence of General Staffs and their technocrats in the design and production of armour?† On the day before he received Dill's paper the first of the 'Tank Parliaments' had assembled, initiated by Churchill in a minute to Ismay which stated: 'I wish to have a conference on tank questions and future developments, to which the commanders of the tank divisions should be invited, as well as representatives of the Ministry of Supply. . . . *The officers of the tank forces should be encouraged to prepare papers of suggestions, and are to be*

---

* The memorandum in full, and the substance of Churchill's reply, are printed in *The Second World War*, Vol. III, p. 373 foll.

† 'Churchill had no love for the Foreign Office, one of the very few Departments of which he had never been head. He suspected them of pursuing their own policy, irrespective of what the Government might wish, and he mistrusted their judgement. One evening, after he had abused the Foreign Office . . . with unusual vehemence, I reminded him that during the afternoon he had been equally harsh about the Treasury. Which, I asked, did he dislike the most? After a moment's thought, he replied: "The War Office!"' Colville, *op. cit.*

free to express their views. . . .'* Yet Martel, then commanding the Royal Armoured Corps—a man of ineffable self-satisfaction—has confessed in his autobiography† that 'I arranged for all the armoured divisional commanders to meet me just before the meeting at No. 10 and at that preliminary meeting we agreed as to what we would say if the Prime Minister descended to these detail matters. General Hobart did not usually join in our general agreement but all the other divisional commanders agreed to voice the same view if they were asked for their opinion. After all, the Prime Minister could not himself know anything about the technique of armoured warfare, and such matters were far best left to the Royal Armoured Corps to settle'. No wonder his own generals sometimes seemed to represent the enemy!

No previous study of Churchill's conduct of the war has sufficiently emphasised the effect on his thinking of his constant interest in the latest information about the enemy. Readers of his memoirs will have noted incidental references to 'the secret intelligence' in his communications with his commanders overseas. He made it a matter of principle that he should be supplied with such intelligence 'raw'—that is, not in the doctored précis of a staff assessment but as it had come to hand. Thus he felt, often with good reason, that in his central position he was exceptionally equipped for keeping himself 'in the know'. All that was romantic in him, moreover, thrilled to the excitement of intercepted signals, Delphic reports from agents, the broken codes, the sense of participation. This knowledge is essential if one is to understand his decisions and, at a lower level, his impatience with his commanders. In the Civil War, Corelli Barnett has written in *Britain and Her Army*, 'The Parliamentary Commander-in-Chief, the Earl of Essex, controlled neither grand strategy nor even all the Parliamentary armies, for he and his fellow-commanders were subjected to a stream of messages and letters from the Westminster politicians'. How much more is this true of Churchill and his commanders! And yet, when the matter is placed in perspective, how comprehensible becomes the intolerance of a man who, feeling he had the enemy's cards in his hands, could not grasp why his generals or admirals were not acting as *he* would have done—ruthlessly, swiftly, and finally! A man, nevertheless, who also failed to grasp that sometimes a local condition may thwart what seems logically inevitable.

Harmonious reconciliation of these attitudes was impossible, and now they overwhelmed Wavell. It seemed plain to Churchill that Tobruk was

* Author's italics.
† Lieut.-General Sir Giffard Martel, *An Outspoken Soldier*, p. 178.

fulfilling its function of 'a thorn in the side of the enemy', and that Rommel's evident shortages of fuel, men, and equipment were not going to be made good by the German High Command, whose eyes were fixed on Russia. In London, therefore, the *Afrika Korps* appeared to be ripe for destruction. Moreover, the Prime Minister took a personal interest in the tanks which the *Tiger* convoy had delivered—his cubs, as he called them. Here were riches for Wavell—why could he not immediately exploit them? It was useless for Wavell to explain that the weary relics of the divisions which had eliminated an Italian army, and themselves been shattered in Greece, needed time to re-organise, and that many of the tanks which had reached Alexandria were disgracefully unsound. Churchill harried, and Wavell succumbed: the result was BATTLEAXE, the engagement on the Egyptian frontier which Wavell initiated under pressure, having warned the C.I.G.S. that 'I think it right to inform you that the measure of success which will attend this operation is in my opinion doubtful'. Action began on 15 June. Rommel displayed a tactical skill far more sophisticated than the inept arrangements of the British, and the upshot was a message from Wavell to Dill which started, 'I regret to report failure of BATTLEAXE'.

Resentment and distrust now coalesced in Churchill's mind. Twice, in 1940 and 1941, Wavell had opposed shipment of armour through the Mediterranean; though he had accepted support for Greece, he had failed to submit to London a precise military appreciation to justify that acceptance, and Crete appeared to have collapsed because energetic measures for its defence had not been undertaken from Cairo; over Iraq, and again over Syria, he had been reluctant to intervene when instant action seemed critically important: and now, in an operation which, for Churchill, was the inevitable preliminary to the relief of Tobruk and the abolition of the Axis in Africa nothing had happened but fumbling and defeat. Yet Rommel, on the information in Churchill's hands, looked like a sitting bird. The consequence was:

Prime Minister to A. P. Wavell   *21.6.41*

I have come to conclusion that public interest will best be served by appointment of General Auchinleck to relieve you in command of armies of Middle East. I have greatly admired your command and conduct of these armies both in success and adversity, and victories which are associated with your name will be famous in the story of the British Army and are an important contribution to our final success in this obstinate war. I feel, however, that after the long strain you have borne a new eye and a new hand are required in this most seriously menaced theatre. . . .'

Perhaps the comment in the memoirs of Lord Ismay—a perceptive and loyal supporter of Wavell—is the correct conclusion about a sad failure of inter-communication between two great men. Ismay says that 'there are limits to human endurance, and it was felt by many people in London, including some of his close friends and ardent admirers, that Wavell was mentally and physically tired, and in need of a respite from the tremendous responsibilities which he had borne so resolutely for so long'. Still, what happened between Wavell and Churchill—and was to happen between Churchill and Auchinleck—supplies a case-history: a documented example of how a War Lord, insistent on action, can so misunderstand the realities of the battlefield that he not only fails to comprehend the qualities of his commander but even forces him, against his will, to undertake an abortive operation. Hitler's generals on the eastern front now learned what this could mean, and for them the intolerable pressure was even more disastrous.

On the day before Wavell was sacked Colville records that he was walking with Churchill on the croquet lawn at Chequers 'when he said that he was now sure Hitler would attack Russia. Remembering the part he had played in inspiring the pro-White expedition to Archangel in 1920, and his detestation of Communism, I enquired whether this event might not put him in an awkward predicament. He replied: "If Hitler invaded Hell, I would at least make a favourable reference to the Devil in the House of Commons".' At 4 a.m. on the 22nd the anticipated news was telephoned to Chequers. Colville prudently refrained from alerting his master until breakfast-time: the only response was 'Tell the B.B.C. I will broadcast at 9 tonight'. Here was a situation which, in Churchill's own words, 'altered the values and relationships of the war'.

Drama is one thing, and reality is another. Much is made—and much was made by Churchill himself—of his radio talk that evening in which he proudly proclaimed that 'the Russian danger is therefore our danger, and the danger of the United States, just as the cause of any Russian fighting for his hearth and home is the cause of free men and free peoples in every quarter of the globe'. Stirring, generous words. But in fact he knew, that night, exactly what he was doing: this was no sudden, emotional response to a new and cataclysmic event. As far back as April it was becoming clear that Russia was Hitler's next target, and long before BARBAROSSA was launched Churchill had warned Stalin—without receiving any reply—

that invasion was on the way. (Stalin had, of course, been advised from his own sources, and the enigma as to why he ignored his intelligence is a large question, only relevant here in that it must have puzzled Churchill. 'Why,' he must have asked himself, 'doesn't the man act as I do? How could anyone have been so taken by surprise?' In July 1941 he did not foresee that some critics would later consider that Singapore was to himself as BARBAROSSA was to Stalin.) Thus Churchill had weeks in which to weigh the contents of his broadcast: moreover, when he publicly turned his coat, and committed his country to the support of a régime he had so often vilified, he knew, even before he spoke, that this would also be Roosevelt's policy. As indeed it was. On 8 July the schedule of Russian requirements from the United States (estimated to be worth some two billion dollars), was delivered by the Soviet Ambassador in Washington. On 21 July Roosevelt ordered an urgent review of this formidable indent, and gave instructions that he must receive, *within forty-eight hours*, a list of what could be immediately supplied.* By 26 July Harry Hopkins was at Archangel, alone, having reached there by a Catalina flying-boat along a route only just opened, and within 24 hours he was in Moscow, with Stalin, announcing that he 'came as personal representative of the President. The President considered Hitler the enemy of mankind and therefore wished to aid the Soviet Union in its fight against Germany.'

For Churchill this opening of a vast new front was a particular benediction, because it coincided with a strong feeling in Washington that British concentration on the Middle East was a policy of sending good money after bad. There were many indications, but the trend of thought was perhaps expressed most nakedly at a meeting at 10 Downing Street before Hopkins left for Russia. The Chiefs of Staff were present, as well as some important American emissaries in London, Admiral Ghormley, General Chaney, and the attaché who had done so much to integrate Anglo-American effort, General Lee. Hopkins frankly defined American doubts about the Middle East and added, 'I don't want to overstate the case, but it is vitally important that we come to an understanding on this matter so that the people in authority in Washington will really know why we must get supplies to the Middle East and then develop and carry through a programme to that end'. The doubters, the 'people in authority in Washington', included the American Chief of Staff, George Marshall.

---

* 'He saw to it that these orders were heeded. Despite opposition in the Army and Navy, and hesitation within the State Department, he got the first list through the mill by notes to his defence assistants that were straight commands.' Herbert Feis, *Churchill, Roosevelt, Stalin*, p. 11.

Many views may be taken about this devaluation by the Americans of British—and in particular Churchill's—strategy, but certainly German intervention in Russia came at a critical point. The threat of a swift Russian collapse, and the consequent menace to the Canal and the vital oilfields, gave a new focus to the Army of the Nile. Moreover, though in the eyes of sceptics nothing solid seemed to have been achieved in an area where Churchill had so deeply committed himself, another front had been opened: and here, it seemed to him, he could demonstrate to the men about him, to the Washington *galère* he was wooing and to the world at large, that words might be followed by deeds.

Yet from those men who surrounded him, from the carefully considered appreciations of the Chiefs of Staff, he received little comfort—for Russia, it was assumed, would be defeated at least within a few months. In America, as in London, the professionals were pessimists. As the weeks passed this mood persisted. When Ismay returned to London from Russia in October, having accompanied the Beaverbrook Mission, there was a discussion about Hitler's promise to the German people that Moscow would fall by Christmas. Dill thought the odds were five to four on: Churchill thought it was even money. (Ismay, fortified by what he had seen in Russia, was ready to lay ten to one against.) Nevertheless, Churchill accepted the consequences as well as the responsibility of bringing the Soviet Union into the ambit of an alliance. Along the benches of the Conservative party, and in the *coulisses* of the military establishment, there were those who knew better: but one of his virtues as a War Lord was a broad back. Reinforcement of Russia became his preoccupation.

But how could this be achieved? He sometimes fell into moods of doubt. Lord Butler was present at a dinner-party in the Edens' new flat above the Foreign Office on 5 July when Churchill burst out: 'What can we do to show the Russians we are in earnest? Remember that on my breast are the medals of the Dardanelles, Antwerp, Dakar and Greece, and I cannot support any more adventures or expeditions like that. I do not believe our generals could manage a major raid. They have not got beyond Crécy and Dettingen.' This was the result of an order he had given the Chiefs of Staff on 23 June, the day after BARBAROSSA was launched, to explore the viability of a raid on the Pas de Calais. 'I have in mind something of the scale of 25 to 30 thousand men—perhaps the Commandos plus one of the Canadian divisions.' (A curious foretaste of Dieppe.) But with the landingcraft then available only 6000 troops at the most could have been put ashore, and in any case all assault shipping was earmarked for the force continually standing by to capture the Atlantic Islands in the event of a German thrust through Spain. This was thought to be a probable follow-up to a German victory in Russia—and the appreciation was correct, for at this time Operation FELIX–HEINRICH, aimed at Gibraltar, was scheduled for the autumn of 1941. Nothing effective, therefore, could be contemplated across the Channel.*

Nevertheless, convoys must carry to Russia all that could be spared: crumbs from the poor man's table, for this, in 1941, was Britain's meagre capacity. Those advising the Prime Minister were reluctant: an invasion was still, in their view, a possibility, and during these months a tank seemed to Dill and Alanbrooke not so much a crumb as a lump of gold. Ismay recalled that 'it was like having all one's eye-teeth drawn out at the same time'. And there was a further consideration—Singapore, to whose importance Dill had drawn Churchill's attention in his May memorandum. On 28 August the Chiefs of Staff minuted to the Prime Minister, on the issue of Hurricanes for Russia: 'The direct military value to us of Russia having these aircraft, only a proportion of which would reach the first line, is not high. . . . These aircraft would pay a better dividend if sent to the Far East and to the Middle East and/or Turkey. . . . On the other hand, the Chiefs of Staff realise that political considerations may be over-riding.' Churchill, therefore, was torn between intolerable options—those which only a War Lord can effectively evaluate. Others have accused, as the Chiefs of Staff implied, that Churchill (and Roosevelt), were prone to take 'political' decisions which, in some sense, conflicted with the relevant 'military' facts. But what is a War Lord for? To make judgements at the very summit of strategy. At this level of decision 'political' and 'military' converge, and every act of Churchill's in relation to Russia in 1941 demonstrates the point. For what, in essence, was he trying to achieve? To maintain an ally. By taking calculated risks, to keep in the fight an enormous auxiliary, with whose survival Britain's was now linked. Every endeavour to that end was politico-military: the two strands of the thread were inextricably interwoven.† Indeed, the fallacy of a *simpliste* opposition of the two terms can be easily indicated. Was Churchill's decision to drop the royalist Mihailovitch in favour of the Communist Tito 'political' or 'military'? And his decision to send British troops into Attica, in December 1944, to support the royalists and thwart the communist ELAS—was this 'military' or 'political'?

* In September, however, the C.-in-C. Home Forces was asked to consider what he called 'a mad scheme put up by the Joint Planning Staff for a feint attack on the Cherbourg peninsula to relieve the pressure on the Russians'. Alanbrooke, *Diary*, 8 September 1941.

† 'The distinction between politics and strategy diminishes as the point of view is raised. At the summit politics and strategy are one.' Churchill, *The World Crisis, 1915*.

Yet many judged, and still judge, Churchill's sustained support of Russia as merely, and in the worse sense, 'political'. It was certainly unpalatable: unpalatable to him, as much as to the Chiefs of Staff, to provide the odious Stalin with a single Hurricane or even a soldier's boot—though hundreds of aircraft and millions of boots were in fact dispatched. Moreover, after the convoys were started and losses mounted it seemed to the sceptics, on a strict analysis of cost/effectiveness, that they were an investment without dividends.* Britain's stocks of the paraphernalia of war for her own purposes were desperately low: the diversion of naval escorts from the inadequate flotillas elsewhere looked, to some admirals, like lunacy:† and there was always the knowledge that America was switching to Russia much of the *matériel* which Pittsburg and Detroit should be sending to Britain herself. Nor, in retrospect, does it appear that the convoys were as justified, in practical terms of tons delivered, as it seemed at the time. The supplies which ultimately reached Russia through Persia were at least a comparable contribution. Nevertheless, for Churchill the convoys were inescapable. In 'the after-time', as he liked to call it, it is difficult to recapture the pressing sense, in 1941, that the panzers might slice through to Russia's heartland—still more difficult to realise how, even after the winter's snows had preserved Moscow, both Prime Minister and President were haunted by the fear that Stalin might make another deal with Hitler. The pact of 1939 was unforgettable. To the Marshal's imperious demand for a Second Front, which struck a key-note for all Anglo-American strategic discussions until 1944, there could be no immediate answer. Might Russia, then, in spite of everything, request an armistice? These were hard-headed, pragmatic estimates. They were almost certainly wrong. Nobody, on the evidence now available, could find it conceivable that Stalin might have capitulated. In 1941 and 1942, however, Churchill and his advisers thought that this was not only credible but probable. Their fear, incidentally, goes far to explain Churchill's almost desperate readiness to ignore the mounting signs of Russian intransigence. In his bulldog way he barked. But, in the event, everything had to be swallowed—the inefficient arrangements in Russian ports, the

* In 1941/42 90% of the merchantmen in the Russian convoys were British or American. The escorts were British. The climax of loss occurred in July 1942, when 23 ships were sunk from P.Q.17, a convoy of 35, and the sailings were temporarily suspended.

† On 18 May 1942 Pound wrote to his opposite number in America, Admiral King: 'These Russian convoys are becoming a regular millstone round our necks and cause a steady attrition in both cruisers and destroyers. . . . The whole thing is a most unsound operation with the dice loaded against us in every direction, but at the same time I do, of course, recognise the necessity of doing all we can to help the Russians at the present time. What we do not know is how much what we are sending them really means to them.'

refusal to co-operate at sea or in the air, the obscurantism about plans or orders of battle, the curt, contemptuous, and constantly renewed demands for more.

The paradox about Churchill's conduct of the war is that, in any given period, his mind could traverse the whole spectrum of strategy from firm commitment to the obdurately non-committal. Critics have found this phenomenon puzzling and even reprehensible. Yet the practice of keeping options open while undertaking the irreversible seems to be a habit, and perhaps a necessary function, inherent in the nature of a War Lord. Granted their differences in temperament and modes of thought, both Hitler and Roosevelt behaved with a similar inconsistency. So did Stalin: and in this same year the Japanese endeavoured in a most extreme fashion to mix open-ended policies with irrevocable decisions. Certainly Churchill, in the summer and autumn of 1941, oscillated. There were two constants —the fundamental requirement of bringing the United States into the war, and the practical necessity of victory in the Middle East. Now (though less dominant), there was Russia. But about Singapore (see Chapter Six), he was decided only to be indecisive, and his views about the strategic air offensive (see Chapter Five), were becoming increasingly ambivalent. In regard to another long-term issue he was equally cautious. This was at once the dilemma, and the duty, of a man running a war with insufficient assets.*

The long-term proposition about which Churchill had reservations was outlined in a Review of Future Strategy produced, on his orders, by the Future Operations Section of the Joint Planning Staff, and submitted on 14 June. It was a purblind forecast of what was to follow—pardonably so, in the current circumstances—for its central thesis was based on the dogma that 'the effort involved in shipping modern armies with the ground staff of Air Forces is so great that even with American help we can never hope to build up a very large force on the Continent'. A Germany possessing 250 divisions and interior lines of communication could never be beaten in the field, unless attrition could diminish this overwhelming superiority. Blockade and bombing must therefore proceed—at increased rates. The last section of the report was entitled The Distant Future. Whenever this

---

* 'When Dorman-Smith was Commandant of the Staff College in the Middle East in the early part of the Second World War he very properly, as Commandant, used to deliver the lecture on the Principles of War himself. On one occasion when the time for a general discussion was reached a Polish officer stood up and in halting English said that the Commandant had omitted one important principle. Dorman-Smith was mildly surprised, but courteously asked him to explain. "You must," said the Pole, "be stronger." '

Brigadier Shelford Bidwell, *Gunners at War*

might be, the planners proposed that patriots in occupied countries should be organised and armed to co-operate with a slender Allied expeditionary force of 10 or so divisions, mainly armoured. Here was a pessimistic anticipation of OVERLORD! The Chiefs of Staff, however, while refusing to ratify the final proposal until it had been more carefully examined, did recommend that the paper as a whole should be circulated to the Dominion Prime Ministers, and Commanders-in-Chief abroad. There was much in it that chimed in with Churchill's own thinking—American allies, intensive bombing, no European Armageddon. Nevertheless, as the weeks passed he rejected the report as too academic, and overtaken, anyway, by BARBAROSSA. There were too many imponderables. To circulate such a paper would be an implicit commitment to a specific policy. The options must be kept open.

But the chameleon soon changed colour. Reluctance in one field of strategy was succeeded by obsessive enthusiasm in another, for Churchill's Norwegian syndrome supervened. In both Great Wars his propensity for yearning to do the wrong thing in the wrong place was never more painfully revealed than in his Baltic or Scandinavian projects. This had happened in 1940. Now Stalin encouraged him. On 19 July, when the Russian crisis was at its height, the Marshal sent the Prime Minister a personal message in which he requested the opening of a Second Front not only across the Channel but also in the north. At first Churchill made the only sensible reply, pointing out that 'it would be impossible to land troops, either British or Russian, on German occupied territory in perpetual daylight without having first obtained reasonable fighter air cover. We had bitter experiences at Namsos last year, and in Crete this year, of trying such enterprises'. All he could offer was the news that air strikes on German shipping off the coast of Norway were in hand, while cruisers and destroyers were being dispatched to Spitzbergen, and a flotilla of submarines would operate in northern waters, 'although owing to perpetual daylight this service is particularly dangerous'. But his enthusiasm was only temporarily restrained: the passion for what Ismay once called 'an Arctic Gallipoli' soon returned.

In September Home Forces carried out a major exercise, BUMPER, to make ready for the invasion which, it was thought, might well follow a Russian collapse. The exercise had hardly ended, and the conference to evaluate its lessons had not yet been held when, at midnight on 3 October, a special messenger from the War Office arrived to inform Alanbrooke that he must prepare immediate plans for an attack on Trondheim. He reported to Chequers for further instructions. 'The plan was to be sufficiently ready only to require the order to start. I was given one week to prepare it.' During that week Alanbrooke tidied up BUMPER and wasted many hours of study and consultation in producing what was inevitably a pessimistic appreciation. His recollection of the conference on Sunday 12 October—at which Churchill observed that 'I sometimes think some of my generals don't want to fight the Germans!'—is worth quoting at length, for it describes graphically the Churchillian technique so often employed when he took on the professionals single-handed.

When we were all assembled he shoved his chin out in his aggressive way and, staring hard at me, said: 'I had instructed you to prepare a detailed plan for the capture of Trondheim, with a commander appointed and ready in every detail. What have you done? You have instead submitted a masterly treatise on all the difficulties and on all the reasons why this operation should not be carried out.' He then proceeded to cross-question me for nearly two hours on most of the minor points of the appreciation. I repeatedly tried to bring him back to the main reason—the lack of air-support. He avoided this issue and selected arguments such as: 'You state that you will be confronted by frosts and thaws which will render mobility difficult. How can you account for such a statement?' I replied that this was a trivial matter and that the statement came from the 'Climate Book'. He at once sent for this book, from which it became evident that this extract had been copied straight out of the book. His next attack was: 'You state that it will take you some twenty-four hours to cover the ground between A and B. Explain to me exactly how every hour of those twenty-four will be occupied?' As this time had been allowed for overcoming enemy resistance on the road, removal of road-blocks and probably reparation to demolition of bridges and culverts, it was not an easy matter to paint this detailed picture of every hour of those twenty-four. This led to a series of more questions, interspersed with sarcasm and criticism. A very unpleasant gruelling to stand up to in a full room, but excellent training for what I had to stand up to on many occasions in later years.

The meeting finished shortly after 8.30 p.m. and for the second time Winston had been ridden off Trondheim. . . .

Ridden off: but not unseated. Throughout 1942 and 1943 Churchill continued, vainly, to press for a Norwegian expedition, JUPITER, and even made rash committal promises to Stalin. The Chiefs of Staff maintained a solid front: but as late as 24 August 1943 the project may still be found preserved, like a fly in amber, in paragraph 13 of the 'Final Report to the President and the Prime Minister' after the Quebec Conference. 'In case circumstances render the execution of OVERLORD impossible, it may be necessary to consider JUPITER as an alternative. Plans for this operation, with particular reference to an entry into Southern Norway, should therefore be made and kept up to date.' Yet it is an ironical fact that the Prime Minister's persistence is paralleled by a sequence of attempts to persuade the Germans that an invasion of Norway *was* imminent. In the autumn of 1941 the War Office initiated just such a scheme, and *via* two double agents, MUTT and JEFF, a number of reports were fed to German intelligence suggesting that an assault force was in being. In the autumn of 1942, again, another Norwegian threat was 'disclosed' as part of the cover plan for TORCH. In the following year there was even more activity. 'Norway was a favourable playground for deception, and even the most retentive memory would have difficulty in recalling just when and how often our agents helped to put into effect a threat against that country. The bulk of this work fell on MUTT and JEFF, who originated a threat in April, in August, and again in October of 1943.'* In the event the paper tigers of deception were probably as effective as, and certainly more economical than, the real forces which Churchill sought to launch in an Arctic Gallipoli: for Hitler, like his opponent, became obsessed by the opportunities which Norway offered to an invader, and locked away, far in the north, divisions which would have been invaluable in Russia or on D Day. This was a fruitful reversal of Canning's dogma that 'a menace not intended to be executed is an engine which Great Britain could never condescend to employ'.

It is essential, however, to keep these essays of Churchill the Generalissimo in perspective: to remember that they represent the efforts of an over-burdened man genuinely and desperately attempting to identify an area of the possible in what was an impossible situation. Moreover, although they appear impractical in retrospect, and were certainly wearisome for his staffs at the time, they were all tangential. At the centre of decision he remained cool, clear-headed and realistic. He might yield under pressure, but he never broke. The maximum strain came at the beginning of September. By now the Russians had lost half the Ukraine, Leningrad was encircled, and Moscow endangered. On 4 September Maisky, the Soviet Ambassador in London, delivered to Churchill another personal message from Stalin which spoke of Russia's diminishing strength and the 'mortal menace' of the Germans. The Marshal demanded 'a second front somewhere in the Balkans or France, capable of drawing away from the Eastern Front 30 to 40 divisions'. There was more than a hint that, if help were not provided, the Soviet Union might capitulate. Churchill carefully explained the impossibility of military action and his intention, already being implemented, of urgently supplying weapons and raw materials: but when Maisky overstepped the mark the Prime Minister curtly re-

* Sir John Masterman, *op. cit.*

minded him that four months earlier 'we in this Island did not know whether you were not coming in against us on the German side'. 'Whatever happens', he added, 'and whatever you do, you of all people have no right to make reproaches to us.' The same night he replied to Stalin, more politely, but without compromise. And next day he wrote to Stafford Cripps, who, in his Moscow embassy, was taking the colour of his surroundings. 'If it were possible to make any successful diversion upon the French or Low Countries which would bring back German troops from Russia, we should order it even at the heaviest cost. All our generals are convinced that a bloody repulse is all that would be sustained. . . . Nothing that we could do or could have done can affect the terrible battle proceeding on the Russian front. Arrangements can still be made to provide for the campaign of 1942 . . . I sympathise keenly with your feelings as you watch the agony of Russia at close quarters, but neither sympathy nor emotion will overcome the kind of facts we have to face.'

In that letter the key sentence was 'arrangements can still be made to provide for the campaign of 1942': they were, in fact, in hand, and all stemmed from that day at the beginning of August when Churchill, sailing to Placentia Bay in Newfoundland on Britain's latest battleship, the *Prince of Wales*, first confronted Roosevelt. The most productive result of their meeting was not the Atlantic Charter, a worthy statement of mutual good intent which had no discernible impact on the conduct of the war. It was not their discussion of the situation in the Far East, for though Churchill reported to the Cabinet that he was confident about Roosevelt's agreement to warn the Japanese that 'any further encroachment by Japan in South-West Pacific would produce a situation in which the United States Government would be compelled to take counter measures even though these might lead to war between United States and Japan', the President, on his return to Washington, succumbed to Cordell Hull, who felt that the text was 'dangerously strong'. The word 'war' was therefore eliminated, and all the Japanese received was a polite reference to 'safeguarding the legitimate rights and interests of the United States and American nationals'. Apart from renewal of trust between the two leaders, and the reassurance Churchill drew from the sheer fact of the meeting, the main by-products of the conference were specific and determinate. One, for example, was of direct aid in the Battle of the Atlantic—the device whereby, so long as a United States warship was escorting at least one American vessel, any number of British merchantmen could join the safety of the convoy. But the most important decision was embodied in a joint telegram sent to Stalin on 12 August:

'. . . The needs and demands of your and our own armed services can only be determined in the light of the full knowledge of the many factors which must be taken into consideration in conjectures that we make. In order that all of us may be in a position to arrive at speedy decisions as to apportionment of our joint resources, we suggest that we prepare a meeting to be held at Moscow to which we would send high representatives who would discuss these matters directly with you. If this conference appeals to you, we want you to know that pending decisions of that conference we shall continue to send supplies and material as rapidly as possible.

For Stalin this proposal and this promise, signalled to him by the two Heads of State even before the conclusion of their symbolic meeting, confirmed and amplified the many gestures of good will and intent which he had received from both sides of the Atlantic since the day of BAR-BAROSSA. On the British and the Americans it imposed, immediately, the need to examine exactly what could be sent to Russia, and how: and on the British in particular the painful experience of realising, as each category of *matériel* was scrutinised, precisely what Russia's gains from the American 'arsenal of democracy' would mean in terms of Britain's loss. The moment of truth came in mid-September when, at talks in London between Beaverbrook and Averell Harriman, the estimated total of supplies which the United States would have available over the next nine months was reviewed in the light of British and Russian requirements. This provided a basis for the Anglo-American Mission, offered at Placentia, which reached Moscow on 28 September. Its reception was frigid but business-like, and in two days a consolidated list had been mutually agreed of items to be supplied on a monthly rate from the combined resources of the U.S.A. and Britain: 400 aircraft, 1000 tanks, 5000 scout cars over nine months, some 1200 anti-tank guns over nine months, a requirement of 10,000 lorries per month to be investigated in the States . . . and so on. Here, at last, was a detailed charter of commitment. And in November it began to look as though the German flood had been dammed. In the south, the Russians had held at Rostov and Sevastopol: in the centre, though spearheads had thrust to within 65 miles of Moscow, they had been parried: in the north counter-attacks were being launched around besieged Leningrad. Churchill therefore had solid grounds for self-congratulation on the course he had followed tenaciously since June —a course involving diplomacy and argument on three fronts, with the Russians, with the Americans, and with his own Chiefs of Staff.

Within a month, however, two great issues left unresolved at Placentia would come to a head—the capacity of the British, which the Americans doubted, to achieve victory in the Middle East: and the intentions of the Japanese. In the meantime the only instrument with which Churchill could hope to damage Germany, the heavy bomber force, seemed to have reached an *impasse*.

4

Dragon Ascendant
The Strategic Air Offensive
1940-1945

'I know a bird can fly, a fish can swim, and an animal can run. For that which runs a net can be made; for that which swims a line can be made; for that which flies a corded arrow can be made. But the dragon's ascent into heaven on the wind and the clouds is something which is beyond my knowledge.'

Confucius

'Whatever we may wish or hope, and whatever course of action we may decide, whatever the views held as to the legality or the humanity or the military wisdom and expediency of such operations, there is not the slightest doubt that in the next war both sides will send their aircraft out without scruple to bomb those objectives which they consider the most suitable.'

Marshal of the R.A.F. Lord Trenchard, 1927

'When victory was celebrated but little was said of the part played in it by the strategic air offensive. The Prime Minister did, it is true, pay a tribute to Bomber Command in a special message to Sir Arthur Harris, in which he spoke of their "decisive contribution to Germany's final defeat" and praised the "fiery gallant spirit" of their crews. But no tribute was paid to that campaign in the Prime Minister's victory broadcast of 13th May except for a cryptic reference to the attack on V-weapons, and no campaign medal was struck to distinguish those who took part in the strategic air offensive. The Prime Minister and others in authority seemed to turn away from the subject as though it were distasteful to them and as though they had forgotten their own recent efforts to initiate and maintain the offensive ... Sir Arthur Harris was not allowed to issue his Despatch on one of the greatest campaigns of the war. ... The short official history of the Royal Air Force, which was published under the auspices of the Air Ministry, has done much to inform the general public, but it had not sufficient space and did not rest on a sufficient background of research to go very deeply into the problems of the strategic air offensive, and on this subject there is surprisingly little in Sir Winston Churchill's war memoirs. Thus, in the absence of any authoritative or highly informed account, myth and mis-conception have grown and been unassailed.' With this mordant protest the *Official History* begins its concluding survey.*

It is a just comment. With the operations of Bomber Command against Germany—operations sustained from May 1940 to April 1945—Chur-chill's connection was close but ambivalent. This was, and will remain, the most remarkable continuous assault by manned aircraft in the history of the world. Its price, in crews and material, was enormous: some 56,000 officers and other ranks were killed in action or on active service, while it has been calculated that 'the British strategic air offensive over Western Europe cost, on an average, 7 per cent of the manpower effort directly absorbed by the fighting services during the war'. It is therefore easy to understand why, for many reasons, the Prime Minister was intimately involved in its direction. But it is much harder to comprehend or to feel any sympathy for his final rejection of its chief architect and indeed of Bomber Command itself.† Churchill's revulsion from Sir Arthur Harris in the spring of 1945 is uncomfortably reminiscent of Falstaff, and Henry the Fifth's merciless *volte face*:

> 'I know thee not, old man: fall to thy prayers; . . .
> Presume not that I am the thing I was;
> For God doth know, so shall the world perceive,
> That I have turned away my former self. . . . '

Though the offensive is normally called 'strategic' it was only inter-mittently that it entered into top level discussions about the higher conduct of the war. (This is equally true of the United States Strategic Air Forces in Europe. Its historians observe that 'the strategic air offensive at no time enjoyed official recognition in U.S. war plans except as a preliminary to the invasion of Western Europe or a programme undertaken in support of that invasion'.‡) Here is one—though not the only—explanation for the paucity of references to it in Churchill's memoirs. In other important volumes too—in, say, the Alanbrooke papers or the 'Grand Strategy' portion of the *Official History*—the offensive is often conspicuous by its absence. Yet the reason for this anomaly is in fact a chief reason why Churchill had to bear so large a responsibility for the offensive: as it

---

* Webster and Frankland, *The Strategic Air Offensive against Germany 1939-1945*, Vol. 3, p. 284.

† The short passage on pp. 468-9 of Vol. 5 of *The Second World War*, beginning 'But it would be wrong to end without paying our tribute of respect and admiration to the officers and men who died in this fearful battle of the air, the like of which had never before been known, or even with any precision imagined', has a perfunctory flavour.

‡ Craven, W. E. and Cate, J. L., *The Army Air Forces in World War II*.

developed, and particularly as it developed from 1942 onwards under Sir Arthur Harris, it acquired more and more the character of a self-contained, independent enterprise. (On 16 June 1942 Alanbrooke actually recommended that the Chiefs of Staff 'should periodically review and make recommendations as to our bomber effort: it should not be treated as a thing apart'.) The lonely detachment of the crews, on their remote East Anglian airfields or during their prolonged airborne vigils, was a symbol of the separateness of the operations in which they were engaged. The Admiralty was in direct, functional control of the Royal Navy. Alanbrooke dominated his field commanders—even Montgomery. But it was only in the most notional way that the Chief of Air Staff, Portal, was able to impose his will on Harris, whose empire was substantially private. In such a situation it became inevitable that the Prime Minister was cast, not unwillingly, in the role of arbiter and overseer.

His readiness to accept this role was due to his acceptance of what seemed a self-evident fact—one as apparent to his professional advisers, the Chiefs of Staff, as to himself: that, during the opening phases of the war, Bomber Command was the only,* and during the later years a primary, method of so gravely injuring Germany that she would accept defeat. Thus it was that, at least during 1942 and 1943, Harris became a court favourite. But it is certainly a mistake to assume, as some do, that Churchill was *at all times* devoted to the bombing of Germany as the *only* instrument of victory: there is abundant evidence to prove that his scepticism as to its efficiency and validity steadily increased. And here, perhaps, may be found a deep-seated reason for his ultimate *volte face*.

Churchill thought of Bomber Command as being essentially a tool—just as (in his relations with his personal staff) he could think of men as units to use and discard. He never identified himself emotionally with the Command. In the case of the Navy he was rarely so happy as when he embarked on a battleship or went touring in a destroyer along the invasion beaches. He loved to mingle with the Army: this was the recovery of his past. And in the special circumstances of the summer and autumn of 1940 he felt an empathy for Fighter Command, visiting its control rooms and studying with fascination the progress of the Battle for his Britain. But the bomber force never fired his imagination in the same vivid way. It was not, for example, his custom to drop in at an airfield before a raid and

---

* 'There is one thing that will bring Hitler down, and that is an absolutely devastating, exterminating attack by very heavy bombers from this country upon the Nazi homeland. We must be able to overwhelm them by this means, without which I do not see a way through.' Prime Minister to Minister of Aircraft Production, 8 July 1940.

speed his 'minions of the moon' on their way with a hopeful V sign. Thus he was able to regard their efforts clinically and dispassionately, and when, in April 1945, it appeared that there were no more worthwhile targets left in Germany, and the strategic offensive guttered out, there was no inherent difficulty for him in consigning it and its executants to limbo. Moreover, as the teams of investigators began their probing into the true effects of the offensive, it became depressingly evident that these, in the event, had been far less than had been anticipated: that 'the progressive destruction and dislocation of the German military, industrial and economic systems' had really only come to a kind of consummation in the final months of the war—that Speer and German morale had won a victory concealed within an apparent defeat. As Churchill considered the campaign with the hindsight of the post-war years he had good grounds for being cankered by disappointment. They were among the factors which explain—though none excuses—his dismissive attitude towards Bomber Command and its commander.

But in May 1940 there was no room for doubt. It was a case of 'action this day'. One of Churchill's most urgent problems when he became Prime Minister was to discover for Bomber Command that effective combatant role which had been denied it under Chamberlain—partly because of French pressure to avoid attacks on German cities, in fear of retribution, and partly because of the British government's own inhibitions. Unescorted daylight raids had proved disastrous: the dropping of propaganda leaflets had been no more than a useful training exercise. Churchill required a rôle that was meaningful.

On 15 May the War Cabinet gave its authority for an attack, launched the same night, by 99 bombers on the Ruhr. This was the first practical expression of the faith declared by the Chiefs of Staff on 25 May, in their estimate for the Prime Minister (made *before* Dunkirk), of Britain's future 'in a certain eventuality': an estimate which affirmed not only that the country might survive, but that Germany might be defeated by 'a combination of economic pressure, the bombing of economic and psychological objectives, and the creation of widespread revolt in the occupied territories'. Unfortunately, however, the faith was without foundations. Indeed, it might reasonably be argued that the period between that night of 15 May and the day in February 1942 when Air Marshal Harris took up his appointment as C.-in-C. Bomber Command provided little more than the opportunity for Churchill to discover the absolute incompetence of the Command, as it then was, to achieve its objectives: 'a time', as the *Official History* puts it, 'of progressive disillusionment as the limitations which beset the night bomber were gradually and ruthlessly revealed'. During these months, of course, the foundations of future success were being laid: but in terms of concrete achievement all the operational effort and all the sacrifice of lives led, in the end, to that moment of truth on the night of 7 November 1941 when, of 400 planes sent to bomb Berlin, the Ruhr, Cologne and Boulogne, and to carry out various subsidiary operations, 37 failed to return—a disastrous conclusion which caused Churchill at Chequers the following night to tell the then C.-in-C., Sir Richard Peirse (soon to be *limogé* to the Far East), that 'he did not think we had done any damage to the enemy lately', and to impose on the Secretary of State for Air and the Chief of Air Staff his decision that the Command must be conserved: that it was, in fact, 'the duty of both Fighter and Bomber Command to re-gather their strength for the Spring'.

For this anticlimax Churchill cannot be held responsible. The initial failure of Bomber Command was built into its structure. Parsimonious politicians, and inadequate preparation by the Air Staff during the pre-war years, had provided a force of planes and pilots which in 1940 and 1941 lacked both the *expertise* and the strength necessary for a successful offensive. Heavy bombers had, it is true, been designed and ordered during the 'thirties, but Stirlings, Halifaxes and Lancasters were not significantly available until 1942. The Hampdens, Whitleys and Wellingtons which, until then, sustained the main effort were both short in range and also relatively feeble load-carriers—moreover, the bombs they carried were inefficient. Far too little attention had been paid to the basic crafts of navigation and night flying, while a failure to protect air-crews against the cold of high altitudes was in its way as hampering a deficiency as the initial failure to protect troops in the Far East against malaria.

Such was the tool placed in the Prime Minister's hand. It was an early model, and with a Mk. I version he could not be expected to finish the job. Nor was the professional intelligence he received from the Air Staff and the Ministry of Economic Warfare about the targets suitable for attack, and the right methods of reaching them, in any way reliable. There was a plethora of proposals—the German oil complex, communications, naval targets to reduce the sinking of shipping, cities whose destruction might undermine their citizens' morale. It is sad, nowadays, to look back on Bomber Command groping like some ardent but blinded animal from one 'panacea' target to another. The Prime Minister's function was not to evolve but to ratify a workmanlike, overall plan of campaign, and during this period none of those offered to him could be properly so described. Of course Churchill was himself to blame for encouraging a spirit of optimism and expecting too much. After the first attack on Berlin,* executed on 25 August 1940 in response to the first German attack on London the previous night, he was advocating that 'the Germans should get as good as they are giving' and that 'Bomber Command should henceforth spread its bombs as widely as possible over the cities of Germany', while his general directive on the munitions situation, addressed to the Cabinet on 3 September 1940, began with the flat declaration that 'The Navy can lose us the war, but only the Air Force can win it. Therefore our supreme effort must be to gain overwhelming mastery in the air. The Fighters are our salvation, but the Bombers alone provide the means of victory. We must therefore develop the power to carry an ever-increasing volume of explosives to Germany, so as to pulverise the entire industry and scientific structure on which the war effort and economic life of the enemy depend, while holding him at arm's length from our Island'. He may be considered blameworthy, too, for himself issuing from time to time an impulsive directive or request for a switch of targets. But in the circumstances it is difficult to see what other course could have been followed by a man devoted to the urgent and total prosecution of the war, pre-occupied by many other conflicting problems, and compelled to lean on advice and weapons both of which, as the months passed, seemed less and less reliable. However that may be, it was wholly due to Churchill that in the autumn of 1941 the failure of the air offensive was first brought undeniably into the open.

It was Churchill—and Churchill alone—who was responsible for appointing Lord Cherwell as his scientific adviser. And it was Cherwell, passionately hostile to Nazi Germany, who posed in a telling fashion the central question emerging from his growing concern about the effectiveness of Bomber Command. 'Late in 1940,' Churchill wrote in *The Second World War*, 'Professor Lindemann had begun to raise doubts in my mind about the accuracy of our bombing, and in 1941 I authorised his Statistical Department to make an investigation at Bomber Headquarters. The results confirmed our fears'. What had happened provided the Prime Minister with a classic illustration of the dictum by Lord Blackett (who

* Churchill has often been criticised for this attack (an immediate response to the first German bombing of London *owing to a navigational error*), on the grounds that it stimulated Hitler into large-scale bombing of British cities. Apart from the fact that this saved Great Britain, by diverting the *Luftwaffe* from its primary target of R.A.F. fighter and sector stations to cities which could soak up bombs, there was a good precedent. After the first Gotha raids on London in 1917, Lloyd George's immediate reaction was to demand the bombing of Mannheim: and the raids led directly to the famous Smuts Report, Trenchard's Independent Air Force formed for the strategic bombing of Germany, and the foundation of the R.A.F.

himself so brilliantly applied operational research to the practice of war), that 'the scientist can encourage numerical thinking on operational matters and so avoid running war by gusts of emotion'. At Cherwell's instigation Mr. Butt of the War Cabinet Secretariat studied 633 photographs taken by bombers during night attacks in the two months of June and July 1941. His conclusion was that when the moon was full two-fifths of the planes reported to have attacked their targets were hitting within five miles of them, but that in the absence of a moon the figure was one-fifteenth. Butt's sample was small. His calculations could be, and were, criticised on a number of grounds. But neither he nor Cherwell claimed that his results were *absolutely* correct. What mattered, in spite of a strong rebuttal by Air Marshals, was that at last a broad and factually based estimate of Bomber Command's performance had reached the Prime Minister's hands. It could no longer be pretended that aircraft were not dropping their bombs, in the words of the poet Gerard Manley Hopkins,

'At God knows when to God knows what.'

Churchill's reaction was uncompromising. As he wrote in his memoirs, 'The air photographs showed how little damage was being done. It also appeared that the crews knew this, and were discouraged by the poor results of so much hazard. Unless we could improve on this there did not seem much use in continuing night bombing'. A minute followed.

Prime Minister to Chief of Air Staff

This is a very serious paper, and seems to require your most urgent attention. I await your proposals for action.

In his reply Portal recognised that an improvement in the accuracy of his bombers was 'perhaps the greatest of the operational problems confronting us at the present time', but the remedies he proposed, though promising, were not such that they could bear fruit in the short term: for there was, indeed, no quick answer available. Neither operational research, nor better training, nor an increase in tactical subtlety nor the benefits of science could achieve a miracle cure. For the short term there appeared to be only one solution—a sacrifice of the concept of precision bombing, and an acceptance of that principle of indiscriminate plastering of German cities which, it had once been laid down, was 'contrary to British policy'. 43 towns containing 15 million people were picked out for destruction, and if this holocaust could be achieved with the aid of the 4000 bombers he demanded—a wholly unrealistic figure—he could, Portal informed Churchill on 25 September, 'break Germany in six months'.

Though this proposition was no more likely than Portal's other suggestions to produce a short or even long term decisive result, it did have an important consequence: Churchill was not convinced, and his subsequent debate with Portal caused him not only to clarify his thoughts about the Bomber Offensive but also to put them in writing, in a document which marks a turning-point in his ideas regarding its strategic feasibility. This paper, full and explicit, is reproduced in the *Official History*.* Its key passage reads:

> Everything is being done to create the Bombing force desired on the largest possible scale, and there is no intention of changing this policy. I deprecate, however, placing unbounded confidence in this means of attack, and still more expressing that confidence in terms of arithmetic. It is the most potent method of impairing the enemy's morale we can use at the present time. If the United States enters the war, it would have to be supplemented in 1943 by simultaneous attacks by armoured forces in many of the conquered countries which were ripe for revolt. Only in this way could a decision certainly be achieved. Even if all the towns of Germany were rendered uninhabitable, it does not follow that the military control would be weakened or even that war industry could not be carried on. . . . One has to do the best one can, but he is an unwise man who thinks there is any *certain* method of winning this war, or indeed any other war between equals in strength. The only plan is to persevere.

What Churchill was saying, in effect, was that there could be no final victory without an OVERLORD. He had travelled a long way in twelve months: there was a fundamental difference between this view and his declaration to the Cabinet in the previous September, 'The Navy can lose us the war, but only the Air Force can win it'. Out of the debate emerged a tacit permission for Portal to proceed, but in the Prime Minister's eyes he and the Air Staff were now on trial. What could they deliver? The answer was, by the end of 1941 . . . virtually nothing. Bomber Command required an impresario and a showman, and this, as has been seen, was achieved by the sacking of Peirse and the substitution of Harris. It was a sad but inevitable termination to a year in which, it is now believed, one bomber had been lost for every ten tons of bombs dropped. 'The strategic air offensive of 1940-1,' remarks A. J. P. Taylor, 'killed more members of the R.A.F. than German civilians'.

Harris was a remarkable man who still awaits a perceptive biographer. Neither in his own memoirs nor in any other book is his curious combination of qualities fully displayed. He was the only commander in history who, over a very long period, has frequently committed to action virtually the whole of his main force and sometimes his reserves as well. Like that

* Webster and Frankland, *op. cit.*, Vol. 3, pp. 184 and 195.

brilliant general of the First World War, Plumer, he had the superficial appearance of a Blimp. Abrupt and spiky in manner, he projected himself by a racy slang—'panacea targets', 'barnyard bombing'. But this was all on the surface. Behind the façade lay not only moral courage, and a tenacity which verged on monomania, but also, as in Plumer's case, the rare gift, in a commander, of infinite patience. The arch-priest and the architect of area bombing, Harris well knew that it would be months and perhaps years before the quantity of aircraft could be assembled, and the scientific devices perfected, to enable him to win the war single-handed. He was prepared to wait, and in the meantime to exercise that talent without which wars are rarely won—the ability to send young men to their death without, apparently, turning a hair. Here was a tool which, Churchill realised, was shaped to his hand: for although the Prime Minister's scepticism about the strategic value of the bombing programme was now confirmed, it was essential for him, in 1942 and 1943, to make use of it to the maximum. The Americans and the Russians, and the British public and parliament, had to be constantly convinced that Britain was not only in the war but also fighting tooth and nail. So Harris enjoyed a honeymoon period of close relationship with Churchill, aided by the fortuitous fact that High Wycombe, the headquarters of Bomber Command, was near to the Prime Minister's retreat at Chequers. And this occurred even though there is little evidence to suggest that the marriage was more than one of convenience, or that Churchill found in Harris a boon companion like, say, Bracken or Beaverbrook.

The instrument which Harris employed is summarily described in the *Official History*.

> During this period there was virtually no quantitative expansion in the available front-line strength of Bomber Command. In November 1941 the daily average of aircraft available with crews for operations was 506. In January 1943 it was 515. But the force of January 1943 had undergone an important qualitative improvement. In terms of aircraft available for operations, it included a daily average of 178 Lancasters and seventeen Mosquitoes. It did not include any Blenheims, Whitleys or Hampdens, which had been taken out of service between May and September 1942 and which, together, had accounted for more than half of the available force in November 1941. Moreover, the force of November 1941 had no radar aids to navigation and bomb aiming. That of January 1943 was extensively equipped with *Gee*, it had a small *Oboe* Mosquito element and some of its aircraft had been fitted with *H2S*.
>
> These developments, however, had more bearing upon the operations of 1943 than upon those of 1942. Apart from the introduction of *Gee*, which

began in March 1942, they occurred towards the end, and in the case of the introduction of *H2S*, after the end of the year. Though Lancasters came into operational service in March 1942, only an average of seven per night were available in that month and it was not until November that this figure rose above a hundred. Nevertheless, Bomber Command was an incomparably more effective weapon in 1942 than it had been in 1941.

In other words, it was under Harris that what Churchill called 'the Wizard War' at last began to come into its own.

The problem immediately facing the Air Staff, Portal and Harris was how to extract the Prime Minister from a crisis of confidence. During the spring and summer of 1942 he was oppressed not only by uncertainty as to the ability of Bomber Command to justify the huge inroads it was making on the human and material resources of the country, but also by external events, whose implications radically affected the bomber programme. These were the incidence of the Battle of the Atlantic, disaster in the Far East, and Rommel's successful offensive in North Africa which, by July, was to carry him to the threshold of the Nile Delta. For each of these widely separated areas of conflict there were urgent demands and good reasons for a diversion of heavy bombers from their main front, Germany: and Churchill alone could wield the casting vote.

The Battle of the Atlantic was a special case. Defeat by the Japanese or the *Afrika Korps* might involve unpalatable consequences: the severing of the transatlantic lifeline meant extinction. A considerable effort by Bomber Command had already been deployed against the *Scharnhorst* and *Gneisenau* in their anchorage at Brest. But though their dash up-Channel on 12 February 1942 terminated the 'Brest question' which, in Churchill's words, 'settled itself by the escape of the enemy', and though he was able on 14 February to declare to Portal and the Secretary of State for Air, in a crucial minute, that he was 'entirely in favour of the resumption of full bombing of Germany, subject always, of course, to our not incurring losses owing to bad weather and enemy resistance combined', the issue, nevertheless, remained unresolved. A debate continued (and continues today), about priorities: about whether more heavy bomber squadrons should be diverted to Coastal Command or otherwise employed to support the Navy in the defence of the Atlantic lifeline. Though the First Lord expressed agreement with the bombing policy which was made explicit after Churchill's minute of 14 February, in fact the Admiralty maintained its indents on Bomber Command's strength, while other voices could be heard arguing that logic was in the Admiralty's favour. The 'pro' and the 'con' of this debate raise complicated technical questions too elaborate to evaluate here—the question, for example, of the capacity of pilots and aircraft, inadequate for precision bombing over Germany, to perform an effective role over the sea—but the short point is that the pressure was there, and that Churchill had to adjudicate.*

Churchill's second major preoccupation was with the consequences for Bomber Command, which he had outlined to Portal in his paper of 7 October 1941, of America's entry into the war. It was not only that this, combined with Russia's survival during the winter, had made an ultimate British return to the continent a probability rather than a pipe-dream, and that therefore the land forces, in coming years, would require an even larger proportion of the gross national product: there were also serious implications for Britain in the impact of Pearl Harbour on the *psyche* of the American people and the war plans of Roosevelt and his Chiefs of Staff. It was essential that Britain's offensive operations should appear to be sufficiently energetic, and sufficiently promising, to overcome the natural instinct of the United States to concentrate on Japan. It was equally essential to ensure that American policy in the air did not castrate British plans and production programmes. The second of these aims was the more difficult to achieve.

American staff thinking, which from 1937 onwards had given priority to an offensive on Germany rather than on Japan in the event of a war with both powers, envisaged that the offensive would be carried out over Germany by the U.S.A.A.F. as a complement to, but not as a substitute for, conventional operations by land. In spite of the trauma of Pearl Harbour this policy was upheld, and as a result of the Washington Conference, in January 1942, Churchill was able to report to the Chiefs of Staff and the Defence Committee that 'The United States Air Force, already powerful and rapidly increasing, can be brought into heavy action during 1942. Already it is proposed that strong bomber forces, based on the British Isles, should attack Germany and the invasion ports . . .'. But if the fundamental basis of Anglo-American strategy—Germany first—had been preserved, its implementation was temporarily threatened. Under a 1941 arrangement known as the Arnold-Portal Agreement American production in 1942 was to be shared between the U.S. and British air forces—with a

---

* A partial resolution of the debate was achieved by Churchill when he set up the Cabinet Anti-U-boat Warfare Committee. This, which included the Ministers and Service officers most concerned, as well as scientists and American representatives (Averell Harriman and Admiral Stark, U.S.N.), was to meet weekly. Its purpose, in Churchill's words, was 'to give the same impulse to anti-U-boat warfare as had been applied to the Battle of the Atlantic and night A/A defence'. It provided a valuable forum where the conflicting needs of the Admiralty and Bomber Command could be thrashed out at the highest level.

minor allocation to Russia and China. Between 700 and 1000 planes per month were emerging from American production lines through the backing of British resources and as the result of British initiative. Now all was called into question, for to maximise their effort over Europe the American airmen considered themselves entitled to the output of American factories. 'It was obvious', General Arnold informed Roosevelt, 'that the number of airplanes the British were receiving must be reduced'. Arnold came to London to argue the matter, and as a result Air Vice-Marshal Slessor was sent back to the States with Arnold to thrash out an agreed principle of allocation. After intensive discussion a satisfactory document was composed, and by an ironical twist it was handed over on 21 June, the terrible day on which Churchill received in Washington the news of the surrender of Tobruk. Slessor has described the scene. 'We were duly shown into the President's study with our agreed document for the great men's approval. Poor Mr. Churchill, I have never been so sorry for any-one—that Tobruk, after its splendid resistance the year before, should have fallen thus unexpectedly, and when he was actually in Washington. It was a very hot day and he was sitting there by the side of the President's desk, looking rather crumpled in his siren suit and with a face of gloomy thunder. Mr. Roosevelt, in grey flannel trousers and an open-necked shirt, also looked rather dishevelled. They were in no mood to interest them-selves in details, but asked whether we were satisfied, heard what we had to say, initialled our report and dismissed us.'

The thorny question which lay at the core of these considerations was once again tabled by Cherwell. On 30 March 1942 he addressed to the Prime Minister a famous minute which, beginning 'The following seems a simple method of estimating what we could do by bombing Germany', went on to argue that if some half of the 10,000 bombers which he assumed would be produced by the middle of 1943 were to drop their loads on the built-up areas of 58 German towns, of over 100,000 population and con-taining over 22 million inhabitants (each bomber having a notional life of 14 sorties), then 'there seems little doubt that this would break the spirit of the people'. This document was fiercely assailed, especially by the scientists—though Portal and Sir Archibald Sinclair, the Secretary of State for Air, found it 'simple, clear and convincing'. The scientists were, in fact, already profoundly sceptical, as may be judged from an entry in Tizard's diary for 17 February. 'Wrote a note urging use of long-range bombers for anti-ship work rather than night bombing of Germany. The latter is ineffective unless done on a scale very much larger than at present. It will only be really effective when American production gets into full swing. . . . Blackett came to see me with his note about civilian deaths in Germany. He makes out a good case for these not being much higher than our own losses of trained crews of bombers. Bernal left his summary of the results of German bombing of England. Taken as a whole the effect on production and morale has been surprisingly small.' Now Blackett declared that 'Lord Cherwell's estimate of what can be achieved is at least six hundred per cent too high', while Tizard both criticised the mathematics by which Cherwell had calculated the probable result and questioned his assumption as to the number of planes which might be produced. He told Cherwell, bluntly, that 'I am afraid that I think that the way you put the facts as they appear to you is extremely misleading and may lead to entirely wrong decisions being reached, with a consequent disastrous effect on the war. I think, too, that you have got your facts wrong'.

Cherwell's response was specious. He argued that he had only submitted a general proposition, with figures designed 'partly to save the Prime Minister the trouble of making arithmetical calculations', and that in any case, however inaccurate his sums might be, an attack on the scale envisaged must prove catastrophic. Once again this vital issue was brought to Churchill for settlement, since only he could decide it. The trouble was that, short of launching an attack and seeing what happened, nobody *really* knew exactly how many bombs could be dropped in the right place, or what effect, assuming they were aimed accurately and in the right quantity, they would have on Germany's economy and morale*: for, as Churchill observed in *The Second World War*, 'experience shows that forecasts are usually falsified and preparations always in arrear'. But his mind was already clear: he had reached a firm conclusion in February, and now he backed Cherwell and the Air Staff against Tizard and the doubters. 'Because of the position which he occupied and the time at which he submitted his minute', says the Official History, 'Lord Cherwell's intervention was of great importance. It did much to insure the concept of strategic bombing in its hour of crisis'.

For the proper prosecution of the war the necessary requirement, of course, was that the bomber offensive should actually have teeth: but for the future of Bomber Command, in the spring and summer of 1942, it was mainly important that it should appear to have them. This appearance,

---

* This hard fact was conclusively demonstrated by the Singleton enquiry. Following the Cherwell minute, on 16 April Churchill invited a judge, Mr Justice Singleton, to consider ' . . . what results are we likely to achieve from continuing our air attacks on Germany at the greatest possible strength during the next 6, 12 and 18 months respectively?' Singleton's findings were inevitably cast in general terms, and were virtually useless. Not surprisingly: gazing into a crystal ball is not a judicial function.

which disguised a different reality, was skilfully contrived by Sir Arthur Harris, and his success provides a background to the directive which later emerged from the Casablanca conference. Approved by the Combined Chiefs of Staff on 21 January 1943, it began: 'Your primary object will be the progressive destruction of the German military industrial and economic system, and the undermining of the morale of the German people to a point where their armed resistance is fatally weakened.' Here was an explicit Charter, underwritten by the Allied military directorate and authorised by Roosevelt and Churchill. Thereafter the practice of strategic bombing, though interrupted occasionally for sound reasons, was never so seriously called into question until the end of the war.

Harris began his campaign with an assault on Germany and continued it with an assault on his Prime Minister. On 28 March Lübeck and a month later Rostock (on four successive nights) were subjected to incendiary attacks by substantial forces. Unusual precision and concentration were achieved. These medieval towns, 'built', as Harris put it, 'more like a firelighter than a human habitation', went up in flames. Though each was (strategically) a minor and (lying on the coast) an easily identifiable target, the dramatic holocausts captured the imagination of the public and the Prime Minister, while the technical efficiency of the attacks provided solid encouragement for the future. Greater drama, and a wider promise, were presented during the night of 30 March, when 1046 aircraft were sent to bomb Cologne, more damage was done to the city than by 1346 sorties made during the previous nine months, and only 40 planes were reported missing. The British public, the enemy and the Allies could not know, at the time, that Harris had only been able to launch this historic operation by committing both his whole front line and most of his reserve—in the shape of hundreds of planes drawn from Training Groups and conversion units: the present and the future of Bomber Command were hurled simultaneously into the air. In a sense, therefore, the affair was deceptive: nor was it immediately repeatable, for two subsequent 1000-bomber efforts were less successful, and in any case the strain imposed on resources was intolerable. But it was the immediate impact, on Churchill and the world, that counted. By the courage of his convictions, and imaginative stage-management, Harris thus created an effect which put in the shade such contemporary failures as the eight large-scale attacks on Essen, during March and April, of which 212 photographs showed only 22 bomb-loads within five miles of the city.

Burning faith and growing self-confidence now caused Harris to risk a gambler's throw. With cool effrontery he sent to Churchill on 17 June a long personal minute in which he spoke of knocking Germany out of the war in a matter of months. 'The success of the 1000 plan,' he claimed, 'has proved beyond doubt in the minds of all but wilful men that we can even today dispose of a weight of air attack which no country on which it can be brought to bear could survive. We can bring it to bear on the vital part of Germany. It requires only the decision to concentrate it for its proper use'. This grandiose and inaccurate assertion was accompanied by demands outrageous in their scope—'the immediate return to Bomber Command of all bomber aircraft in Coastal Command, which he regarded as "merely an obstacle to victory", the return of all Middle East bombers as soon as the battle there was stabilised, the return of all suitable aircraft and crews from Army Co-operation Command, the extraction of every possible bomber from America, an approach to Stalin to transfer his bomber force to Britain and the highest possible priority for the production of heavy bombers in Britain'. But Harris survived: he was neither sacked nor reprimanded.

Perhaps Churchill warmed to an aggressiveness akin to his own, for it was his principle that none of his generals ought to suffer for *attacking*: perhaps, too, he responded to the fear expressed by Harris, which he also shared, that an invasion of Europe would entail vast casualties 'in the mud of Flanders and France'. He spotted that Harris had over-called his hand, but—with an important qualification—he endorsed the thesis that bombing must remain a chief weapon in Britain's armoury. His attitude was made clear in a paper composed for the War Cabinet on 21 July. 'We must regard the Bomber offensive against Germany as at least a feature in breaking her war-will second only to the largest military operations which can be conducted on the Continent until that war-will is broken. Renewed, intense efforts should be made by the Allies to develop during the winter and onwards ever-growing, ever more accurate and ever more far-ranging Bomber attacks on Germany. In this way alone can we prepare the conditions which will be favourable to the major military operations on which we are resolved'. This statement might well be described as an early draft of the Casablanca directive. But 'by the Allies': here was a crux. Before the end of the year, before a blue-print for victory could be produced at Casablanca, one vital question must still be clarified—the rôle of the American bombers which, in 1942, began to accumulate in, and operate from, the British Isles.

In spite of Churchill's enthusiastic report after the Washington conference in January the United States Air Force was not 'brought into heavy action in 1942', nor was the proposal that 'strong bomber forces, based on the British Isles, should attack Germany' implemented. All that happened was that under fighter escort relatively small forces bombed relatively safe targets in occupied France at a price of relatively small casualties. But this proved nothing, for the basic American belief was that when it came to bombing Germany large groups of Fortresses, flying in self-protecting 'boxes', would be able to fight their way to and from their targets, unescorted, against all opposition. Their French experience convinced the American air generals Spaatz and Eaker, fallaciously, that this possibility had been proved: but it did not convince Portal—or Churchill. Slessor records that 'hating heavy casualties, as ever, and remembering our costly experience in 1940, he was cross-examining us as early as August 1942 about the American ability to bomb by day, and exploring various alternatives such as turning over to night bombing (which involved flame-damping engines) or using the American bombers for the air-sea war in the Atlantic. This attitude caused us in the Air Staff some anxiety ...'. The anxiety derived from a dilemma: Portal felt strongly, as a result of British disasters in 1939 and 1940, that unescorted day-time bombing was not a viable operation of war, but on the other hand the whole of American theory, training and equipment, based on the pre-war introduction of the Flying Fortress and the evolution of the Norden bomb-sight, was irreversibly committed to the thesis that such operations were viable. Moreover, there was the grave and major risk that British dubiety might cause the Americans to switch their main air effort to the Pacific. In the event Slessor, then Assistant Chief of the Air Staff for Policy, put up a minute to Portal in which he declared that 'The view of the Air Staff is that the Americans and the R.A.F. will be able to bomb Germany in daylight. Given sufficient strength to saturate the defences, they think it quite possible that our losses on the aggregate will be no heavier than by night and that the results, combined with night attack, should be doubly effective'. Slessor has subsequently admitted that he was backing a hunch rather than following a rational judgement: but in spite of their reservations this was the view which Portal and Churchill adopted, so that early next year, at Casablanca, an Allied bombing policy was approved without schism. 'Some who have studied the contemporary records far more carefully than I have had an opportunity of doing', Slessor has written, 'think it possible that, if I had not taken that line at the time, the American bomber offensive in Europe might have been still-born'. Churchill puts his own part in the affair succinctly. In January 1943 he was visited by Eaker, Commander of the American Air Forces in England (at the latter's request), and the whole issue was carefully dis-

cussed. 'I decided to back Eaker and his theme . . . General Eaker afterwards said on several occasions that I saved the Fortress bombers from
abandonment by the United States at the moment when they were about
to come into their own. If this is true I saved them by leaving off opposing
them'. They were not about to come into their own: this would not happen
till 1944. But then it happened triumphantly, and Eaker's faith, Slessor's
hunch and Churchill's calculated risk were eminently justified.

Before Casablanca occurred, however, it was also necessary to achieve
further clarification of British policy, and in this achievement Churchill's
exceptional capacity as War Lord was once again abundantly demonstrated
—his capacity, that is, to hold a central position at which he kept in focus
all the conflicting demands of his advisers, and of the battle-fronts, and
rejected secondary considerations for the sake of maintaining the essential
objective. This was the defeat of Germany. In the latter months of 1942
there was a powerful move by Portal and the Air Staff to reinstate bombing
as the prime agent of victory—to the extent of giving Bomber Command
over-riding priority over British resources and the U.S.A.A.F. priority, in
regard to transatlantic shipping, over the American army. Churchill put
his foot down, firmly. Not only was he convinced, by now, that a Second
Front would have to be opened sooner or later: in August 1942 he assured
Stalin that if possible one would be opened in 1943. Thus—and he was
certainly right—he refused *carte blanche* for the bombers, and this reservation was reflected in a final memorandum of the Chiefs of Staff on 31
December which was, in effect, the brief that was carried to Casablanca.
In reviewing Churchill's handling of this debate the *Official History* uses
words which describe so well his overall practice that they are worth
quoting in full. 'He was concerned to preserve a balance between the
various possibilities and, perhaps, above all, he was anxious to preserve a
freedom of choice. Though he did not deny the necessity for long-term
planning, he was also ever watchful for opportunities which might be
exploited in unexpected ways. He, therefore, tended to be cautious about
doctrinaire strategies which might result in over-specialised production
and mobilisation, and might, therefore, in turn, destroy, or at any rate
reduce, the freedom to exploit unforeseen opportunities. It is, perhaps,
because these thoughts were constantly in his mind that the Prime
Minister's attitude has so often been misunderstood and misrepresented.
He had to examine many sides of many questions and more often than not
his rulings and advice were addressed to subordinates who were often and
necessarily considering only one side of one question'.

Coming as the culmination of a prolonged period of heart-searching and mind-clearing, the Casablanca directive for a joint bomber offensive provided a sufficiently stable statement of principle for Churchill to declare, at the second Washington conference in May 1943, that there was no need to discuss any more than the details of the Battle of the Atlantic or that over Germany because 'there were no differences of opinion on these subjects'. And, in general, Churchill was not so intimately involved, during the course of that year, in crucial questions of air policy. Nor is this surprising, for with a steady proliferation of scientific aids, a powerful reinforcement of Lancasters and Mosquitoes, and a rich harvest of crews from the Empire Air Training Scheme Harris appeared to be achieving spectacular results. During the 'Battle of the Ruhr', between March and July, 43 major raids were launched; 17,000 sorties in 33 major raids between July and November constituted the 'Battle of Hamburg'; and in the 'Battle of Berlin' more than 20,000 sorties were flown between November and the following March in attacks on the capital and other prime targets. This was a new order of magnitude, and it was certainly not evident at Washington in May, or indeed until later, that the underlying spirit of the Casablanca policy was not being implemented.*

But there was no Combined Bomber Offensive; and the divergent operations of Bomber Command and the U.S.A.A.F. led each into what seemed, for a time, to be a dead end. The directive, though ambitious, was vague—perhaps inevitably, for otherwise it might never have been issued. But its vagueness allowed of variant interpretations such that, in 1943, Harris pursued by night a policy of area bombing and Eaker, by day, one of unescorted precision bombing, neither with reference to a co-ordinated scheme and each carrying within it the seeds of defeat. In the case of the 8th Air Force this was made plain on 14 October, when of 291 Fortresses which attacked the ball-bearings factory at Schweinfurt 60 were destroyed and 138 damaged, an appalling ratio of loss which was only the high point of a week in which 148 were shot down. The losses of Bomber Command also steadily escalated, reaching a point of no return rather later, in the raid on Nuremberg of 30 March 1944, when out of 795 bombers 94 were destroyed and 71 damaged, an unacceptable proportion. The fact was that by day and night the German fighters seemed to be winning a conclusive victory.

But before that became evident, the threat of another conclusive

---

* The plan was modified by the issue on 10 June 1943 of the *Pointblank* directive, which began 'the Combined Chiefs of Staff have decided that first priority in the operation of British and American bombers based in the United Kingdom shall be accorded to the attack on German fighter forces and the industry upon which they depend': but the theory of a *combined* offensive remained.

victory had been faced and dispelled—that of the German submarine. The heavy and continuing loss of merchant shipping was one of the most urgent issues at the Casablanca conference in January, and the figures speak for themselves—between January and May 1943, in all theatres of war, 298 merchant ships were sunk, and of those theatres the Atlantic was the vital area. From January onwards, therefore, Bomber Command was ordered—in spite of resistance from Harris—to concentrate effort on the U-boat bases in the Bay of Biscay and on the building yards in Germany. (Harris, it can now be seen, was justified in his protests, for in fact no submarine pen in a Biscay base was ever penetrated by a bomb and no completed U-boat was destroyed in Germany until April 1944.) But the scale of effort was considerable—3568 bombing sorties over the Biscay ports between January and May, and 3414 over the German yards, involving a total loss of 266 aircraft.

The inevitable tension between the Navy and the R.A.F. created by this situation was suddenly intensified when, on 30 March and without prior warning, the Admiralty presented to the U-boat Committee a demand for 190 aircraft from Bomber Command to work in a maritime role. This *démarche*, founded on calculations by the naval Operational Research team under Blackett, produced a strong reaction, particularly from Air Marshal Slessor, now C.-in-C. Coastal Command. A former 'bomber baron', he would nevertheless have supported the Admiralty case if bombers had been the right answer: but the right answer was Very Long Range aircraft from America. Once again, only Churchill could cut the Gordian knot. He thought the demand excessive and inopportune. 'Winston fairly rounded on poor old Dudley Pound', Slessor recalls.* ' "Here are our Russian allies desperately hard pressed and you want me to agree to decimate the only arm which is bringing direct pressure on Hitler," etc., etc.' The result was that the Admiralty had to accept a smaller contribution from Bomber Command, while pressure was brought to bear on the Americans to supply more V.L.R. Liberators for the Atlantic routes. Slowly sufficient aircraft were provided, to make a valuable contribution in that rapidly attained victory in the Battle of the Atlantic which transformed the prospects of the Allies.†

For the war on land, for OVERLORD and its aftermath, victory over the German fighter force was as fundamental as the defeat of the submarine in the war at sea. With each of these weapons, unchecked, the Germans had the power to produce irreversible disaster. But the climacteric triumph

* Private communication.
† See Chapter 7, p. 185 foll.

of the *Luftwaffe's* day and night fighters was short-lived, for the introduction by the Americans, during the winter of 1943/44, of the Mustang was decisive. As far back as the summer of 1941 Churchill had foreseen the need for a long-range fighter when, in June of that year, he warned Portal that without one 'You will be helpless in the West and beaten in the East'. Now, largely thanks to British development, the Mustang emerged as an aircraft capable of escorting bombers in daylight as far, in its latest version, as Berlin. The effect was so immediate and so powerful that Spaatz was even able to encourage his bombers to invite the opposition of the *Luftwaffe*, and with freedom of the air Fortresses were able to start destroying oil installations and aircraft factories with relative impunity. This sudden, and unexpected, conquest of the daytime skies had important consequences for Bomber Command, since lack of oil and shortage of skilled pilots also began to impair the efficiency of the German night fighters—just at the point when the strategic offensive had reached a nadir. In the short term, however, it was the requirements of OVERLORD which saved the Command from the consequences of its defeat, and Churchill from what would certainly have been one of the most agonising re-appraisals of the war.

Although by the spring of 1944 the U.S.A.A.F. was establishing air superiority over Western Europe, its benefits would have been gravely reduced if, in their preparations for D Day, the Allies had failed to incorporate in their invasion plan an effective means of exploiting their air power. The place of this within the master plan was by no means self-evident, and in the vigorous and sometimes violent discussions which finally evolved a satisfactory solution Churchill's rôle was dominant and constructive. A general authorisation was to be found in the Casablanca directive, which instructed the Cs.-in-C. of Bomber Command and the U.S. 8th Air Force that when Allied troops invaded Europe 'you will afford them all possible support in the manner most effective'. But this left unanswered two vital questions—who was to exercise overall control of the heavy bombers and relate their operations to the pattern of OVERLORD, and by what method could they best lay foundations for D Day? The answer to the second question was found in the answer to the first.

When Eisenhower took up his position as Supreme Commander, the C.-in-C. of the projected Allied Expeditionary Air Force was Air Marshal Sir Trafford Leigh-Mallory. He had been so nominated at the Quebec conference in August 1943, to supply *tactical* support to OVERLORD. But his Expeditionary Air Force would only contain light bombers and fighters, and Leigh-Mallory's present post was C.-in-C. Fighter Command. Was this the man, and had he the essential experience and authority, to knit Harris and the U.S. Strategic Air Force into a comprehensive scheme? Moreover Eisenhower, carrying the supreme responsibility, not unnaturally refused 'anything short of complete operational control of the whole of Bomber Command and the U.S.A.A.F.E.'; and this, even if it could be granted, could certainly not be granted to Leigh-Mallory. That, observed Churchill, was 'not what was meant at all': nor, in spite of the magnitude of OVERLORD, could a British Prime Minister be expected to hand over his heavy bombers lock, stock and barrel. There were other priorities as well as OVERLORD . . . the counter-offensive against the V weapons, the unremitting Battle of the Atlantic. In the event it was Churchill who produced the solution, by proposing that the Deputy Supreme Allied Commander, Air Chief Marshal Sir Arthur Tedder, should be 'complete master of all the air operations'; a proposal thoroughly acceptable to Eisenhower, who had seen Tedder's work at first hand in the Mediterranean. Tedder was not, however, to be 'complete master'. The Chiefs of Staff saw lurking behind the idea a subtle American scheme to subordinate what should remain British and independent. Churchill accepted their argument, and at a meeting with Eisenhower and Portal on 29 February he laid down that 'there can be no question of handing over the British Bomber, Fighter or Coastal Commands as a whole to the Supreme Commander and his Deputy'. This did the trick: on 10 March Portal was able to inform Churchill that an accommodation had been reached with Eisenhower whereby Tedder would evolve the strategic air plan, as a preliminary to OVERLORD, in *consultation* with Harris and Spaatz, while the tactical plan for the actual invasion would be handled by Leigh-Mallory under Tedder's *supervision*. Any further indents by Eisenhower on the strategic bombers would have to be approved by the Combined Chiefs of Staff. Churchill found all this 'very satisfactory'.

Tedder was now in a strong position to impose his own policies. From his experience of the Mediterranean campaigns (fortified by an Operational Research report by Professor Solly Zuckermann on the results of bombing in Sicily and Italy), he had firmly decided that the most fruitful use of heavy bombers was against the enemy's transportation—bridges, railways, marshalling yards, etc. This was the basis of the Interdiction programme which so profitably preceded and accompanied OVERLORD. He was met by dogmatic opposition from Harris, and serious but not bigoted objections from Spaatz. The latter believed that attacks on the German oil system would be more effective, but arguments that any results achieved could only be long term gained his co-operation. Harris was beaten from the start. His theory that his bombers could not attain the precision necessary for hitting the small targets offered by a transportation complex was disproved practically, while his reiteration of the boast that sustained area bombing of Germany was all that was necessary met with a cold reception. Churchill's previous suspicions had been confirmed by the performance of Bomber Command in 1943, tremendous though that was. Harris had lost the ear of the master, while Portal and the Air Staff were now severely critical of his pretensions. Thus it was that in April, May and June 1944 Bomber Command undertook no less than 12,949 sorties in preparation for OVERLORD (quite apart from the many operations carried out against flying-bomb sites): at times its deflection from Germany was absolute, just when major attacks on the previous scale were passing beyond the acceptable rate of loss. It was an invaluable breathing-space.

Before the Interdiction programme could gather momentum, however, Churchill had second thoughts. On 3 April he wrote to Eisenhower: 'The Cabinet today took rather a grave and on the whole an adverse view of the proposal to bomb so many French railway centres, in view of the fact that scores of thousands of French civilians, men, women, and children, would lose their lives or be injured.' Eisenhower replied immediately and firmly that 'We must never forget that one of the fundamental factors leading to the decision for undertaking OVERLORD was the conviction that our overpowering Air Force would make feasible an operation which might otherwise be considered extremely hazardous, if not foolhardy . . . I and my military advisers have become convinced that the bombing of these centres will increase our chances for success in the critical battle . . .'. But Churchill remained uneasy. The nub of dispute was a plan, ratified by Eisenhower and the Chiefs of Staff, for bombing 74 selected railway targets in France and Belgium: Churchill wished this number to be reduced to three, as several of the targets lay among a large population. (It is relevant to note that he had not expressed anxiety with a similar passion when it was a question of bombing the French ports which harboured German submarines and capital ships.)*

The plan was therefore cut down in scale, Portal now estimating that before D Day French civilian casualties would amount to 10,500 killed and

---

* The issue was raised by Pound in January 1943, when the bombing of the Biscay ports was renewed. He pointed out the dangers for the local population to the War Cabinet: 'we must balance the loss of French lives against those of our own merchant seamen'. The Cabinet endorsed the policy. When it was laid before the Combined Chiefs of Staff at Casablanca on 21 January, they ruled that area bombing must be unrestricted, even if the inhabited areas of the French ports were devastated. Thus Churchill did not stand alone in this matter.

5500 badly injured. But this was still not enough for the obstinate Prime Minister. 'He told Eisenhower on 29 April that the War Cabinet was nearly unanimously against it. He deplored the killing of 10,500 to 15,000 French civilians and said that experience in Italy had shown how difficult it was to stop traffic by bombing marshalling yards. He pointed out that the plan had been opposed by Bomber Command Headquarters, by the United States Strategic Air Forces,' (see above for the views of Harris and Spaatz), 'by the Directorate of Bomber Operations in the Air Ministry, the "railway experts" at the War Office, the Ministry of Economic Warfare, the Joint Intelligence Committee and various civilian railway experts. He said that the railway system of Northern France was estimated to have a capacity of seven to eight hundred trains a day, but that the German army only required about ten per cent of that number. It would, therefore, Mr. Churchill argued, be necessary to knock out ninety per cent of the system before any valuable effects began to occur'.* Nobody could say that five years of conducting a war at the highest level had diminished his capacity to fight, and fight again! On 7 May, indeed, he took the final step of laying the issue before Roosevelt, in a long and statesmanlike letter which set out the contradictory arguments lucidly but reasonably, and which ended by saying 'Whatever is settled between us, we are quite willing to share responsibilities with you'.

But would the responsibilities be shared? An important passage in the letter stated that 'The War Cabinet could not view this figure without grave dismay on account of the apparently ruthless use of the Air Forces, particularly of the Royal Air Force, on whom the brunt of this kind of work necessarily falls, and the reproaches that would be made upon the inaccuracy of night bombing'. It seems clear, in fact, that Churchill was not only impelled by compassion, but also by a concern that in the liberated France which would emerge after D Day the British, because of the scatter effect of night bombing, would be held guilty of civilian slaughter in a larger measure than the Americans whose daytime bombing was assumed, without justification, to be inexpensive in non-combatant lives. Roosevelt, however, concluded the debate in magisterial terms. 'However regrettable the attendant loss of civilian lives is, I am not prepared to impose from this distance any restriction on military action by the responsible commanders that in their opinion might militate against the success of OVERLORD or cause additional loss of life to our Allied forces of invasion.' The Prime Minister gave in: but it was noted that 'he kept a sharp and sometimes even suspicious eye upon the estimates of French dead which were supplied

* Webster and Frankland, *op. cit.*, Vol. 3, p. 37.

by Sir Arthur Tedder. Bomber Command was often warned of the need to keep this roll of honour as short as possible'.

After OVERLORD had been successfully launched and the Allied armies advanced eastwards Bomber Command discovered that it could join the U.S. 8th Air Force, and the 15th operating from Italy, in a united offensive on Germany which could be conducted with an unprecedented freedom. It was not only the progressive collapse of the German oil complex, and with it the steady decline of the *Luftwaffe*, that created conditions so favourable. The advance of the armies had a double effect: as they moved from France into Belgium and Holland the continental early warning system on which the German fighter controllers relied was driven eastwards, while the stations from which guidance was provided for Allied bombers could operate now from the far side of the Channel, with a significantly extended range. This culmination of an offensive which Churchill had consistently supported, even in periods of disaster, doubt and despondency, relieved him of a considerable burden. At no time between D Day and the end of the war was he required to settle, or even to intervene in, disputes over policy or practice such as had perhaps inevitably marred the growth of Bomber Command. Not even the head-on collision between Harris and Portal during the winter of 1944/45 (in which Portal sought to pin Harris down to undertaking selective and precision bombing while Harris insisted on pursuing his policy of area bombing up to the point of offering his resignation), seems to have disturbed the Prime Minister. It is, indeed, ironical that the event in the bombing campaign which, occurring at its close, was to cause the greatest controversy after the war, and has left a name for history as doom-laden as Hiroshima, happened without any important preliminary debate. This was the destruction of Dresden. The origins of the murder of this ancient and exquisite city are multiple, and though Churchill was certainly an accessory before the fact posterity will be unjust if it retains him alone in the dock. Indeed the story of Dresden, so complicated and so tragic, can best be summarised in the words inscribed by a fatalistic soldier on a board which he hung across the main street of Péronne in March 1917, as the Germans, to the accompaniment of their 'burnt earth' policy, withdrew to the Hindenburg Line. *Nicht ärgern, nur wundern*, pleaded the inscription. 'Do not be angry, only wonder.'

The idea of a cataclysmic blow struck at a German city or cities, at a carefully chosen moment when the enemy was on the knife-edge of defeat, had been mooted by Portal as early as August 1943, but that moment had not yet arrived, and the plan, later to be called THUNDERCLAP, was held in suspense. On 25 January 1945, however, the Joint Intelligence Committee recommended that such an attack on Berlin might effectively aid the Russians in their progress towards the capital and might, indeed, have 'a political value in demonstrating to the Russians, in the best way open to us, a desire on the part of the British and Americans to assist them in the present battle'. On the eve of the Yalta conference, and with only the Ardennes battle to offer as a contribution by the Allied armies, Churchill seized on the proposition with avidity. That night he rang Sinclair, the Secretary of State for Air, and asked what the R.A.F. intended to do about 'basting the Germans in their retreat from Breslau'. This caused a flurry of consultation, and next day Sinclair minuted back that to continue attacking oil targets seemed the best policy, though it would not prevent occasional area bombing. 'These opportunities', he wrote, 'might be used to exploit the present situation by the bombing of Berlin and other large cities in Eastern Germany such as Leipzig, Dresden and Chemnitz, which are not only the administrative centres controlling the military and civilian movements but are also the main communication centres through which the bulk of the traffic moves'. This was no good for Churchill, who replied acidly, 'I did not ask you last night about plans for harrying the German retreat from Breslau. On the contrary, I asked whether Berlin, and no doubt other large cities in East Germany, should not now be considered especially attractive targets. I am glad that this is "under examination". Pray report to me tomorrow what is going to be done'. There followed immediately a clear and direct instruction to Harris from the Air Staff to launch major attacks on the cities mentioned by Sinclair and 'any other cities where a severe blitz will not only cause confusion in the evacuation from the East but will also hamper the movement of troops from the West'. This was, in effect, Dresden's death-certificate: but in evaluating responsibility it must be observed that Churchill's expressed wishes, amounting to a directive, were general rather than specific, and it cannot be maintained that it was he who selected Dresden for annihilation from among the various possible targets. Nor can the Russians, as is sometimes claimed, be faulted, though there is little doubt that had they felt an operational necessity they would readily have underwritten the application of THUNDERCLAP to any remaining city in the Reich. It is true that at Yalta the Deputy Chief of Staff of the Red Army, Antonov, tabled a request for the use of heavy bombers against communications and for the paralysis of Berlin and Leipzig. But no record can be traced of a demand that Dresden in particular should be 'taken out'. In any event, on the night of 13 February some 800 aircraft of Bomber Command attacked

Dresden in 'one of the most devastating attacks of the war in Europe'. Next day over 400 bombers from 8th Air Force followed, the next day over 200, and over 400 again on 2 March.

The Greeks would have understood the tragedy of Dresden: their Prometheus who, caring for men, brought them fire also brought them the gift of numbers—to count their murders.

5

The Artificial Coalition 1941-1942

'A war begun by Germany will immediately call into the field
other states than the one she has attacked, and in a war against a
world coalition she will succumb and for good or evil be put at
that coalition's mercy.'

General Beck, in a private memorandum, *Germany in a
Future War*, written after his rejection by Hitler in 1938

'In the whole of world history there has never been a coalition
which consisted of such heterogeneous elements with such
diametrically opposed objectives. Ultra-capitalist states on the one
hand; ultra-Marxist states on the other. On the one side a dying
world-empire temporarily supported by one of its ex-colonies
anxious to take over the inheritance. The United States is determined to take over Britain's place in the world and the Soviet
Union is anxious to get hold of the Balkans, the Dardanelles and
Persia. These three states are already at loggerheads with one
another and a great victory on the Western Front will bring down
this artificial coalition with a crash.'

Hitler to his generals, before the Ardennes offensive in 1944

During the winter of 1941/1942 Churchill reached both a high point and a
nadir in his career as a War Lord. The strategic bomber offensive with
which he was so closely identified had come to a dead end, as he admitted
in November, with his order that it was 'the duty of both Fighter and
Bomber Command to re-gather their strength for the Spring'. Auchinleck's offensive in the desert, CRUSADER, which opened on 18
November, was only rescued from disaster by the intervention of the
Commander-in-Chief: its final success, moreover, proved to be transient,
for Rommel's counter-offensive in January drove the British back to the
stalemate of the Gazala Line, the airfields essential for interdiction of the
Axis convoy-routes were surrendered, and the Mediterranean Fleet was
savagely wounded. Much of what went wrong in the CRUSADER
offensive, from which he anticipated so many gains—the partnership of
Vichy North Africa, the seizure of Sicily—was ascribed to Churchill
himself. And the sudden collapse of British power in the Far East was felt
by contemporaries, as well as by their successors, to have been the direct
result not only of persistent and wilful blindness on the Prime Minister's
part to what was impending but also of his foolish and precipitate inter-

ference. These are partial judgements: but they have been professed with the vehemence of partiality.

Nevertheless, the Japanese assault in the Pacific brought the United States into the war as Britain's ally on terms almost beyond belief—the agreement that priority should be given to *Germany first*. Churchill's immediate reaction to the news of Pearl Harbour was understandable. 'So we had won after all! . . . I had studied the American Civil War, fought out to the last desperate inch. American blood flowed in my veins. I thought of a remark which Edward Grey had made to me more than thirty years before—that the United States is like "a gigantic boiler. Once the fire is lighted under it there is no limit to the power it can generate". Being saturated and satiated with emotion and sensation, I went to bed and slept the sleep of the saved and thankful.' But his reaction was also justified. The linkage of Great Britain, the United States and the Soviet Union may have appeared, in Hitler's eyes, to be an 'artificial coalition', but the effective reality of the alliance and the fact that its first and common enemy was Germany were due primarily to Churchill's insight and statesmanship. If a main function of a War Lord is to seek and preserve victorious combinations of allies, Churchill had not failed. This achievement was fundamental: it, alone, if set in the scales against the sum of his errors, will be seen to prevail.*

Among the errors for which he has been held accountable was his treatment of Auchinleck who, like Wavell, survived as Commander-in-Chief Middle East for little more than a year. The pressure imposed by the Prime Minister—imposed from the moment the two changed post—was indeed severe. He respected both. In Wavell's case, respect became corroded by distrust. Auchinleck, with the character of the *preux chevalier* to which Churchill always responded, handsome, open, frank, a soldier of the firing-line, suffered not so much from distrust as from dissatisfaction. Like Lincoln in the crisis of the Civil War Churchill sought commanders who could deliver, and Auchinleck's tragedy was that his great and manifest gifts aroused too great hopes—some of which, unfortunately, might have been fulfilled had the Prime Minister been less exigent, and his general more sophisticated in both his relations with Downing Street and his conduct of the battle. Dill was no deranged Cassandra when he observed, at the time of the switch of appointments, that 'Auchinleck, for all his great qualities and his outstanding record on the Frontier, was not the coming man of the war, as the Prime Minister thought'. Dill was, in fact,

---

* 'The manoeuvre which brings an ally into the field is as serviceable as that which wins a great battle.' Churchill, *The World Crisis*.

Auchinleck's friend. And to his friend, before he left Delhi for Cairo, he sent a long sagacious letter in which he issued a warning: 'The fact is that the Commander in the field will always be subject to great and often undue pressure from his Government. Wellington suffered from it: Haig suffered from it: Wavell suffered from it. Nothing will stop it. In fact, pressure from those who alone see the picture as a whole and carry the main responsibility may be necessary'.

Nothing could stop it. From July until November, when CRUSADER was launched, Auchinleck was urged to attack. Justifiably? On many grounds the answer must be 'No'. The battle began too soon. The Eighth Army, as it was now named, was insufficiently trained and had only been lashed together at the last minute: it lacked unity and cohesion. Churchill could not be blamed for the selfish intransigence of an Australian government which insisted, in spite of his vehement pleading, on the withdrawal of one of its divisions from Tobruk: but Auchinleck suffered from the consequent distraction of effort by the Navy and the Desert Air Force. Nor could Churchill be blamed for the death in an air-crash, on the eve of the battle, of Major-General Pope, who was to command the British armour, and of his senior staff officers: but Auchinleck, who had risked the Prime Minister's displeasure by previous postponements, was compelled to make readjustments in a rush—and they were not good enough. The combination of Cunningham as Army commander (Auchinleck's own and unfortunate choice), and Willoughby Norrie as a replacement in charge of the armour produced dispositions so inept that they threatened defeat. In all this the frequency and the tone of Churchill's hectoring signals played their part. Montgomery, in his time, would insist on fighting a 'balanced' battle at Alamein: but in far too many respects the Eighth Army in CRUSADER was unbalanced, and, to a degree which it is still difficult to assess, this was because Churchill felt unable to grant his commander the essential gift of time.

Yet it was Churchill alone who could see the picture as a whole, and Churchill who carried the main responsibility. Dill, over-strained by service under his master, was nevertheless a man without venom, and in this matter his cool mind grasped facts which neither Auchinleck nor his protagonists could appreciate. On the very day Churchill wrote to Auchinleck to order him to take over the Middle East the Germans invaded the Soviet Union. In that same summer Churchill had digested the Butt Report, and knew that Bomber Command, blind, weak and inaccurate, was unable to mount a strategic offensive which could yet do much for Britain, or anything for Russia. As the weeks of the summer and autumn went by it became progressively clear to him that cross-Channel expeditions on more than a trivial scale were impossible, while intervention in Norway, much though he desired it, was only a dream. From September onwards invasion of Britain was once more considered a serious threat, while Gibraltar and the mouth of the Mediterranean seemed to be in jeopardy. And all the time Stalin clamoured for help. Moreover, from the secret traffic Churchill obtained first-hand evidence of Rommel's own difficulties and shortages. These considerations go far to explain his impatience with Auchinleck and his intense concentration on CRUSADER. Success, he thought, 'might bring the rallying from Vichy of Tunis, Algeria and Morocco, and perhaps even the accession of Vichy itself. This purpose was only a hope built on a hope. . . . If we got Tripoli, and France would not move, our possession of Malta would enable us to descend on Sicily. . . . Once Rommel was beaten and his small, audacious army destroyed and Tripoli was ours it was not thought impossible for four divisions of our best troops, about 80,000 men, to land and conquer Sicily'. An extravaganza: but what would have been Britain's posture in the year of the locusts if Churchill had not consistently played for high stakes and kept confidence ablaze? On the day of BARBAROSSA Dill was heard to remark, 'I suppose you realise this means we shall lose the Middle East'. This was neither Churchill's reaction nor his intention.

By the beginning of December the prospect seemed brighter. After CRUSADER's clumsy opening gambit and Cunningham's loss of nerve Auchinleck had taken grip of the battle with the order 'Attack and pursue. All out everywhere'. Victory loomed within reach. And in Russia the Germans had been halted: on 5 December Hitler abandoned his Moscow offensive for the winter, and the next day the Soviet counter-offensive was launched. But in the Far East the Japanese carrier fleet had already sailed. On 7 December Pearl Harbour was attacked, Singapore bombed, and landings began in Thailand and Malaya. During the next two days Hong Kong, Guam, Midway, Wake Island, and the Philippines were assaulted, and *Repulse* and the *Prince of Wales* were sunk. The war suddenly entered a new dimension.

Early in 1941 the Prime Minister of Australia, Robert Menzies, had flown to London via Singapore for the sole purpose of discussing what he considered to be the Japanese menace. Before the meeting at the Foreign Office on 26 February at which he presented his views he jotted down some notes. The last one read:

7. We must as soon as possible tell Japan 'where she gets off'. Appeasement

is no good. The peg must be driven in somewhere. I must make a great effort in London to clarify this position. Why cannot *one* squadron of fighters be sent out from North Africa? Why cannot some positive commitment be entered into regarding naval reinforcement of Singapore? At this stage, misty generalisations will please and sustain the Japanese, and nobody else.

No peg was driven in. Between February and November Japan was never told 'where she gets off'—never faced by a threat of military response to aggression powerful enough to shift her war party from the course it was determined to follow. In essence the issue was simple: it was presented nakedly in Menzies' note. But the reason for failure to face the issue was equally simple. It was in the last analysis the responsibility of the Prime Minister and the President of the United States. And each, in a different way, was impotent.

Churchill saw clearly why Roosevelt was powerless. As the climax approached he defined the problem in a careful letter addressed to Smuts on 9 November:

> I do not think it would be any use for me to make a personal appeal to Roosevelt at this juncture to enter the war. . . . We must not underrate his constitutional difficulties. He may take action as Chief Executive, but only Congress can declare war. He went so far as to say to me, 'I may never declare war; I may make war. If I were to ask Congress to declare war they might argue about it for three months'. The Draft Bill without which the American Army would have gone to pieces passed by only one vote. . . . Public opinion in the United States has advanced lately, but with Congress it is all a matter of counting heads. Naturally, if I saw any way of helping to lift this situation on to a higher plane I would do so. . . .

He saw, equally, that had it been possible power would have been exercised. 'Roosevelt, Hull, Stimson, Knox, General Marshall, Admiral Stark, and, as a link between them, Harry Hopkins, had but one mind.' For they knew the reality, not only from what was obvious to any percipient observer, but also from the invaluable intelligence about the attitude and intentions of the Japanese High Command which they obtained from MAGIC, that cryptanalytical triumph which enabled the Americans to read the most 'secure' Japanese naval and diplomatic signals. 'The intercept services missed little. Of 227 messages pertaining to Japanese–American negotiations sent between Tokyo and Washington from March to December 1941, all but four were picked up'.* Roosevelt was powerless, in fact, not because of ignorance but because of the dead weight of Ameri-

---

* David Kahn, *The Codebreakers*, p. 13. He provides a detailed account of MAGIC. The British shared this information. The misuse of it by the Americans before Pearl Harbour is a part of their history, and lies outside the scope of this book.

can public opinion. All the protestations and proposals, therefore, all the warnings and sanctions initiated by Washington in 1941—even the economic embargo imposed in July—lacked final authority (and in Tokyo were seen to lack it), because Roosevelt was unable to threaten or even to hint at the ultimate sanction of war. His spirit had conquered his polio, but this was a more subtle form of paralysis. So grave, in fact, was the limitation on his powers that Churchill and his Chiefs of Staff and their counterparts in Washington were haunted by the possibility that Japan might declare war on Britain alone, thus presenting the President with a grave and perhaps insuperable problem—that of committing the first act.

Nor can it be maintained that Churchill, in 1941, was ignorant—either from lack of information or because of his own blindness. Whatever his *laissez-faire* attitudes about the Far East may have been in the past, in 1941 he was briefed and aware. His responsibility for what occurred was that of a man with open eyes. It is naive to dismiss his policy as one of disregard: it was conscious, and deeply considered. One should not reject it contemptuously—or lightheartedly, as Menzies did. 'Of the Far East he knew nothing, and could not imagine it. Australia was a very distant country which produced great fighting men, and some black swans for the pond at Chartwell, but it cannot be said that it otherwise excited his imagination or his interest. I sometimes think that he regarded the Japanese attack in the south-west Pacific as a rather tiresome intrusion, distracting attention from the great task of defeating Hitler.' This is not true in the sense that he was blind to the gravity of the situation. Menzies in February, Dill in May,* the Chiefs of Staff over aircraft for Russia— these and others, in 1941, compelled him to face facts and to pursue a policy.

The facts, as he saw them, made him as impotent as Roosevelt. Britain's existing commitments were so great, her resources so slender, that nothing significant could be spared for the Far East. The little that could be spared would be irrelevant, in the absence of America as an ally. Better not waste that little, but deploy it where it could be profitably used—in the Middle East, in Russia. If America did become an ally, then all would be well in the end. On this point Churchill was explicit, and unrepentant.

> I confess that in my mind the whole Japanese menace lay in a sinister twilight, compared with our other needs. My feeling was that if Japan attacked us the United States would come in. If the United States did not come in we had no means of defending the Dutch East Indies, or indeed our own

---

* In May the Chiefs of Staff warned Churchill that three months' notice would be required if Singapore was to be reinforced. They never received such a notice.

Empire in the East. If, on the other hand, Japanese aggression drew in America I would be content to have it. On this I rested. Our priorities during 1941 stood: first, the defence of the Island, including the threat of invasion and the U-boat war; secondly, the struggle in the Middle East and the Mediterranean; thirdly, after June, supplies to Soviet Russia; and, last of all, resistance to a Japanese assault.*

This was a basic policy decision, and it is impossible to deny its force. It is certainly fair to argue that if Churchill had felt the Far East on his pulses, as he felt France or the Western Desert—if he had experienced some personal, emotional involvement—if he had, say, been a correspondent not in Cuba, or the Sudan, or South Africa, but in the Russo–Japanese war—he might have applied a larger energy and a deeper intuition. He might have observed that the military and civil administration in Singapore was lethargic, wrapped in a cocoon of self-deceit. He might have tightened up arrangements in this place and brought minor reinforcements to that. But the facts were inescapable: so long as the American Pacific Fleet was absent, either because it was neutral or, as turned out, because it was neutralised, there was no action he could take, military or otherwise, which could hold up a Japanese advance for more than a short time longer than it was in fact delayed. The decisions about the defence of Singapore in the 'twenties, the wasted 'thirties, and the success of Hitler since 1939 had made this inevitable.

Churchill did, however, make two major miscalculations, the first of which caused the second—with tragic consequences. All through 1941 he persisted in the assumption that when it came to the crunch the Japanese would behave like rational beings and avoid the suicide which must follow war in the Pacific. He forgot the national predilection for *hara-kiri*. As late as 10 November he pointed out in an important speech at the annual Guildhall Banquet: 'If steel is the basic foundation of modern war, it would be rather dangerous for a Power like Japan, whose steel production is only about seven million tons a year, to provoke quite gratuitously a struggle with the United States, whose steel production now is about ninety millions . . .'. On rational grounds, this was undeniable. Nevertheless, perhaps because of a lack of empathy, he failed to penetrate the mentality of his enemy and to realise that the Japanese were in a box from which they must inevitably strike out. The containment was psychological and economic. If the price of accommodation exacted by the United States was to be a surrender of the Japanese strangle-hold on China, it was inconceivable that the High Command in Tokyo would accept the

* Churchill, *op. cit.*, Vol. III, p. 522.

consequent loss of face. And unless the economic embargoes imposed in July by America, Britain and Holland were lifted, the Japanese nation must fight or wither. (So limited were stocks that when the blockade was instituted the Emperor was informed that existing oil supplies could only maintain the fleet in war conditions for a year and a half.) Thus the increasing tension which preceded Pearl Harbour, and the stroke itself, caught Churchill off balance and caused him to make hasty, off-the-cuff dispositions. 'Madness', he observed in his memoirs, 'is an affliction which in war carries with it the advantage of SURPRISE'. But foresight, he might have added, puts a man on the QUI VIVE.

The disaster Churchill helped to precipitate was the result of a curious chain of cause and effect. From Placentia Bay he signalled that as a result of the Atlantic Conference Roosevelt would shortly be warning the Japanese that any further advance to the south would entail hostilities. (As has been seen, the President in fact had second thoughts.*) In consequence the Admiralty reviewed the possibility of reinforcing the Eastern Fleet. There was a long-term plan to establish in the Indian Ocean, by March 1942, 7 capital ships, 1 aircraft-carrier, 10 cruisers and some 24 destroyers. But spare ships were few, and in the short term Pound proposed to get four old battleships into the Ocean and later to send three more, all to be based on Ceylon. This was no good for Churchill. He wanted a fast modern ship, to operate as a general deterrent within the Simonstown-Aden-Singapore triangle. The Admiralty case was argued fully, firmly, and for many weeks, but it was over-ruled by the Prime Minister. There is no doubt about this. He confessed the truth in his signal to the Commonwealth Prime Ministers at the end of October:

> 3. In the interval, in order further to deter Japan, we are sending forthwith our newest battleship, *Prince of Wales*, to join *Repulse* in the Indian Ocean. *This is done in spite of protests from the Commander-in-Chief Home Fleet, and is a serious risk for us to run.* (Author's italics: after 'Home Fleet' he should have added, 'and the First Sea Lord and his staff'.) *Prince of Wales* will be noticed at Capetown quite soon. In addition the four 'R.' battleships are being moved as they become ready to Eastern waters. Later on *Repulse* will be relieved by *Renown*, which has greater radius.

> 4. In my view, *Prince of Wales* will be the best possible deterrent, and every effort will be made to spare her permanently. I must however make it clear that movements of *Prince of Wales* must be reviewed when she is at Capetown, because of danger of *Tirpitz* breaking out and other operational possibilities before *Duke of York* is ready in December.

These paragraphs raise two significant points. The first is the absence of

* See p. 86.

any reference to an aircraft-carrier: yet, as Churchill himself admitted,*
'an essential element' in his plan was the inclusion of the new armoured
carrier *Indomitable*. But though *Indomitable* was damaged on 3 November,
by running aground off Kingston, Jamaica, the plan was allowed to
proceed.

The phrase 'reviewed when she is at Capetown' is also important. The
intention is specifically recorded in the minutes of the Defence Committee meeting on 20 October. 'The Committee: Approved the First Sea
Lord's proposal that *HMS Prince of Wales* should be sailed forthwith to
Capetown and agreed to take a decision as to her subsequent movements
when she had arrived at her destination'. 'And yet,' in the words of the
Official History, 'if a review of her future movements then took place no
record of it has been found in the Admiralty's or the Prime Minister's
papers; the Chiefs of Staff and Defence Committees certainly did not
consider the matter again'.† On the contrary: *before* the ship reached
Capetown the Admiralty, on 11 November, 'ordered the *Prince of Wales*
and the *Repulse* to meet in Ceylon and proceed in company to Singapore'.
There is only one possible explanation which accounts for these extraordinary facts: Churchill, in a private meeting with Pound, insisted on the
order being issued. Pound's Naval Assistant subsequently recorded that he
showed 'silently, but unmistakably that he had been overborne on a
matter . . . of considerable weight. He was more severely upset on this loss
than we ever saw him'. The end of the story is well known. At the first
sign of Japanese landings in Malaya Admiral Sir Tom Phillips took his
two battleships into action without air cover—not that anything relevant
was available. On 10 December they were attacked by a force of Japanese
high-level and torpedo bombers which had been specially trained for
anti-shipping work, and both were sunk between 11.00 a.m. and 1.20 p.m.
A third of 3000 officers and men were lost. Afterwards Churchill wrote:

> I was opening my boxes on the 10th when the telephone at my bedside rang.
> It was the First Sea Lord. His voice sounded odd. He gave a sort of cough
> and gulp, and at first I could not hear quite clearly. 'Prime Minister, I have to
> report to you that the *Prince of Wales* and the *Repulse* have both been sunk by
> the Japanese—we think by aircraft. Tom Phillips is drowned.' 'Are you sure
> it's true?' 'There is no doubt at all.' So I put the telephone down. I was
> thankful to be alone. In all the war I never received a more direct shock.
> The reader of these pages will realise how many efforts, hopes, and plans
> foundered with these two ships. As I turned over and twisted in bed the full
> horror of the news sank in upon me. There were no British or American

* *Op. cit.*, Vol. III, p. 524.
† Roskill, *op. cit.*, Vol. I, p. 557.

capital ships in the Indian Ocean or the Pacific except the American survivors of Pearl Harbour, who were hastening back to California. Over all this vast expanse of waters Japan was supreme, and we were everywhere weak and naked.

Many serious judges now consider that this bitter episode was unnecessary and that Churchill was its architect. This is, in one sense, probably true. But one must ask questions, questions which in the nature of things can never be resolved. How far was Pound the guilty man in that he, the operational commander of the Navy, failed to give Admiral Phillips explicit instructions about the dangers of air attack, and the need for air cover, in any engagements he might undertake when he reached his Far Eastern station? How far was Phillips himself responsible—a man notorious for his belief in the ability of capital ships to sustain air attack? And how far was what happened off the Malayan coast a distortion of Churchill's intentions, which were, undoubtedly, that the battleships should disappear into the distant seas, offering a hidden menace, rather than get entangled in some tactical, close-to-the-shores, observable manoeuvre?

The intricate inter-relationships of global warfare soon became plain. During the latter part of the year the German High Command was increasingly concerned about the fortunes of the *Afrika Korps* and, in particular, about Italian inability to guard its supply routes. This produced an easement on two fronts. On 5 December Hitler ordered the transfer of a whole *Fliegerkorps* from Russia to the Mediterranean. From the Atlantic, groups of U-boats were steadily re-directed through the Straits of Gibraltar, so that by mid-December there were 18 inside the Mediterranean and 10 under orders to sail there. This movement had an immediate effect on the Atlantic convoys: in November, and again in December, losses from all causes fell to just over 50,000 tons as against three times that amount in October. But on 16 October the carrier *Ark Royal* was torpedoed after flying-in Hurricanes to Malta. On 25 November the battleship *Barham*, in passage from Alexandria, blew up after a U-boat attack, and on 14 December the cruiser *Galatea* was sunk. Worse was to follow. On 18 December Italian 'human torpedoes', penetrating the harbour at Alexandria, so damaged the battleships *Queen Elizabeth* and *Valiant* that they were put out of action for months. The same day Malta's famous 'Force K' was obliterated in an unsuspected minefield off Tripoli: one of its three cruisers, and a destroyer, were lost and the two others damaged. Thus it was that an easement in the Atlantic was followed by disaster in the Mediterranean, and this in turn meant that, as Cunningham was only left with three cruisers and a few destroyers, nothing could be done to send aid to the Far East, while the loss of two battleships off Malaya, combined with these other sinkings, had repercussions on all the main sea-routes where British interests were involved: nor could any succour be anticipated from the U.S. Navy—indeed, American warships were now withdrawn from the Atlantic. Moreover, while Russia was helped by a *Fliegerkorp's* departure, this menaced Auchinleck's Eighth Army at the very time when, because of Japan's entry into the war, reinforcements of men and aircraft destined for Africa were being urgently switched to the Far East. Such was only part of the complicated background to ARCADIA, the first Washington Conference.

'When so much was molten,' in Churchill's words, he might reasonably have been tied to London. Nevertheless, as soon as he heard of Pearl Harbour, just as one instinct impelled him to the side of his friend the President, so another warned him that Roosevelt must be turning his attention and energies to the Pacific. British interests must therefore be preserved, common strategies must be concerted, and an assurance must be won that a fair share from American factories would continue to flow across the Atlantic. He was off immediately: within a week, on 14 December, his party embarked on the new battleship *Duke of York*. The winter gales were violent, and they sailed with hatches battened down, abandoning their destroyer escort. Beaverbrook said they might as well have been in a submarine.

In November Churchill had at last unseated the overstretched Dill, replacing him as C.I.G.S. by Alanbrooke: but Dill was on the *Duke of York*, deputising for his successor, while Alanbrooke held the fort in London. This was because Churchill intended to leave him in Washington as his personal representative—initially with the title of Deputy Defence Minister, though this was altered to Head of the British Military Mission when the Combined Chiefs of Staff organisation was conceived during ARCADIA. These were the two most important appointments made by Churchill in the course of the war. About Alanbrooke he was right from the start, but he nearly erred over Dill, and it is ironic that the successor was responsible for the new role of the man he had just supplanted. 'This agreement', Alanbrooke wrote, 'was not arrived at without a good deal of discussion. . . . I had to press for this appointment and point out to him that, with Dill's intimate knowledge of the working of the Chiefs of Staff Committee and of our strategy, there could be no better man to serve our purposes in Washington at the head of our Mission. Thank heaven I succeeded in convincing Winston, as few men did more in furthering our cause to final victory than Dill. From the very start he built up a deep friendship with Marshall and proved to be an invaluable link between the British and American Chiefs of Staff. . . . I look upon that half hour's discussion with Winston at 10 Downing Street on December 11 as one of my most important accomplishments during the war or at any rate amongst those that bore most fruit'. This verdict is universally accepted; most notably by the Americans who, when Dill died in November 1944, accorded him, at Marshall's suggestion, the exceptional tribute of burial in Arlington National Cemetery.* There is no disagreement, either, about Churchill's selection of Alanbrooke, which, against all probability, resulted in one of the most remarkable combinations in British history. Two mercurial temperaments miraculously discovered a common ground in spite of profound differences in training and attitude. It is, for example, instructive to compare Churchill's reactions in May 1940, when he became Prime Minister, with the entry in Alanbrooke's diary on the day that his appointment as C.I.G.S. was announced. 'I had never hoped or aspired to reach those dizzy heights, and now that I am stepping up on to the plateau land of my military career the landscape looks cold, bleak and lonely, with a ghastly responsibility hanging as a black thundercloud over me. Perhaps I am feeling liverish for want of exercise today!' But that vein of pessimism and uncertainty, so dominant in Alanbrooke's private papers, was an invaluable complement to his Prime Minister's occasional euphoria and constant self-confidence. Churchill's 'Black Dog' moods were only intermittent: in Alanbrooke optimism never galloped on a free rein.

As the *Duke of York* ploughed across the Atlantic Churchill was certainly not cast down. He and the Chiefs of Staff seized the opportunity of the voyage to review and define the principles of strategy and programme of action which must be presented in Washington as a firm basis of discussion by the new allies in their first War Council. They worked independently. Churchill has described his own method. 'In order to prepare myself for meeting the President and for the American discussions and to make sure that I carried with me the two Chiefs of Staff, Pound and Portal, and General Dill, and that the facts could be checked in good time by General Hollis and the Secretariat, I produced three papers on the future course of the war, as I conceived it should be steered. Each paper took four or five hours, spread over two or three days. As I had the whole picture in my mind it all came forth easily, but very slowly.' For their part, the Chiefs of Staff had already available a survey of the current military situation which had been produced for them by their Directors of Plans.

---

* Wingate was also buried at Arlington. This was consequent on an Anglo-American agreement about the siting of war graves. The aircraft in which he died belonged to the U.S.A.A.F.

The three papers which Churchill composed emerged under the heads of 'The Atlantic Front', 'Notes on the Pacific', and 'The Campaign of 1943'.* Taken together, however, they constitute a single document, which surveyed the future course of the war and should certainly be considered as one of the more remarkable British State Papers—remarkable for its range, its prescience, its cogency, clarity, and majestic mastery of its theme. It would seem astonishing if judged simply as the product of a hard-pressed man in his sixties, working on a storm-tossed battleship in mid-Atlantic, who had just heard terrible and personally grievous news from the Far East and who was nerving himself for one of the most important confrontations of his career. But it also supports Ismay's observation about Churchill†, that 'in his grasp of the broad sweep of strategy— "the overall strategic concept" as our American friends called it—he stood head and shoulders above his professional advisers'.

The document provided both a forecast and a blueprint for action. As the main Allied effort in 1942 Churchill advocated the clearing of the whole of the southern coast of the Mediterranean, which in turn would involve an Anglo-American entry, peaceful or otherwise, into Vichy North Africa. The United States must send divisions to Ireland which would release better trained British divisions for active operations. The bombing of Germany must continue, intensified by the participation of the U.S.A.A.F. And the basis for all this would be the maintenance of the Atlantic supply-lines. In the Pacific, a general fleet action must be avoided. 'We must expect to be deprived one by one of our possessions and strong points . . . in this interim period our duty is one of stubborn resistance at each point attacked. . . .' One of Churchill's most notable previsions is to be found in paragraph 5 of 'Notes on the Pacific'. Here he stated that 'the warfare of aircraft carriers should be developed to the greatest possible extent', and went on to argue that 'it takes five years to build a battleship, but it is possible to improvise a carrier in six months. Here then is a field for invention and ingenuity similar to that which called forth the extraordinary fleets and flotillas which fought on the Mississipi in the Civil War'. He could not then know it, but he was anticipating the battles of the Coral Sea and Midway, on 7 May and 4 June respectively, when in a few hours American carrier-borne aircraft destroyed for ever the Japanese domination of the South Pacific: anticipating, also, that phase of the Battle of the Atlantic in 1943 when hastily built, improvised escort carriers played a

---

* See Gwyer, *Grand Strategy*, Vol. III, Pt. I, pp. 325-336, for the complete text: a somewhat reduced version is in Churchill *op. cit.*, Vol. III, p. 574 foll.

† Ismay, *op. cit.*, p. 163.

considerable part in the final defeat of the U-boats. Lastly, Churchill considered,

> We have to prepare for the liberation of the captive countries of Western and Southern Europe by the landing at suitable points, successively or simultaneously, of British and American armies strong enough to enable the conquered populations to revolt. By themselves they will never be able to revolt, owing to the ruthless counter-measures that will be employed, but if adequate and suitably equipped forces were landed in several of the following countries, namely, Norway, Denmark, Holland, Belgium, the French Channel coasts and the French Atlantic coasts, as well as in Italy and possibly the Balkans, the German garrisons would prove insufficient to cope with the strength of the liberating forces and the fury of the revolting peoples. . . . We must face here the usual clash between short-term and long-term projects. War is a constant struggle and must be waged from day to day. It is only with some difficulty and within limits that provision can be made for the future. Experience shows that forecasts are usually falsified and preparations always in arrear. Nevertheless, there must be a design and theme for bringing the war to a victorious end in a reasonable period. . . .

In some respects Churchill's vision was faulty. His ideas about North Africa, for example, predicated a victorious advance by the Eighth Army but Rommel's riposte in January destroyed this illusion. Equally illusory was the notion of ultimate Anglo–American landings at many widely scattered points around the periphery of Europe. Nevertheless, in terms of 'grand strategy' his survey had a breadth and an accuracy which transcended the pessimistic conclusions of the Chiefs of Staff. They, following the estimates of their Directors of Plans, found themselves unable to penetrate the forest of difficulties in the foreground and envisage the 'broad shining uplands' of the future. It was undoubtedly their professional duty to be cautious: but, in effect, they reverted to the narrow policies formulated in the darkest hours after Dunkirk, of bombing, blockade, and subversion. Churchill would have none of this, asserting that it was important 'to put before the people of both the British Empire and the United States the mass invasion of the Continent of Europe as the goal'. His more optimistic views prevailed and the paper jointly produced for submission to the Americans represented, at all substantial points, the Prime Minister's intentions. Here, it may be observed, is the first, conclusive documentary evidence—of which much more was to follow—demolishing the *canard* that Churchill was 'soft on the Second Front'. And, unlike his advisers, he had outlined the design for bringing the war to a victorious end which the Allies were to adopt.

The Americans came to the conference with no design. This was not surprising. Since 1939 Marshall and his colleagues had been mainly, and in recent months overwhelmingly, concerned with arming their own naked nation, as well as supplying Britain and Russia. Until Japan struck, until America was actually in the war, realistic plans could hardly be formulated, for strategy is related to facts. Moreover, the team at ARCADIA was unbalanced. Marshall was dominant. It was only by subterfuge on his part that General Arnold, representing the Army Air Force, sat as an equal at the table, while Admiral King, now head of the Navy, was still in process of replacing Admiral Stark. Additionally, there had been no intensive preliminary discussions with the President such as Churchill shared with his advisers. And 'the staff organisation was less than desirable. The delay of the opening session because the officer in charge of arrangements had selected a room too small for the meeting reflected a lack of preparation that General Marshall was determined to eliminate'.* It is understandable, therefore, that the American attitude at ARCADIA was tentative and suspicious. If there was a common purpose it was to avoid being cozened into serving merely British interests. There was no plan to be argued point to point, but only a principle to uphold, and though the conference ended with agreed formulae the Americans were inevitably left with a vague but pervasive sense of unease. Somehow, they suspected, they had been overborne. As the war advanced this small cloud would develop the proportions of a thunderbank.

There was a genuine basis for the nagging resentment which long persisted in the War Department in Washington. On the first night after his arrival Churchill had a meeting with Roosevelt during which, he has recorded, 'I immediately broached with the President and those he had invited to join us' (Halifax, Beaverbrook, Hull, Stimson, Hopkins and Sumner Welles—no Chiefs of Staff), 'the scheme of Anglo-American intervention in French North Africa'. The result was reported by him to the Cabinet the next day. 'The President said that he was anxious that American land forces should give their support as quickly as possible where they could be most helpful, and favoured the idea of a plan to move into North Africa being prepared for either event, i.e., with or without invitation.' Although Roosevelt cooled off in the course of the conference, during which technical evidence revealed that it would be premature to think of invading North Africa, Churchill had nevertheless sowed a seed which would germinate the following summer and cause the President, over the heads of his own staff, to commit the United States irrevocably to Operation GYMNAST—as the landings were called until TORCH was

* Pogue, *op. cit.*, p. 270.

substituted. Marshall and those close to him never forgot. Whereas Eisenhower gave himself wholeheartedly, once GYMNAST was firm and he was appointed commander, Marshall never lost his reservations about a matter which seemed to him, as Auchinleck's delay in mounting CRUSADER had seemed to Churchill, to be at once 'a mistake and a misfortune'. The American Chiefs of Staff were always nervous thereafter, whenever Churchill and Roosevelt met in private, lest the Prime Minister should bewitch the President into paths of which they disapproved.

All the same, the results of ARCADIA were positive and constructive. With certain minor adjustments the British paper was accepted as the basis on which the military operations of the alliance would be conducted —the principle of *Germany first*, for which alone Churchill would have travelled to Washington, being agreed without qualification. But there were two other decisions, both American-inspired, which should have caused enough satisfaction to remove their lingering doubts, since each was fundamental in the future conduct of the war. It was Marshall who proposed the appointment of a Supreme Commander for the Far East, and Marshall who, by suggesting Wavell for the post, overcame the strong opposition of Churchill, his Cabinet, and his Chiefs of Staff. Though the Far East was already an impossible theatre for any Supremo this conception provided the command structure under which Germany was finally conquered. But to whom should the Supreme Commander be responsible? The British feared that they were being asked to provide a scapegoat for further disasters. Alanbrooke, the new C.I.G.S., was distracted by a desire for 'spheres of influence', with the Americans in charge of the Pacific and the British responsible for Burma, India, the Indian Ocean and the Middle East. It was Marshall, again, who was practical and statesmanlike. In spite of prejudices on his own side, especially within the U.S. Navy, he declared that 'we cannot manage by co-operation. Human frailties are such that there would be emphatic unwillingness to place portions of troops under another service. If we can make a plan for unified command now, it will solve nine-tenths of our troubles'. And it was Marshall who resolved a fractious debate about the Supreme Commander's responsibilities by recommending that he should act under the directives of a combined council. This led immediately to the institution of the Combined Chiefs of Staff and the establishment in Washington of a permanent Joint Staff Mission, headed by Dill, to represent the British Chiefs in regular meetings with their American counterparts. About this proposal, too, Alanbrooke was sceptical—though in later years he was compelled to confess, as is now accepted, that the Combined Chiefs of Staff organisation was 'the most efficient that had ever been evolved for co-ordinating and correlating the war strategy and effort of the Allies'. In these negotiations, during which the Americans displayed an almost missionary fervour, it was Churchill and not his C.I.G.S. who was prepared to be flexible and shift his position, realising that an American involvement in Europe would sooner or later produce similar problems of co-ordination and control.

He arrived back in England on 16 January. It was characteristic that having travelled down to Bermuda in a Boeing flying-boat, to join the *Duke of York*, he should have suddenly decided to proceed across the Atlantic in the same aircraft, although Portal, his Chief of Air Staff, at first thought the risk unjustifiable: characteristic, too, that 'I woke up unconscionably early with the conviction that I should certainly not go to sleep again. I must confess that I felt rather frightened. I thought of the ocean spaces, and that we should never be within a thousand miles of land until we approached the British Isles. I thought perhaps I had done a rash thing, that there were too many eggs in one basket'. Lord Moran has described how, after committing himself to a dangerous flight, Churchill would have a *frisson* of fear. In this case the fear was a true premonition, for after ten hours of blind passage through cloud and mist the aircraft only just avoided the hostile defences of Brest and, as it approached its landfall, was mistaken for an enemy bomber. Six Hurricanes were sent up, unsuccessfully, to shoot it down. While Churchill, like Hitler, was hard on his commanders, and was always prepared to order men to stand at their posts and die, at least it can be said that unlike Hitler he too was ready, if need be, to die. Some consider that he was merely making the irresponsible gestures of an insatiable romantic: but it may also be thought that his bravado, or indeed his bravery, help to explain why he was both respected by the seasoned men of war who surrounded him and revered by millions to whom he appeared to be not so much a remote War Lord as a larger and more heroic version of themselves.

Certainly Churchill required courage after his return. For the next six months—from the Washington conference until Rommel was halted in the first battle of Alamein—the sequence of disaster was continuous in the Far East, in Africa, in the Atlantic, even in the English Channel. The British, Gandhi mordantly observed, were 'on the toboggan'. Moreover, whereas during the swift fall of France Churchill's leadership had been indisputable, a succession of stunning defeats, in each of which British incompetence became appallingly evident, now undermined his personal position. Twice, in January and July, he had to defend himself in the House of Commons, once on a vote of confidence and once on a motion of censure. His system of war direction was criticised on all sides. But there was this difference: in 1940 the issue had been the simple one of survival, whereas in 1942 the observant could recognise that the real problem was one of organisation for victory. At the time the superficial impression was bound to be one of *ad hoc* reactions to one crisis after another, the response of a muscle to a blow. It was difficult to discern either a pattern or a plan. Yet, as in 1941, it was not the episodes which mattered but the underlying trends. The autumn was the watershed of the war. Allied victories at Alamein, at Stalingrad, at Guadalcanal and in the Barents Sea marked the beginning of the end.

It was not courage that Churchill lacked, but patience—sometimes with his staff, always with events. He was human, he was pugnacious, he was patriotic. It is not surprising, therefore, if at a time of crisis he did not always appear to be the calm centre of the whirlwind—if he hit out at those nearest to him and tried to hit out at the enemy. But it is dangerous to generalise from his frailties, since he could so often be at his best immediately before or after behaving at his worst. During the tense spring of 1941, for example, Captain Charles Lambe, the naval Director of Plans, noted in his diary for 2 April how brilliantly Churchill had pulled together the scattered strands of war production.* 'With a stroke of the pen he has done the whole thing himself. . . . These are decisions which have long been wanted, which even the most powerful committee would have funked taking and required endless study in many separate directions. . . . His knowledge of technical matters apart from politics, strategy and history, combined with his personality and readiness to shoulder responsibility and his intuitive flair for a situation mark him out as an outstanding man whatever his faults'. Yet shortly afterwards, on 19 April, Lambe wrote: 'The news from Greece and Jugoslavia and Libya was bad and the P.M. came in ten minutes late very depressed. He was puffy and very pink and white, pig-like. . . . He was very depressed and desperately tired—in a sort of coma almost. His speech was rather slobbery and very slow. . . . It was a terribly depressing interview.' Only those who could hold these antitheses in balance could appreciate Churchill as a whole. Fortunately this was Alanbrooke's gift. While he was still only C.I.G.S. designate, on 4 December 1941, he realised the problem.

We were told that we did nothing but obstruct his intentions, we had no ideas of our own and, whenever he produced ideas, we produced nothing but

* See page 60 *foll.*

objections, etc., etc. Attlee pacified him once, but he broke out again; then Anthony Eden smoothed him temporarily, but all to no avail. Finally he looked at his papers for some five minutes, closed the meeting and walked out of the room. It was pathetic and entirely unnecessary. We are only trying to save him from making definite promises which he might find it hard to keep later on. It is all the result of over-working himself and keeping too late hours. Such a pity! God knows where we should be without him, but God knows where we shall go with him.

Next morning Churchill issued a memorandum to the Chiefs of Staff on virtually the lines which they had been pleading with him to accept! Similar outbursts appear regularly in Alanbrooke's diary for the spring of 1942. 'Have you not got a single general in the Army who can win battles . . . ?' 'Pray explain, C.I.G.S.,' (*in the middle of a Cabinet meeting*), 'how is it that in the Middle East 750,000 men always turn up for their pay and rations, but when it comes to fighting only 100,000 turn up. Explain to us exactly how the remaining 650,000 are occupied?' And then there was the craving for action. On 30 March, 'I had to go round to see P.M. at 10.30 p.m. and was kept up till 1 a.m. discussing possibilities of some form of offensive in North France to assist Russia'. And Norway, always Norway. 'Why he wanted to go back and what he was going to do there . . . we never found out. The only reason he ever gave was that Hitler had unrolled the map of Europe starting with Norway and he would start rolling it up again with Norway'. Churchill kept no diary. He exteriorised in open anger the dreams and frustrations which Alanbrooke secretly committed to the private page.* But in practice the C.I.G.S. understood, and preserved a balanced view of his master. This was his triumph.

By July, Hopkins noted, 'the Prime Minister's powers of emotional endurance were now being tested to the limit after six months of mortification'. The state of *angst* started much earlier in the year, as almost daily signals revealed the skill and speed of the Japanese advance and, by contrast, the lack of British preparation.

Prime Minister to General Ismay, for C.O.S. Committee   *19.1.42*

I must confess to being staggered by Wavell's telegram of the 16th and other telegrams on the same subject. It never occurred to me for a moment, nor to Sir John Dill, with whom I discussed the matter on the

---

* Alanbrooke wrote that 'I considered it essential never to disclose outwardly what one felt inwardly. . . . My diary acted as a safety valve, the only safety valve I had'. On the other hand Captain Butcher, Eisenhower's A.D.C., records Churchill as saying, at Algiers in 1943, 'it was foolish to keep a day-by-day diary because it would simply reflect the change of opinion or decision of the writer, which, when and if published, makes one appear indecisive and foolish'.

outward voyage, that the gorge of the fortress of Singapore, with its splendid moat half a mile to a mile wide, was not entirely fortified against an attack from the northward. What is the use of having an island for a fortress if it is not to be made into a citadel? To construct a line of detached works with search-lights and cross-fire combined with immense wiring and obstruction of the swamp areas, and to provide the proper ammunition to enable the fortress to dominate enemy batteries planted in Johore, was an elementary peace-time provision which it is incredible did not exist in a fortress which has been twenty years building. If this was so, how much more should the necessary field works have been constructed during the two and a half years of the present war? How was it that not one of you pointed this out to me at any time when these matters have been under discussion?

It is impossible to analyse briefly the complicated reasons for the fall of Singapore. Up to a point the Chiefs of Staff had done their duty: they had warned. But they never *fought* Churchill over the issue of giving an over-riding priority to a Far Eastern Strategy, and, in so far as they considered it a vital interest, they must certainly carry a share of the blame, as professionals, for not seeing that at least the best possible arrangements were made to defend the island with all resources available, inadequate though they may have been. In justice to them it must be recalled that they, like Churchill, were always aware, with terrifying clarity, that Britain could not sustain alone a war with Germany, Italy and Japan. But neither they nor he did the best that could have been done, and in Churchill's contemporary minutes one can detect a note not only of mortification but also of a disguised yet conscious guilt.

When the imminent disaster became evident, however, it was he who faced it with the most brutal realism, and he who proposed that, since Singapore was now a wasting asset, it might be best to cut losses and 'at once blow the docks and batteries and workshops to pieces and concentrate everything on the defence of Burma and keeping open the Burma road'. His colleagues argued successfully against so desperate a move: indeed, Churchill himself was torn by doubt. But once the decision to stand and fight had been taken, he was ruthless.

Prime Minister to General Wavell   *10.2.42*

... There must at this stage be no thought of saving the troops or sparing the population. The battle must be fought to the bitter end at all costs. The 18th Division has a chance to make its name in history. Commanders and senior officers should die with their troops. The honour of the British Empire and of the British Army is at stake. I rely on you to show no mercy to weakness in any form. With the Russians fighting as they are and the Americans so stubborn at Luzon, the whole reputation of our country and our race is involved. . . .

It must, however, be added that when, four days later, nothing seemed left but the useless slaughter of street fighting, Churchill sent Wavell an unqualified instruction to use his own judgement about a surrender.

The strain of the situation was increased by the attitude of the Australian government, who clamoured for their far-flung divisions to be brought home and made importunate demands for Anglo–American action. Their hysteria was understandable, though understanding was not advanced by a message from Curtin, the Prime Minister, declaring that evacuation of Singapore would be 'an inexcusable betrayal'. Churchill was in the intolerable position which Dill had described to Auchinleck, of 'those who alone see the picture as a whole and carry the main responsibility'. All military wisdom requires the concentration of available forces at the vital point, and in the global war which Churchill was now facing Australia was not an immediate risk—except in the imagination of Australians. How much more important, for example, was Burma, seen from a higher viewpoint—and in the eyes of the Americans, on whose good will and assistance the Australians laid such emphasis—Burma, the outpost of India and supply-route to China? A sort of compromise was achieved, in which Churchill never surrendered his responsibility for central decision or allowed Australia to forget her own larger obligations: a painful but inevitable episode, which would certainly have been resolved with less heat and loss of dignity if Menzies had still been Prime Minister, for Menzies could look beyond the Antipodes.

It was fortunate for the Prime Minister that the debate in which he insisted on demanding a vote of confidence from the House of Commons was not held a month later. As it was, he emerged from the three-day discussions of 27–29 January with a majority of 464 to one and a message of congratulation from Roosevelt: 'It is fun to be in the same decade with you'. But under the shock of domestic as well as distant disaster Parliament, at the end of February, might well have seen nothing funny about a month during which Singapore had been lost, Auchinleck had been driven back to Gazala, and the *Scharnhorst* and *Gneisenau*, by their passage of the Channel, had inflicted on Britain the most searing humiliation since Von Tromp sailed up that same Channel with a broom at his mast-head.

The result of the debate was to fortify Churchill's personal position but to impel him to reconstitute his administration. The pent-up feelings of frustration and defeat which expressed themselves in attacks on his conduct of the war, and which were renewed in February in both the Lords and the Commons, led not so much to a demand for Churchill's replacement as to attempts to prevent him doing so much. But the difficulty, for his critics, was to produce a viable alternative method. There were various proposals—a Great General Staff, a Deputy Prime Minister, an independent chairman of the Chiefs of Staff. Hankey spoke along these lines in the House of Lords—but Hankey was a star in decline, and warped by a sense of rejection. The distinguished scientist A. V. Hill spoke cogently in the Commons. 'Nor can the sort of technical knowledge which is necessary for those who have to guide our strategy now be acquired as a part-time job by an elderly statesman whose historical outlook inevitably leads him to think in terms of earlier wars. It requires the full-time attention of a technical section of a combined General Staff, composed for the main part of young and able officers of all arms who have grown up with modern methods and equipment.' But Hill was a member of the Tizard faction, and what he was really saying was 'Cherwell must go'. The fact was that Churchill was unique, 'a vast species alone', and since it was accepted that he was irreplaceable it was useless to dream of deputies whom he would never tolerate.

The Chiefs of Staff were a different matter. Here it was a question of the best functional arrangement. But again the critics were at a loss, for none of the alternatives proposed was an improvement. Alanbrooke later summed it all up in *Notes on My Life*.

> Frequently when the situation was bad there were suggestions that a separate Chairman for the Chiefs of Staff should be found or a Deputy Defence Minister interposed between the P.M. and the Chiefs of Staff. None of these alternatives was either possible or necessary. To my mind the P.M. in war must always deal direct with the Chiefs of Staff and the members of the C.O.S. must defend their actions personally in the Cabinet, using their Chairman as spokesman. The introduction of an outside Chairman will never smooth over differences between members of the C.O.S. if these exist. Should there ever be such differences there is only one course, to change all or some of the members of the C.O.S. It is essential that these three men should work as a perfect trinity.

The problem was one of personalities rather than one of patterns or structures. Pound was the chairman of the Chiefs of Staff Committee, and Pound was slow, somnolent, and essentially a seadog, prone to nod off during a meeting, as Alanbrooke put it, 'like an old parrot asleep on his

perch'. Normally Pound would have retained the chair until his retire-
ment, but on 5 March Churchill replaced him by Alanbrooke. This was
the answer: henceforth the Prime Minister and his professional advisers
were more closely integrated than at any time in British history, and none
of the alternatives ventilated by critics (all of whom only saw part of the
whole, and many of whom were disappointed men), could conceivably
have produced a more efficient or indeed a more harmonious result. In
any event debate cleared the air, and the changes in his governmental
team which followed (of which the most important was the introduction of
Lyttleton in the new post of Minister of Production), left Churchill better
placed to tackle the considerable strategic decision which was now impending.

The Washington conference had hardly concluded before the attitude of
Marshall and his War Department began to harden about GYMNAST.
By late January Eisenhower, whom Marshall had just made Chief of War
Plans Division, was writing 'We've got to go to Europe and fight, and we've
got to quit wasting resources all over the world—and still worse—wasting
time. If we're to keep Russia in, save the Middle East, India, and Burma;
we've got to begin slugging with air at West Europe; to be followed by a
land attack as soon as possible'. This summarised the views of all in the
U.S. Army whose main preoccupation was not the Pacific. Germany
first, certainly: but to destroy Germany all must be concentrated on a
single, massive, cross-Channel attack, and minimum forces must be
diverted to what from the American point of view were secondary theatres.
This thesis was crystallised in a memorandum which Marshall submitted
to Roosevelt on 1 April. It contained a preamble, in which the broad
principle was stated that 'The bulk of the combat forces of the United
States, United Kingdom, and Russia can be applied simultaneously only
against Germany, and then only if we attack in time. We cannot concentrate against Japan'. To this a plan was attached for landings between
Le Havre and Boulogne in April 1943 with 48 divisions on a six-divisional
front supported by 5,800 aircraft. Marshall also wanted a preliminary
landing to occur in 1942. Roosevelt ordered Marshall to fly to London to
present the American case, and sent both a letter and a signal to Churchill
telling him that the proposal, which he hoped would please Stalin, had
'his heart and *mind* in it'.

Since arguments about the nature and timing of a Second Front were to
bedevil the coalition for the next two years it is worth pausing to consider
some relevant facts, now known, which could hardly be foreseen in their
entirety—though some were clear to the British—during the early stages

of the debate. What, it may be asked, was essential for a successful OVERLORD in 1944 which could not have happened in 1942 or 1943? These are at least some of the factors:

1. In the earlier years, Marshall might well have been Supreme Commander. Superb as a Chief of Staff, he would almost certainly have proved inferior to Eisenhower as a battle commander. Whenever he intervened with tactical proposals he was wrong—over North Africa, over Sicily, over D Day: in each case Eisenhower had to put him right.

2. In 1942 and 1943 Bomber Command was still not fully developed. The U.S. 8th Air Force, operating under the initial doctrine of self-defence, was shot out of the skies in 1943: it was not till 1944 that the long-distance Mustang day-fighter enabled the 8th Air Force to destroy the German day-fighters, achieve the air superiority by day which was essential for OVERLORD and, as a by-product, so affect the German night-fighter that Bomber Command could work more safely by night. Also, the techniques of precision bombing which were so critical for the interdiction programme before D Day were not adequately evolved until 1944.

3. Until 1944 neither *Mulberry*, nor *Pluto*, nor the specialised assault armour of 79 Division would have been available.

4. Before 1944 German reserves for defence in the West would have been more substantial. The drain on the Russian front and in North Africa, Italy and the Balkans was enormous in 1942 and 1943.

5. The Battle of the Atlantic was not won till mid-1943.

6. Until 1944 the Allies, and particularly the Americans, were short of senior commanders, and of staffs, and of divisions sufficiently battle-trained in combined operations.*

7. In 1942, and to a lesser but still important degree in 1943, shortage of landing-craft would have been critical.

British resistance to American pressure for an earlier OVERLORD is often ascribed, especially by American analysts, to British self-interest of a political character. What tends to be forgotten is that the *practicality* of the American proposals is the nub; that the British, who since Dunkirk had been examining the possibilities of a continental landing from a practical point of view, were deterred by what seemed to be the impossibility of an

---

* The shrewd Harry Hopkins made this point effectively when he once observed: 'In trying to figure out whether we could have got across the Channel successfully in 1942 or 1943, you've got to answer the unanswerable question as to whether Eisenhower, Bradley, Spaatz, Patton, Beedle Smith, and also Montgomery and Tedder and a lot of others, could have handled the big show as they did if they hadn't had the experience fighting the Germans in North Africa and Sicily?' See Robert Sherwood, *The White House Papers*, Vol. II, p. 797.

early success in action. Churchill, who so often pressed his Chiefs of Staff to undertake continental adventures, was the first to be aware of the inherent difficulties. He never weakened in his determination to re-enter Europe *at an appropriate moment*. Indeed, as will be seen, he can be observed in conflict with reluctant Chiefs of Staff on this very point. This is a matter which justifies the use of hindsight. In view of what is now known about D Day and the Normandy campaign it can hardly be denied that Churchill was correct in resisting the enormous pressures from Russia and America for a premature Second Front. It was fortunate that by securing an invasion of North Africa in 1942 he made an invasion of Northern France—though he sought one for 1943—impossible until 1944. A cross-Channel offensive in 1942 would have been a guaranteed, and in 1943 an almost certain, failure.

The so-called 'Marshall Plan' which was examined in London in early April contained three elements. BOLERO was the code-name for the transatlantic build-up of men and munitions on the launching pad of the British Isles. ROUNDUP (a name criticised by Churchill as being pretentious and boastful, though OVERLORD was hardly modest!), stood for an invasion of Europe in 1943. But what should happen in 1942? Here was the main area of controversy: here Marshall was inflexible. He wanted SLEDGEHAMMER, a form of emergency operation to be conducted in 1942 for the apparent purpose of aiding the Russians: although, as the months passed and Marshall clung to his conception, he visualised it more and more as an insurance policy, since so long as planning proceeded for a SLEDGEHAMMER in 1942, ROUNDUP in 1943—his dominant aim— could hardly be in jeopardy. For Roosevelt this scheme for a limited attack by a few divisions, perhaps no more than an extended raid in strength, had the further attraction that it would bring American troops to battle before the year's end.

The British were only too clear about how limited the operation would have to be. For Churchill it seemed a trivial alternative to the capture of Vichy North Africa and control of the Mediterranean. 'Throughout the sessions, in which winning charm, cold persuasion, rude insistence, eloquent flow of language, flashes of anger, and sentiment close to tears were called on by Churchill to advance his cause, the Chief of Staff stuck to his basic contentions for a strategy that suited the interests of the United States, carefully reiterating American problems, American pressures, and American determination.'[*] The British Chiefs relied on facts and figures. Alanbrooke thought that the forces which could be landed

* Pogue, *op. cit.*, p. 313.

would be too small to hold a bridgehead and that evacuation would be impossible. Portal was unable to guarantee air support over the zone of action. Mountbatten, now a member of the Chiefs of Staff Committee as Chief of Combined Operations, rested on the technical difficulties. Nevertheless, late in the evening on 14 April Churchill declared that 'he had no hesitation in cordially accepting the plan', 'a momentous meeting', as Alanbrooke put it, 'at which we accepted their proposals for offensive action in Europe in 1942 perhaps, and in 1943 for certain'.

Alanbrooke's private 'perhaps' was a key word, for in seeking the accommodation with the Americans which he felt to be essential Churchill had gone too far. In his memoirs he admitted that while he was prepared to give SLEDGEHAMMER 'a fair run', nevertheless he was 'almost certain the more it was looked at the less it would be liked'. These reservations were never properly expressed or registered in the final stages of the discussions, so Marshall departed with the conviction that he had achieved a commitment which the British felt they had not accepted either on paper or, more importantly, in their hearts. Lip-service was paid to the concept of SLEDGEHAMMER, in the schedule for operations in Europe which was now prepared for and approved by the British Chiefs of Staff; provisional force commanders for SLEDGEHAMMER were nominated; but the British were carrying out an exercise while Marshall thought he had ensured a reality.

It is ironic that what Marshall himself knew to be a limiting factor for his project, and what was a major concern for Churchill during the spring and summer of 1942,* was to a large degree the fault of the Americans. This was the catastrophic rise in shipping losses. The tonnage of British, Allied and neutral merchant shipping sunk by U-boats in all theatres increased at a steady rate from over 300,000 tons in January to 700,000 in July. But the real significance lay in the area of American responsibility—roughly, the western Atlantic. Here well over a quarter of a million tons was sunk in January, rising to a peak just short of 600,000 tons in June, and the worst feature was the fact that in every month the greater proportion of the loss occurred within 300 miles of the American coasts. Professor Morison, in his magnificent history,† is uncompromising. 'This writer cannot avoid the conclusion that the U.S. Navy was woefully unprepared, materially and mentally, for the U-boat blitz on the Atlantic coast. He further believes that . . . this unpreparedness was largely the

---

* As Hitler appreciated. 'Time and again, Churchill speaks of shipping tonnage as his greatest worry.' Führer Naval Conference, 13 February 1942.

† S. E. Morison, *The History of United States Naval Operations*, Vol. I, p. 200.

Navy's own fault.' Yet Churchill and the Admiralty had done their utmost. From the time that a powerful American naval mission arrived in London in August 1940 everything the British learned about the new war at sea was handed over without reservation—including the latest radar devices— as part of the traffic the Prime Minister had approved. Immediately after Pearl Harbour Pound was in America for a whole month to co-ordinate the policies and practices of the two navies. Nevertheless, with that curious inability to make use of the experience of others which characterised all three of the American armed services when they too had to fight, the U.S. Navy began by rejecting the methods which had been proved, over and over again, to be the best anti-U-boat defence—convoys and escorts. Tactfully but firmly Churchill tried to put matters right. On 12 March he wrote to Hopkins, in outlining the form that British assistance could take, that 'I am most deeply concerned at the immense sinking of tankers west of the 40th meridian and in the Caribbean Sea. . . . Please let me know whether you think it well to bring all this before the President straight away . . .'. But Roosevelt, who was not incapable of instant action, re- mained strangely inert. 24 anti-submarine trawlers and 10 corvettes were transferred by the British, convoy cycles were modified, and the Director of Anti-Submarine Warfare, with the Air Vice-Marshal in charge of a Group of Coastal Command, was sent to the States to advise on all aspects of the battle. But concrete results came slowly. The first properly organised convoy down the East Coast to Florida did not sail until 14 May, and it was not until the end of the year that a fully effective system, covering the waters from Canada to South America, was in operation. Meanwhile it was galling for Churchill, and even more so for those directly concerned, to know that precious merchant ships were being safely shepherded across the Atlantic only to be destroyed in dozens as their voyage drew to an end.

In the Arctic, also, the pressures of coalition warfare were now taking their toll. The early convoys to Russia arrived safely, but during the spring and summer of 1942 the situation changed so gravely that Churchill was presented with another politico-strategical dilemma. It was as if, in some way, the Führer had a telepathic understanding of the Prime Minister's deepest volitions, for by the end of December he was so convinced about the possibility of a combined operation against his northern flank that on the 29th he ordered: 'The German fleet must therefore use all its forces for the defence of Norway. It would be expedient to transfer all battle- ships there for this purpose. The latter could be used for attacking con- voys in the north, for instance.' A month later he described Norway as 'the zone of destiny in the war'. A concentration of the German battlefleet in Norwegian harbours and fiords was effected. Then, at the beginning of March, he demanded vigorous action against the Murmansk convoys which, he pointed out, had hardly been touched. By the middle of April he was declaring that 'attacks on the Murmansk convoys are the most important thing at the moment'. The consequent offensive by German U-boats, aircraft and surface vessels had its reward in a rising graph of loss not only of merchant ships but also of the escorting cruisers and destroyers. In the Navy professional opinion increasingly opposed the continuance of something which, by the narrower standards of a staff appreciation, no longer appeared to be an operation of war. And what, anyway, were the Russians doing to help? 'Though there are no grounds for suggesting that, within the limits imposed by their somewhat primitive conceptions of maritime war, the Russians did not do what they could with what they had, it is none the less the case that they never relieved the Home Fleet of any appreciable share of the responsibility for defending any Arctic convoy.'*

Churchill, however, had to look far beyond the mathematics of a staff solution. On the one hand there was Stalin, whom it was vital to sustain, and to whom he wrote, on 9 May, 'We are resolved to fight through to you with the maximum amount of war materials'. Hitler might call the coalition artificial but Churchill was a realist, and an undefeated Russia was worth the gravest risk. But could Russia survive? The thaws of spring had released the Germans on every front in the east; by the end of May most of the Crimea was in their hands, by 1 July Sevastopol had fallen, and in May and June they not only held Timoshenko's offensive around Kharkov, but regained the initiative. The Donetz basin was crumbling, Rostov was threatened, and by mid-July Halder was already noting in his diary 'the forthcoming battle of Stalingrad'. Moreover for Roosevelt, as for Churchill, the dangers in the east were an almost daily preoccupation. Allied supplies for Stalin were given high priority in Washington, and during April and May there was a tense exchange of telegrams about 'the log jam', with the President arguing powerfully for more frequent convoys—'Our problem is to move 107 ships now loaded or being loaded in the United Kingdom or the United States prior to June 1'—and Churchill fighting a delaying action, as in his signal of 2 May:—'With every great respect, what you suggest is beyond our power to fulfil. . . . I beg you not to press us beyond our judgement in the operation, which we have studied most intently, and of which we have not yet been able to measure

* Roskill, op. cit., Vol. II, p. 128.

the full strain'. But the pressures were too great, and Churchill, who had to endure them, grasped their consequences more clearly than his admirals.

Prime Minister to General Ismay, for C.O.S. Committee   *17.5.42*

Not only Premier Stalin but President Roosevelt will object very much to our desisting from running the convoys now. The Russians are in heavy action, and will expect us to run the risk and pay the price entailed by our contribution. The United States ships are queuing up ... I share your misgivings, but I feel it is a matter of duty.

The bill was soon presented. At the end of May convoy P.Q.16 and the homeward bound Q.P.12 survived, against all expectations, continuous attack from the air with the loss of only seven out of 50 ships. But when the next convoy was planned, for the end of June, it seemed probable that P.Q.17 would have to face not only aircraft, U-boats and destroyers, but also the *Tirpitz*. Admiral Tovey, Commander-in-Chief of the Home Fleet, disliked the arrangements, but the convoy sailed, with disastrous consequences. The dust of controversy over the Admiralty order to scatter (given by Pound himself, apparently without Churchill's knowledge), and the withdrawal of the escorts will probably never settle. Many of the merchantmen were American, as were some of the supporting warships. There was an inevitable wave of indignation, and a natural criticism which tended to overlook the recent record of the British Navy. More importantly, a decision had now to be taken to suspend further operations until the perpetual daylight of the summer had contracted. Stalin's reply to Churchill's elaborate explanation was frigid:—'the British Government refuses to continue the sending of war materials to the Soviet Union via the Northern route. ... Our naval experts consider the reasons put forward ... wholly unconvincing'. Churchill himself has been much condemned for the tragic losses: but it should be observed that so heavy a price was not inherent in the P.Q.17 operation itself, although everybody knew that sooner or later it must be exacted. Pound made a misjudgement. As to Churchill, it would be more correct to say that his whole policy over the Russian convoys was on trial, for the P.Q.17 disaster was essentially a part of a whole. It is difficult, at this distance, to see how anyone in Churchill's place could have done anything different, granted the scale of the issues involved: and equally difficult to calculate the consequences if anything different had been done. Of his dispatching of the two battleships to Singapore some might observe, with Talleyrand, that 'it was worse than a crime: it was a blunder'. He bore the responsibility. But in the Russian convoys Stalin and Roosevelt were co-partners.

If the tendencies were to matter more than this succession of adverse episodes a victory in the desert was mandatory, for the strategical scheme which Churchill had delineated in December, as he tossed across the Atlantic towards ARCADIA, pivoted on the clearance of the Mediterranean shore. So the Eighth Army had hardly sorted itself out after its retreat to Gazala before he became avid for a new battle. On 26 February he wrote to Auchinleck:—'I have not troubled you much in these difficult days, but I must now ask what are your intentions. According to our figures you have substantial superiority in the air, in armour, and in other forces over the enemy'. But Auchinleck was not to be stampeded. He considered that 1 June was the earliest possible date, since 'to launch major offensive before then would be to risk defeat in detail and possibly endanger safety of Egypt'. With good reason—for between O'Connor and Montgomery the Eighth Army suffered from deficiencies of command, at all levels, which fitted it ill for offensives against Rommel. But Auchinleck's attitude infuriated Churchill, who 'looked to the Eighth Army to repair the shame of Singapore', and it troubled the Chiefs of Staff for the more practical reason that Malta was now under great strain: a desert offensive was desirable both as a cloak for the supply convoy which must be fought through to the island, and also to capture the airfields in Cyrenaica from which the approaches to Malta could be protected. Auchinleck remained adamant. The situation was not eased by his imprudent refusal to fly to London for consultations, or by the visit of Stafford Cripps and General Nye, the V.C.I.G.S., to Cairo in mid-March. Churchill had employed them as inquisitors to discover why Auchinleck was wrong, but their judgement, on the spot, was that he was right. An unprofitable debate continued until on 10 May, as Churchill wrote, 'it was decided to send General Auchinleck definite orders which he must obey or be relieved. This was a most unusual procedure on our part towards a high military commander'. He was instructed to attack as soon as possible, and at the very latest by a date 'which provides a distraction in time to help the passage of the June dark-period convoy'. Auchinleck did not resign, as was anticipated, but acquiesced. Nevertheless, he refused Churchill's request to take command in the field himself.

In the event, he was compelled to do so. Churchill's instinct was confirmed. On 26 May Rommel forestalled Auchinleck with a typically dashing offensive whose objectives were the Delta and the Canal: with luck, perhaps a link-up with other panzer divisions thrusting south from the Caucasus through Turkey. The Eighth Army retreated. It became clear that General Ritchie was inadequate at the level of Army commander, and Auchinleck himself at last took charge of the battle, halting Rommel along the Alamein Line which had been roughly prepared after the first assault of the Afrika Korps in 1941. And Auchinleck could not complain: he had not been repulsed because he had been pressed into a premature attack but because the commander of his own choice, and his subordinates, had thrown away a possible victory in those early stages of the fighting when even Rommel was anticipating defeat. Where he and all subsequent critics have ground for dissatisfaction is in Churchill's persistent failure to recognise the skill and determination with which Auchinleck, during the last phase of the battle, prevented the ejection of the British from Egypt. This was no temporary pique. Long after the war, when Churchill published the fourth volume of his memoirs, Dorman-Smith (who at the time was Auchinleck's Deputy Chief Staff Officer), challenged the implications of the text, and Churchill agreed to the insertion of a qualifying passage. Liddell Hart acted as 'honest broker' between Dorman-Smith and those representing Churchill. It is obvious from the file in the Liddell Hart Papers that whatever verbal adjustments the Prime Minister—as he then again was—may have accepted he had not modified his fundamental belief. And that, of course, was reflected in the decision he made in Cairo, in August 1942, to replace Auchinleck by Alexander—of which Ismay, a profound admirer of 'the Auk', wrote regretfully that 'there was an undercurrent of feeling both at home and in the Middle East that a change was advisable'.

Apart from changes in the high command, however, by August two events had already occurred which, together, led to that clearance of the southern shores of the Mediterranean which Auchinleck failed to achieve —the provision of American armour which made Montgomery's victory at Alamein, and its aftermath, possible: and a final Anglo–American agreement about GYMNAST/TORCH.

After the presentation and modification of the 'Marshall Plan' in London, during April, Roosevelt's eagerness to get American troops into action increased at the same time as the British Chiefs of Staff, and Churchill, became more and more convinced that a European operation in 1942 was out of the question. By June the Cabinet had affirmed that nothing must be undertaken unless German morale had been enfeebled by defeat in Russia: unless, also, any lodgement made by the Allies in France could be retained. A visit to Washington early in the month by Mountbatten, with the professional authority of Chief of Combined Operations, helped to persuade Roosevelt that in any case the landing craft available were insufficient for anything more than a suicide squad. And so when Churchill decided to cross the Atlantic once again, on 17 June, with Alanbrooke to support him, Roosevelt's mind was already turning back to North Africa as a sphere where Americans might get into the German war. Churchill's attention had never been diverted. It was not that he opposed an invasion of France—when the time was ripe. His aggressive attitude can be clearly seen in the long paper he addressed to Ismay on 15 June,* just before he left for Washington, in which he outlined the appropriate tactics for a ROUNDUP in 1943. 'I was especially anxious that the gigantic scale of the operation should be understood from the outset and plans made accordingly. I threw myself into the mental proposition with such strength as I had. I wanted to give a picture of the size and character of the enterprise, and of the spirit in which alone it could be undertaken. Whatever may be thought about the detail, it struck the note of supreme effort.' Considering that the paper was composed at a time when Churchill was distracted daily by the depressing reports of Rommel's successes outside Tobruk, it provides yet another striking example of his capacity to rise *au-dessus de la mêlée*. But the difficulty was that Marshall had not tackled the mental proposition of a landing in France in 1942 with an equivalent insight or grasp of the inherent military problems.

As the Combined Chiefs of Staff reviewed the future together, immediately after Churchill and Alanbrooke arrived in Washington, Marshall's concepts dominated the discussion. GYMNAST was dismissed, while SLEDGEHAMMER still retained a reserved place. It was curious that Alanbrooke should have committed himself to the unanimous conclusions of the meeting, in view of the way policies had been developing in London: it was more than curious, it was dangerous. The immediate rejection of these proposals of the Combined Chiefs of Staff, followed so soon by decisions for action the exact opposite of what they had recommended, did much to keep alive the American sense of suspicion and frustration already generated at ARCADIA. The proposals were:

a. That United States and Great Britain should adhere firmly to the basic decision to push BOLERO with all possible speed and energy.

b. That since any 1942 operation would inevitably have some deterring effect upon Continental operations in 1943, it should be undertaken only in case of necessity or if an exceptionally favourable opportunity presented itself.

* Churchill, *op. cit.*, Vol. IV, p. 316 foll.

c. That GYMNAST should not be undertaken under the existing situation.

d. That the locality, strength and availability of needs for any 1942 attack on Western Europe should be studied further. But when the most favourable of these had been decided upon, plans should be developed in anticipation of conditions compelling its initiation.

Moreover, though it was agreed that assaults on Norway, Cherbourg, Brest or the Channel Islands would carry a risk, 'any of these plans', it was felt, 'would be preferable to undertaking GYMNAST . . .'.

While generals may propose their political masters dispose. Alanbrooke was aware of the omens, noting in his diary that he and his American colleagues 'fully appreciated that we might be up against many difficulties when confronted with the plans that the Prime Minister and President had been brewing up together at Hyde Park. We fear the worst and are certain that North Africa and North Norway plans for 1942 will loom large in their proposals, whilst we are convinced that they are not possible'. The 'worst' had indeed occurred, for Churchill worked effectively on Roosevelt, pointing out that no responsible military authority had so far presented a plan for a SLEDGEHAMMER blow in 1942 which could conceivably succeed unless the Germans lost their nerve—which was improbable. Had the Americans such a plan? He for his part would welcome one. Since there was, of course, no such plan available, Churchill was able to proceed triumphantly to the conclusion that 'it is in this setting and on this background that the French North West Africa operation should be studied'. The logic was remorseless, and Roosevelt was swayed. The carefully drafted record of the decisions reached on 21 June, during a prolonged discussion between the President and the Prime Minister, Marshall, Alanbrooke, Ismay and Hopkins, marked a new and critical phase in the anxious debate, for while it made a diplomatic genuflection towards SLEDGEHAMMER, it continued with the flat statement that 'the possibilities of Operation GYMNAST will be explored carefully and conscientiously, and plans will be completed in all details as soon as possible . . .'. Churchill had, in effect, defeated Marshall: from this point onward SLEDGEHAMMER was dead, while GYMNAST thrived.

21 June was also, however, the day when Roosevelt, sitting in his study, handed to Churchill the news of the fall of Tobruk. The reaction was tersely summarised by the American War Secretary, Stimson, who wrote that the blow 'shifted the attention of the Washington meeting from grand strategy to immediate repair work'. Without hesitation Roosevelt made his memorable request to be informed what he could do to help, and

Churchill asked for Sherman tanks. By the end of the day Marshall had held no less than three meetings in the White House, and he emerged with an offer to send to the Middle East a fully equipped armoured division, even though this meant switching tanks from units they had just reached. 'It is a terrible thing to take the weapons out of a soldier's hands', he told Churchill, 'but if the British need is so great they must have them'. (This, incidentally, marks the appearance of Patton on the Anglo–American scene, for it was Patton whom Marshall ordered to prepare 2 Armoured Division in readiness for Egypt, adding that he wanted nothing said about a corps. The next morning Patton blithely suggested that a second division should be sent! Marshall immediately dismissed Patton to California, where, on reflection, he decided that he could manage with a single division. He was then summoned back to Washington, 'and that', Marshall used to say, 'is the way to handle Patton'.)

Meanwhile, second thoughts suggested that *matériel* would be more use to the Eighth Army than men: as a result, Marshall offered the dispatch in fast convoy of 300 tanks and 100 105 mm. self-propelled guns. Their arrival in September was a prime factor at Alamein. Not enough weight has been paid by British writers to the significance of this transfer. It was an extraordinary gesture on the part not only of the warm-hearted and spontaneous Roosevelt, but also of the cold and calculating Marshall, to provide such equipment at a time when the U.S. Army was still in a fledgling state and when, on a strict analysis, American shortages in the Pacific might have been held to be a more insistent priority. In another sense, it was an extraordinary achievement on Churchill's part. The fact that he obtained this succour so swiftly, on the very day when he was skilfully destroying the dearest ambitions of the U.S. War Department, is something probably unparalleled in the history of military alliances. It was an expression of confidence in his partnership, fostered now over so many months, which transcended all superficial feelings about his malign influence or backstairs gossip about perfidious Albion. Yet these sentiments persisted: and when, after his return, Churchill sent a message to Roosevelt on 8 July that SLEDGEHAMMER was unacceptable for 1942, and that all concentration should be on GYMNAST, the American Joint Chiefs of Staff were driven to a desperate move. Two days later Marshall and King (Marshall, as he later admitted, bluffing but King fully resolved), stated to the President that:

If the United States is to engage in any other operation than forceful, unswerving adherence to BOLERO plans, we are definitely of the opinion that we should turn to the Pacific and strike decisively against Japan; in other words, assume a defensive attitude against Germany, except for air operations; and use all available means in the Pacific.

On the following Sunday Roosevelt reacted by requiring *that same afternoon* 'a full statement of the Pacific alternative, with estimated times of landings, total numbers of ships, planes, and men, proposed withdrawals of men, planes, and ships from the Atlantic, and the effect of the change on the defence of the Soviet Union and the Middle East'.*

This volley gave him game, set and match. Instead of opting for the Pacific he ordered Marshall, King and Hopkins to proceed immediately to London and make a final deal with the British. Stimson nevertheless made a subtle extra ploy on behalf of the Army *v.* the President by putting in Roosevelt's hands a copy of Field Marshal Sir William Robertson's *Soldiers and Statesmen*, in which the C.I.G.S. of the First World War trounced Churchill over Gallipoli—in particular, for diverting forces from a main to a secondary theatre. It was no use. The party left on the 16th, taking with them a draconic memorandum from their Commander-in-Chief entitled 'Instructions for London Conference, July 1942'. The seventh paragraph contained the sting:—'If SLEDGEHAMMER is finally and definitely out of the picture I want you to consider the world situation as it exists at that time, and determine upon another place for U.S. troops to fight in 1942'.

After three days of intensive discussion with the Chiefs of Staff Marshall found the British unwilling to budge. The issue was laid before a formal meeting of the War Cabinet on 22 July, and it was obvious that since a deadlock had been reached Roosevelt must be consulted. Privately informing Churchill that 'a Western front in 1942 was off', and that he was influencing his Chiefs in the direction of an invasion of North Africa, the President instructed his London delegation to settle for one of five possibilities:—an Anglo–American landing in North Africa, an American operation against French Morocco, Norway, or the reinforcement either of the Eighth Army or of Persia. Marshall naturally settled for GYMNAST, with qualifications: in the tactfully phrased agreement of the Combined Chiefs of Staff, called CCS 94, the operation, now named TORCH, was accepted on the basis that no final decision should be taken until mid-September. Roosevelt, however, stimulated by Churchill through Hopkins' agency, imperiously ignored the qualification: on 25 July he signalled that he was delighted by the 'decision' and that the target date for TORCH should be 30 October. 'By ignoring the carefully framed conditions in

* Pogue, *op. cit.*, p. 341.

CCS 94 and in suggesting a date for launching TORCH, the President actually made the decision. In so doing, he effectively jettisoned ROUND-UP for 1943, though he probably did not fully realise it at the time.'* Eisenhower certainly did. He thought that Wednesday, 22 July 1942, might well be recognised as 'the blackest day in history'. But history, and Eisenhower, were to prove otherwise.

The Allies had at last been brought to the point of action and Churchill was the man mainly responsible. In retrospect it seems that these months of protracted argument and final resolution represent the peak of his performance, since the undertaking of TORCH brought to an end the period of his independence. When Eisenhower, at the beginning of August, was appointed Supreme Commander for TORCH his direct responsibility was to the Combined Chiefs of Staff, and as an American general in charge of a force that was substantially American his lines ran straight to Marshall and Roosevelt. Over TORCH, Sicily, Italy, OVERLORD, Churchill could no longer talk, in an absolute sense, of 'my' generals. Still, the concept and the conclusion were his achievement, and there was something anomalous in the fact that on 1 July, in the midst of these crucial discussions and immediately after his great successes in Washington, he should have had to face a motion in the House of Commons which stated 'That this House, while paying tribute to the heroism and endurance of the Armed Forces of the Crown in circumstances of exceptional difficulty, has no confidence in the central direction of the war'. The motion, of course, collapsed under its own weight. Churchill's majority was 475 to 25, 'les vingt-cinq canailles', as he used to call them, 'qui ont voté contre moi'.

But in the robust defence of his administration which he offered to the House there was one matter, of vital importance for Britain both during and after the war, about which he was necessarily silent. During his meetings with Roosevelt in Washington he had made a compact about TUBE ALLOYS.

* Leo J. Meyer, 'The Decision to Invade North Africa', in *Command Decisions*, p. 143.

6

Germany Contained 1942-1943

'I cannot help feeling that the past week represented a turning point in the whole war and that now we are on our way shoulder to shoulder.'

Roosevelt to Churchill, 24 July 1942

'The days of plugging holes are over.'
Preamble to the Report by the Chiefs of Staff Committee on *American-British Strategy in 1943*, 31 December 1942

'The time was ripe for the emergence of the master plan, the blueprint for how to set about winning the war.'
Marshal of the R.A.F. Sir John Slessor, of the Casablanca Conference, January 1943

The three foolscap pages of the Frisch–Peierls paper, produced at Birmingham University in the spring of 1940, 'stands as the first memorandum in any country which foretold with scientific conviction the practical possibility of a bomb and the horrors it would bring'.* From then until the final explosion at Hiroshima the threat of an atomic weapon was a permanent background to the war, a menace whose dimensions increased as the years passed by. And for most of those years the Allies were haunted by the reasonable probability that German work in this field, known to be taking place, might well produce the first operational results. In fact, when the Allies entered Germany they apprehended the leading group of experts who had been striving to achieve a result, including the famous physicist Werner Heisenberg, and transferred them to Farm Hall, a country mansion near Huntingdon, where they were informed, in due course, about the success at Hiroshima. At first they flatly refused to believe what they were told, since they were unable to accept, on the basis of their own research, that the Allies could conceivably have designed a bomb that worked. Nothing like this, however, could be predicted before 1945. The responsibility for TUBE ALLOYS, the cover name for the project by which the British provided 'a specious air of probability', was nerve-wracking. As Pontecorvo rightly observed about atomic energy,

* Kenneth Jay, introductory chapter in Margaret Gowing, *Britain and Atomic Energy, 1939–1945*.

'toute l'affaire ne cessera jamais d'être à la fois passionante et déplaisante'.

For Churchill, especially during the latter half of the war, the nervous strain was immense. As a considered act of policy he insisted that all information about atomic development should be restricted to the smallest of circles, and he himself handled many of the main negotiations privately and personally. Brooding on the implications of this new and incalculable source of energy not only for the immediate war effort, but also for post-war Britain, he was obsessed by the need for secrecy. Indeed, by a curious paradox far more scientists than statesmen were aware of what was in train. For example the *doyen* in the field, Niels Bohr, was smuggled out of Denmark to Sweden in the autumn of 1943, flown from Stockholm to Britain in the empty bomb-bay of an unarmed Mosquito, and put fully in the picture: but Attlee, Churchill's Deputy Prime Minister, knew virtually nothing about the bomb until he attended the Potsdam Conference in July 1945. (Roosevelt pursued a similar policy: as Vice-President, Truman was kept in the dark.) It is therefore essential to remember, when assessing Churchill's day-by-day performance as Prime Minister and Minister of Defence, that he continually carried in his mind a secret which, unlike his other problems, he was unable to share with even his closest confidants. And the questions which perplexed him were grave. Might the Germans move first? Might the Russians receive a leak?

Most daunting of all, might the Americans, with their vast industrial strength and their supreme self-confidence, decide to go it alone? Churchill had long ago agreed—one of his most far-sighted decisions—that British advances in atomic research should be shared with the United States: without such a sharing, perhaps America would have been left as far behind as was Germany. But now, in the summer and autumn of 1942, another intolerable possibility emerged, and it may be argued that Churchill's conversation with Roosevelt about TUBE ALLOYS in Washington that June was one of his most important and decisive contributions during the whole of his wartime administration. He made it, moreover, alone: and its consequences were wholly due to the special relationship which he had so carefully cultivated with the President. He has described how, during their discussion, he urged that 'we should at once pool all our information, work together on equal terms, and share the results if any equally between us. The question then arose as to where the research plant was to be set up ... the President said he thought the United States would have to do it. We therefore took this decision jointly and settled a basis of agreement'. Nothing was committed to writing, nor did Churchill inform his colleagues on his return to London.

14 *With the Fleet, 1942. The ships have just returned from a Russian convoy*

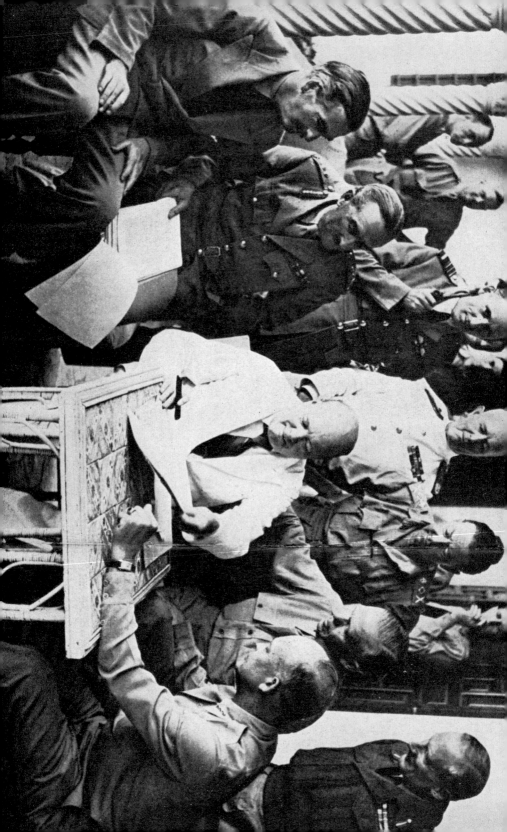

Nevertheless, the conversation was crucial. During the following months everything went wrong. The rapidly expanding American research and development projects were handed over to the military for surveillance and General Groves, the chief executive, began a rigorous policy of exclusion. British scientists and technicians no longer had parity of esteem. Furthermore in December Dr James Conant, the chairman of the U.S. National Defence Research Committee, made proposals which Roosevelt accepted but of which Sir John Anderson, in charge of the British effort, observed when communicating them to the Prime Minister, 'This development has come as a bombshell and is quite intolerable. I think you may wish to ask President Roosevelt to go into the matter without delay'. 'In future the British and the Canadians were to be given no more information about electro-magnetic separation, about the production of heavy water, about fast neutron reaction, or about the manufacture of the bomb itself.' In February, therefore, Churchill sent a personal message to Hopkins in which he pointed out that 'when the President and I talked on the matter at Hyde Park in June 1942, my real understanding was that everything was on the basis of fully sharing the results as equal partners'. But a long silence followed. Then came news of further American intransigence, and information that a deal had been made with Canada whereby the total output of Canada's heavy water plant and uranium mines—vital for Britain, if she were ostracised by her ally—was to be made available to the United States.

This unhappy state of affairs continued until July 1943, when Roosevelt suddenly decided to keep his word—under pressure from Hopkins, who advised him that 'I think you made a firm commitment to Churchill when he was here and there is nothing to do but to go through with it'. Roosevelt had good grounds for reneguing. His chief scientific aides, and the military *bloc*, were firmly opposed to anything but minimal co-operation. Nevertheless, now it had come to the moment of truth Roosevelt honoured his un-witnessed pledge to his friend and ally and issued instructions to 'renew, in an inclusive manner, the full exchange of information with the British government regarding tube alloys'. As a result, Sir John Anderson was able to draft an agreement preserving all British rights for the period of the war—post-war arrangements were to be made 'on terms to be specified by the President of the United States to the Prime Minister of Great Britain'—and it was this text which Churchill carried to the Quebec Conference and which was signed by himself and Roosevelt, unamended, on 19 August 1943. Thereafter harmony prevailed: British scientists and engineers took a full and uninhibited part in the subsequent development of the bomb,

15 *The Casablanca Conference, 1943.* l. to r., *Eden, Alanbrooke, Tedder, Cunningham, Alexander, Marshall, Eisenhower, Montgomery*

and Britain was launched into the post-war world with an *expertise* which could hardly have been acquired if America had left her in the cold. For what was the alternative? In the spring of 1942 Sir John Anderson made an estimate of the requirements if Britain were to act independently and a gaseous diffusion and heavy water plant were to be erected in the United Kingdom. The conclusion was that *within five years* it would be possible to produce one kilogram of Uranium 235 per day, at the tolerable cost of some fifty million pounds. But this implied a peak labour force of about 20,000 men, half a million tons of steel, and an extra supply of half a million kilowatts of electricity. Britain's resources of manpower and *matériel* were already stretched to the limit, and it can hardly be doubted that, if the question had ever arisen, Churchill and his Cabinet would have been compelled to abandon a speculative proposition which, in any case, could not be expected to pay dividends before the defeat of Germany. The immense significance of that brief and unconfirmed declaration of intent in June 1942 is therefore apparent; and this achievement on Churchill's part, together with the securing of the Shermans and self-propelled guns for the Eighth Army, invests with a special irony the debate in the House of Commons to which he returned, in which his conduct of the war was called into doubt and the name of the Duke of Gloucester was seriously put forward for the post of Commander-in-Chief.

It was to the desert that Churchill now gave an absolute priority. There was a saying at the time, 'all's not right with the Eighth Army': and this was true. Auchinleck's aggressive backs-to-the-wall defensive actions in July had saved the Delta and brought the *Afrika Korps* to the point of exhaustion, but within the Eighth Army itself there were fundamental defects. The men were brave enough, certainly: but, as Churchill observed, they were baffled. Ritchie and Norrie had been failures, and their inadequacy had a fatal consequence. The troops began to doubt the competence of their commanders. Moreover, during recent months petty bickering and jealousies among the more senior officers had produced not only an unhealthy atmosphere, but also inefficiency. The infantry mistrusted the armour, and the armour still looked on itself as a private army. Cohesion and common doctrines were lacking. About this time the young Julian Amery, then serving in the Middle East as a Captain in S.O.E., had to visit London. He obtained a personal interview with Churchill, to whom he had the *entrée* as Leo Amery's son, and, telling him of the *malaise* among the junior officers of his acquaintance, he pleaded with the Prime Minister to fly out to Egypt and re-invigorate his army. As he already had a visit in mind Churchill needed no persuasion: nor, for that matter, did Alanbrooke, to whom all was evident. 'It was quite clear', he subsequently wrote, 'that something was radically wrong but not easy at a distance to judge what this something was, nor how far wrong it was. . . . The crisis had come and it was essential that I should go out to see what was wrong. But for this I wanted to be alone.'

The problem of how to persuade the Prime Minister to allow his C.I.G.S. to leave his side and visit an exciting theatre of war led Alanbrooke into reflections which provide a valuable insight into the relationship between Churchill and his advisers. 'I had by then learnt', he wrote, 'that if you wanted to get Winston's agreement to something, you might have to wait several days for a propitious moment. To ask at the wrong moment was to court disaster. Once you had received a negative reply it was almost impossible to get him to alter his verdict. I had been waiting for days, very precious days, to ask him if I might go to the Middle East on my own. I knew that the odds would be heavily against getting his sanction. That he would say that he could not spare me, whilst in the back of his mind the real reason would be that he would hate me to go off on my own without him. . . . Meanwhile the situation in the Middle East was not improving . . .'. This technique of playing the waiting game was one also evolved by Pound. When one praises Churchill for the basic *rapport* between himself and the Chiefs of Staff, one must remember that much of this was due to the patient wisdom and shrewdness of the men themselves. Pound's method has been analysed by Professor Marder. 'The First Sea Lord was a master-hand at patiently weaning or diverting Churchill from his wilder, or shall we say more imaginative, projects, usually perfectly desirable tactically or strategically, but completely impracticable from entire lack of resources. . . . The *modus operandi* was never to show any obstructive response, but to indicate that the proposition would be fully investigated. This was done, by a groaning staff, which already had more on their plate than could be done efficiently. They produced an "appreciation" and a statement of "forces required" which argued against the project. This method, instead of provoking obstinacy, usually allowed the project to die quietly.'* Marder makes too much of a Machiavelli out of Pound. He was more Churchill's helot than he realised. But after the Admiral's death Churchill's distress was marked: he once declared that there were only four men whose minds were in tune with his own, Smuts, Beaverbrook, Bracken—and Pound.

Alanbrooke's day-dream was soon disrupted. On 30 July, the eve of his departure, he was informed at the Chiefs of Staff Committee that the Prime

* Arthur Marder, *Winston is back : Churchill at the Admiralty*, p. 5.

Minister had decided to accompany him. There were two considerations in Churchill's mind. First there was the *Afrika Korps* and, looming in the north, the threat of a German advance southwards from the Caucasus. A few weeks later Sir Ian Jacob would find him pacing his room in Cairo and shouting, 'Rommel, Rommel, Rommel, Rommel! What else matters but beating him?'* But secondly there was Stalin. Now that SLEDGE-HAMMER had been abandoned and TORCH agreed, with typical courage and honesty Churchill felt that he must personally inform the Marshal of this unpalatable fact. That same morning, therefore, he sent a signal to Stalin proposing that he and Alanbrooke should meet him after their task in Cairo was completed. Stalin replied immediately, suggesting a meeting in Moscow. And so, on 2 August, in spite of the remonstrances of the Cabinet and the doubts of his doctors, Churchill set off in the bomber 'Commando'. 'The bomber was at this time unheated, and razor-edged draughts cut in through many chinks. There were no beds, but two shelves in the after cabin enabled me and Sir Charles Wilson, my doctor, to lie down.' His departure had been preceded by a 1 a.m. discussion with Alanbrooke during which the Prime Minister had expounded his plan for disguising himself, when they touched down at Gibraltar, with the dubious assistance of a grey beard.

Churchill had no doubt that Auchinleck must be replaced. He was thus faced with a double problem . . . who should command in the Middle East, and who should command the Eighth Army? The first was easily solved.† From the First World War, from Dunkirk and Burma Harold Alexander had earned a reputation for cool courage—'unflappability', as the jargon had it—and these qualities, added to his patrician air of detachment, seemed to equip him ideally for the multifarious but delicate duties of the C.-in-C. Churchill adored him and Alanbrooke respected him. But when it came to a titular commander for the battle Churchill was seriously misled: had it not been for the intervention of chance his choice, though it might not have resulted in disaster, would certainly not have produced the clean-cut victory at Alamein. Alanbrooke's diary makes it clear that from the start his own candidate was Montgomery—a judgement based on his extensive knowledge of the man, his observation of Montgomery's hand-

---

* Diary of Lieut.-General Sir Ian Jacob, 8 August 1942.

† Easily by Churchill. But he was muddled before and during the Cairo Conference, thinking that if he gave Alexander the Middle East as his fief his hero would also take over the battlefield. He was blurred about the distinct functions of C.-in-C. Middle East and Commander, Eighth Army. 'Surely Alex. will not remain in Cairo doing things a Minister or a Quartermaster could do! When a battle impends he will take the field.' So Jacob heard him say, at the time: but he was misjudging the realities.

ling of 3 Division in the Battle of France, and his subsequent approval of the way Montgomery had grown in stature as a more senior commander responsible for the anti-invasion defences of South East England.

On the evening of 3 August Alanbrooke was summoned by Churchill and held in discussion till 1.30 a.m. Churchill favoured Gott, the old desert hand now commanding 13 Corps. The C.I.G.S. argued that Gott was worn out . . . an opinion now shared by all serious analysts. A fine straightforward officer, universally admired within the desert army, he had acquitted himself well, during the previous campaigns, at all levels of command up to that of a corps: but his batteries needed re-charging. Churchill therefore countered by offering Alanbrooke himself the post, which, the latter recalled, 'gave rise to the most desperate longings'. Next morning, however, the C.I.G.S. consulted Auchinleck—who at this stage had no knowledge that he was doomed—and found that he too thought Montgomery was the right choice. On the following day he and the Prime Minister went up into the desert to be given breakfast by Auchinleck at his fighting headquarters 'in a cage', Churchill acidly observed, 'full of flies and high military personages'. The tone of the meeting was not inspiring, and Churchill left in a black mood, ordering Gott, whom he had just met for the first time, to drive him to his aeroplane. During the journey Gott significantly said that he was tired, and spoke of a long leave in England. That afternoon Alanbrooke went down to 13 Corps H.Q. for further talk with Gott, and found his doubts confirmed. Gott said he had used up most of his ideas and that what was required was new blood.

Early on the 6th, while Alanbrooke was still dressing, Churchill burst in on him with the news that his thoughts were taking firm shape. He proposed to split the Middle East Command, making a Persia Iraq Command that would be offered to Auchinleck and a Near East Command which he offered to Alanbrooke, with Montgomery at Eighth Army. Alanbrooke's reasons for rejecting what, as a genuine fighting soldier who preferred battles to the conference table, he would have sacrificed almost anything to possess do him very great honour.

> I could not put the real reasons to Winston. . . . Whether I exercised any control or not, I knew by now the dangers to guard against. I had discovered the perils of his impetuous nature. I was now familiar with his method of suddenly arriving at some decision as it were by intuition without any kind of logical examination of the problem. I had, after many failures, discovered the best ways of approaching him. I knew that it would take at least six months for any successor, taking over from me, to become as familiar with him and his ways. During those six months anything might happen.

I would not suggest that I could exercise any real control over him. I never met anybody that could, but he had grown to have confidence in me, and I had found that he was listening more and more to any advice I gave him. They were reasons which I could not put before Winston. I had therefore to rely on other arguments such as my lack of knowledge of desert warfare. I should, however, have been ready to chance this shortcoming and do not believe that it would have rendered me unfit for the appointment.

During the day, however, Churchill changed front—possibly owing to the influence of Smuts, who strongly supported Gott. Alanbrooke was summoned to the British Embassy where, sitting with Smuts, Churchill showed him a telegram which was to go off to Attlee, the Deputy Prime Minister and, in Churchill's absence, the chairman of the Cabinet. This signal proposed the division of the Middle East Command and recommended Alexander for the Middle East, Gott for Eighth Army, and Montgomery for TORCH. The C.I.G.S. agreed to the formula, though he retained misgivings about Gott. 'I may have been weak; in any case Fate took the matter in its hands within twenty-four hours of our decision.' On the 7th Gott was flying back to the army by a route so safe that no escort had been provided for Churchill when he had used it. A chance German fighter, driven from on high, came across the lumbering transport in which he was travelling, and Gott was killed.

The news reached Churchill and Alanbrooke that evening. After prolonged discussion with Smuts, and consultation with Auchinleck, a cable was despatched.

Prime Minister to Deputy Prime Minister   *7.8.43*

C.I.G.S. decisively recommends Montgomery for Eighth Army. Smuts and I feel this post must be filled at once. Pray send him by special plane at earliest moment. Advise me when he will arrive.

And thus it was that Montgomery, who on 5 August was at South Eastern Command in England, and on the 6th was appointed to lead the British First Army to N.W. Africa in TORCH, found himself, on the 10th, flying out to Cairo and immortality. It only remained to dispose of Auchinleck, which was summarily effected by means of a letter from Churchill conveyed by Sir Ian Jacob. 'I felt as if I were just going to murder an unsuspecting friend,' Jacob wrote in his diary. 'After offering the condolences of the Prime Minister and C.I.G.S. on the death of General Gott, I handed the C.-in-C. the letter I had brought. He opened it and read it through two or three times in silence. He did not move a muscle and remained outwardly calm and in complete control of himself. . . .' This sequence of events demonstrates strikingly how the notion that Montgomery was 'Churchill's man' is a misapprehension. He was not the Prime Minister's first choice for command: nor, indeed, was it until the *end* of Alamein that Churchill fully surrendered his confidence. Only victory made Montgomery *persona grata*.

But *persona grata* was not how Churchill appeared to Stalin when he presented himself at the Kremlin on 12 August. 'I have a somewhat raw job', he had written to Roosevelt before he left London. In his memoirs he makes the point more emphatically:—'it was like carrying a large lump of ice to the North Pole'. Marlborough's heir and the former Joseph Vissarionovich Djugashvili from the Theological Seminary of Tiflis, both veterans in the poker game of politics, played their hands with different but carefully calculated techniques. Stalin's method, used so frequently by the Russians that it lost the value of surprise as it hardened into a ritual, was to handle the first session with a surly amity designed to elicit the main points over which battle must be engaged. In mid-conference there came a change of front, into a stony-faced and contemptuous rejection of one who was now being treated more like an adversary than an ally. At the final stage the mood unexpectedly switched to drinks and a midnight dinner, tête-à-tête in Stalin's private apartments, of which the 1.30 a.m. culmination was 'a considerable sucking-pig'. The purpose was to extract as many concessions as possible by a last-minute display of sweet reasonableness. Churchill, by contrast, decided to get the worst over first, making it plain that there could be no cross-Channel assault in 1942—not, as he argued, that one had ever been definitely promised. Stalin, not unnaturally, became glum and restless. Then, by degrees, the Prime Minister led his listener towards the news of TORCH, whose potentialities he illustrated with the famous drawing of a crocodile and the declaration that 'it was our intention to attack the soft belly of the crocodile as we attacked his hard snout'.

During the Moscow conference Churchill made notable gains. He looked Stalin in the eyes without flinching—an investment which would bear fruit in the future. Though the Marshal accepted the disappointing '*non possumus* in 1942' with bad grace, he accepted it, and the invasion of Vichy North Africa made a good impression. Moreover, Churchill was able to return with the conviction that whatever the Russian dissatisfaction with Anglo–American planning there was no visible sign, not even a threat, of an intention to make a separate peace. He also felt certain—and rightly, as it proved, though Alanbrooke was less confident—that the Russians would never permit the Germans to break through the barrier of the

Caucasus. On the other hand Stalin won the poker game, for Churchill committed the error of issuing a post-dated cheque which was bound to bounce. Though Alanbrooke was non-committal in his talks with the Russian military staff, Churchill himself halted only just short of a formal promise in his references to Anglo–American intentions in 1943. Defending the abandonment of an invasion in 1942 he declared that 'it was important . . . not to expose the people of France by a withdrawal to the vengeance of Hitler and to waste them when they would be needed in the big operation of 1943'. As to this operation, he spoke of a plan to 'hold the enemy at this point or that and at the same time attack elsewhere, for instance in the Loire, the Gironde or the Scheldt'. Though he later admitted that he had been too optimistic (while claiming that he did not 'deceive or mislead Stalin'), he had gone too far. For this he had no warrant. The Chiefs of Staff would certainly not have endorsed his enthusiasm, while the Americans, as will be seen, were at this stage of the war turning their attention steadily towards the Pacific. 'Nevertheless at this first meeting in Moscow Mr Churchill, while yielding nothing to Stalin's taunts and bullying,' (surely an overstatement), 'did succeed in creating with the man some form of human connexion, rooted in mutual respect for the other's courage and firmness. At least a sufficient understanding was built up to provide some degree of concert . . .'.*

There were, however, three other important respects in which ideas for aiding Russia, though raised at the conference, led either to nothing or to no immediate results. During the nocturnal dinner-party in the Kremlin Churchill's favourite theme was ventilated—JUPITER, a British landing in Norway with Russian support. The notes on this conversation suggest that Churchill promised an intervention in Northern Norway, during November 1942, by two British divisions, to be assisted by three from Russia. (The interpreter, Major Birse, has however stated that the record of this conversation should only be accepted as *rough* notes.) And indeed Churchill subsequently pushed the idea further, encouraged by Stalin's apparent agreement. In mid-September he obtained a report on a possible plan from General McNaughton, who was in charge of Canadian troops in Great Britain. With this in hand, and lukewarm though it was, he informed the Chiefs of Staff that 'it may well be that JUPITER, with all its costs and risks, will be found not only necessary but cheapest in the long run'. Then he tackled Stalin again, signalling to him on 8 October that 'it would of course greatly help you and us if the Germans could be denied the use of the airfields in Northern Norway. If your staffs could make a good plan

* J. R. M. Butler, *op. cit.*, p. 666.

the President and I would at once examine the possibility of co-operating up to the limit of our ability'. Unfortunately Stalin's interest, if it was ever genuine, had now waned, and no positive response was forthcoming. November brought TORCH, and for the time being Churchill allowed the scheme to be forgotten. Quite apart from the logistical difficulties of an operation of this nature, it seems highly likely that Churchill's hopes for a joint enterprise were doomed from the start: the last thing Stalin wanted was for the British to obtain a foothold in this sensitive area so close to Russia's frontier. Here was a nuance which did not escape the Germans, and may well have been one of the factors which contributed to the failure of the deception efforts, in 1944, to persuade Hitler that Norway would be part of OVERLORD.

The second idea took longer to reach its inevitable conclusion. Throughout 1942 various attempts had been made to bring support to the Russians along their southern front by sending troops into Persia or transferring aircraft from the Middle East to assist in the defence of that perennial preoccupation, the Caucasus. Russian reluctance, and concern for the fortunes of the Eighth Army, made all of them abortive. However, while he was in Moscow Churchill seized the opportunity to re-open the plan for establishing an Anglo–American air force in Transcaucasia—subject to the defeat of Rommel. But many predictable difficulties supervened—the Americans lacked enthusiasm, the commanders in Cairo were unhappy about losing a certain strength for the sake of an uncertain advantage, and when an Anglo–American air mission was sent to Moscow in November to examine the project the Russian Chief Air Staff officer pretended to know nothing about it. By the end of the year the scheme was moribund. Conditions had suddenly changed. Alamein, TORCH and Stalingrad gave the war a new aspect and now, in addition to his normal xenophobia, Stalin was unwilling to risk sharing with others the glory, beginning to seem within his grasp, of expelling the Teuton invader from the soil of Mother Russia.

There was a third question, raised by Stalin, to which Churchill replied in his best vein.

Presently we talked about the convoys to Russia. This led him to make a rough and rude remark about the almost total destruction of the Arctic convoy in June. I did not know as much about it then as I do now. 'Mr. Stalin asks', said Pavlov, with some hesitation, 'has the British Navy no sense of glory?' I answered, 'You must take it from me that what was done was right. I really do know a lot about the Navy and sea-war.' 'Meaning,' said Stalin, 'that I know nothing.' 'Russia is a land animal,' I said; 'the British are sea animals.' He fell silent and recovered his good humour.

But there was nothing humorous about the actual situation. It was not until 2 September that convoy P.Q.18 was despatched, after the pause which followed the disaster to its predecessor. From this convoy 13 merchant vessels were lost out of a total of 40. And now TORCH was imminent. Churchill and the Chiefs of Staff were therefore compelled, in spite of pressure from Roosevelt, to defer any further convoys until January 1943. Ships were sailed independently, during the last quarter of the year: but out of 13 only five reached harbour. And these, it should be remembered, were the months of Stalingrad. Nevertheless, in the incalculable way of warfare, a vast change for the better occurred at the end of the year. Taking advantage of the short winter hours of daylight the Admiralty hazarded a further convoy operation in the latter half of December. The Germans made a considerable but ineffective effort to intercept with the heavy ships which, because of Hitler's fears for Norway, had been gathered in the north. One pocket-battleship, one heavy cruiser and six destroyers were kept away from the convoy for four hours by five destroyers of the Royal Navy, and finally dispersed by two six-inch cruisers: the convoy itself was barely damaged. This alone was a major triumph, but of far greater importance was Hitler's rage at the ignominy of the battle in the Barents Sea, his decision to pay off his heavy ships of war, and the consequent resignation of Admiral Raeder, leaving the field free for Dönitz to pursue a policy of U-boat attack which, within a few months, would be fully and finally frustrated.

These events were a relief to the Prime Minister and the President—and to Stalin. But in the long term the arrangement made between Averell Harriman and Churchill during his Cairo visit was of greater significance. On 22 August Churchill sent a message to Roosevelt accepting the President's proposal that the American Army should take over the Persian railways and extending it with the suggestion that they should also operate the ports. These ideas were rapidly implemented, and though various technical problems prevented an immediate rapid increase in overland supplies to Russia the graph rose dramatically throughout 1943. In January the figure was 51,285 long (U.S.) tons; in July 178,742; in December 248,018. Even more dramatic was the increase in the scale of shipments from the United States to the Far East of Russia. These quadrupled within a year, from 78,616 tons in August 1942 to 313,479 in September 1943. (One reason was a change in the emphasis of Russian requirements, after Stalingrad, from military to civilian supplies, which could be more easily ferried overland from Vladivostock to European Russia.) Nothing like these amounts reached port in the Arctic convoys, and arithmetic suggests, in retrospect, that Churchill—and Roosevelt—were guilty of grave misjudgement in forcing through the convoys of 1942. The losses of ships and men seem vain. But 'ripeness is all'. If the issue is to be assessed objectively, Stalingrad and its consequences must be dismissed from the mind, and the desperate state of the Soviet Union in the early months of 1942 recalled. Psychologically, and practically, the convoys were at that time inescapable.

Any disappointments, however, were balanced by two great counterweights. First, the battle of Alamein began on 23 October, and within 12 days Montgomery had driven Rommel into retreat.

General Alexander to Prime Minister   *6.11.42*

Ring out the bells! Prisoners estimated now 20,000, tanks 350, guns 400, M.T. several thousand. Our advanced mobile forces are south of Mersa Matruh. Eighth Army is advancing.

But history, as usual, jogged Churchill's memory. He recalled how the successes in the first substantial armoured action, at Cambrai in 1917, had set England alight with expectation: and how, within a short space, German divisions recovered all the ground that had been gained. He therefore thought it prudent to withhold public rejoicing until the second counterweight had been thrown into the scale. This was TORCH. On 8 November the landings were announced.

The day after Alanbrooke heard that Montgomery had checked Rommel in his final attempt to break through, at Alam Halfa in the first days of September, he noted in his diary that 'my next trouble will now be to stop Winston from fussing Alex and Monty and egging them on to attack before they are ready'. But in his relations with Churchill Montgomery proved to be less malleable and more self-confident than either Wavell or Auchinleck. He has described in his *Memoirs* how he ensured a victory by first defeating his Prime Minister.

I had promised the Eighth Army on arrival that I would not launch our offensive till we were ready. I could not be ready until October. Full moon was the 24th October. I said I would attack on the night of 23rd October, and notified Alexander accordingly. The come-back from Whitehall was immediate. Alexander received a signal from the Prime Minister to the effect that the attack must be in September, so as to synchronise with certain Russian offensives and with Allied landings which were to take place early in November at the western end of the north African coast (Operation TORCH). Alexander came to see me to discuss the reply to be sent. I said that our preparations could not be completed in time for a September offensive, and an attack then would fail: if we waited until October, I guaranteed complete success. In my view it would be madness to attack in September. Was I to do so? Alexander backed me up as he always did, and the reply was sent on the lines I wanted. I had told Alexander privately that, in view of my promise to the soldiers, I refused to attack before October; if a September attack was ordered by Whitehall, they would have to get someone else to do it. My stock was rather high after Alam Halfa! We heard no more about a September attack.

Churchill was, in fact, in a state of high tension—so overwrought that when he received a signal from Alexander firmly advocating the postponement which Montgomery proposed he interrupted the only brief holiday Alanbrooke had taken that year to summon him to the telephone. '"You have not seen it! Do you mean to say you are out of touch with the strategic situation?" I replied, "I told you I was going grouse shooting today, and I have not yet solved how I am to remain in touch with the strategic situation whilst in a grouse-butt." ' Churchill was not mollified. A wretched Contact Officer had to ride through the night on a motor-cycle from Whitehall to Darlington with a copy of the signal for the C.I.G.S.

The reasons for this agitation were manifold. Apart from his Russian preoccupation Churchill had domestic problems. He had emerged triumphant from the Vote of Confidence debate in the summer, but he was aware of a constant rumble of dissatisfaction at a time when, for too many months, he had been able to offer the nation little but the news of defeat. And the Lord Privy Seal, Sir Stafford Cripps, was now so concerned about the organisation for the higher direction of the war that he was threatening to resign. The staunch support of the President of the United States was endangered by the impending Congressional election. Then there was Malta. Alanbrooke estimated that the island's resources could only hold out until mid-October and that its very survival depended on Montgomery's coming offensive, and TORCH. 'If neither succeed God knows how we shall keep Malta alive.' On 14 September Hitler ordered a fresh attempt by the *Luftwaffe* to eliminate the island and this, beginning on 11 October, was sustained for ten days on a scale of 200/300 planes per day. The solution was obvious. Eighth Army must advance as fast as possible to a point so far westwards along the African shore that the R.A.F. would again be able to work from airfields which would enable it to regain control over Malta. It is not surprising that under so great a strain Churchill's imagination became over-heated. Irked by his generals' delay, he began to think that it was allowing Rommel to fortify 'a belt twenty miles deep by forty miles broad'. He was only released from his fantasies when he received from Alexander the pre-arranged codeword.

C.-in-C. to Prime Minister   *23.10.42*
   Zip!
Former Naval Person to President Roosevelt   *23.10.42*

The battle in Egypt began tonight at 8 p.m. London time. The whole force of the Army will be engaged. I will keep you informed. A victory there will be most useful to our main enterprise. All the Shermans and self-propelled guns which you gave me on that dark Tobruk morning will play their part.

By 28 October, however, it seemed to the remote observers in London that the battle was at a standstill. Montgomery had always affirmed that its initial stage would involve what he called a dog-fight. Now, to recover the initiative and make a breakthrough, he started to extricate some of his forces in order to build up a reserve for a new assault. The fact that divisions were coming out of the line soon reached Cairo and London, and caused great alarm. Alanbrooke vividly described Churchill's reactions on the morning of the 29th. 'What, he asked, was *my* Monty doing now, allowing the battle to peter out. (Monty was always my Monty when he was out of favour.) He had done nothing now for the last three days, and now he was withdrawing troops from the front. Why had he told us he would be through in seven days if all he intended to do was to fight a half-hearted battle?' A Chiefs of Staff meeting was summoned for 1230, at which Alanbrooke had to defend Montgomery against the strictures of Churchill and the Cabinet. His defence had little effect until Smuts, who was fortunately present, gave the C.I.G.S. his unqualified support. Nevertheless, in his heart even Alanbrooke had doubts. 'On returning to my office I paced up and down, suffering from a desperate feeling of loneliness.'

This misapprehension was in part the fault of Montgomery, to whom all things were self-evident. One of his weaknesses as a commander (which undoubtedly led to misunderstanding between himself, Eisenhower and Churchill during the Normandy campaign), was his refusal to make explicit to his seniors the real intention in his mind. It caused Churchill to draft a sarcastic communication to Alexander which he did not reproduce in *The Second World War* and which was not, in fact, dispatched until it had been tactfully touched up by Ismay. It was inaccurate, ill-timed, and improper, but it is worth quoting as evidence of Churchill's state of mind.

> We are glad the battle started well and are sure that you intend to press it remorselessly to a finish. We have nothing to fear from a *bataille d'usure*. . . . The enemy is hard run for petrol and ammunition, and our air superiority weighs heavily upon him. . . . We do not of course know what you have in

mind and therefore were somewhat concerned to see that on the 27th the attack on Kidney Ridge by two battalions was the only substantial thrust. And now by your latest Sitrep most units appear to be coming back into reserve. . . . We should be grateful if you could tell us if you have any large-scale attacks impending because we feel that the intensity and scale of the battle will be hard for the enemy to bear.

Of course it must be understood that his intelligence service kept Churchill informed about Rommel's grave shortage of men and supplies. In particular, the information available to him about the meticulously conducted campaign against the Italian convoys made it clear to him that the *Panzerarmee* must soon run out of fuel. The man was obviously on his last legs. Why could he not be given the *coup de grâce*? But all became plain, and all was pardoned, when he received the signal of victory. 'Overnight Generals Alexander and Montgomery became popular military heroes of a kind hardly known in Britain since the days of Kitchener and Roberts; and the Eighth Army itself and the airmen who fought with it acquired a nimbus of glory which was not to be without its effect on the subsequent shaping of Allied strategy.'*

The Allies also had solid grounds for self-congratulation over the immediate results of the invasion of North West Africa, for the risks had been enormous. The vast convoys converging from the British Isles and across the Atlantic might so easily have been intercepted, and, until all was over, there was justifiable uncertainty about the way the invaders would be welcomed. But the Germans were deceived—though not the Italians, as Ciano noted in his diary on 7 November, the eve of the landings. 'What will the various convoys do that have left Gibraltar and are eastward bound? According to the Germans the provisioning of Malta or an attempt at landing in Tripolitania in order to fall upon Rommel's rear. According to our General Staff the occupation of French bases in North Africa. The Duce, too, is of this opinion; in fact, he believes that the landing will be accomplished by the Americans who will meet with almost no resistance from the French.' By the 11th Hitler had moved into occupied France: in consequence 73 French warships were scuttled in Toulon harbour, and on the 23rd the Governor of French West Africa came over to the Allies, bringing with him the valuable gifts of Dakar, the battleship *Richelieu*, and three cruisers. Even the infinitely complicated political skein was to some degree disentangled, first by Eisenhower's bold acceptance of Admiral Darlan as *de facto* head of French Africa, with the rival Giraud as his Commander-in-Chief, and secondly by Darlan's assassination. It is true

* Michael Howard, *Grand Strategy*: Vol. IV, p. 69.

that recognition of Darlan gave rise to bitter protests in Britain and the United States, but it was vigorously defended by Churchill in the House of Commons and even gave satisfaction to Stalin, who wrote to Roosevelt, in December:—'In view of all sorts of rumours about the attitude of the U.S.S.R. towards the use made of Darlan . . . it may not be unnecessary for me to tell you that in my opinion, as well as that of my colleagues, Eisenhower's policy . . . is perfectly correct. I think it a great achievement that you succeeded in bringing Darlan and others into the main stream of the Allies fighting Hitler.'

But all this optimism was premature. By Christmas the situation was a stalemate. Final plans for TORCH had not been agreed without controversy, in which Churchill himself was compelled to join, and one of the chief bones of contention had been the Americans' refusal to commit large forces east of Gibraltar. The British (and Eisenhower), saw the need: but Marshall was blind. The result was that not enough mobile troops were available to advance eastwards, over the hills and rough going, in the lightning thrust which was necessary to forestall the ruthless German reinforcement. As the winter rains destroyed communications and turned their airfields into mud the Allies were able to establish no more than a thin circlet round the *enceinte* of Tunis, into which the Germans were pouring men and armour daily by sea and air. Eisenhower's only course was to postpone further offensive operations until the spring, though he was characteristically modest in declaring that his campaign had 'violated every recognised principle of war . . . and will be condemned . . . for the next twenty-five years'. This was certainly not the impression of Rommel, who was already convinced that the war in Africa was lost—indeed, the war itself was lost, and in the aftermath the main danger would be Russia. It was about this time that he remarked to one of his confidants, Major von Luck, that 'Winston Churchill is the only man who can save Europe'.

Still, it is not surprising that during the early weeks of TORCH Churchill's mood was one of euphoria. It was his own achievement. He had predicted the campaign in the strategic survey which he had composed on the *Duke of York* during his winter voyage to Washington: he had formulated it as a practical operation of war, fought for it against reluctant Chiefs of Staff and adamant Americans, and now he was observing what at first appeared to be its successful execution, while Montgomery was advancing steadily westward from Alamein. His mind galloped into the future. A fortnight after the landings, on 25 November, he circulated a 'Note By The Minister Of Defence' of which the third paragraph read: 'There are therefore two phases—consolidation and exploitation. Dealing with consolidation first, we may hope that General Alexander will become master of the whole of Cyrenaica during the present month, and that he will be pressing the enemy in the Agheila position, or even at Sirte. We may also assume that in the same period or not long after the American and British forces will become masters of the whole of French North Africa, including Tunis, provided they press forward with their present energy and violence.' He went on to advocate a combined air offensive against Italy by Bomber Command, from England, and the U.S.A.A.F. working from bases in Tunisia. This was to be followed by the occupation of either Sardinia or Sicily: 'from either of them continuous intensified short-range attacks on Naples, Rome, and the Italian fleet bases would raise the war against Italy to an intense degree'. The surgery on the underbelly of the crocodile which he had described to Stalin in Moscow could now, he thought, be started.

These assumptions were patently too large. Their significance is that they were made at a moment when a long and vigorous debate between himself and his Chiefs of Staff, about the strategy to be pursued in the following years, was reaching a point of resolution. Its roots lay far back, in June and July—in that other debate with Roosevelt, Marshall and their staffs which had inveigled them into the very operation, TORCH, whose progress now filled Churchill with such high hopes. The issues have been dramatically defined in the *Official History*.*

> Relief at having reached a decision at all after such arduous debate, exhilaration at the prospect of action, increasing concern with the formidable complexities of the projected operation, these emotions, for several weeks, filled the minds of the British commanders and statesmen responsible for taking and implementing the decision; not least that of Mr. Churchill himself. Only gradually did it become clear that agreement to mount the operation had been secured with the Americans only by ignoring more profound disagreements, or by making commitments which it would be difficult or impossible, when the moment came, to fulfil. Like figures in some Faust legend, the Chiefs of Staff Committee had, to gain an immediate advantage, signed a contract which deferred, but did not abolish, the disagreeable need for payment.
>
> The contract in question was C.C.S. 94, with its explicit statement:
>
> 'That it be understood that a commitment to this operation renders ROUNDUP in all probability impracticable of successful execution in 1943 and therefore that we have definitely accepted a defensive, encircling line of action for the Continental European theatre, except as to Air operations and blockade. . . . '

* Michael Howard, *op. cit.*, p. 191.

16 'You can always take one with you'. Eisenhower, Churchill and Bradley try their skill – 39 hits from 45 shots at a target 200 yards away

BEFORE D DAY 1944

17 Ready for the assault (Unit identifications were blanked out for security)

18 *By destroyer to Normandy*

'A JOLLY DAY ON THE BEACHES'

19 *With Alanbrooke and Smuts at Montgomery's headquarters in the beachhead*

a statement which acquired all the more force when taken in conjunction with the provision, also made in C.C.S. 94, for the transfer of fifteen groups of U.S. aircraft from BOLERO 'for the purpose of furthering offensive operations in the Pacific'.

The profound effect of these conclusions on the thinking of the Americans became frighteningly clear in the following weeks. On 11 August the British Joint Staff Mission in Washington sent a warning message to London in which they declared that the Americans felt let down in their struggle to maintain the policy of winning the war in Europe first. Little real faith in TORCH was apparent, and none at all in the possibility of subsequently attacking Germany across the Mediterranean. When Dill, the faithful guardian of British interests in Washington, sought to mollify Marshall he was told without compromise that the requirements for TORCH definitely precluded offensive operations against Germany. Here was a new, a fundamental and, for the British, an immensely dangerous divergence of opinion, which protracted exchanges between the two Staffs failed to resolve. For Churchill the situation was further complicated by the fact that his own Chiefs of Staff, with Alanbrooke actively in the lead, were explicitly proposing an extension of effort in the Mediterranean in 1943 to the complete exclusion of a major assault in Northern France. 'It would seem', as he wrote of a later *impasse*, 'that the sum of all American fears is to be multiplied by the sum of all British fears, faithfully contributed by each service'.

The dangers were compounded by a change in American practice as well as in policy. Notions that the United States held undeviatingly to the principle of *Germany first* are a myth. A year after Pearl Harbour the Army in the Pacific was roughly equivalent to that in the United Kingdom and North Africa . . . some 346,000 as against some 347,000 . . . and the figure for the Pacific was greater by some 150,000 than the number originally planned for the end of 1942 when BOLERO, the transference of American troops across the Atlantic, was initiated. Indeed, the official American historians have themselves pointed out that the total Army forces deployed in the war against Japan exceeded by some 50,000 the total deployed against Germany.* Moreover in Marshall's proposals made in the spring of 1942 for a ROUNDUP across the Channel in 1943 3250 aircraft were contemplated: but by the end of 1942 hardly half of these were available—because of the Pacific.

* Maurice Matloff and Edwin M. Snell, *Strategic Planning for Coalition Warfare, 1941–1942*, pp. 359-61.

In effect, as the Army planners emphasised, strength and resources originally earmarked for the main effort, BOLERO-ROUNDUP, had served in 1942 as a pool from which aircraft, as well as air units, had been diverted to secondary efforts. . . . The trend . . . was towards the continued diversion of planes to the Pacific, the secondary theatre, rather than towards a concentration of air forces against Germany, the main enemy.

Alert to every menace, Churchill appreciated far more sensitively than his Chiefs of Staff the width of the opening gulf. It was evident to him, but not to them, that though a Mediterranean strategy in 1943 was certainly something to be undertaken, it would not in itself be enough. If the Americans were to be persuaded to co-operate the British must demonstrate that they were prepared to fight à outrance: in effect, they must urge a ROUNDUP in 1943, as well as a movement through Sicily or Sardinia towards Italy, as the natural and intended consequence of TORCH. Only a strategy as positive as this would convince Marshall, and only in this way could the Americans be pulled back from the Pacific to the long-established principle of Germany first. Furthermore it was only by such a strategy, as he was well aware, that he could fulfill the unfortunate promise he had made to Stalin in Moscow.

> . . . for the rest of 1942 Mr. Churchill urged and worried the Chiefs of Staff Committee to admit the possibility of carrying out ROUNDUP in 1943 with a pertinacity which gives the lie to the belief, so widespread in certain quarters after the war, that he consistently favoured a predominantly Mediterranean strategy. Paper after paper was put up by the Chiefs of Staff arguing the impossibility of ROUNDUP in 1943, which the Prime Minister analysed line by line, challenged in minutest detail and reluctantly accepted; only to question their conclusions a few days later when some fresh victory spurred his unquenchable optimism, or a cold reminder from Stalin stung him into examining once more the alleged impossibility of fulfilling the assurance he had so rashly given.*

From the many possible examples one instance illustrates the acumen and tenacity with which Churchill developed his case. On 18 November he composed a paper in which he dexterously pointed out that under the agreement reached with Marshall about ROUNDUP and BOLERO 27 American and 21 British divisions were to be available for the Continent by April 1943, as well as the necessary landing-craft. TORCH was only employing 13 divisions. No ROUNDUP in 1943 implied a reduction in the Allies' striking intention against the enemy of 35 divisions.

It is no use blinking at this or imagining that the discrepancy will not be

* Michael Howard, op. cit., p. 208.

perceived. I have no doubt myself that we and General Marshall overestimated our capacity as measured by shipping and also by the rate at which United States forces as well as special landing-craft etc. could be ready. But there is a frightful gap between what the Chiefs of Staff contemplated in the summer of 1942 for the campaign of 1943 and what they now say we can do in that campaign. . . . We have in fact pulled in our horns to a most extraordinary extent, and I cannot imagine what the Russians will say or do when they realise it. My own position is that I am still aiming at a ROUNDUP retarded till August. I cannot give this up without a massive presentation of facts and figures which prove the physical impossibility.

In a strictly technical sense Alanbrooke and his colleagues were correct in reiterating that the resources of the British allowed for no more in 1943 than intensification of the Strategic Bomber Offensive and an expanded effort in the Mediterranean. This was the truth in November 1942: it became still more obvious as the North African campaign dragged on into the late spring of 1943. Their duty was to be hard-headed. Yet if it had been the unqualified views of the Chiefs of Staff alone that was communicated to the Americans in the 'transatlantic essay competition' which continued throughout the latter months of 1942, who can say whether Admiral King and MacArthur might not have won an even more impressive victory over the protagonists of a European strategy . . . whether even more American shipping, and men, and aircraft and armour might not have been directed to the Pacific? As it was, by the end of the year Marshall had veered right back to the concept of an invasion of France. And by that time all were agreed that these huge questions could only be properly answered at a summit meeting between Roosevelt, Churchill, and the Combined Chiefs of Staff. This was shortly to occur, at Casablanca. If, again, the unqualified ideas of the British Chiefs of Staff had been all that Churchill could lay on the table at Casablanca it may be doubted whether the result of that conference would have been as satisfactory as it proved to be. For though in the final preparations of the British case for the conference Churchill came very far to meet the professional advice of the Chiefs, his militancy and his powerful advocacy of a Second Front injected into the British paper a note of determination which the Chiefs of Staff themselves were inhibited from uttering. 'For the first time the British were able to present their allies with a reasoned and realistic programme for the defeat of Germany. Its realism was due solely to the Chiefs of Staff; but the positive, offensive spirit which inspired it was largely the work of the unwearying and merciless interventions of the Prime Minister himself.'*

* Michael Howard, *op. cit.*, p. 216.

As it happened, by the end of 1942 a summit conference also seemed urgently desirable to bring Anglo–American strategy in the Far East into harmony. Once the flood of Japanese expansion reached its limits the British found themselves at a dead end. During the rest of the year neither in action nor in policy was any important progress achieved. So far as the British were concerned the limits of expansion were easily definable: the Japanese held Burma, but for the time being the land frontiers of India were reasonably safe. As to the sea, the Japanese had certainly penetrated, in April, far into the Indian Ocean, attacking from the air the naval bases at Trincomalee and Colombo, and even raiding the mainland coast of India. But American victories in the Coral Sea and in the decisive action at Midway in June immediately destroyed any further threat from Japanese sea-power. With their rear and their seaward communications secure the British forces in India could now concentrate on counter-attack. The problem was how, where, when, and with whose support?

One stumbling-block was China. At this stage of the war all British thinking up to the level of Churchill himself was clouded by a failure to appreciate two fundamental factors—the utter commitment of the American administration to the support of Chiang Kai-shek, and the utter unreliability of Chiang himself, who, as later events were to prove, was more interested in stock-piling such supplies as he could extort from his co-belligerents, for use in future power-struggles with the Communists, than in conducting joint operations against the common enemy Japan. Inevitably, therefore, the main interest of Chiang and the Americans lay in the re-opening of the Burma Road, the only overland route along which a large flow of aid could be pumped into China. In March General Stillwell had taken post in Chungking as head of the Military Mission and of all U.S. Army forces in China, Burma, and India. His immediate report to his superiors in Washington was conclusive: 'unless positive action is taken to reopen Burma, the offer of U.S. help to China is meaningless'. But in all this there was nothing, so far, which conflicted with British aims. In April Churchill had ordered the Chiefs of Staff 'to frame plans for a counter-offensive on the Eastern Front in the summer and autumn', and Wavell, now restored from his abortive ABDA Command to that of Commander-in-Chief, India, had similarly instructed his staff to prepare for the recovery of Burma. Chiang Kai-shek, after much bargaining with Stilwell, was also persuaded to concentrate on the same objective, but this, he indicated on 1 August, would mean that the 'British should occupy the Andamans, give support to a landing at Rangoon and control the Bay of

Bengal. It is therefore deemed necessary that the attitude of Great Britain in this case should first be ascertained and that she be urged to act'.

Of all people, Churchill least required an urge to action. Nevertheless, as the months passed, fine intentions had to be surrendered, one by one, as the realities were revealed. No operations were conceivable in the north. A hundred miles of mountain-barrier between Assam and Upper Burma, the monsoon rains and the prevalent malaria made this an impossible theatre of war for troops who had not yet learned, as they would later do, that neither mountains, monsoons, nor malaria are ultimate impediments. In the south the only landward approach lay through the difficult country of the Arakan, and for the support of an offensive in this area the communications back into India by road, rail, and across the broad Brahmaputra were barely adequate for the meagre traffic of peacetime. Everything, therefore, would have to centre on an assault from the sea, on the southern regions of Burma and the main objective, Rangoon. Churchill, taking the view which he was later to expound in regard to the Mulberry harbours, that the difficulties would look after themselves, pressed in every direction, on the Chiefs of Staff, on Wavell, with the same relentless and meticulous attention that he displayed over the Second Front. No argument about logistic problems could convince him. No suggestion for more limited enterprises could seduce him. On 12 June he signalled to Wavell:

> All these minor operations are very nice and useful nibbling. What I am interested in is the capture of Rangoon and Moulmein and thereafter striking at Bangkok. For this we should have to fight our way along the coast amphibiously from Chittagong to Akyab and at the right moment launch an overseas expedition of 40 or 50,000 of our best British troops with suitable armour across the northern part of the Bay of Bengal. . . . This would be seizing the initiative and making the enemy conform instead of being through no fault of your own like clay in the hands of the potter.

This has rightly been described as 'cigar-butt strategy'. It is a perfect example of those propositions which Pound, according to Professor Marder, manipulated so capably, 'his wilder, or shall we say more imaginative projects, usually perfectly desirable tactically or strategically, but completely impracticable from entire lack of resources'. Wavell's response, however, was a skilful variant of the Pound manoeuvre. He refrained from politely unveiling the fallacies in his Prime Minister's assumptions. Instead, he riposted with a definite scheme of attack. He proposed to use the Long Range Penetration Group, under Wingate (later to win fame as the 'Chindits'), to create a diversion in the north by operating behind the Japanese lines. In the south he intended first to seize airfields on the

Arakan, from which cover could be provided for a seaborne assault on Rangoon. The sting lay in his provisos: he must have enough aircraft, landing-craft, and other assault-shipping, which he well knew were lacking in the Far East, and there must be a further diversion of Japanese strength by Allied activity in the Pacific. This obviously meant that the offensive, to be named ANAKIM, would have to be held over until 1943. Churchill struggled manfully, but the combined influence of Wavell, the Chiefs of Staff, and the inescapable logic of the facts finally wore him down. On 12 July he issued a Directive which stated that:

> Unless . . . the Japanese Air Force available for the regions affected by ANAKIM is cut down to below present level and their military forces cannot be greatly reinforced, we need not commit ourselves to the enterprise. Nothing will have been risked or lost, and all the preparations will be helpful in the future.

It was fortunate that he capitulated—as, in truth, he normally did when after a fair fight he had failed to win over his advisers to his way of thinking. A rapid sequence of events reduced still further the possibility of immediate large-scale operations from India. Planning for TORCH was now gathering momentum, which meant that shipping would be at a premium. The increasing threat of a German breakthrough in the Caucasus involved a transfer of men and equipment from India to Iraq, in a prudent policy of insurance. And Wavell's firm base, India, itself began to show signs of crumbling, for the August riots initiated by the Congress Party caused such disruption that all military preparation, the Commander-in-Chief reported, would be delayed by at least one month owing to interruption of communications, and troop-training must be postponed. In every respect, therefore, the British were in no posture to meet the rigorous prerequisites for his co-operation which Chiang Kai-shek formulated on 1 August. And the situation was further bedevilled by a communication gap. On 14 September Wavell wrote to Churchill:

> I should like your advice as to the extent to which I should take the Americans into my confidence as to future operations. Present situation most unsatisfactory since Americans here under Stilwell who is at Chungking and everything tends to be referred there with delay and damage to security. Would it be possible to get Americans to order Stilwell to Delhi with deputy to Chungking and instructions issued to him to take part in action from India? I have naturally said nothing to Chiang Kai-shek at present but feel he may before long ask what is being done from India towards re-occupying Burma. This will not be an easy one to answer.

Confusion was worse confounded by a meeting of the Combined Chiefs of Staff in Washington four days later at which it was decided that 'the Combined Staff Planners should study the possible action to retake Burma and open the Burma Road, and that Chiang Kai-shek should be told that this was being done'. The news caused much distress in London. It was felt that the Americans must have exercised improper pressure, in what was an inter-Allied Staff, about a theatre which was not their direct concern. 'Burma', Dill was stiffly reminded, 'is a British sphere and any operation for its recapture and for reopening the Burma Road must be undertaken almost exclusively by British forces'. In Washington Dill brilliantly carried out his task of interpreter for both sides, boldly explaining the American view to Alanbrooke and tactfully presenting to Marshall the reasons for British resentment. The outstanding feature of the Anglo–American alliance, which Churchill had done so much to cement, was that when misunderstandings were brought to the surface and not allowed to fester under the skin a compromise was often the result—but never an open, catastrophic break.* So it now proved. On 7 October Dill was able to report that Marshall 'denied all desire to butt in but explained how impossible it was to separate Indian and Chinese interests in Burma, and for good or ill he feels that Americans can handle China better than we can'.

If Marshall's first point had some validity, the next three months demonstrated that even an American general as hard-boiled as Stilwell was incapable of making Chiang Kai-shek collaborate effectively in a combined operation. Much anxious discussion in Delhi between Stilwell and Wavell produced an agreement that an assault on Lower Burma and Rangoon, as adumbrated in the ANAKIM plan in June, should be amplified by a more powerful drive by the British into Upper Burma, assisted by the operations of 20,000 Chinese in the far north. But there was a crux. Wavell signalled that 'I propose therefore to work on lines of combined effort with stipulation of single command over all land forces operating from Burma', while Stilwell was noting in his diary 'We have now got both the Limies and the Chinese working at it. If we can keep a fire lit under Wavell and horn in on command and training on this side, the job is in a fair way to get done'. But it was not. Detailed investigation revealed what was only too obvious—that sufficient supplies could not be delivered to the Chinese, and that Chiang was blithely, but incorrectly, assuming that Rangoon would be captured before the end of the year,

---

* 'Our close relationship made it possible to have the most heated professional discussion and even rows without affecting our personal relations to each other.' Alanbrooke, *Notes on My Life*, in Bryant, *The Turn of the Tide*, p. 547.

while the Burma Road would be re-opened in one massive sweep. He then changed ground: aided by the attractive advocacy of his wife in Washington he attempted, with some success, to persuade Roosevelt that the real route to victory lay in a build-up of American bombers to work from bases in China. (The logistics of such a scheme would, of course, have rendered any sustained military operations on the ground impossible.) By the end of the year everything was once again fluid, even in terms of a spring offensive. Stilwell himself wrote in his diary a private confession: 'A damn good thing March 1st is off. We'd have been hung'. It was thus fortunate that a summit conference, seen to be necessary to unify Anglo-American strategy in the West, but equally essential for the evolution of a common doctrine in the East, was now imminent.

Roosevelt was deeply conscious of the need. The meeting at Casablanca derived, in fact, from a telegram he sent to Churchill on 26 November. 'I believe', he stated, 'that as soon as we have knocked the Germans out of Tunisia we should proceed with a military strategical conference between Great Britain, Russia, and the United States.' Churchill immediately and wisely lifted the idea on to a higher level by recommending a meeting not simply between staffs but between principals: 'Stalin talked to me in Moscow in the sense of being willing to come to meet you and me somewhere this winter, and he mentioned Iceland'. But Stalin was now unwilling to leave Russia while the battle for Stalingrad was in a critical state, and the consequence was an Anglo–American assembly, Prime Minister, President, and the Combined Chiefs of Staff, at what Churchill described to Roosevelt as 'a satisfactory and safe place just north of Casablanca'. With his flair for apt nomenclature he proposed for it the code-word SYMBOL—a happier choice than the cover which, on security grounds, Roosevelt selected for himself: 'Admiral Q'.

Former Naval Person to President   *3.1.43*

However did you think of such an impenetrable disguise? . . .

It is instructive to contrast the approach of the two national groups to what was perhaps the most important of all the wartime councils. Under Churchill the British team had spent weeks of intensive preparation during which, as has been seen, an agreed line of action was hammered out in a merciless dialogue between the Prime Minister and his advisers without quarter being either given or taken. It was a natural part of their careful organisation that they were accompanied by H.M.S. *Bulolo*, which had been specially equipped as a headquarters ship for combined operations. The facilities it provided for staff-officers, ciphering and communications meant, in effect, that Whitehall had moved to Morocco. And Churchill was at pains to brief his subordinates about procedure. 'They were not to hurry or try to force agreement, but to take plenty of time; there was to be full discussion and no impatience—"the dripping of water on a stone".'* The Americans, on the other hand, arrived with neither the appropriate dispositions† nor a properly formulated programme. Marshall still considered some form of cross-Channel attack in 1943 to be a main priority, but Roosevelt himself was open-minded about the Mediterranean and he had certainly not sought, like Churchill, to tease out in discussion with his advisers a single agreed strategical concept. Admiral King, for his part, thought primarily of the Pacific. General Arnold, the Chief of the Army Air Force, had as his main concern the maiming or destruction of Germany by bombing. In many ways, indeed, it seemed as though the Americans had still not advanced beyond the unsophisticated state of the British Chiefs of Staff Committee which Churchill described to Baldwin in a letter dated 19 March 1926: 'we have in fact the meeting of three tribal chiefs, all working for the common victory, but allowing no inroad upon the vested interests of their tribe'. Yet neither the rivalries nor the anti-British feelings of the triumvirate were absolute. Marshall's desire for a 1943 SLEDGEHAMMER had been weakened to some degree by his own planners' emphasis on the difficulty of making it effective. King, so long as he was assured that his essential requirements for the Pacific were secure, was not unwilling to proceed from that point to examine Mediterranean opportunities, while Arnold was well aware that Mediterranean bases offered his bombers the best route to southern Germany and the oil-fields of Rumania. There was, in fact, room for manoeuvre.

It took five and a half days, however, to discover an area of consent. The conference formally opened on 13 January. Alanbrooke's diary for the 17th began: 'A desperate day. We are further from obtaining agreement than we ever were.' And on the 18th: 'From 10.30 to 1 p.m. a very heated Combined Chiefs of Staff meeting at which we seemed to be making no progress.' Underlying the debate was fear . . . justifiable fear, on both sides. The controversial months of 1942 had confirmed in the minds of the Americans the suspicion that British self-interest was centred on the West:

* Bryant, *op. cit.*, p. 544.

† 'What was completely lacking in the American party was any kind of staff who could tackle the problems that were bound to arise in the course of the conversations, and to produce detailed solutions for the Chiefs of Staff. When the U.S. Chiefs saw how the land lay and the size of our party, they suddenly woke up to the fact that they had left most of their clubs behind.' Sir Ian Jacob, Diary, 13 January 1943.

that they had little enthusiasm for energetic action in the East and, furthermore, that if and when Germany was defeated they would not be forthcoming as partners in the defeat of Japan. The British were equally afraid that the military and political leaders of the United States were already concentrating on the Pacific rather than Europe and that this tendency might be irreversible. Each side had sufficient evidence to support its fears.

In the terrible aftermath of the great German offensive of March 1918 the moment arrived, as Pétain coldly announced that he proposed to withdraw his divisions southwards for the protection of Paris, when Haig, Foch and their political superiors suddenly realised that a fatal fissure was about to destroy the coherence of the Allied front. By the morning of the 18th, after five days of exposition, argument and *impasse*, it seemed as though the Combined Chiefs of Staff were similarly splitting: the prospect was appalling. Slessor, now Air Vice Marshal, had been brought out by Portal in the role of aide and uncommitted observer. Sitting on the sidelines, he could see more clearly than his seniors that a chasm was opening. He acted.

After lunch I repaired to the roof of the hotel with a scruffy little notebook and scribbled down a draft of a memorandum which I thought might form a bridge between the two points of view. The Pacific hurdle was jumped by the words:

'Operations in the Pacific and Far East shall continue with the forces allocated, with the object of maintaining pressure on Japan, retaining the initiative and attaining a position of readiness for the full-scale offensive against Japan by the United Nations as soon as Germany is defeated. These operations must be kept within such limits as will not, in the opinion of the Combined Chiefs of Staff, prejudice the capacity of the United Nations to take any opportunity that may present itself for the decisive defeat of Germany in 1943.'

Portal altered a word or two and said he thought it might do the trick. There were a bare ten minutes to go before the conference reassembled, but when we met again in the long room three or four copies of the draft . . . were laid on the table. No one but Portal had seen it, and the C.I.G.S. suggested that the meeting should take a few minutes to read it. I can still see Marshall and King poring over it, exchanging a few words in undertones, Marshall making some notes on it in pencil. After about five minutes Marshall said that the U.S. Chiefs were prepared to accept it, subject to a few minor amendments and the addition of paragraphs to the effect that the defeat of the U-boat should remain a first charge on our resources, and that supply to Russia must continue. There was a short discussion, and then Ismay and I, with General Hull of Marshall's staff, were told to take it out and get it into final form. . . .'.*

The ground had, in fact, already been prepared by Dill. After the morning meeting Alanbrooke confessed to him 'It is no use, we shall never get agreement with them'. They retired to Alanbrooke's room and sat on his bed. Dill rehearsed all the points over which there was no dispute, and those which were unresolved. As to the latter, the C.I.G.S. stated that he refused to move an inch. Dill replied. 'Oh yes, you will. You know that you must come to some agreement with the Americans and that you cannot bring the unresolved problem up to the Prime Minister and the President. You know as well as I do what a mess they would make of it'. At this moment Portal appeared with Slessor's draft. It was decided to adopt it, and Dill, the honest broker, departed to brief Marshall before the conference reassembled.

Churchill, whose account of Casablanca in *The Second World War* is partial and perfunctory, was demonstrably incorrect in writing that 'the differences did not run along national lines, but were principally between the Chiefs of Staff and the Joint Planners'. The differences arose because of a divergence of national interests and national attitudes, voiced by the Chiefs of Staff themselves in open conflict. Nevertheless, at 5.30 that afternoon Churchill and the Combined Chiefs met Roosevelt at his villa and Alanbrooke was asked to describe the results of the discussions. 'It was a difficult moment. We had only just succeeded in getting the American Chiefs of Staff to agree with us. However, the statement went all right, was approved by the Americans and the President and P.M. and received a full blessing. . . .'

The dripping-of-water-on-a-stone technique had succeeded, for the decisions reached at the SYMBOL conference, unlike those for TORCH, were the result of direct negotiation between the professional staffs, not the edict of President and Prime Minister. They thus had a firmer base, for the master plan which the Chiefs of Staff took back to their respective countries was their own. Superior British preparations and more efficient organisation may have left the Americans with a suspicion that they had somehow been out-manoeuvred, but at least they could not claim, on this occasion, that they were merely the residuary legatees of a private piece of horse-trading between Roosevelt and Churchill. Admiral King, indeed, was heard to remark on the evening of the 18th: 'The document that is now in preparation goes a long way towards establishing a policy of how we

* Slessor, *The Central Blue*, p. 446.

are to win the war.' From that hard man, who shared with his President the joke that he was tough enough to shave himself with a blow-lamp, this was an accolade.

The document to which King referred, the memorandum by the Combined Chiefs of Staff of 19 January, entitled 'Conduct of the War in 1943',* certainly represented a triumph for Churchill and his team. On the 20th Alanbrooke noted in his diary 'we have got practically all we hoped to get when we came here'. 'Brigadier Jacob, whose business it was to draft the final agreement, wrote that if before the Conference he had had to write down what he hoped its decisions would be, he could never have written anything so sweeping, comprehensive and favourable to British ideas as in the end he found himself writing.'† Yet even now the insatiable Churchill was dissatisfied. He reported to the War Cabinet that

> . . . it must be admitted that all our military operations taken together are on a very small scale compared with the mighty resources of Britain and the United States, and still more with the gigantic effort of Russia. I am inclined to think that the President shares this view, as Hopkins spoke to me on the subject yesterday, saying in effect, 'It is all right, but it is not enough'.

Was he, perhaps, anticipating the text of the response he thought he might receive from Stalin?

Only a man like Churchill, consumed by a passion for victory, could have registered discontent, for the heads of the agreement were unexceptionable. The defeat of the U-boat came first, followed by the sustenance of Russia with the greatest volume of supplies that could be transported without prohibitive cost in shipping. Nor could Churchill reasonably complain that the third paragraph read 'Operations in Europe will be conducted with the object of defeating Germany in 1943 with the maximum forces that can be brought to bear upon her by the United Nations'. To this end Sicily would be occupied, thus securing the Mediterranean sea-way, diverting German forces from Russia, and threatening Italy. Turkey—the Prime Minister's King Charles's head—was not forgotten: the aim would be 'to create a situation in which Turkey can be enlisted as an active ally'. From the United Kingdom the heaviest possible bomber offensive against Germany would continue, amphibious attacks would be launched on a limited scale, and the strongest possible force

---

* This memorandum, together with the subsequent Directive of 21 January, 'The Bomber Offensive from the United Kingdom', and the final report on SYMBOL, 'by the Combined Chiefs of Staff as approved by the President and Prime Minister', dated 23 January, are to be found in full as Appendices (D), (E) and (F), in Michael Howard, *op. cit.*

† Bryant, *op. cit.*, p. 561.

would be assembled 'in constant readiness to re-enter the continent as soon as German resistance is weakened to the required extent'. In the Far East the recapture of Burma was scheduled to begin in 1943, together with forward moves in the Pacific not greater than the British thought desirable: moreover, written into the memorandum was the all-important condition that 'these operations must be kept within such limits as will not, in the opinion of the Combined Chiefs of Staff, jeopardise the capacity of the United Nations to take advantage of any favourable opportunity that may present itself for the decisive defeat of Germany in 1943'.* By achieving this accord the Casablanca conference had restored Anglo–American strategy to the basis on which it had first been established at the Washington meeting which followed Pearl Harbour.

It will be observed, however, that there is no reference in the document to 'unconditional surrender'. The world first heard that this was an Anglo–American war aim during the Press Conference on 24 January when Roosevelt observed:

> Some of you Britishers know the old story—we had a General called U.S. Grant. His name was Ulysses Simpson Grant, but in my and the Prime Minister's early days he was called 'Unconditional Surrender' Grant. The elimination of German, Japanese and Italian war power means the unconditional surrender by Germany, Japan and Italy. This means a reasonable assurance of future world peace. It does not mean the destruction of the population of Germany, Italy or Japan, but it does mean the destruction of the philosophies in those countries which are based on conquest and the subjugation of other peoples.
>
> This meeting may be called the 'unconditional surrender' meeting.

Roosevelt's announcement was endorsed by Churchill on the spot. His own account, in *The Second World War*, of the origins of the declaration is uneasy and evasive. And his statement to the House of Commons after the war that 'the phrase "unconditional surrender" was not brought before me to agree to in any way before it was uttered by our great friend, our august and powerful ally President Roosevelt' may be described either as the result of an ageing man's lapse of memory or as a terminological inexactitude. For the facts are clear and documented. Roosevelt himself had stated at a meeting of his Joint Chiefs of Staff on 7 January, well before Casablanca, that he intended to support Unconditional Sur-

---

* Any American doubts about British determination in regard to Japan should have been dispelled by the solemn pledge given by Churchill on the 18th, before a full session of the conference, that 'if and when Hitler breaks down, all of the British resources and effort will be turned towards the defeat of Japan'.

render as the Allies' priority. Churchill explicitly mentioned the matter in his report to the War Cabinet on 20 January, asking the view of his colleagues as to whether the announcement should include Germany and Japan but omit Italy. The Cabinet replied favourably, the only qualification being that it was felt that Italy should also be included—a course Roosevelt in fact followed in his statement. There can be no question about the sharing of responsibility, as Churchill indeed accepted in his memoirs. But what seemed right at the time has now been so distorted by hindsight that it is almost impossible to evaluate a commitment which, in spite of its enormous importance, has the air of something undertaken à l'improviste. Far fewer man-hours were devoted to its consideration than, for example, to TORCH.

Whatever its consequences, in January 1943 it was a symbol of SYMBOL. The landmarks indicated in the quotations at the head of this chapter had all been passed. The war was beyond its turning point, the days of plugging holes were over, a blueprint for victory had been designed, and after Casablanca the Allies seemed to be truly on their way, shoulder to shoulder.

7

Atlantic and Mediterranean 1943

'An operation of war cannot be thought out like building a bridge;
certainty is not demanded, but genius, improvisation, and energy
of mind must have their parts. ... Everywhere the British and
Americans are overloading their operational plans with so many
factors of safety that they are ceasing to be capable of making any
form of aggressive war. ... That is the position to which we are
reduced and which you should labour sedulously to correct.'
Winston Churchill, in a minute to the Chiefs of Staff,
3 March 1943

The popular conception of a War Lord is of a man who is master of events:
a Titan. But no War Lord in history has been able to dominate events
in an absolute sense. They have a way of taking their own unpredictable
course, and one of the difficulties for the man who seeks to impose his own
pattern upon them is that he never has enough information. What he
thinks he knows is often inadequate, and his ignorance may be of critical
importance. The intuition of a War Lord is always limited by the competence of his advisers—and by the unexpected. He may be led to hope for
more than is possible: on the other hand, the swings and roundabouts of
events can bring him unexpected profits, since the war he is waging may
sometimes, for reasons too subtle or too complex for him to anticipate,
suddenly take a turn in his favour. This was Churchill's experience in the
months after the Casablanca conference.

The optimistic plans which were tabled and ultimately agreed at
Casablanca included a miscalculation. In the Mediterranean, in the Far
East and for a cross-Channel invasion Anglo–American strategy depended
on ships, and ships were in short supply. Churchill and Roosevelt were
warned, but not warned enough, about this essential requirement if
effective offensives were to be launched in all or any of these theatres. The
warning was insufficiently supported by evidence. It never drove home. In
consequence the President and the Prime Minister parted in a glow of good
will and high hope which, during the following months, was to wane
before recovering some of its original strength.

It is difficult to condemn the Combined Chiefs of Staff. Casablanca was one of those occasions when nerves are on edge, and where a settlement between allies was of over-riding importance. Niggling could easily have delayed, damaged, or destroyed the possibility of strategic harmony, and some things were best left in the pending tray. Still, to defer a problem is not necessarily to deal with it, and much that was deferred at Casablanca soon, and insistently, demanded to be faced. There was, however, another reason for the reticence of the Combined Chiefs: they themselves were ill-informed. This was largely the fault of the Americans, arising from their failure to prepare themselves properly for the debate and to provide themselves with an adequate infrastructure of medium-grade staff officers who could produce, immediately, the information on which top-level decisions are based.

> From the American side, no representative of the War Shipping Ad-ministration was present, and shipping questions were handled by General Somervell who showed, in the words of the U.S. official historians, 'a degree of confusion' about the arrangements that had already been made between the shipping authorities of the two countries. General Somervell was working on the assumption that the United States would be required to provide ship-ping to carry 3.6 million tons of British imports. In fact the figure was nearly double—7 million tons. At Casablanca the confusion was compounded by the impression which General Somervell gained in discussion with Lord Leathers that the United Kingdom could find 1.6 million tons of shipping to help out with the movement of U.S. forces to the United Kingdom. This double misunderstanding involved a total of nearly six million tons of shipping, or 'almost a fourth of the entire tonnage that was actually to be shipped overseas to the U.S. Army in that year'.*

Quis custodiet ipsos custodes? But this grave error, allied to a harsh but inescapable fact, appeared to nullify much of what had been agreed at Casablanca even as Roosevelt returned to Washington and Churchill, in his irrepressible way, flew off to the east in another endeavour to lure Turkey into the battle.

The fact which neither Churchill nor his planners could evade was the current rate of loss in the Atlantic. Dönitz was now free to wage a sub-marine war without inhibition. By the end of January no less than 100 U-boats were active in the north and central Atlantic and the toll they were taking was appalling. The centre of the ocean was the significant zone: an area still without cover by allied aircraft—waters in which a kill could be easily achieved.

Churchill came under enormous pressure from the Admiralty to divert

* Michael Howard, *op. cit.*, p. 293.

Bomber Command, primarily for the abolition of U-boat bases and construction yards. Slowly and reluctantly he yielded, authorising a considerable offensive. The figures are:

January/May 1943: operations by R.A.F. and U.S.A.A.F.
  Biscay bases: sorties 3568, 98 planes lost.
  German yards: sorties 3414, 168 planes lost.

No fully manufactured U-boat was destroyed in Germany until 1944. In the Biscay ports no submarine shelter was ever penetrated by a bomb. What, then, was the quality of the Admiralty's judgement? At Casablanca and at the routine meetings in Whitehall the spokesmen for the Navy, headed by Pound, failed to impress on Churchill and Roosevelt the paramount necessity for closing the Atlantic gap because the Navy's eyes were often elsewhere. Of course voices were raised: but not loudly enough. Churchill generally apprehended the message conveyed by an urgent voice. He liked men who shouted in a good cause. And the Americans usually understood a vital issue when it was lucidly presented to them. The vital issue now, the closing of the Atlantic gap, could only be settled swiftly by an exceptional provision of American Very Long Range aircraft. This was the kind of 'crash action' which Churchill enjoyed arranging, and was dexterous in arranging when he had grasped the need for an arrangement. Roosevelt, too, was delighted to respond to genuine calls for help (tanks after Tobruk, for example), if he could comprehend the scale of the emergency. He was always capable of giving the Atlantic priority over the Pacific, switching some squadrons of the very-long-range Liberators, and backing the decision with the full weight of his authority as Commander-in-Chief. Something could have been done. But the sailors got their priorities wrong. In the circumstances of the time it was understandable that they should have wished to have targets which they thought vital included in the broad programme of the Strategic Air offensive: the bombing would go on, so why should they not take their cut?

But the essential issue was not one of sending bombers over the ports and U-boat yards: it was to get aircraft over the Atlantic and the Bay of Biscay. Though the case for this was certainly presented at Casablanca and in London its vital implications were never so impressed on Churchill that he was prepared, as he would have put it, to lift the matter on to the highest level. It is not surprising, therefore, if in this sphere of the Battle of the Atlantic his efforts were less than supreme, for the critical months of the Battle in 1943 were precisely those when it seemed to Bomber Command, and to him, that new technical aids and an increasing supply of efficient aircraft were about to enable the Command to inflict on Germany a long-deferred punishment. Yet what was immediately required was a sufficient switch of squadrons from Bomber Command to release the long-range Liberators working over the Bay of Biscay for conversion to very-long-range types which could cover the Atlantic gap and, at the same time, sustained pressure on the President by the Prime Minister for the transfer of further V.L.R. squadrons from the United States forces.

The result was a half-hearted compromise. Some bomber squadrons were diverted to the Bay. As for further V.L.R. planes, although the Combined Chiefs of Staff had declared at Casablanca that 'the defeat of the U-boat must remain a first charge on the resources of the United Nations', and though it had been agreed there that 80 V.L.R. aircraft should be made available, American action was tardy. In February only 18 were operating: in mid-April, only 41. It was not until the Chiefs of Staff sent a formal appeal to Washington on 21 April, and followed it up with a visit by Air Marshal Slessor to Admiral King, that the log-jam broke. By July many American V.L.R. aircraft were covering the Atlantic, but by then many lives and ships had been lost—and the battle had been won. The figures speak for themselves. In February U-boats sank 359,328 tons: in March 627,377. The Admiralty believed that the Germans never came so near to disrupting communications between the New World and the Old as in the first 20 days of March 1943: and it is the considered opinion of Captain Stephen Roskill that 'in the early spring of 1943 we had a very narrow escape from defeat in the Atlantic; and that, had we suffered such a defeat, history would have judged that the main cause had been the lack of two more squadrons of very long range aircraft for convoy escort duties'. The margin was as narrow as that; and the presence of more Very Long Range aircraft over the Atlantic gap in the spring of 1943 must surely have prevented the loss of many lives and many tons of merchant shipping. Nevertheless, in May what proved to be an irreversible victory was suddenly and unexpectedly achieved. The date can be pin-pointed—22 May, when Dönitz decided to withdraw his U-boats 'to avoid unnecessary losses in a period when our weapons are shown to be at a disadvantage'. How did such a *bouleversement* occur?

Several factors miraculously converged: but the dynamism and organisation behind the allied offensive were due, in great part, to Churchill, who on 4 November 1942 had instituted the Cabinet Anti-U-boat Warfare Committee. He took the chair himself. The Committee included not only the service chiefs and ministers—First Lord of the Admiralty, First Sea Lord, Secretary of State for Air, Chief of Air Staff, Minister of Transport and C.-in-C. Coastal Command—but also (and this was the secret of its success) a high-level group of scientists among whom were Watson-Watt, the radar expert; Cherwell, of course; and Professor P. M. S. Blackett, the *doyen* of Operational Research. It met weekly until mid-April and thereafter fortnightly until, in August 1943, its job was done. Its function was not operational: this was the task of the Navy and the Air Commands. But it brought within its purview every aspect of the Battle, however minute; it provided a forum where inter-service differences about policy, tactics or supply could be settled without undue acrimony; and, in particular, it was able to assess and implement the results of a remorseless scientific examination of developments within the Battle whose outcome was an immense increase in the efficiency of operations. For this is the point: the Battle of the Atlantic, in its final victorious stages, was as much a Wizard War (Churchill's description of the Strategic Air Offensive), dependent on technical superiority and scientific sophistication, as was the Strategic Air Offensive itself. None of the dictators, nor Roosevelt for that matter, fashioned an instrument as flexible and comprehensive as did Churchill with his Anti-U-boat Committee. Professor Blackett makes the point well:

> These decisive successes put operational analysis 'on the map': the opera-
> tions of Coastal Command, now under Air Marshal Slessor, became increas-
> ingly statistically and scientifically controlled; statistics on U-boat densities,
> sighting probabilities, rates of search, lethality of attacks, flying hours per
> aircraft per month, became the standard agenda for the periodical joint
> Admiralty and Coastal Anti-submarine meetings and of the regular . . . meet-
> ings of the Cabinet Anti-U-boat Committee. . . . Probably the anti-submarine
> campaign in 1943 was waged under closer scientific control than any other
> campaign in the history of the British Armed Forces . . . .*

But battles are not won by Committees. At sea it was the sudden and simultaneous fruition of months (in some cases years), of profound scientific research and intensive tactical training which defeated Dönitz. At the turn of the year U-boats were able to identify the less sensitive form of radar then employed by Coastal Command and to sink beneath the surface before they were attacked. But patrols were being fitted with the new and more efficient ten-centimetre radar. In February and March aircraft with this equipment began to take their toll. Moreover, escort groups specially trained for their function now began to appear in the Atlantic: by March five were operational. The killing-power of a trained

* P. M. S. Blackett, *Studies of War*, p. 238.

and integrated escort group was out of all proportion to its numbers. At the same time the first escort carriers (whose value Churchill had emphasised so many months ago) started to accompany convoys. New weapons and new techniques emerged. And, dominating all, there was the part played by the Navy's Operational Intelligence department, now at the pinnacle of its performance, whose nerve-centre was Captain Rodger Winn's submarine tracking room in the Admiralty. These developments were decisive. During April and May no less than 56 U-boats were sunk, on 22 May Dönitz threw in his hand, and the Naval Staff noted that S.C.130, which reached harbour on 25 May, 'was the last convoy to be seriously menaced'. This was a *dénouement* which could not have been anticipated either at or after Casablanca, and well illustrates that unpredictability of events which will always make a War Lord less than absolute master of the field.

Before victory brought relief, however, Churchill experienced months of grave strain in both his capacities, as Prime Minister as well as Minister of Defence, for the slaughter of shipping seemed to imperil not only the Casablanca military programme but also the very survival of the United Kingdom as a base of war. Nor was the Atlantic the only wound. Fighting in North Africa, prolonged beyond expectation, made further inroads into the inadequate fleets of merchant and escort vessels. The original plan for TORCH had assumed 66 ship-voyages per month from the U.K. to North Africa: in fact the rate was 105 per month until the end of January, 92 in February and 75 in March. At the same time, of course, the hoped-for opening of the Mediterranean route, and consequent saving on sailings round the Cape, was deferred.

The only immediate solution was to cut to the bone. In January it was decided to reduce by half, or to 40 sailings a month, the traffic to the Indian Ocean which supplied the Middle and Far East. 'There are 400,000 tons of ammunition alone in the Middle East and 220,000 in India or on the way there,' Churchill observed. 'Only 25,000 tons were fired in the first month of the campaign that began at the battle of Alamein. Generally speaking, Eighth, Ninth and Tenth Armies and India must live on their tail, on their stocks, and their share of the 40 ships a month.' And when on 16 February the Minister of War Transport reported a long list of pressing demands from Mauritius, Reunion, the Seychelles, South Africa, Rhodesia, Kenya, Iran, Turkey, and Ceylon, Churchill's response was brusque. 'I hope you will be as stiff as you can. There is no reason why all parts of the British Empire should not feel the pinch in the same way as the Mother Country has done.' The fact was that 'in the spring of 1943 the stock-pile resources of the United Kingdom reached their lowest point of the entire war'.*

Furthermore, Churchill and his advisers felt that they were not getting a fair deal from the Americans. The situation was summarised in a message sent by Dill from Washington in March. 'We *think* that the Americans misuse ships in the Pacific, but we do not know. They *think* that we may be using too many ships for British imports, but they do not know. In fact neither side feels the other is being quite open and there is distrust.' Once again it was Churchill who rose to the emergency and Churchill's carefully cultivated relationship with Roosevelt which provided an avenue of escape. A Shipping Mission was sent over to Washington, but this alone was not enough. It happened that Eden was due there later in the month for discussion with Roosevelt. He took with him a long paper, entitled 'The Shipping Position', which Churchill had composed with Cherwell's aid. This presented the British case with compelling and unanswerable eloquence: the sting lay in the final paragraph.

We have undertaken arduous and essential operations encouraged by the belief that we can rely on American ship-building to see us through. But we must know where we stand. We cannot live from hand to mouth on promises limited by provisos. This not only prevents planning and makes the use of ships less economical, it may, in the long run, even imperil good relations. Unless we can get a satisfactory long-term settlement, British ships will have to be withdrawn from their present military service even though our agreed operations are crippled or prejudiced.

Roosevelt, always a more responsive ally than his military entourage, immediately promised Eden that 'the American Chiefs of Staff must be told of the decision that American share of [the British import programme] must be fulfilled.' As a result, British imports in 1943 reached more or less the required level. It also happened that in July the curve of Allied shipping construction (chiefly American), crossed and rose above the more slowly rising curve of loss, never to fall below it thereafter. A battle had been won. But this was a phase of great tension.

Though the Battle of the Atlantic culminated in a victory it was essentially a defensive campaign. But in 1943 Churchill was aware that the tide of war was turning and must be taken at the flood. His mood, therefore, was even more offensive than in previous years, and during these months he may be observed consistently endeavouring to whip on his commanders, and to overcome the brute force of circumstances, in a search for positive triumphs rather than defensive successes. His spirit is summarised in his

* Michael Howard, *op. cit.*, p. 291.

minute to the Chiefs of Staff of 3 March. 'Everywhere the British and Americans are overloading their operational plans with so many factors of safety that they are ceasing to be capable of making any form of aggressive war. . . . That is the position to which we are reduced and which you should labour sedulously to correct.' And if the strategy which he pursued in 1943 is compared with his pre-Casablanca conflict with his advisers it will be seen that his focus, shifting from North West Europe, was firmly transferred to the Mediterranean. But there was no contradiction in this renewed concentration on the inland sea and southern Europe. He never believed, like Marshall, in a logical but inflexible strategy—a plan derived from first principles. For him, strategic concepts must always be malleable. He was the supreme opportunist. In 1943, therefore, he naturally devoted himself to the area in which he now scented success. This quest for local victories in the short term by no means implied that he had abandoned the long-term aim of an assault across the Channel, but in 1943 it imposed great strains on the Anglo–American alliance.

The debate was embittered by American suspicions that the British intended somehow to sidetrack, weaken, or indefinitely postpone the invasion from the north-west, subordinating it to peripheral and indecisive ventures in the Mediterranean that would serve their own long-range political ends. Since the British consistently disclaimed such intentions, the issue of OVER-LORD versus the Mediterranean could not be debated on that basis—and, indeed, cannot now be proved even to have existed outside the minds of the Americans. For them, nevertheless, it was the real issue. . . .*

The shift of emphasis in Churchill's mind was not immediate. It was not until 8 February that he was back in London, after an abortive trip to Turkey and a return journey *via* Cairo which enabled him to take a triumphal parade of Eighth Army through the newly captured streets of Tripoli. He was then struck down by pneumonia. 'I passed the next week in fever and discomfort, and I sometimes felt very ill. There is a blank in my flow of minutes from the 19th to the 25th.' He was, after all, 68. Casablanca had been a hard grind and might well have been considered enough: but it was typical of Churchill's unquenchable optimism and indomitable spirit that he must shuttle to and from Turkey before paying the physical price for his efforts. And then Alanbrooke in his turn succumbed to an influenza with which he had long struggled. He was in bed from 14 to 24 March. Two days later he was summoned.

During the meeting the P.M. sent for me. By the time I . . . reached him

---

* Richard M. Leighton, 'OVERLORD versus the Mediterranean', in *Command Decisions*, p. 182.

in the annexe he was in his bath. However, he received me as soon as he came out, looking like a Roman centurion with nothing on except a large bath-towel draped round him. He shook me warmly by the hand in this get-up and told me to sit down while he dressed. A most interesting procedure. First he stepped into a white silk vest, then white silk drawers, and walked up and down the room in this kit looking rather like 'Humpty-Dumpty', with a large body and small thin legs. Then a white shirt which refused to join comfortably round his neck and so was left open with a bow-tie to keep it together. Then the hair (what there was of it) took much attention, a handkerchief was sprayed with scent and rubbed on his head. The few hairs were then brushed and finally sprayed direct. Finally trousers, waistcoat and coat, and meanwhile he rippled on the whole time about Monty's battle and our proposed visit to North Africa. However, the main thing he wanted to say was that he thought I looked tired last night at the meeting we had, and that I was to take a long weekend.

Which Brooke did: and on his return to London 'the two convalescents, sitting in arm-chairs in the Prime Minister's drawing-room, dined tête-a-tête on "plover's eggs, chicken broth, chicken pie, chocolate soufflé and with it a bottle of champagne, followed by port and brandy".'* Comic: but an immensely informative vignette. It is impossible to imagine Hitler, Stalin, Mussolini or Roosevelt on terms of such affectionate intimacy with a Chief of Staff who, nevertheless, never truckled to his master's whim.

The consequence was that Churchill was unable to recover his grip on affairs until early April, by which time much had happened. Montgomery had encircled the Mareth Line by 26 March, on 6 April the defences at Wadi Akarit had been penetrated, and on the 7th Eighth Army linked up with 11 U.S. Corps in the west. The Germans in North West Africa were now surrounded: but there were still some quarter of a million men in the mountain *enceinte* of Tunisia. After Casablanca Churchill had dreamed of a rapid end to the African campaign, a swift and brutal thrust at the stepping-stone of Sicily, and then Italy's *coup de grâce*. But now, while much hard fighting still lay ahead in Africa, the planning for HUSKY, the invasion of Sicily (and for its follow-up), appeared to have fallen into disarray.

The reasons were predictable, but none was properly anticipated. In the first place a command structure had been created for HUSKY which, from Churchill's chauvinistic viewpoint—concerned, as he increasingly was, to retain at least parity of esteem for the British—was admirable. Under Eisenhower, Alexander was Deputy Commander-in-Chief and also

---

* Bryant, *op. cit.*, p. 587.

commander of all land forces, while Tedder and Cunningham became C.-in-C. respectively of all air and naval forces. The eastern landings were the responsibility of Montgomery, the western of Patton, while the central planning staff at Algiers was also under a British general, Gairdner. But there was a snag. Most of these men were still preoccupied with the unfinished battle in Tunisia and had to start their preparations with deputies. (Montgomery's planners, for example, worked as far away as Cairo.) Thus the realism which is injected into plans by the actual commander of an operation was lacking—a weakness which would later be revealed in the planning for D Day. Moreover, unlike Churchill the men who were responsible for HUSKY realised that a successful invasion could not be cavalier in spirit: caution was paramount, and all contingencies must be examined.

By 19 March Eisenhower was observing that 'the HUSKY thing has got planners really in a turmoil'. He had already declared his own view— that the need for training in amphibious techniques precluded an attack before July: and on 7 April he informed the Combined Chiefs of Staff that if more than two German divisions were present in Sicily 'the operation offers scant promise of success'. Such was the situation which faced Churchill on his return from the sick bed, and he was scandalised. On 8 April he addressed to his own Chiefs of Staff what has been described as 'one of the most memorable minutes of the war'.

> . . . If the presence of two German divisions is held to be decisive against any operation of an offensive or amphibious character open to the million men now in North Africa, it is difficult to see how the war can be carried on. Months of preparation, sea power and air power in abundance, and yet two German divisions are sufficient to knock it all on the head. . . . I trust the Chiefs of Staff will not accept these pusillanimous and defeatist doctrines, from whoever they come. . . . I regard the matter as serious in the last degree. We have told the Russians that they cannot have their supplies by the Northern convoy for the sake of 'Husky', and now 'Husky' is to be abandoned if there are two German divisions (strength unspecified) in the neighbourhood. What Stalin would think of this, when he has 185 German divisions on his front, I cannot imagine.

This was less than just to Eisenhower, who was tackling with his usual sense of responsibility the situation as he saw it. A swift sequence of signals from London to Washington and Washington to Algiers soon elicited from him this stately reply: 'Operation HUSKY will be prosecuted with all the means at our disposal. While we believe it our duty to give our considered and agreed opinion of relative changes under conditions as stated in our previous messages, there is no thought here except to carry out our orders to the ultimate limit of our ability.' In any case it was his *British* subordinates who were arguing over the right course of action—arguments which, in the end, threw up no less than eight sets of plans for HUSKY.

The commanders and their staffs were, in fact, learning from harsh experience something which had never occurred to Churchill—that they were committed to the largest amphibious operation against a defended coast ever undertaken in history. Growing awareness of this reality naturally made them cautious about the tactics of the assault, for they well knew how doggedly the Germans were still fighting in Africa, even though their cause was lost. And they were also aware that had the TORCH landings been adequately opposed the result might have been disaster, since at certain points inexperience of troops and inefficient preparation had produced chaos. (34% of the assault craft on American beaches were lost.) Moreover, there was the problem of resources.

It was a venture of extreme complexity, more so even than TORCH which had preceded it by eight months. It involved transporting in more than two thousand ships, under an escort of twelve hundred naval vessels, including eight battleships and two aircraft-carriers, a force of 160,000 men with 1,800 guns, 600 tanks and 14,000 other vehicles. These had to be carried through waters heavily mined, guarded by U-boats, a powerful battle-fleet and German and Italian air forces operating from shore airfields, to storm open beaches and conquer an island defended by more than twice as many troops, a substantial part of them German.*

In mounting this venture there was not only the general problem of shipping shortage caused by losses in the Atlantic and the urgent requirement in those waters for escort vessels: there was the special, and critical, problem of landing-craft. Their provision was almost entirely an American responsibility, and the Americans were neither sufficiently equipped nor willing to transfer a proper number to the Mediterranean. Lack of foresight in planning production, together with the decision of the Casablanca Conference to give priority in the building yards to escort vessels, meant that the craft constructed were not enough for a global war, while Admiral King's stranglehold on their employment, and Marshall's continuing dislike for Mediterranean enterprises, caused the great majority of them to be sent to the Pacific. In consequence the Chiefs of Staff came to realise that HUSKY would, at best, only be possible if all thought of a cross-

* Bryant, *op. cit.*, p. 663.

Channel offensive in 1943 were abandoned, since the former operation would pre-empt the landing-craft essential for the latter. Their decision was communicated to Churchill on 13 April.

As usual he professed astonishment. 'It had certainly not been made clear at Casablanca that the mounting of HUSKY would entail their sacrifice'—a shrewd point. Alanbrooke countered by observing that it was not simply HUSKY but also its exploitation that must be taken into account. The normal Churchillian probing and interrogation followed before the Prime Minister accepted defeat. (This was the moment when Churchill committed himself wholeheartedly to the Mediterranean for 1943.) It is, however, an index of Marshall's desire to be freed from this obnoxious entanglement as soon as possible that he should have sent a signal on 17 April proposing the launching of HUSKY even before North Africa had been cleared. This absurd suggestion was nicely calculated to make Churchill lose his head, and it was at times like these that Alanbrooke proved his worth. 'Quite mad and impossible,' he noted in his diary, 'but P.M. delighted with this idea, which showed according to him a high strategic conception. I had half an hour's row with him on the telephone'.

All these uncertainties bore directly on the other option which, at this time, was a continual preoccupation for both Churchill and the Chiefs of Staff—the possibility of forward moves in the Eastern Mediterranean. As they looked ahead to the not too far-distant future when North Africa would be fully occupied, Sicily captured, and Italy tottering or defeated, the whole area seemed ripe for exploitation. The Turks, it is true, had been no more than lukewarm during Churchill's post-Casablanca visit to Adana, but he was convinced that 'we have got our foot in the door, and we mean to keep it there'. For the British, however, the key to Turkey was the Dodecanese, since control of the island complex enabled the Axis to neutralise Smyrna, the only port through which military aid could be fed to Turkey in large quantities. This was fully understood in Whitehall. On 5 April Churchill proposed to Roosevelt that if the Germans in Italy held up an allied advance, 'we must be ready for an attack on the Dodecanese for supporting Turkey if she gets into trouble'. Two days later the Joint Planning Staff went further, suggesting that if Italy collapsed the Dodecanese should be occupied and footholds secured in the Balkans, while if Italy held out the Dodecanese should nevertheless be seized. But everything, it was evident, would turn on what happened in Italy—and on the availability of landing-craft.

The Balkans also began to seem a 'growth prospect'. Churchill's policy in this area has been frequently debated and too frequently falsified: it is best considered not so much in terms of the Prime Minister's hopes as of Hitler's fears. For Germany the significance of the peninsula was at once military, political, and economic. A high proportion of her chrome, copper, nickel and bauxite—all essential for the war industries—was drawn from the Balkans, whose proximity to Rumania also offered a potential threat to her main source of oil. In early 1945 this treasure-house seemed to Hitler to be at risk—on two grounds. First there was the increasing military/political menace of Tito. In Yugoslavia his Partisans were now emerging as the real force to be reckoned with, in contrast to the supporters of Mihailovitch, bedevilled as they were by their leader's policy of inaction against, and even collaboration with, the occupying powers of Germany and Italy, and of active hostility to their communist partners in resistance. Secondly the Führer was convinced, and continued to be convinced, that sooner or later, and probably sooner, the Allies would invade. In the early months of 1943, therefore, the Germans launched a vicious all-out offensive against Tito, whose survival is one of the minor epics of the war. At the same time they maintained an anxious watch for any signs of an Allied move.

As he recovered from his illness and devoted himself progressively to Mediterranean affairs Churchill was only vaguely aware of the true situation. The Foreign Office was obsessed with Mihailovitch, and it was not till later in the year, as a result of the missions of Captain Deakin and Brigadier Fitzroy Maclean,* that sufficient information was garnered about Tito's strength and the unreliability of Mihailovitch. Nevertheless, Churchill grasped the central fact—that the Balkans were the Achilles Heel of the Axis—and, indeed, increase in information and support for the Partisans owed much to the personal intervention of the Prime Minister. (Until he passed through Cairo on his Turkish visit, for example, the Middle East unit of S.O.E. responsible for the Balkans had only a trivial allotment of aircraft, without which it was virtually useless: it was due to Churchill that six invaluable Halifaxes were extracted from a reluctant Middle East Command.)

At no time, however (either then or later), did Churchill advocate a military penetration of the Balkans *on a major scale*. The full records now in the hands of historians have destroyed this wartime (and post-war) figment—largely the by-product of American fears. But he certainly and consistently argued that the Achilles Heel should be shown for what it was by every kind of aggressive activity short of a set-piece invasion. At Adana in January, in the long document of intent which he handed to the Turkish

* See F. W. D. Deakin, *The Embattled Mountain, passim.*

President, he observed that 'The breaking down of Italy would lead to contact with the Western Balkans and with the highly hopeful resistance maintained both by General Mihailovitch and the Partisans in Croatia and Slovenia.' This objective seemed more and more desirable as the spring months passed. 'Neither in Cairo nor London was there any more doubt that the Balkans now constituted a fully active theatre of war; and this knowledge was to have its effect on the proposals which the Chiefs of Staff took with them to the Washington Conference in May 1943.'*

The second Washington Conference, TRIDENT, was initiated by Churchill because, as he wrote to Roosevelt on 29 April, 'It seems to me most necessary that we should all settle now first HUSKY and exploitation thereof and secondly future of ANAKIM in light of Burma campaign experience and shipping stringency.' For the fallacies in the Casablanca forecast had been revealed: no cross-Channel operations in 1943; difficulties in the Mediterranean because of a lack of ships; and now a deferment of ANAKIM, the offensive which was intended to recover Rangoon and open up North Burma. The causes were several, but a world-wide shortage of shipping was pre-eminent. One reason was the Chinese. Chiang Kai-shek's insistence on unattainable amounts of aid meant that little could be expected in the northern theatre: moreover, the Americans themselves were divided—Roosevelt inclining to support the Generalissimo's contention that the build-up of air forces in China should have priority, and Marshall favouring a land operation to free the Burma Road. Some of the British, in turn (curiously unaware that to the Americans Burma, apart from the question of the Road, represented at best a secondary front), began to feel reservations about anything large-scale on land and to seek for other targets. Wavell summarised these in a note of 15 April, '. . . the objective I have in mind for such a blow is the control of the Sundra Straits between Sumatra and Java. This would threaten Singapore and the whole Japanese position in the Netherlands East Indies. If we could at the same time seize a base in Northern Sumatra from which to control the Malacca Straits we should have gone far towards the defeat of Japan.'

On land, indeed, the auguries were poor. The limited attack in the Arakan, which opened in January, had culminated by the end of February in a disastrous Japanese counter-offensive, a loss of morale among British troops, the sacking of the Army and divisional commanders involved, and a further diminution of Churchill's confidence in Wavell. On 24 March he wrote to Alanbrooke:

* Michael Howard, *op. cit.*, p. 391.

This campaign has ended in a complete failure resulting in our being out-manoeuvred and outfought by smaller numbers than those of which we disposed. . . . Field Marshall Wavell seems to take a very detached view of the whole business. But he is directly responsible for inspiring the necessary vigour into the operations and making sure that the right men are in charge of them.

In every quarter, therefore, it seemed that the strategy, methods and forward planning of the Allies required an urgent and searching examination. The two weeks of the TRIDENT conference in Washington (12–25 May), set a pattern which would be followed at the Quebec conference in August and the meetings at Teheran and Cairo in November and December. After Casablanca the mood of the Americans was once again resentful. Marshall's chief adviser there, General Wedemeyer, observed that '. . . we lost our shirts . . . we came, we listened, and we were conquered'. And so at TRIDENT, and thereafter, the Americans donned their armour. '. . . they went to these "summit" meetings with the British . . . armed to anticipate and counter every imaginable argument of the British and backed by ranks of experts whose brief cases bulged with studies and statistics; and they devoted themselves to getting Mr Roosevelt to throw his weight in their favour. They concentrated their growing argumentative skill and resourcefulness on getting from the British an inescapable commitment to a cross-Channel invasion in force in the spring of 1944.'* Churchill's policy, by contrast (and indeed that of Alanbrooke and the Chiefs of Staff), was to retain the maximum number of options in the Mediterranean and the Far East—though the Americans never felt, until Teheran, that this was merely the maintenance of a flexible strategy and not a surreptitious defaulting on OVERLORD. In the strategic review which Churchill drafted for the Chiefs of Staff in the *Queen Mary*, on the way to TRIDENT, he remarked about Burma that 'my impression is that the Americans will require to be satisfied that the maximum action is taken in this theatre and that it is not being displaced in its importance in our minds, and that once reassured on these points they will be ready to consider variants and alternatives. It is for this moment that our studies must be ready'. The failure concealed within his victory of 1943—for he contrived to secure the main part of his options—was that in doing so he never provided the Americans with a convincing reassurance about North West Europe. And this happened in spite of the fact that in his opening address at TRIDENT he bluntly stated: 'He wished to make it absolutely clear that His Majesty's Government earnestly desired to undertake a full-

* Kent Roberts Greenfield, *op. cit.*, p. 32.

scale invasion of the Continent from the United Kingdom as soon as a plan offering reasonable prospects of success could be made.' The Americans' suspicions were so deep-seated that they paid more attention to the qualifications than to the promise.

But if the Americans needed reassurance so did the British, for their ally's behaviour was equally ambivalent. An entry in Alanbrooke's diary for 7 May, written on the *Queen Mary*, reads: 'There is no doubt that, unless the Americans are prepared to withdraw more shipping from the Pacific, our strategy will be drastically affected. Up to the present the bulk of the American Navy is in the Pacific and larger land and air forces have gone to that theatre than to Europe in spite of all we have said about the necessity of beating Germany first.' In other words, it was no use for the Americans to strike attitudes and insist on an absolute priority for OVER-LORD unless they were ready to provide the means: yet there was still an unresolved dualism in the thinking of their Joint Chiefs of Staff. Nor was the local climate of TRIDENT favourable for the British. Some of Eisenhower's officers visited Washington at this time: impressed by the amount of interest displayed in the Pacific as compared with their Mediterranean problems, they reported back that public opinion was 'veering . . . to lick the Japs first and let Hitler wait'. All the same the right note was struck at the very start of the conference, for on its opening day, 12 May, when the principals assembled in Roosevelt's study to discuss its agenda, Churchill received a message from Alexander which began, 'The end is very near,' and the next day his famous signal arrived.

Sir:
   It is my duty to report that the Tunisian campaign is over. We are masters of the North African shores.

Here were the fruits of Churchill's strenuous fight for TORCH in the previous year when conditions had been so much more adverse. For, as Alanbrooke noted, 'I could not help wandering back to eleven months ago when P.M. and I were alone with the President in that room and Marshall came in with the news of the surrender of Tobruk. I could see us standing there, and the effect it had on us. And then I wandered through the last eleven months with all their anxieties, hopes, disappointments and worries. And now!'

The real effect of the news, nevertheless, was to emphasise even more powerfully the need for clear-cut decisions about the next step, and these were hard to find during the fortnight's debate, which was mainly conducted at the level of the Combined Chiefs of Staff, with Roosevelt and

Churchill in the background. 'I remember feeling the absolute hopeless-
ness of it,' Alanbrooke recalled. Marshall, supported by Admirals Leahy
and King, was adamant in his view that an invasion of Italy 'would preclude the assembly of sufficient forces in the United Kingdom to execute
a successful cross-Channel invasion', and that assault on Italy should be
confined to the air, preferably from bases on Sardinia. In spite of
Churchill's advocacy nothing could be done to interest the Americans in
the Eastern Mediterranean. It was only after prolonged skirmishing that a
compromise was reached, acceptable to both sides but, in effect, a clear
victory for the British, since their chief objective was secured. This will
be seen from the second paragraph of the final agreement.

>   (b) That the Allied Commander-in-Chief, North Africa, should be in-
> structed to mount such operations in exploitation of HUSKY as are best
> calculated to eliminate Italy from the war and to contain the maximum number
> of German forces. Each specific operation will be subject to the approval of
> the Combined Chiefs of Staff. The Allied Commander-in-Chief North Africa
> may use for his operations all those forces available in the Mediterranean area
> except for four American and three British divisions which will be held in
> readiness from the 1st November onwards for withdrawal to take part in
> operations from the United Kingdom, provided that the naval vessels required
> will be approved by the Combined Chiefs of Staff when the plans are sub-
> mitted. The additional air forces provided on a temporary basis for HUSKY
> will not be considered available.

The Americans had at least obtained safeguards—no action without
authority from the Combined Chiefs, no more troops to be committed:
the British had offered hostages to fortune (as would become clear in 1944,
when the withdrawal of the seven OVERLORD divisions from Italy had a
ruinous effect), but they had gained their point.

Over policy in the Far East it was the British, however, who demanded
and obtained a safeguard. The Americans wanted the final agreement,
after referring to the primary objective of 'an unconditional surrender of
the Axis in Europe', to continue 'Simultaneously . . . to maintain and
extend unremitting pressure against Japan with the purpose of continually
reducing her military power and attaining positions from which her
ultimate unconditional surrender can be forced. . . .' The British rightly
considered that this was yet another example of the dualism in their
American colleagues' minds, and rejected the formula because it clearly
gave the United States a blank cheque on which to draw for the Pacific.
Alanbrooke wanted the sentence to be qualified by the insertion of 'and
so far as is consistent with (a) above' after 'maintain' (a) being the clause

referring to the Axis. The Americans, and Admiral King in particular, refused. There was stalemate, which was resolved at last by Pound's proposal that a final sentence should be added—'The effect of any such extension of the overall objective to be given consideration by the Combined Chiefs of Staff before action is taken.' This was accepted.

The methods by which operations in the Burma theatre should be conducted within this general brief for the Far East had also been settled, after hard bargaining in which the British had to agree that an offensive from Assam into Burma should be undertaken, in conjunction with the Chinese in the north, 'as an essential step towards the opening of the Burma Road', as well as amphibious operations in the south for the capture of Akyab and Ramree Island. The air route to China (which depended, of course, on airfields and supply bases in India), was also to be increased to a capacity of 10,000 tons per month. This was a substantial commitment in view of the limited amount of shipping then available for the eastern run. But in this respect the future looked brighter, for on 24 May Churchill was able to observe that 'Today we meet in the presence of a new fact'—evidence of a victory won or imminent in the Battle of the Atlantic. After a careful review, indeed, the Combined Staff Planners were confident enough to state that 'On the assumption that future losses do not exceed the agreed estimate, personnel ships will be available to permit of the optimum deployment of United Nations forces up to the limits imposed by the availability of cargo shipping.' As to the latter, 'the deficiencies are small and, if properly spread over all the programmes concerned, the effect will not be unmanageable'. Here was a freedom which only a few months ago Churchill would hardly have dared to anticipate.

But the freedom promised in a further paragraph of the final report on TRIDENT was far too optimistic. This read: 'Provided the casualties in operations are no greater than we have allowed for, and provided that the United States and British planned productions are maintained, all the assault shipping and landing-craft required can be made available. . . .' The claim would be disproved by every major amphibious operation subsequently contemplated or undertaken—including OVERLORD. This can be calculated immediately from the fact that at TRIDENT the number of assault divisions for OVERLORD was fixed at five because there would not be enough landing-craft to provide a lift for more, and it was on this basis that COSSAC was instructed to prepare an outline plan for submission to the Combined Chiefs by 1 August. Yet when, in due course, Eisenhower and Montgomery took executive charge of the plans for D Day, their first demand was for a broadening of the front of the assault, and the extra requirement of landing-craft led to endless controversy. Nevertheless one major achievement at TRIDENT was undeniable: into the final report was written the target date for D Day—1 May 1944.

But when Churchill informed London that an agreement most satisfactory to the Chiefs of Staff was being reached over the whole strategic field, and added that 'This is a tribute to the authority of the President and to my close contact with him, the Staff differences of view at one time being most serious', he was prevaricating about both his own feelings and his own part in the discussions. Undoubtedly he supplied the impulsion which ultimately produced the result, but without Alanbrooke's determined stand the British might have come off far worse, while the Prime Minister's contributions were not always diplomatic. His desire to alter the final draft and include a statement that operations in the general area of the Balkans opened up very wide prospects was certainly justified, but its timing was as certainly ill-chosen. Alanbrooke exploded.

> *May 25th. Washington.* I went over to the office early to find out result of P.M.'s attempts to alter wording of our agreement. I discovered from Ismay that the P.M. had produced an impossible addition to our agreement which would have crashed the whole discussion, as we would never have got the American Chiefs of Staff to agree. Luckily, however, Harry Hopkins succeeded in getting him to withdraw it at the last moment, and he finally only put up a matter of wording, which only altered details and none of the principles. We were therefore exactly as we started so far as the paper we had submitted to the President and the P.M. was concerned, but the P.M. had done untold harm by rousing all the suspicions, as regards ventures in the Balkans, which we had been endeavouring to suppress.

Nevertheless Churchill was right in feeling concerned, for at the end of TRIDENT Allied policy about Italy was as vague as at the beginning. In the spring of 1941 he had been compelled to play the War Lord and endeavour to grip a generally disintegrating situation; in the summer and autumn of 1942 his energy and realism had forced agreement over TORCH; now he saw that if the African victory was to be consummated in Italy he must act decisively, directly, and personally. The Combined Chiefs of Staff had remitted to Eisenhower a decision about the operations 'best calculated to eliminate Italy from the war': very well, he and Alanbrooke would immediately fly to Algiers to lobby the Allied Commander-in-Chief North Africa. 'The President had not seemed ready to press his advisers to become more precise on the invasion of Italy, but as this was the main purpose for which I had crossed the Atlantic I could not let the matter rest. Hopkins said to me privately, "If you wish to carry your point you will have to stay here another week, and even then there is no certainty." I was deeply distressed at this, and on May 25 appealed personally to the President to let General Marshall come with me.' This was a prudent insurance. Had Churchill and Alanbrooke travelled alone a purely British intervention would have had a disastrous effect in Washington, and by confirming the false but deep-seated suspicions of Marshall might well have driven him further into the arms of Admiral King.

Between 29 May and 4 June, therefore, Churchill and the two Chiefs of Staff held a series of meetings in Algiers at which he found all the British senior commanders in favour of a forward policy in Italy, while Eisenhower, though reluctant to emerge from Marshall's shadow, proved open to persuasion. And Marshall himself was friendly. Perhaps it was the setting of the discussions, far from the hectic atmosphere of Washington, which caused Churchill to observe that 'I have no more pleasant memories of the war than the eight days in Algiers and Tunis'. It cannot have been the conclusions of the conference, for Marshall's views prevailed. He was not against an entry into Italy, but insisted that the actual decision about it should depend on progress in Sicily. When he pointed out that the shortage of shipping would limit amphibious attacks against the Italian coast, Churchill went so far as to offer to make a cut in Britain's rations in order to provide more ships: but this wild gesture had no effect. Once again the Prime Minister tried to demonstrate that 'the aiding, within the limits proposed, of the patriot bands in Yugoslavia and the fomenting of revolt in Greece and Albania are measures of high importance', covering himself by re-asserting that 'His Majesty's Government do not contemplate or desire the provision of any organised armed force for the Balkan theatre, either in this year or in any period with which we are now concerned.' Marshall was unmoved.

It is worth noting, however, that Churchill's appreciation of the best course open to the Germans if the Allies invaded Italy was exactly that advocated by Rommel (when he became responsible for the army of northern Italy), and almost adopted by Hitler himself until Kesselring persuaded him to stand south of Rome. In the 'Background Notes' for the conference which Churchill submitted on 31 May he said of the Germans that 'they would be wiser to fight only delaying actions, stimulating the Italians in these regions and retiring to the line of the Po, reserving their strength to hold the Riviera and the Balkans . . .'. But the upshot was that Churchill sensibly accepted the facts. In any case Sicily should be a success, and Italy would automatically follow. The future would take care of itself. 'I felt that great advances had been made in our discussions and that everybody wanted to go for Italy. I, therefore, in summing up, stated the conclusions in a most moderate form and paid my tribute to General Eisenhower. I said I should take home the feeling of confidence and comradeship which characterised action in this theatre. I had never received so strong an impression of co-operation and control as during my visit. It would be impossible to embark on an undertaking under better augury.' But there was another augury. The Americans were growing in self-confidence and flexing their muscles. The War Lord was assuming his inevitably secondary role in the Allied directorate.

This shift in balance was more than a nuance. Influence in summit conferences is usually a reflection of power, and by mid-1943 Great Britain was stretched. More fully mobilised than any other belligerent, she had, by now, an Air Force the equivalent of the *Luftwaffe*; her navy was the second largest in the world; she had some 5,000,000 men in the armed services. But the limit had almost been reached. Alanbrooke knew this.

> *July 9th.* .... We have now reached a stage when all three Services, and industry supplying them, are living beyond their means. .... Cuts must be made; unfortunately, while recognising that cuts must be made, Winston won't face up to reducing formations. It is useless retaining emaciated formations which we cannot maintain, and I refuse to do so, and that leads to differences of opinion of the severest nature with Winston.

Meanwhile the multitudinous preparations for an invasion of North West Europe were nowhere near their peak, and demands on manpower would be prodigious. For example, it has been estimated that more sailors were required to man the landing-craft than comprised the whole pre-war Navy. The building, equipping and staffing of supply bases, airfields, roads, camps and harbours needed huge numbers of labourers, technicians and troops. The Strategic Air Offensive must continue to grow. This situation, whose effect progressively diminished Churchill's influence in the Allied councils, may be summarised by the fact that in November 1943 a Ministerial Committee decided that the only way left was to assume an ending of the war by December 1944 and, by reducing munitions output accordingly, to make more reinforcements available for the services: even this remedy was founded on a miscalculation. At the same time the war effort of the United States was steadily expanding. In mid-1943, for example, there was only one U.S. division in the British Isles, and some 150,000 other personnel. By the spring of 1944 it was estimated that BOLERO would have produced 1,000,000. Thus the relative power of the British Isles was declining while their physical existence remained essential as a launching-pad for OVERLORD.

But suppose that existence was once again threatened from the air. In 1940 the Germans had tried to prepare the way for their own invasion by bombing. Suppose they now tried to destroy OVERLORD's base.

For the British—and for Churchill—there was nothing new in the concept of a long-distance guided missile. It is not generally known that in the Twenties, during Churchill's reign as Chancellor of the Exchequer, the government refused to supply a sum of under a million pounds for the development of a promising project.

> The weapon had the code-name 'Larynx'. It looked like a conventional aircraft and was fitted with a normal Armstrong-Siddeley Lynx aero-engine of 180 h.p. When first catapulted off a destroyer in Swansea Bay in the late Spring of 1927, carrying half the load of a day-bomber of the period, the missile was guided by its automatic pilot to a point within five miles of the pre-arranged target. The 'Larynx' had a range of 200 miles; but this, for practical security reasons, was cut by half during the firing trials. Wireless signals emitted from the enclosed cockpit, every ten miles, enabled a chain of direction-finding stations along the coasts of Somerset, Devon and Cornwall to track its course. Trenchard and the Air Staff were delighted at the early promise of this deadly and relatively cheap form of a 'catapulted bomb'.*

In the spring of 1943, however, it began to be evident that the Germans had advanced from the pioneer phase to the efficient production of some such weapon. An accumulation of evidence was presented to the Chiefs of Staff. As a result, Ismay minuted on 15 April,

> *Prime Minister*
> The Chiefs of Staff feel that you should be made aware of reports of German experiments with long-range rockets. The fact that five reports have been received since the end of 1942 indicates a foundation of fact even if details are inaccurate.
>
> The Chiefs of Staff feel that no time should be lost in establishing the facts, and, if evidence proves reliable, in devising counter-measures. . . .

The task of co-ordinating further investigation was given to Churchill's son-in-law, Duncan Sandys, who had commanded the first experimental rocket regiment. Within a month he reported that

> It would appear that the Germans have for some time past been trying to develop a heavy rocket capable of bombarding an area from a very long range. This work has probably been proceeding side by side with the development of jet-propelled aircraft and airborne rocket torpedoes. Very little information

* Andrew Boyle, *Trenchard*, p. 565.

is available about the progress of this development. However, such scanty evidence as exists suggests that it may be far advanced. London, in view of its size, is much the most likely target. . . .

Sandys also reported that Peenemünde, on the Baltic coast, seemed to be the centre of rocket development and that this opinon was supported by recent photographs.

When Churchill returned from Algiers at the beginning of June, therefore, he was greeted by a terrifying prospect. An intense intelligence and scientific effort was devoted to establishing the truth, and every week produced new indications of some massive, novel threat to the island base. On 3 June, for example, Cherwell informed the Prime Minister that photographs had revealed a series of large structures, similar to gun emplacements, in the Calais region. 'Whether or not we take seriously the story about new weapons for bombarding London, would it not be a good thing to bomb these emplacements before concrete roofs over them are finished?' One of the difficulties, for Churchill, was the scepticism of his adviser: Cherwell flatly rejected the technical possibility of constructing an effective long-range rocket with a large warhead—in which he was wrong—and thought the most probable menace was a form of flying bomb (a more sophisticated version, in fact, of LARYNX)—in which he was right.* Churchill, however, was more impressed by the evidence than by Cherwell's deflationary tactics—which derived, to some degree, from the Professor's unconcealed jealousy of Sandys. The critical date was 29 June, when Churchill summoned a full meeting of the Cabinet Defence Committee (Operations), before which Sandys and his staff debated with Cherwell the pros and cons of the situation. The result was that the Committee, with Churchill's full approval, decided that all northern France within a radius of 140 miles from London should have constant surveillance and that Peenemünde should receive the heaviest possible attack by Bomber Command.

Though in 1944 the flying bomb was to strike first, and though of the 1000-odd V2s ultimately launched only some 500 reached Greater London, causing not 108,000 fatalities per month, as was at one time estimated, but only 1,500 in all, Churchill and the Chiefs of Staff were justified in their concern. (In July plans were drawn up for the evacuation from London of 100,000 priority cases, particularly mothers and children, and

---

* 'I remember going to see Cherwell and asking him why a ten ton warhead was out of the question. He said, "If you came and told me that you had in your Company a man 10 feet tall I should call you a liar. If you said you had a man who was 7 feet tall I might believe you. A rocket of the size and weight suggested is so far beyond present capability that I regard it as out of the question now. A one-ton warhead is a possibility." ' Sir Ian Jacob, private information.

30,000 Morrison shelters were quietly stock-piled in the capital.) This is no place to tell the story of the unremitting effort to destroy Peenemünde and the launching sites, but it is worth recalling the picture as it appeared to Hitler in June 1943. After he visited Peenemünde on 10 June he informed his generals that they need only hold out until Christmas, for by then London would have been razed to the ground. It is also worth recalling the figures for the provisional programme laid down in June 1943 for mass production of the V 1. These were 100 in August, rising to 2,000 in December and 5,000 by June 1944. In the end the incompetence and internecine rivalries of the Germans, combined with British counter-measures, substantially reduced the threat of the guided missile and the rocket, but this in no way diminishes the scale of what then seemed possible.

There is another truth worth recalling. Neither in his own memoirs, nor in the millions of words others have written about him, is full weight given to the daily strain imposed on Churchill as War Lord by his incommunicable knowledge. It was not simply a matter of the non-stop flow he received of information about the enemy's capabilities and intentions in the field. There was always TUBE ALLOYS and the haunting fear that the Germans, in spite of all contrary evidence, might win the race for an atom bomb. (On 23 June 1943 Churchill's office passed to Cherwell a sealed envelope inscribed THIS TELEGRAM IS OF PARTICULAR SECRECY AND SHOULD BE RETAINED BY THE AUTHORISED RECIPIENT AND NOT PASSED ON. This contained a report from an agent in Switzerland that 'The Germans are announcing a devastating and decisive air attack on Great Britain for the month of August. Liquid-air bombs of terrific destructive power would be used. Also other un-defined methods hitherto unexploited. . . .' Cherwell, who was not given to panic, seriously considered that the 'undefined methods' might include an atomic weapon.) And now there was the mystery of Peenemünde, and the sinister concrete objects at Watten and other sites in the French hinterland. It is not surprising, therefore, if Churchill's conduct of the latter stages of the war is characterised by a sense of urgency which some have found frenetic. He was racing against time.

And there was no respite. On 10 July HUSKY was successfully launched. Thirty-eight days later Alexander sent another of his laconic signals.

General Alexander to Prime Minister   *17.8.43*

By 10 a.m. this morning 17, 1943, the last German soldier was flung out of Sicily and the whole island is now in our hands.

Meanwhile, on 25 July, Marshal Badoglio had broadcast the news that he had replaced Mussolini as head of the Italian Cabinet. These dramatic events provided a welcome alternative to contemplating the extinction of London, and Churchill was soon in the saddle. The first days of the invasion of Sicily promised a rapid result. In consequence, the Prime Minister began to campaign ardently for a decisive choice between the two options, Italy or Sardinia, which Marshall had insisted on keeping open. He had already, on 5 July, issued his instructions to the Chiefs of Staff. 'We cannot allow the Americans to prevent our powerful armies from having full employment. Their Staffs seem now to be wriggling away to the idea of Sardinia. We must stiffen them all up and allow no weak- ness. I trust the Chiefs of Staff will once again prevent through the Com- bined Chiefs of Staff this weak shuffling away from the issue.' On the 16th he wrote to Smuts that 'The moment is now approaching when this choice must be made, and I need not tell you I shall make it a capital issue. . . .'

In his selective presentation of the Alanbrooke papers Sir Arthur Bryant has argued that the C.I.G.S. was the chief architect of Britain's Mediter- ranean strategy, 'Neptune's general', the great amphibian. But this is naïve, for though Alanbrooke certainly fought for the British case at staff level with a tenacious and effective advocacy, the motive power was as certainly Churchill's. Just as, in 1941, he had driven forward the attempts to counter Rommel, and in 1942 had dominated the discussions about TORCH, so in 1943 it was Churchill who supplied the essential dynamism.

There are two main considerations. By mid-1943 it was obvious, and accepted, that no cross-Channel assault could be undertaken until 1944, and in the Mediterranean, once Sicily had been captured, no target other than southern Italy made sense. The notion of Sardinia as an alternative to, and not as a consequence of, an Italian campaign was irrational. Though Hitler believed that it and the Balkans would be the Allies' priorities, Churchill was correct in thinking that no more was involved than the acquisition of 'a desirable island' whose main value, as an airfield, was surpassed by that of the Italian mainland. As for the Balkans—and the Dodecanese—nothing substantial could be achieved until the Italian fleet and army had been eliminated and German control of harbours and air- fields reduced. Southern France was hardly worth contemplating. If the many British and American divisions, ships and planes in the Mediter- ranean theatre were not to be left idle—a possibility which both Churchill and Roosevelt rejected—there was really no significant alternative to Italy, and Churchill's broad policy, spelled out by Alanbrooke, must be ap- proved. (This, of course, is not necessarily to endorse the subsequent policy, pursued in 1944, of slogging up the spine of the peninsula.) More-over, from the British point of view there was the ever-present danger that if doldrums supervened in the Mediterranean even Roosevelt might be finally persuaded to abandon 'Germany first' and authorise a massive switch of American resources to the Pacific.

Churchill was not alone, however, in being stimulated by events in Sicily. His own response was characteristically expressed in a minute to the Chiefs of Staff of 13 July . . . 'why should we crawl up the leg like a harvest-bug from the ankle upwards? Let us rather strike at the knee . . .' in which he adumbrated the Salerno landings by stating: 'Let the Planners immediately prepare the best scheme possible for landing on the Italian west coast with the objective the port of Naples and the march on Rome, thus cut off and leave behind all the Axis forces in Western Sicily and all ditto in the toe, ball, heel and ankle.' But Marshall was temporarily with him: when it was clear that Sicily must fall the General began to refer to 'taking unjustifiable risks', and it was at his instance that on 16 July the Combined Chiefs of Staff suggested to Eisenhower the examination of 'a direct amphibious landing operation against Naples in lieu of an attack on Sardinia . . .'. Marshall had taken up his option: but the enthusiasm was no more than temporary. Indeed, it was no doubt more the expression of a wish to finish with the Mediterranean as soon as possible than a recognition of new strategic horizons. In any case, a cold douche followed.

Once again the urgent need to convert desire into reality, to produce an actual plan of attack, demonstrated that amphibious operations cannot be conducted without ships. By the end of July the British Chiefs of Staff were so anxious about resources that they recommended to their American colleagues what amounted to a reversal of the TRIDENT agreement. 'It would be a profound mistake,' they argued, 'to allow anyone or anything which General Eisenhower might need to move from the Mediterranean area until we know the outcome of the examination on which he is engaged and his precise requirements for whatever operation may be decided upon'. At the same time the Commander-in-Chief Mediterranean was instructed to 'hold everybody and everything'. Such a stand-fast was calculated not only to reduce BOLERO, the transatlantic accumulation of U.S. troops for OVERLORD, but also to defer the amphibious operations due to be undertaken by the British in the Far East, against Akyab and Ramree, as a preliminary to the recovery of Rangoon. The Americans reacted with virtuous astonishment. 'They view the British proposal as a conservative and orthodox plan which would require the allocation of additional resources to an indefinite extent and in which the element of calculated risk is lacking.' Moreover, not only was Eisenhower refused the four extra groups of Flying Fortresses he requested for AVALANCHE (Salerno): three groups of Liberators were removed from his support.

For Churchill, and for Roosevelt, these military dissensions were compounded by the looming probability of an Italian offer to consider terms of surrender, whose drafting would involve the weighing of a wide range of factors, political, military, and economic. It was therefore fortunate that at the TRIDENT conference in May it had been decided to reconvene in the early autumn, and that at the end of June the President should have asked the Prime Minister 'What would you think of coming over soon . . . and that you and I with staffs should meet in the Citadel at Quebec?'

8

Quebec to Teheran 1943

'If God decides to end this war in 1943, no doubt he can and will
do so, but it would surely be nice if he could have a little co-
operation from you and the President and Winston.'
From a letter by a Colorado lady to Harry Hopkins,
October 1943

The Prime Minister's party, over 200 strong, which sailed from the Clyde
on 5 August contained many remarkable men, but of those who embarked
on the *Queen Mary* two were certainly unusual choices for a summit conference. The first was Wing-Commander Guy Gibson, V.C., D.S.O.,
D.F.C., the young bomber pilot whose special squadron, the 'Dam-
busters', had recently started its famous career with its attack on the
Möhne and Eder dams. But Gibson's inclusion was essentially pro-
pagandist, for Churchill was aware 'how much the President liked meeting
young heroic figures'. The presence of Brigadier Orde Wingate had a
more subtle purpose.

In May Wingate had returned to India with the remnants of his Long
Penetration Group after his first sortie, of three months' duration, behind
Japanese lines in Burma. The Chindits had captured the imagination of
the world. And their exploits, however unprofitable they may have been
in short-term gains, had two unpredictable consequences. On the one
hand, they so impressed the Japanese with the possibility of penetrating
the mountain barriers ahead of them that they began to plan an offensive
which, by over-running Imphal, might open the gates of India. On the
other, they gave Wingate's ideas about long range penetration an impulsion
which carried them into the highest levels of the Allied command.
Churchill, however, was disingenuous when he described in his memoirs
how Wingate suddenly arrived from the East at No. 10 Downing Street on
4 August as the Prime Minister was dining alone on the eve of his departure
for Quebec, and how the travel-stained 'Clive of Burma' so impressed him
that he instantaneously decided to make him one of the party on the *Queen
Mary* in order that he could 'tell his tale to the Chiefs of Staff'. Churchill
already knew much about Wingate, who had been brought to his attention

by Liddell Hart as early as 1938.* He had been instrumental in sending Wingate to India in 1942, and on 4 August it was already a fortnight since, on 24 July, he had made the extraordinary recommendation to the Chiefs of Staff that Wingate should be promoted to overall command of the army in the Far East. 'There is no doubt that in the welter of inefficiency and lassitude which has characterised our operations on the Indian front, this man, his force and his achievements stand out; and no question of seniority must obstruct the advance of real personalities in their proper station in war.'

The truth is that Churchill was out to make a killing and in Wingate he thought he had discovered a lethal weapon. The old gang in the East must be supplanted. Wavell, in whom he had so little confidence and whom he had recently attempted to *limoger* as Governor–General of Australia, had actually been appointed Viceroy of India on 18 June, with Auchinleck to replace him as Commander-in-Chief. Though Churchill obviously endorsed these appointments he as obviously had his reservations, for BATTLEAXE and First Alamein, however unjustly he may have interpreted them, can hardly have seemed to him to provide a promise of dramatic, offensive action in the Far East. Yet this was what he now required—not only because British arms had so far met little but disaster in this enormous theatre, but also because *Danegeld* must be paid to the American interest in China. How could it be achieved? Auchinleck's first appreciation seemed feeble and pessimistic—no more than an amphibious assault on Akyab, and that at an unacceptably later date. Wingate came to his hand, in fact, just as Churchill was pointing out to the Chiefs of Staff, (on 24 July), that Auchinleck's proposals indicated 'how vital and urgent is the appointment of a young, competent soldier, well-trained in war, to become Supreme Commander and to re-examine the whole problem of the war on this front so as to infuse vigour and audacity into the operations.' The proposals themselves he dismissed with contempt. 'I know the Chiefs of Staff fully realise what a foolish thing it now looks to go and concentrate precious resources from the Mediterranean in order to attack the one speck of land in the whole of this theatre, namely Akyab, where the enemy are making a kind of Gibraltar and are capable of reinforcing up to an entire Japanese division. For this petty purpose, now rightly stripped of its consequential attempt upon Rangoon, we are to

---

* See the letter to Churchill in *The Liddell Hart Memoirs*, Vol. II, p. 182, which begins: 'A few days ago I met Captain Orde Wingate, who is of our G.H.Q. Intelligence in Palestine, and who has been playing a Lawrence-like role (in the opposite way) in combating the Arab Terrorist gangs in Palestine.'

utilise the whole of the amphibious resources in the Bay of Bengal for the whole of the year 1944. Even Ramree is to be left over until after the monsoon. A more silly way of waging war by a nation possessing over-whelming sea power and air power can hardly be conceived, and I should certainly not be prepared to take responsibility for such a waste of effort and above all of time.' It cannot be denied that Churchill had put his finger on the truth, nor that in the end the right combination of youth and military competence was discovered—not, as it turned out, in Wingate, but in the marriage of Mountbatten and Slim.

There was another sense in which Wingate's presence was catalytic. As the Combined Chiefs of Staff drew closer together during the intimate give-and-take of the Quebec Conference, QUADRANT, it became clear that in spite of deep and almost ineradicable suspicions on both sides a *modus vivendi* and, indeed, an agreed schedule of operations could be reached in respect of what seemed the two most sensitive arenas—OVER-LORD and the Mediterranean. It was the Far Eastern Theatre, curiously enough, which proved most intractable. The main divergences as to policy in Europe were settled by the Combined Chiefs themselves during their private meetings: at the plenary sessions of QUADRANT, when Churchill and Roosevelt got down to business with their advisers, it was Burma and the Pacific which dominated the discussions, and though Quebec produced definite and acceptable decisions about a wide range of issues—from the Normandy landings to TUBE ALLOYS—it was precisely the problem of strategy in regard to Japan which had to be left unresolved. It was essential, therefore, that the British should enter this most delicate and controversial area of debate not only in a mood of harmony as between Churchill and his Chiefs, but also with basic ideas about what should be done which would not antagonise and might even be approved by the Americans.

For the United States Burma—and a secure India—were important only in so far as they could provide routes and bases for the supply of China: yet this very fact entailed, in their eyes, the removal of the Japanese block between Rangoon and the Burma Road. For the British Chiefs of Staff the ideal policy was different. It is summarised in a note from their Joint Planners: 'the correct strategy, and one that would make for a speedier end to the war, requires the capture of Northern Sumatra and Singapore to precede the capture of Burma.' Churchill himself, while realising that Singapore was 'an utterly remote objective, more likely to be recovered at the peace table than during the war', passionately advocated an assault on Sumatra, which he sometimes spoke of as the TORCH of the Far East and sometimes, in his more hysterical moments, compared with Gallipoli. Moreover, he had an *idée fixe* about fighting in the Burmese jungles, which he envisaged as an open maw waiting to swallow his armies: the thought of landings at Akyab, as a preliminary to an amphibious operation at Rangoon designed to provide beachheads for the long march up the road to Mandalay, was repellent.

And now all these hopes and theories had to be brought into relationship with another awkward fact, for just as the QUADRANT group was about to leave England it was informed by Auchinleck that sudden floods had seriously affected the lines of communication north of Calcutta, disrupting the main arteries of the railways and the Grand Trunk Road. For Alanbrooke and his colleagues, therefore, the question was, how to reconcile the idea with reality? Pragmatists, they saw that the theoretical perfection of a seaborne advance eastwards, outflanking the Japanese, was not yet 'on': neither the naval resources nor the necessary aircraft were available. Sumatra was still a Prime Minister's cigar-dream. But they also saw that it would be fatal to arrive at Quebec with empty hands. And so it was that out of intensive discussions with Wingate on board the *Queen Mary* there emerged the concept of a large operation by Long Range Penetration Groups in the next dry season, intended to dominate North Burma, effect a linkage with Stillwell and the Chinese, and thus protect and amplify the air and land routes to Chiang Kai-shek's armies. The concept, it must be emphasised, was one adopted by the Chiefs of Staff themselves, in spite of outspoken objections from Auchinleck and other senior officers on the spot: emphasised because it is sometimes alleged that Wingate's second expedition was merely a piece of Churchillian romanticism. This, in essence, was the package sold to the Americans at Quebec: for though Churchill continued to hanker for Sumatra his own advisers' caution and Marshall's opposition defeated him, while Marshall's sustained predilection for a drive northwards from Rangoon was countered with a Sibylline formula devised by the Prime Minister himself: 'To continue preparations for an amphibious operation in the Spring of 1944. Pending a decision on the particular operation, the scale of these operations should be of the order of those hitherto contemplated for the capture of Akyab and Ramree.'

In the large sense, therefore, strategy in Burma remained for the British a future indefinite: it was the Japanese, indeed, who by taking a miscalculated initiative in 1944 created the possibility of their own defeat. But for the meeting of that initiative, and for the final victory over Japan, Churchill won his way at QUADRANT over two important issues. The first was the question of a Supreme Commander. The Prime Minister and Chiefs of Staff were anxious that a plenipotentiary should be appointed, on the analogy of Eisenhower in the Mediterranean—but with two differences: he should be British, and unlike Eisenhower should function under the British and not the Combined Chiefs of Staff. The Americans could hardly deny the validity of the principle: it was Marshall, after all, who had been responsible for Wavell's elevation to the A.B.D.A. Command in early 1942. Fortunately Mountbatten's name was welcomed by Roosevelt, and Churchill thus secured what he was after—the removal of operational matters from the hands of Wavell and Auchinleck; the assurance of British authority in a theatre where Imperial interests predominated; the appointment of a man who, as he signalled to the War Cabinet, was 'young, enthusiastic and triphibious'. (It is worth noting, however, that just as Montgomery was not the first choice for Eighth Army in August 1942, so at Quebec the candidatures of Sholto Douglas, Tedder and Admiral Cunningham unsuccessfully—for various reasons—preceded that of Mountbatten. Few would argue that of the three even Tedder would have proved a more effective Supremo.)* But if Mountbatten did his job, and if by OVERLORD Germany could be conquered, there would still remain an ultimate campaign against the heart of Japan. Churchill's second achievement at Quebec was to ensure that the doctrine of full British participation in this last phase of the Pacific war was understood and accepted by the lukewarm Americans: he was already looking ahead to VJ Day, and to the intolerable situation that would arise if the United States could argue that after the downfall of Germany perfidious Albion had retired from the field.

For OVERLORD, however, the Supreme Commander would not be British. Roosevelt's mind was moving in this direction even before QUADRANT. His War Secretary, Stimson, recalled in his memoirs that 'he said he wanted to have an American commander and he thought that it would make it easier if we had more men in the expedition at the beginning'. This novel method of deciding the scale of an assault force fortunately proved unnecessary, for Churchill, in his feline way, had sensed what was happening and grasped the imperative need for con-

---

* 'He had made up his mind on the voyage. I can confirm this, as he sent for Hollis and me to his cabin and asked us who we thought would make a good Supremo. It was rather an important question, but we suggested some names. Then he, with a look like a naughty schoolboy, produced Mountbatten's name and asked what we thought of that. I said I thought it a splendid idea, and one which would appeal to the Americans. It was obvious that the P.M. intended to get it accepted.' Sir Ian Jacob, private communication.

forming. At Quebec, therefore, he approached Roosevelt 'voluntarily'—the President's own word—and offered to accept Marshall for OVER-LORD although, as he confessed, he had already promised the post to Alanbrooke. (Not, as he states in *The Second World War*, early in 1943, but *en passant* in mid-June and formally only on 7 July.) His decision was inevitable: but his method of breaking the news to Alanbrooke provides a notable example of that self-absorption which sometimes led him to act with ruthless disregard for the feelings of others. The necessity was obvious: it must, Churchill felt, therefore be obvious to Alanbrooke, and he did nothing to soften the blow. 'I informed General Brooke, who had my entire confidence, of this change and the reasons for it. He bore the great disappointment with soldierly dignity.' That is as it may be. In his *Notes on my Life* Alanbrooke recalled that he had turned down the offer of Eighth Army before Alamein because he felt that it was his duty to do so.

> But now when the strategy of the war had been guided to the final stage—the stage when the real triumph of victory was to be gathered—I felt no longer tied to Winston and free to assume the Supreme Command which he had promised me on three separate occasions. It was a crushing blow. . . . Not for one moment did he realise what this meant to me. He offered no sympathy, no regrets at having had to change his mind, and dealt with the matter as if it were one of minor importance.

This was the Churchill who, for the sake of victory, was prepared to sup with the devil: not the other Churchill, human, quick in empathy, magnanimous.

For whoever might ultimately assume command of OVERLORD there would at least be a plan available, approved both in Whitehall and in Washington. It will be recalled that at the last summit conference, in May, General Morgan (COSSAC), was instructed to submit to the Combined Chiefs of Staff by 1 August proposals for an Allied invasion of Europe. That they should have been in the hands of Churchill and his advisers when they sailed for Quebec in the *Queen Mary* was itself an index of British intentions, for it would have been impossible to produce them in so short a time had not Morgan been able to draw on the vast reservoir of thinking and, indeed, active preparation undertaken in England ever since the fall of France. (The Americans might also have taken it as a proof of serious intent that Churchill was at pains to bring to QUADRANT not only the blueprints for the Mulberries and other artificial harbours, but also the experts who could explain them: for this enterprise, so crucial an element in the OVERLORD plan, committed the British to an enormous expenditure of man-power and material resources at a time when these banks were already overdrawn.) There was little argument at Quebec over Morgan's actual proposals, which were, indeed, to form the skeleton on which the final arrangements for D Day were articulated. But Churchill submitted important reservations and qualifications. It was, for example, prescient of him to observe that he would have preferred the assault forces allotted to be increased by 25% and that the plan should include landings on the eastern flank of the Cotentin peninsula. This extension of the front, and increase in the weight of attack, were precisely the aspect of the plan whose amendment was demanded and obtained by Eisenhower and Montgomery after they were put in executive command of OVERLORD. It was also sensible of him to insist in both the plenary sessions of the conference on one over-riding condition, as the QUADRANT minutes record:

> If it developed that the German ground or air fighter strength proved to be greater than that upon which the success of the plan was premised, the question as to whether or not the operation should be launched would be subject to review by the Combined Chiefs of Staff. In this connection he suggested that the United Nations have 'a second string to their bow' in the form of a prepared plan to undertake Operation JUPITER. He did not in any way wish to imply that he was not whole-heartedly in favour of OVER-LORD; but, at the same time, he wished to emphasise that its launching was dependent upon certain conditions, which would give it a reasonable chance of success.

JUPITER was, of course, the Prime Minister's King Charles's Head . . . an invasion of Norway. The Combined Chiefs humoured him by allowing JUPITER to be written into the minutes, but it is clear that nobody treated it seriously: and rightly so. Of much greater import was the failure of the British Chiefs—and Churchill—to seize immediately on the full significance of an American proposition that the landings in Northern France should be complemented by landings in the south—the embryo of ANVIL, over which the Allies would be locked in controversy for many subsequent months. That the inherent weakness of the proposition was not immediately exposed may be ascribed to the fact that all discussions at Quebec about the southern theatre were dominated by a major theme, the attempt by the British to make the Americans comprehend that a forward policy in the Mediterranean would contribute directly to OVERLORD's success and must not be considered as parenthetic or diversionary.

Marshall and his colleagues had entered QUADRANT in 'the spirit of winning', as the General laid down before the conference opened. That

20 *Dogfight over Normandy. Churchill, Smuts, Montgomery, Alanbrooke*

21 *Setting foot in Normandy*

22 *The Rhine Crossing : on the bridge at Wesel with Montgomery and Simpson, March 1945*

they were induced to shift into an attitude of compromise about a Mediterranean policy was largely due to Alanbrooke, for the pros and cons were thrashed out between the Combined Chiefs themselves, and not in the plenary sessions. Urgency was, of course, provided by the signals flowing into the conference suggesting that an Italian collapse was imminent. But it required much argument, and a closed session on 16 August, before compromise was achieved. Alanbrooke noted that:

> Our talk was pretty frank. I opened by telling them that the root of the matter was that we were not trusting one another. They doubted our real intentions to put our full hearts into the cross-Channel operations next spring, and we had not full confidence that they would not in future insist on our carrying out previous agreements irrespective of changed strategic conditions. I then had to go over our whole Mediterranean strategy to prove its objects which they have never fully realised, and finally I had to produce countless arguments to prove the close relationship that exists between cross-Channel and Italian operations. In the end I think our arguments did have some effect on Marshall.

The effect was that, instead of the Allies settling for a stand-still in the Mediterranean, a certain latitude was accepted for further exploitation of Italy's defeat, whose imminence held Churchill in Washington when the conference dispersed, for he realised that matters might have to be settled on a day-to-day or even hour-by-hour basis between himself and the President. It provided him, also, with a unique experience, a symbol of that sense of Anglo–American unity which under-pinned all superficial cracks in its structure. At the end of his stay, on 11 September, Roosevelt left Washington and placed the White House at the Prime Minister's disposal. Churchill convened there a final meeting between all the American service heads and the representatives of his own Chiefs of Staff. 'It was an honour to me to preside over this conference of the Combined Chiefs of Staff and of American and British authorities in the Council Room of the White House, and it seemed to be an event in Anglo–American history.'

But the *opéra bouffe* of the Italian surrender was no more than a serio-comic interlude whose conclusion marked the beginning of the last act in the world-wide drama of the war. All was now moving into position for a *dénouement*. The policies agreed at Quebec would be altered, and amplified, but they would not be radically distorted. In south Russia, the Germans were pulling back to release more divisions for Italy and the Balkans. First Kharkov was recaptured, and then Taganrog. Indeed, Stalin's telegram to Roosevelt and Churchill, despatched on 14 September, was unusually warm and optimistic:

I congratulate you on new successes, and especially on the landing at Naples. There is no doubt that the successful landing at Naples and break between Italy and Germany will deal one more blow upon Hitlerite Germany and will considerably facilitate the actions of the Soviet armies at the Soviet-German front. For the time being the offensive of the Soviet troops is successfully developing. I think that we shall be in a position to achieve more successes within the next two-three weeks. It is possible that we shall have recaptured Novorossisk within the next few days.

In the Balkans Tito was quick to exploit his opportunity. Disarming or recruiting Italian divisions, occupying the approaches to Trieste and surrounding Zagreb, moving into Split and the Dalmatian islands, he had already (as Brigadier Fitzroy Maclean reported) so improved his situation by the end of October that he now disposed of 26 divisions, about 220,000 men, and was dominating the better half of Yugoslavia. In the Pacific the routes along which the Americans would advance could already be discerned, for the establishment on 5 August of a new Central Pacific Force under Admiral Nimitz meant that in future there would be two great centre-lines; one under MacArthur, proceeding via the Bismark Archipelago and New Guinea; the other, under Nimitz, sweeping through the Gilberts, Marshalls and Carolines. For these operations the ships laid down in the 1940 programme, and subsequently, were steadily coming into service: by the end of 1943, no less than 50 new carriers were available. In Burma, moreover, the Japanese were already evolving the plan of campaign which would draw them to their doom.

It can now be seen, therefore, that in the autumn of 1943 the course of events was transforming Churchill's role. He was no longer a War Lord *tout court*, independent and irresistible. The threat of invasion was over, and whatever the guided missile might portend its demands on the Prime Minister would be very different from those of 1940. The Chiefs of Staff Committee (on which Cunningham had at last replaced Pound),* was by now a far more sophisticated machine for controlling his vagaries and implementing his better judgement. And the days when Churchill could initiate and impose his private strategic concepts had ended. American predominance, and Russia's increasing self-confidence, remained prime factors until the end of the war. At Casablanca, at Washington and at Quebec this had become progressively evident, while soon, at Cairo,

---

* Without Churchill's approval. Cunningham's diary (in the British Museum) records a report to him by the First Lord, A. V. Alexander, to whom the Prime Minister growled: 'All right, you can have your Cunningham. But I warn you that if the Admiralty does not do as they are told I will bring them all down.' See S. W. Roskill in the *R.U.S.I. Journal*, December 1972, p. 53.

Roosevelt would be revealed as having made secret promises to Chiang Kai-shek without troubling to consult his allies; and, at Teheran, as actually avoiding consultation for fear of giving Stalin the impression that he was 'ganging up with the British'. Underlying all was the inescapable fact that mobilisation of the United Kingdom for total war had reached an ultimate. On November 1 Churchill would circulate a significant minute in which he stated bluntly that '... The problem is no longer one of closing a gap between supply and requirements. Our manpower is now fully mobilized for the war effort. We cannot add to the total; on the contrary, it is already dwindling. All we can do is to make within that total such changes as the strategy of the war demands. If we had to carry on the war against Germany and Japan for several more years, the scale of our war effort in terms of manpower would have to decrease progressively....' His freedom as a War Lord had never been absolute. France, the Commonwealth, the United States—there had always been restraints and impediments. But during the last quarter of the war his function became even less that of the spearhead of British power, and more and more that of the guardian of British rights and Britain's future. He could modify; he could oppose: but he found it more and more difficult to dominate.

A few hours after the Italian surrender was formally announced Mark Clark's assault divisions were landing at Salerno while Montgomery's Eighth Army pushed slowly up the eastern coast—and modification of the high hopes entertained at Quebec became immediately imperative. The invasion of Italy was at once too late and too successful. Too late, because dilatory decision-making, American obstinacy, and shortage of assault shipping had combined to prevent the Allies keeping the Germans on the run from Sicily. Too successful, because when Hitler decided to reject Rommel's policy of retiring on the Alps and to accept Kesselring's plea for a stand south of Rome, and when he began to reinforce Italy and the Balkans with units from all over the Continent, and from Russia, the declared aim of the invasion was certainly achieved. Early in July there were six German divisions and one brigade in Italy, and 12 divisions and two brigades in South-east Europe and the Greek islands. By the end of October the figures were—Italy, 25 divisions: South-east Europe, 24. But for the success a price had to be paid. All that Marshall had earlier feared came true. The Italian theatre, instead of proving to be an area of swift conquests, pinned down more and more Allied resources in slow-moving operations whose requirements inhibited freedom of action elsewhere. Churchill began to grapple with this problem even before it became obvious, and continued to do so, defiantly but often successfully, during the months to come.

As early as 26 August he wrote to Alexander, protesting at what he considered to be the intolerably slow rate of build-up envisaged for the Allied armies in Italy.

> I addressed myself to this administrative failure as soon as I got home. [On 19 September] The measures to re-form our armoured divisions which I had asked for on August 2, and which had been pursued by General Brooke, were already producing results, and the pessimistic estimates of which General Whiteley had been the bearer were soon overcome. The British 1st Armoured Division was re-equipped, and became a magnificent fighting force. Two Polish divisions, the New Zealand Division, and the 4th British-Indian Division were brought to the highest pitch and transported to Italy. The extraordinary prowess of the United States Engineers transformed the port of Naples from ruin into a first-class harbour. In the early days of October, a hundred thousand men were added to General Alexander's army. Had this not been achieved a disaster might easily have occurred, for the Germans were arriving in strength.

There seemed three obvious ways in which the collapse of Italy could be exploited: by the use of Allied command of the sea against the vulnerable flanks of the peninsula, by increased support of the Balkan partisans, and by deleting the German forces which controlled the Aegean. From the moment he returned to London Churchill devoted himself to all three objectives, but the combination of American reluctance, the priorities given to OVERLORD, and the insistent demands of the Italian campaign defeated him.

Although a few more heavy bombers and, at Churchill's demand, a limited amount of coastal craft were diverted to Tito's support, no more than 2,050 tons of supplies were landed, in addition to 150 tons dropped before the end of the year, by which time a powerful German counter-offensive had robbed the partisans of most of their gains. They survived, but they were expelled from all but two of the islands and pushed back again into the mountains. Nor could troops be spared from Italy to establish beach-heads through which they might be succoured. As to amphibious operations, the harsh reality is presented succinctly in the *Official History*: 'In the third week of October, the Mediterranean was due to lose eighty per cent of its LST. and LSI., and two-thirds of its landing craft, within the next six weeks. . . . The new pressure for reinforcements, and for landings on the coast of Italy, thus came at a time when the necessary ships and craft were destined to be removed'.

This weakness was compounded by two other factors. At Quebec the British had only retained the principle of flexibility for operations in Italy by avoiding argument with the Americans about the commitment that seven divisions should be brought back to England by the end of November, as part of the build-up for OVERLORD. The deferred payment was now due, while at the same time the Americans imposed an unexpected strain on all services of supply by insisting on the establishment in Italy, before the end of the year, of a minimum of six heavy bomber groups. A wearisome and fractious argument about shipping resulted. The commanders on the spot, Eisenhower and Alexander, were certain that they must be allowed to retain the craft at their disposal for a longer period if even the most modest amphibious operation—the landing of a division—could be contemplated. But it was not until, on 4 November, the Chiefs of Staff pressed Washington to accept Eisenhower's request (because otherwise 'we shall be faced with a long drawn-out campaign involving a series of frontal attacks at a heavy cost'), and not until Churchill himself had sent a similar personal message to Roosevelt, that 68 of the larger landing ships were grudgingly permitted to remain. So the long drawn-out campaign proceeded. 'In the end, everything I asked for was done. . . . What happened however was that the long fight about trying to get these small easements and to prevent the scrapping of one vast front in order to conform to a rigid date upon the other led to prolonged, unsatisfactory operations in Italy.'

The effect of all these inhibiting factors was even more disastrous in the Eastern Mediterranean, where Churchill had to face not only one of his most bitter disappointments but also the brute fact that in the Allied orchestra his place had become that of the second fiddle. As early as 2 August he was minuting to Ismay:

> Here is a business of great consequence, to be thrust forward by every means. Should the Italian troops in Crete and Rhodes resist the Germans and a deadlock ensue, we must help the Italians at the earliest possible moment, engaging thereby also the support of the populations.

The Aegean islands looked like plums ripe for picking. Turkey might at last be lured off the fence. But though it was agreed at Quebec that Rhodes, Leros and Cos should be occupied, the scale of German resistance in Italy, and American intransigence, caused Churchill's great expectations to gutter out in ignominy. It was useless for him to signal to the Commander-in-Chief, Middle East, General Wilson: 'This is the time to play high. Improvise and dare.' The fact was that Wilson was compelled to send to Italy his only sizeable formation, 8 Indian Division, and his resources in naval forces, transports and aircraft were inadequate. Rhodes could not be captured: an assault on Crete could not even be contemplated. The margins were small, but Churchill's most impassioned arguments failed to persuade Eisenhower to shift any of his strength, even temporarily, into the Eastern Mediterranean. Churchill therefore tackled Roosevelt. On 7 October he sent to the President a long and carefully worded document in which he deployed the whole weight of his authority. 'I beg you to consider this and not let it be brushed aside.' The response was unequivocal.

President Roosevelt to Prime Minister   *8.10.43*

I do not want to force on Eisenhower diversions which limit the prospects for the early successful development of the Italian operations to a secure line North of Rome.

I am opposed to any diversion which will in Eisenhower's opinion jeopardise the security of his current situation in Italy, the build-up of which is exceedingly slow, considering the well-known characteristics of his opponent, who enjoys a marked superiority in ground troops and Panzer divisions.

It is my opinion that no diversion of forces or equipment should prejudice OVERLORD as planned.

The American Chiefs of Staff agree.

I am transmitting a copy of this message to Eisenhower.

It was inevitable that sooner or later the British and the Americans should come to a point of absolute, uncompromising disagreement, but hindsight suggests that for the issue of the Aegean to be elevated to such a point was a tragedy. Churchill had to give way. His offer to fly out to North Africa and meet Marshall at Eisenhower's headquarters was coolly rejected by Roosevelt: 'Frankly, I am not in sympathy with this procedure under the circumstances.' All he could do was to signal to Alexander: 'You should now try to save what you can from the wreck . . .' and put the best face possible on evacuation or loss of such British troops as had been landed on the islands, together with six destroyers and two submarines sunk and four cruisers and four destroyers damaged. His pride was wounded. To Eden he wrote on 21 November that 'it is just to say that it is our first really grievous reverse since Tobruk, 1942'.

Yet this (unlike, for example, his schemes for Norway), was not one of Churchill's impractical delusions. On the most hard-headed estimate it can now be seen—as the Germans well knew at the time—that by a slight shift of emphasis their stranglehold on the Eastern Mediterranean and the approaches to Turkey and the Dardanelles could have been eliminated. The percentage of the total Allied power in the Mediterranean which would have had to be temporarily diverted would have been minimal. This was perhaps a classic example of how the American obsession with fixed policies and programmes denied them a flexibility of thought and action whereby sudden opportunities could be swiftly exploited. Alanbrooke, the sternest critic of Churchill's follies, was here at one with him. Not in his sometimes emotional *Diary*, but in his carefully considered post-war *Notes on my Life*, he observed:

> Just when there were fruits to be gained, the Americans selected this moment to damp down our efforts; troops, landing-craft and transport were removed and re-allocated. At very little cost, Crete and Rhodes could have been rendered possible operations without affecting Italy, whereas, as matters stood, these were only possible at the expense of Italian operations, and were consequently ruled out. Success in Crete and Rhodes might have had the happiest repercussions in Turkey and the Balkans without ever committing a single man in the Balkans.

All the same, if someone in Whitehall had leaked to someone in Washington what was being thought and said in London during these months Roosevelt and Marshall could have claimed exemplary justification for their obduracy. What would they have made of the note in Alanbrooke's *Diary*, following a meeting of the Chiefs of Staff on 19 October? 'C.O.S. at which we received a note from the P.M. *wishing to swing the strategy back to the Medtierranean at the expense of the Channel. I am in many ways entirely with him.*' What would they have made of Alanbrooke's comment, on the 25th, about the Americans' 'insistence to abandon the Mediterranean operations for the *very problematical cross-Channel operations?*' Or of the meeting on the 27th, when Churchill and Smuts ... 'gave a long discourse on relative merits of Mediterranean theatre *as opposed to the cross-Channel operations*'? 'You see,' they might have sardonically observed, 'Just as we said. In spite of TRIDENT, in spite of QUADRANT, in spite of solid commitments solemnly undertaken the British are ratting.'

They would have been wrong. It was a matter of *nuance*. At this stage of the war there was never any question of British determination to re-enter Europe.* The record is clear. After the Quebec decisions were known Smuts, who had a uniquely intimate relationship with Churchill, sent him a vigorously critical letter in which he disputed the validity of

---

* When General Sir James Steele was appointed Director of Staff Duties at the War Office in *July* 1943 he was given two main tasks: to prepare the forces for OVERLORD, and to initiate a plan for the structure of the *post-war* army. (Private communication.)

what had been agreed and argued with passion for an all-out policy in the Mediterranean, while 'preparations for Channel plan should be slowed down or put into temporary cold storage . . .'. When Churchill replied, privately, to his old friend, he was not composing a state document 'for the record'. Nevertheless he surrendered no ground. On 11 September he wrote to Smuts that 'there can be no question whatever of breaking arrangements we have made with United States for OVERLORD. . . . I hope you will realise that British loyalty to OVERLORD is keystone or arch of Anglo–American co-operation. Personally I think enough forces exist for both hands to be played, and I believe this to be the right strategy'.

Here is the clue. In spite of Alanbrooke's brilliant expositions and Churchill's own efforts, the Americans could never bring themselves to believe that the British envisaged a forward policy in the Mediterranean as complementary to, and not an alternative for, OVERLORD. They thought too much in terms of black and white, of either/or. And though they recognised, and feared, the British habit of opportunism, which derived from centuries of experience as a small land-power with great capabilities at sea and world-wide commitments to sustain, they could not accept that opportunism has military merits. Nor, as they observed British hesitations about OVERLORD, were they sufficiently sensitive or sophisticated to appreciate that the hesitations were not fundamental. They were not about *whether* France should be invaded, but about when, and under what conditions. If Roosevelt and Marshall had served, like Churchill, as a battalion commander in the trenches of the Western front, or shared his involvement in the great crises of the First World War, they might have understood better how every week that brought him nearer to D Day made him more apprehensive about his responsibilities. They might have appreciated more perceptively the tensions in the mind of a man who had known one holocaust and was about to commit the armies of his country to another: irreplaceable armies. For the British there could only be one OVERLORD.*

All these considerations deeply affected Britain's current relationship with Russia. It was uneasy. During October Churchill was engaged in an outspoken correspondence with Stalin over the resumption of Arctic

---

* ' "You are fighting the ghosts of the Somme," the Prime Minister's doctor said to Marshall. Churchill's dread was such that even into the final months, he seemed to hope for some miracle that would bring the German collapse without an invasion. As late as March and April, he continued to say occasionally to American visitors: "I am hardening on this operation," as if, even then, it might be averted.' Forest C. Payne, in *D. Day. The Normandy Invasion in Retrospect*, p. 13.

convoys, for which the proper treatment of British service men and technicians in Russian ports seemed a prerequisite to the British but curiously unacceptable to the Russians. Matters came to a head during the meeting of Foreign Ministers in Moscow which began on 19 October. Eden's position there was difficult, for on the one hand, as he reported, the Russians were 'completely and blindly set on our invasion of Northern France', and throughout the conference the dominant note was their reiterated inquiry as to whether the British and Americans were really going to honour their promise, made during the Washington Conference in May, that OVERLORD would occur in the early spring of 1944. On the other hand he was receiving qualifications and conditions from Churchill which prevented him from giving the Russians full satisfaction. These were summarised in a message from Churchill to Eden of 26 October, which he asked him to show to Stalin.

> It will therefore be necessary for you to make it clear that the assurances you have given about May OVERLORD, subject to the specified conditions, must be modified by the exigencies of the battle in Italy. I am taking the matter up with President Roosevelt, but nothing will alter my determination not to throw away the battle in Italy at this juncture, so far as the King's armies are concerned. Eisenhower and Alexander must have what they need to win the battle, no matter what effect is produced on subsequent operations. This may certainly affect the date of OVERLORD.

Such being the prevailing atmosphere of uncertainty, suspicion, and irresolution, it was singularly fortunate that after hectic negotiation a meeting between the three heads of government, first adumbrated at Quebec, was finally organised, to open on 28 November in Teheran.

Churchill sailed from Plymouth on the *Renown* on 12 November. He was not to return for over two months, during which most of the main decisions affecting the final stages of the war would be taken. That he could afford to be absent from London for so long, that he could conduct so much important business so far from home, and that, during his absence, the war effort could proceed smoothly is a vivid illustration of how by the end of 1943 the system of administration evolved under his overlordship had reached a peak of efficiency. (In another sense it is a dramatic proof of the stability of his regime: neither Roosevelt, nor Hitler, nor Stalin would have dared to absent themselves from the centre of power for so long a period.) Yet much was in train in Britain during those eight weeks—a critical phase of the Strategic Air Offensive; the unremitting preparations for the advent of the guided missile; the intensive work on plans and preliminaries for D Day.

Teheran was preceded by a conference in Cairo, SEXTANT, for Churchill and Roosevelt sensibly considered that they and their staffs should exchange views and concert policies before facing Stalin together for the first time. Yet the Cairo meeting differed in tone from all previous conferences. Roosevelt was no longer the equal partner: he became the pace-setter. The fatal theory that he could deal more effectively with the Russians on his own, which reached its supreme expression at Yalta, had already conquered him. Indeed he sought to keep discussion at Cairo to a minimum, and even requested the presence of a Russian observer, while the general attitude of the American team was one of avoiding specific commitments until Teheran. The honeymoon was over. This new and almost callous independence of the Americans is well exemplified by the presence of Chiang Kai-shek in Cairo. Churchill assumed, not unreasonably, that the proper priority for heads of discussion would be 1. OVER-LORD, the Mediterranean and the Pacific, and only 2. future operations in South East Asia. But Roosevelt stood these priorities on their heads, and the British were frustrated to find that much invaluable time at Cairo was wasted in arguments over secondary matters of vital interest only to the Chinese.

It was not that there were no Far Eastern issues deserving of urgent discussion. The appointment of the Chief of Combined Operations to the Supreme Command inevitably seemed to open wider horizons for amphibious warfare—at first. Churchill was never willing to allow his favourite projects to remain in discard, and soon after his return from Quebec he re-opened, with his usual *panache*, the question of an assault on Sumatra. As late as 1 October, in Cairo, Alanbrooke noted:

> ... meeting with P.M., Chiefs of Staff, Dickie Mountbatten and Pownall.* This resulted in an hour's pitched battle between me and the P.M., on the question of withdrawing troops for the Indian Ocean offensive. I was refusing to impair our amphibian potential power in the Mediterranean in order to equip Mountbatten for ventures in Sumatra. P.M., on the other hand, was prepared to scrap our basic policy and put Japan before Germany. However, I defeated most of his intentions in the end!

But Churchill soon changed his tune. Once it became clear that amphibious operations in the East would only be possible by denying assault craft to the Mediterranean, and even OVERLORD, he started to oppose what he had so intemperately advocated. On 29 November, indeed, he had already gone so far as to send a formal minute to the Chiefs of Staff: 'The Prime Minister wishes to put on record the fact that he specifically

* Pownall was Mountbatten's Chief Staff Officer.

refused the Generalissimo's request that we should undertake an amphibious operation simultaneously with the land operations in Burma'. Now he began to hedge over his Sumatra scheme, CULVERIN. But there still remained Mountbatten's alternative proposal for a seaborne operation to capture the Andaman Islands, BUCCANEER.

The Americans had come to Cairo in search of some such plan. 'We were prepared,' wrote Admiral Leahy, 'to hear British objections to the Burma operations, but the President seemed determined that we formulate the best possible plans to support the Chinese war-effort'. The President was so determined, and in spite of the known British objections he secretly promised to Chiang Kai-shek at Cairo 'a considerable amphibious operation across the Bay of Bengal within the next few months'. The American Chiefs of Staff therefore refused to discuss BUCCANEER further, treating it as a *fait accompli*, and this delicate and important subject, involving the relationship of the British, the Americans and the Chinese, was carried forward to Teheran unresolved. The affair was a gross aberration on Roosevelt's part.

But a second aberration was firmly and successfully handled by the Prime Minister. The American Chiefs of Staff put up a serious proposition, endorsed by Roosevelt, that a single Supreme Commander should be appointed to control all operations against Germany both from the Mediterranean and from the Atlantic (i.e., OVERLORD). The manifest impracticability of inserting such a man, with a vast staff, between the American and British Governments and their actual commanders in the field was exposed by the British—and notably by Churchill—point by point. But though the grotesque idea was killed at birth, it is possible to see what lay behind it. Roosevelt was seeking for a post big enough to justify to himself, and to the American nation, the removal of Marshall from the position of Chief of Staff. OVERLORD, as will be seen, was not in itself enough.

The auguries for the Teheran conference, on which so much depended, were thus unfavourable. Roosevelt might be in a positive mood, but his advisers were apprehensive. They, certainly, had not 'ganged up with the British': but suppose Stalin were to do so? Suppose he were to support Churchill in mad Balkan projects? Since Churchill had no such plans, and since the last thing Stalin desired was a powerful Anglo–American presence in the Balkans, these fears were groundless: they were no less real. The British Chiefs for their part were equally apprehensive that Russo–American solidarity over a Second Front might force their hand: moreover, they were irritated. Afternoons in Cairo like that described in the *Sitwell Papers* had not sweetened their temper. 'Brooke got nasty and King got good and sore. King almost climbed over the table at Brooke. God, he was mad! I wish he had socked him ... 3.30 p.m. Chinese came in. Terrible performance. They couldn't ask a question. Brooke was insulting. I helped them out. . . .' And Churchill, who was unwell when he left England, spent his first evening at Teheran in bed at the British Legation, the assiduous Lord Moran endeavouring with his sprays to restore to the Prime Minister that essential weapon, his voice. He had also been much disturbed on his arrival by a reprehensible lack of security. 'The people were friendly but non-committal. They pressed to within a few feet of the car. There was no kind of defence at all against two or three determined men with pistols or a bomb.' Rumours spread about a plot. Though these appear to have been unfounded they were enough for Churchill to support Molotov in his proposal that Roosevelt should move into the Russian compound. (The staff in the villa occupied by the President were all N.K.V.D. men, and Ismay was presumably correct in his supposition that microphones had been installed in advance.) Even so, during the first dinner there, at which Roosevelt was host, and for which the meal had been prepared by his own Filipino servants, he had to withdraw because of an acute digestive attack, and for a time it was feared that he might have been poisoned.

It was to the surprise and relief of everyone, therefore, that the conference was conducted in an atmosphere of good will and concluded with positive decisions acceptable to all parties—though they were less definite than was suggested by a final communiqué drafted, as Churchill observed, with 'brevity, mystery and foretaste of impending doom for Germany'.

> The Military Staffs of the Three Powers concerted their plans for the final destruction of the German forces. They reached complete agreement as to the scope and timing of the operations which will be undertaken from East, West and South, and arrangements were made to ensure intimate and continuous co-operation.

The initiative in the discussions was immediately grasped and consistently retained by Stalin, who skilfully lit the fuse to two time-bombs. In the opening Plenary Session he announced almost casually that the moment Germany collapsed Russia would march with the two allies against Japan. By this, which Churchill later called the most important statement made at Teheran, he opened up such new horizons that Anglo–American thinking about the Far East now seemed out-of-date and, in particular, brought further into question the good sense of Roosevelt's rash promise about BUCCANEER. But the Americans were still more astonished to discover that after Churchill and Roosevelt had outlined their policies in regard to OVERLORD and the Mediterranean Stalin chiefly concentrated on the United States proposal, introduced almost incidentally, for a landing in southern France. (They had not, in fact, even come to the conference fully briefed on the project.) Stalin, however, brushed aside any suggestion of operations in the Balkans and boldly suggested that divisions should be moved from Italy to facilitate ANVIL. Furthermore, he welcomed the American idea that ANVIL should actually precede OVERLORD.

In Alanbrooke's afterthoughts on Teheran he pays a warm tribute to Stalin's strategical shrewdness, while suggesting that his support for Roosevelt's notion that ANVIL should start on 1 April and OVERLORD not until 1 May had a political rather than a military purpose—to keep his allies out of the Balkans. This was possibly but not necessarily so, since the concept of the two-pronged attack was by now basic to Russian strategical thinking—as Stalin himself remarked. But when, under Russian pressure, it was finally agreed at Teheran that OVERLORD should be launched 'in May'—which the combined Chiefs of Staff privately interpreted as 1 June—it was certainly all to the good that ANVIL was moved back to coincide with, rather than to anticipate, the D Day for OVERLORD. Nevertheless, this unexpected enthusiasm on Stalin's part for Southern France was his second time-bomb, for ANVIL was to create a rift between the British and the Americans right up to the invasion of Normandy.

In these discussions Churchill's rôle was ambivalent. He was ill, but he fought with undiminished ardour for his personal objectives—the capture of Rhodes; Turkey to be brought in as a belligerent; sustained operations in Italy.

> I wished it to be placed on record that I could not in any circumstances agree to sacrifice the activities of the armies in the Mediterranean, which included twenty British and British-controlled divisions, merely in order to keep the exact date of May 1 for OVERLORD.

Well aware that Roosevelt was leaning heavily towards the Russians, he contrived a talk with Stalin in which he assured the Marshal with some effect that he was fully determined on a cross-Channel invasion; that he had no wish to intrude powerfully into the Balkans; and that his Italian plans stopped short of advancing from the leg of the peninsula into the broad plains of the Po. But why did he accept ANVIL with such apparent equanimity?

He himself disclosed the true answer years afterwards, when he wrote in *The Second World War* that he liked the proposition at first sight because, since both the Americans and Russians favoured it, it would be easier to secure the landing-craft necessary for the success of the Italian campaign and capture of Rome. The Italian capital, rather than the French Riviera, was Churchill's target—Rome, and the Aegean islands. And anyway, as he added: 'All this lay five or six months ahead. There would be plenty of time to make a final choice as the general war shaped itself, if only the life of our armies in Italy was not paralysed by depriving them of their modest requirements in landing-craft. Many amphibious or semi-amphibious schemes were open.'

Here was Churchillian opportunism at its most naked. By agreeing to ANVIL he thought the Americans would be so committed that they would be compelled to bring back landing-craft from the Far East and, it might be, even from the Pacific: once a sufficient fleet was assembled in the Mediterranean there would still be a chance that he might be able to draw on it for other enterprises. The Turks would be meeting him when he got back to Cairo. Suppose that in the end he could acquire Rhodes? Measureless possibilities (his favourite adjective) would open. Chester Wilmot argued with great force in *The Struggle for Europe* that Russia's post-war domination of South East Europe was due to American blunders about the Balkans, as compared with a far-sighted Churchillian determination to establish bastions for future political strength. It is worth noting, therefore, that neither at Teheran nor afterwards did Churchill give any indication of realising that the effect of accepting ANVIL, and re-orientating Anglo–American strategy towards the western Mediterranean, would be to increase very considerably the likelihood of Russian penetration into the Balkans. Nor was this the only casualty—his Mediterranean ambitions would soon reduce to zero all Mountbatten's plans for seaborne operations in South East Asia. These plans were premature and over-ambitious. The Russians were destined to become the masters of South East Europe. But the consequences of Churchill's pre-occupations must be placed in the right perspective.

Having obtained the commitments he required about the opening of a Second Front Stalin next asked if he could be told who was going to command OVERLORD. He put the question during the dinner party given by Churchill at the British Legation on 30 November to celebrate his 69th birthday. 'This was a memorable occasion in my life. On my right sat the President of the United States, on my left the master of Russia. Together we controlled a large preponderance of the naval and three-quarters of all

the air-forces in the world, and could direct armies of nearly twenty
millions of men, engaged in the most terrible of wars that had yet occurred
in human history.' (These were birthday thoughts. In later days Churchill
would observe that Teheran first brought home to him the relative strength
of Britain. 'There I sat with the Great Russian bear on one side of me, with
paws outstretched, and on the other side the great American buffalo, and
between the two sat the poor little English donkey who was the only one
... who knew the right way home.') To Stalin's query Churchill replied
that he assumed the Supreme Commander would be Marshall: the great
Russian bear was obviously satisfied. But Roosevelt had other ideas.

The President was about to take what Robert Sherwood has called 'one
of the most difficult and one of the loneliest decisions he ever had to make'.
It was to Sherwood, when he was working on *The WhiteHouse Papers*, that
Marshall described how, after the Anglo–American contingent had
returned from Teheran to Cairo, he was summoned on Sunday 5
December to Roosevelt's villa:

> I recalled saying that I would not attempt to estimate my capabilities; the
> President would have to do that; I merely wished to make clear that whatever
> the decision, I would go along with it wholeheartedly; that the issue was too
> great for any personal feeling to be considered. I did not discuss the pros and
> cons of the matter. If I recall, the President stated in completing our con-
> versation: 'I feel I could not sleep at night with you out of the country.'

War is an able contriver of coincidences. Nevertheless it is a remarkable
fact that Cairo should have happened to be the place where two great
soldiers were to address their political masters in similar terms—for it was
in Cairo, of course, that Alanbrooke in the previous year had made his
noble renunciation. And so it was that 'against the almost impassioned
advice of Hopkins and Stimson, against the known preference of both
Stalin and Churchill' Roosevelt selected Eisenhower as Supreme Commander for OVERLORD, informing Churchill of his decision as they
drove together from Cairo to the Pyramids on a visit to the Sphinx. 'We
... examined this wonder of the world from every angle,' Churchill
remembered. 'Roosevelt and I gazed at her for some minutes in silence as
the evening shadows fell. She told us nothing and maintained her
inscrutable smile.'

But if the Sphinx could have spoken she would have commended
Roosevelt's choice. Nothing in the mass of evidence available suggests
that Marshall would have improved on Eisenhower's performance, while
there is much to indicate that the man who was superb as Chief of Staff

would have lacked the right touch in OVERLORD. In any event Churchill accepted the decision without demur, and the consequential appointments were rapidly agreed. By the end of the year the selectors had picked the whole of the Allied command. Both Churchill and Eisenhower would have preferred Alexander, but again hindsight makes it certain that Montgomery was the best candidate for the post of overall ground commander. With Tedder as Eisenhower's deputy, Bradley as the senior American battle commander, Wilson as Supreme Commander Mediterranean and Alexander in control of the armies in Italy, the team was as strong a one as the Allies could field.

In the few days at Cairo before Roosevelt returned to Washington a number of the other important issues which had been by-passed at Teheran were either settled or clarified. Policy over the Far East predominated, and there were two factors which enabled Churchill to win the day. The first, of course, was Stalin's declaration of intent about Japan. This, as Churchill pointed out, offered the possibility of far better bases for bombing Japan into surrender than could ever be found in China— though this was a main element in Roosevelt's support of Chiang Kai-shek. The second was the revised plan for BUCCANEER which Mountbatten, now back in India, forwarded to Cairo. Rightly or wrongly he had greatly increased its scope, and Churchill was shocked—as he roundly informed Mountbatten on 9 December. 'Everyone here has been unpleasantly affected by your request to use 50,000 British and Imperial troops, of which 33,700 are combatant, against 5,000 Japanese. I was astounded to hear of such a requirement, and I cannot feel sure that you are getting competent military advice'. In fact there were valid reasons for Mountbatten's estimate, and in *The Second World War* Churchill had the good grace to print a subsequent War Office appreciation which indicated that his first, emotional reaction was unjustified.

Nevertheless the scale of the new proposals for BUCCANEER had a decisive effect, when combined with a steadily mounting suspicion among the military experts that the forces so far allocated to OVERLORD and ANVIL were inadequate. After intensive discussion Marshall and his colleagues began to accept the British case, and by the afternoon of 5 December the Combined Chiefs of Staff had decided to signal to Mountbatten that European operations must have priority and BUCCANEER must be postponed. But their decision had already been overtaken by events. That evening Churchill received from Roosevelt a curt message: 'BUCCANEER is off.' In spite of pressure from his advisers, in spite of all the arguments they had deployed against the British, in spite of his

23 *Victory in Europe, May 1945. Churchill with the Chiefs of Staff in the garden of No. 10 Downing Street*
Front Row: *Portal, Alanbrooke, Churchill, Cunningham*
Rear row: *Hollis, Ismay*

secret promise to Chiang Kai-shek, he had decided to sacrifice his word and the Chinese for the sake of ensuring Allied solidarity in Europe and a sufficiency of resources for OVERLORD and ANVIL. Churchill, of course, was delighted, remarking to Ismay of Roosevelt's *volte-face* 'He is a better man that ruleth his spirit than he that taketh a city.' Formal endorsement was now given to an assault on Southern France. It was agreed that the landing-craft assigned to BUCCANEER should be diverted to OVERLORD and ANVIL. The Final Report of the Combined Chiefs of Staff was initialled, and in a moment of exuberance Churchill declared that 'when military historians came to adjudge the decisions of the SEXTANT conference, they would find them fully in accordance with the classic articles of war'.

If one looks back two years, from those December days in Cairo to the first Anglo-American conference in December 1941, ARCADIA, it becomes evident that Churchill was not merely being bombastic when he spoke of 'the poor little English donkey ... who knew the right way home'. The Teheran and Cairo conferences in the winter of 1943 were the culmination of a prolonged debate. Other controversies would follow— the vapid arguments over ANVIL, the dissensions over Eisenhower's 'Broad Front' policy, the question of a single Land Force Commander in Europe, the ultimate dispute about Berlin. Yet all these were secondary issues. As the Allies entered 1944 the pattern for the defeat of Germany— if not of Japan—had been finally determined, and all subsequent disagreements were about details rather than essentials. If that pattern is carefully scrutinised it will be seen that it conforms with remarkable fidelity to the 'design and theme for bringing the war to a victorious end in a reasonable period' which Churchill drafted, alone, in his cabin on the *Duke of York* as he sailed towards ARCADIA.

24 *V.E. Day 1945. The victory broadcast*

9

The Return 1944

'I had a jolly day on Monday on the beaches and inland. There is a great mass of shipping extended more than fifty miles along the coast. . . . After doing much laborious duty we went and had a plug at the Hun from our destroyer, but although the range was 6000 yards he did not honour us with a reply.'

Churchill to Roosevelt, 14 June 1944

'I noticed that I no longer dried myself after my bath, but lay on the bed wrapped in my towel till I dried naturally.' Readers of Lord Moran's medical memoirs will be aware of the constant attention Churchill paid to his physical symptoms and of the anxieties and premonitions engendered by this obsessive surveillance. It was not, of course, the unfounded concern of a valetudinarian, nor did these anxieties, vivid though they might be, prevent him from facing his duties: Churchill's courage, as Lord Snow has remarked, did not exclude but could overcome fear. And when, on his return to Cairo from Teheran, Churchill observed that he was so weary that he was unable to rub himself down after a bath, there was every reason for misgiving. By the time he reached Carthage, on his way home, he had to send a message to Eisenhower that he was at the end of his tether. X-rays revealed pneumonia. 'The days passed in much discomfort. Fever flickered in and out.' But emergency action and the new drug M. and B. worked their miracle, and a week after his collapse on 12 December he had already had a long discussion with Alanbrooke and was pugnaciously minuting to the Chiefs of Staff in London:

There is no doubt that the stagnation of the whole campaign on the Italian front is becoming scandalous. The C.I.G.S.'s visit confirmed my worst forebodings. The total neglect to provide amphibious action on the Adriatic side and the failure to strike any similar blow on the west have been disastrous. None of the landing-craft in the Mediterranean have been put to the slightest use for three months. . . . There are few instances, even in this war, of such valuable forces being so completely wasted.

This was the first wave in a great flood of contentious debate about strategy in which Churchill would be immersed up to D Day and far beyond—an ever-widening debate, centred initially on SHINGLE (the landings at Anzio). It was extended and continued in the running controversy over ANVIL, of which it has been rightly observed that 'the fate of ANVIL may indeed be regarded as a barometer of strategic thought, tracing the results of events elsewhere that impinged immediately upon it'. Thereafter the flood became almost global in its range as Churchill committed himself to a ferocious and, as it proved, nugatory battle with his Chiefs of Staff about British policy in the Far East and the Pacific after the defeat of Germany—a battle in which the Prime Minister and his advisers came closer to an open break than at any other time in the whole course of the war.

Churchill, Alanbrooke, Eisenhower and Alexander, the four figures most directly involved, were all convinced of the paramount necessity for an amphibious outflanking operation, SHINGLE, whereby the German defences at Cassino could be turned and the road to Rome opened: but they were equally convinced that a weak assault, of less than two divisions, would be fatal. As usual the problem was to find enough landing craft for such a force within the restrictive limits imposed by the Americans on allied resources in the Mediterranean. In the event, 36,000 men and 3,000 vehicles were on shore by the evening of the first day at Anzio, 22 January—30 miles from Rome and 60 miles north of the Germans' mountain line. Even so this substantial corps and its reinforcements were nearly thrown back into the sea, and it was not until 4 June, 35 hours before the Normandy landings, that Mark Clark's troops finally rode into the Piazza Venezia.

A student of Churchill's military conduct of the war who consulted Sir Arthur Bryant's edition of the Alanbrooke papers for information about the Prime Minister's part in this enterprise would find himself misled. The C.I.G.S., who bore the burden of an Atlas during Churchill's absence and illness, not surprisingly convinced himself that the vision of Anzio and the action which made it possible were his and his alone—as the entry in his diary for 20 January implies.

> Oh! how I hope that the Rome amphibious operation will be a success. I feel a special responsibility for it as I resuscitated it after my visit to Italy. It may fail, but I know it was the right thing to do, to double the amphibious operation and carry on with the out-flanking plan.

But Bryant's glosses on Alanbrooke's self-communings, and his partisan suggestion that at this time Churchill, in his seventieth year and exhausted by sickness, 'found difficulty in concentrating and making up his mind', are contradicted by the documentary evidence. A review of this as quoted by Churchill himself in *The Second World War* and, more substantially, in the *Official History** shows that it was Churchill's own meticulous and remorseless examination of the shipping situation, his refusal to be deterred by pessimistic specialists or dubious Chiefs of Staff, which finally produced the armada on which SHINGLE was launched. It was he who pressed the issue home on the Americans, even though the Chiefs of Staff informed him, on 27 December, that 'we feel we should not conceal from you the difficulty we expect with the United States Chiefs of Staff, if we tell them frankly the true position as we see it'. It was the Prime Minister's personal message to Roosevelt (in which, as he says, he was 'careful to state the root fact bluntly'), that elicited the President's permissive signal of 28 December, beginning 'It is agreed to delay the departure of 56 L.S.T.s schedules for OVERLORD for mounting Anzio on January 20. . . .' Churchill, not his C.I.G.S., was the prime mover over SHINGLE: its near failure, and delayed success, were due to inadequacies of generalship beyond his control. A detached observer, indeed, might well consider that the record of his military judgement and persuasive negotiation between 12 December 1943, the onset of his pneumonia, and the start of SHINGLE on 20 January was an astonishing achievement for an aged man in his fourth year as War Lord.

The commitment of Anzio, particularly the unexpected delay in breaking out from the beachhead, had many consequences, and Churchill was compelled to accept cancellation or deferment of projects which in some cases he had cherished. Any lingering hopes of an attempt on Rhodes now faded: by early February the Chiefs of Staff were writing of the 'virtual abandonment of effort to get Turkey into the war as soon as possible'. In the Far East plans which Mountbatten had devised for PIGSTICK, an amphibious operation on a smaller scale than his ambitious BUCCANEER, were also frustrated. On 28 December, when Churchill received from Roosevelt the 'All Clear' for Anzio, he signalled to London 'I quite agree that it should be "Pigstuck" and not "Pigstick".' (But this, as will be seen, was *reculer pour mieux sauter*.) Most important of all, the stalemate of SHINGLE and at Monte Cassino created such vast demands for reinforcements and therefore shipping—in February a movement of 276,000 men and 34,000 vehicles was forecast during the next two months—that on 22 February General Wilson, the Commander-in-Chief, Mediterranean, informed the Chiefs of Staff: 'I recommend that ANVIL be cancelled'.

Here, at least, was something that Churchill could approve. While he

* See John Ehrman, *Grand Strategy*, Vol. V, pp. 214–221.

was convalescing at Marrakesh Montgomery looked in, *en route* to England and his OVERLORD command: on New Year's Eve Churchill handed him the COSSAC plan, about which Eisenhower had already warned Montgomery that he was unhappy. He studied it overnight and next morning gave Churchill a report which began: 'My first impression is that the present plan is impracticable.' The two commanders who would actually have to fight the battle had, in fact, reached the same conclusion as Churchill himself when he first examined Morgan's proposals at the time of the Quebec conference: the front of the OVERLORD assault must be extended, and the weight of the landings increased. The British Chiefs of Staff were already feeling a similar disquiet. But this wider front, these extra divisions implied more landing craft, more cargo vessels, more warships, more aircraft. How else, in January 1944, could they be furnished unless ANVIL were cancelled or postponed and the May date for OVERLORD, so firmly promised to Stalin, deferred?

By the time Churchill returned to London from the Mediterranean considerable progress had been made. Under Montgomery's impulsion an intensive review of the original OVERLORD project, by COSSAC himself and by the Chiefs of Staff, confirmed the new requirements. On 10 January Montgomery urged Eisenhower to 'hurl yourself into the contest and what we want, get for us'. By 23 January the Supreme Commander (who had long supported ANVIL) was so convinced that he signalled to the Combined Chiefs of Staff, his executive authority, that the OVER-LORD plan must be amplified; a reduced ANVIL must be merely retained as a threat; and, if necessary, OVERLORD itself must be put off for a month. (Churchill alone seems to have understood, at this stage, that the crucial factors of moon and tide meant that delay *must* entail a month's postponement.) Weeks of transatlantic argument followed: weeks which reflect most gravely on the military judgement of Marshall and his staff. The Americans, for whom a second front in northern France had long been Top Priority, were now struggling in defence of a subsidiary operation which could have no important immediate significance for OVERLORD while Churchill and the British Chiefs, the arch-advocates of a Mediterranean strategy, fought to ensure that the cross-Channel invasion might have a chance of success. Dr Johnson's principle applies (if a man is going to be hung in a fortnight it clears his mind wonderfully), for there can be little doubt that if Marshall had come to England as Supreme Commander, instead of Eisenhower, he too would have rapidly grasped the realities and turned against ANVIL.

Meanwhile the bitter and inconclusive conflict at Anzio and in the

Italian mountains dragged on, giving no hope of early results or a consequent fall-off in the demand for men and ships. There were simply not
enough to go round: but it was not until 24 March, after a second request
from General Wilson, that the Americans at last agreed to postpone
ANVIL until July and to transfer from the Mediterranean the extra
assault craft required for OVERLORD. Yet these dissensions between the
Allies were as nothing by comparison with what had been happening
between the British themselves. On 4 March General Ismay, Churchill's
shrewd and loyal Chief of Staff, wrote to him in confidence that

> ... we are faced with the practical certainty of a continued cleavage of
> opinion between the War Cabinet and their military advisers; nor can we
> exclude the possibility of resignation on the part of the latter. A breach of
> this kind, undesirable at any time, would be little short of catastrophic at the
> present juncture. OVERLORD is, in all conscience, a sufficiently hazardous
> operation. It must be given every chance.

When Ismay wrote 'the War Cabinet' he meant, of course, 'the Prime
Minister'. The ordinary citizen, remembering 1940, the cigars, the 'V'
signs, the rasping broadcasts, little realises that only three months before a
'D' Day which was the culmination of Churchill's achievement as a War
Lord he and his Chiefs of Staff, whose relationship had withstood so many
strains, were so perilously near to parting. In the end, moreover, their
schism proved to be about a non-event.

For this battle in London the background was a prolonged and dis-
couraging conflict in the Far East. The plans which Churchill and his
Chiefs had reluctantly accepted in 1943 for a major offensive to recover
North Burma were already hanging fire when the Japanese themselves
struck, ferociously, unexpectedly, and with initial success. A diversionary
attack in the Arakan opened in mid-February. This, however, was only
an overture to their main offensive which, starting on 12 March, had as
its objective the huge base areas of Imphal and Dimapur. Capture of these,
and further penetration westwards, would have had incalculable consequences not only for the British and Chinese forces on the Central and
Northern Fronts but also for the continuation, let alone the expansion of
the American air lift to China and, more importantly, for the political
situation in India—a powder barrel, which only awaited the lighting of its
fuse. Ultimately, of course, a combination of Slim's generalship and
Mountbatten's imperious grasp of authority brought victory out of defeat,
but even after the launching of OVERLORD on 6 June the issue on the
threshold of India remained uncertain.

Here, then, was a curious context, it might be thought—Normandy unconquered, the Indian frontier aflame—for a deadlock engagement between the Prime Minister and the Chiefs of Staff on British long-term strategy in the Far East. This, however, had already been treated by Churchill as a major issue at Quebec, and even during his convalescence in Africa signals were flying east to Mountbatten and north to Whitehall. On 19 January, immediately after his return to London, the Defence Committee was summoned and battle was joined.

At the time the issues involved seemed to be enormous. Churchill, still avid for landings in Sumatra, insisted that for at least the next 18 months the correct course was 'to keep the centre of gravity of the British war against Japan in the Bay of Bengal': as resources increased, particularly after the collapse of Germany, major amphibious operations should be undertaken against the Andamans, Sumatra and further to the east in the direction of Singapore and the China sea. Thus the great bases established in the Middle East and India would continue to be used productively. The threat of the Japanese main fleet, which on 24 February moved to Singapore, would be countered. But there was another consideration. As Prime Minister, if not as Minister of Defence, it was Churchill's duty in 1944 to be weighing with ever-increasing care the post-war political implications of each new military commitment. The strategy he now advocated had the virtue that it carried the British flag back into the conquered zones of the British Empire, and for this reason his colleagues in the War Cabinet solidly supported his proposals. The Foreign Office was particularly vehement, minuting on 21 February

> A strategy which until a later date leaves the Japanese virtually unassailed in those regions which mean most to the peoples of Asia and to the Japanese themselves will cast a considerable strain upon the already stretched endurance of the occupied territories and will materially retard their rehabilitation upon recovery ... if there is to be no major British role in the Far Eastern war, then it is no exaggeration to say that the solidarity of the British Commonwealth and its influence in the maintenance of peace in the Far East will be irretrievably damaged.

It is not surprising that Mountbatten, the Allied Supreme Commander in the Far East, held the same view and was prepared to implement it with specific plans.

But the Chiefs of Staff looked elsewhere. United, and buttressing their case with formidable technical arguments, they maintained that elements of the British Fleet should be dispatched forthwith to work with the Americans in the Pacific, and that thereafter, as the German war allowed, a considerable force of British divisions and aircraft should be built up in Australasia to press northwards 'on the left or southern flank of the main American advance against the Philippines, Formosa and ultimately Japan'. This entirely new theatre of war would be supplied from a transformed Australia in which great camps, training areas and administrative centres would be created, and by a large Fleet train which, on the American pattern in the Pacific, would constitute a seaborne mobile base.

Both sides were uncompromising. In the counter-thrust of argument the strengths and weaknesses of two incompatible propositions were rehearsed in long, careful and eloquent papers. By the beginning of March, as Ismay's tactful warning to the Prime Minister indicated, disagreement was reaching danger-point. Churchill might say or do something unforgivable or irrecoverable: the Chiefs of Staff might resign. Our knowledge of Hiroshima makes their dispute seem irrelevant, for in one convulsive second the atom bomb destroyed the premises on which the conflicting arguments were constructed. But to think so is to misuse hindsight. In the spring of 1944 the quest for the bomb was still at a critical stage. None of the small circle secretly aware of its progress would have dared to found a strategy on the certainty of its success. Indeed 'the design of the weapon was not frozen until March 1945 and even then feverish activity was necessary at Los Alamos to get the weapon ready for the test which had been scheduled for July'.* Both Churchill and his Chiefs thought, and were right to think, only in terms of conventional warfare.

On those terms, whether from the military or the political point of view, Churchill was more justified in his stance than were his chiefs. With hindsight, again, it can be argued that neither he nor the Foreign Office realised the extent to which the war had released and fostered aspirations in the Far East, Marxist, nationalist, anti-colonial, which no demonstration of British power could hope to restrain. Granted that, it may nevertheless be observed that the 'Indian Ocean' policy sponsored by the Prime Minister presented a better possibility of containing the post-war revolution than did the 'Pacific' strategy advocated by their military advisers. And from the strictly military angle it is difficult to estimate how the British might have gained in the Pacific a profit commensurate with the vast outlay of effort, men and resources such a strategy postulated. All the lines of advance from Australia examined by the Chiefs of Staff were eccentric to the true strategic objectives which, not unnaturally, were already the target of the United States. This was evident to the Americans.

* Margaret Gowing, *Britain and Atomic Energy, 1939–1945*, p. 369.

National pride and national self-interest inevitably conditioned their thinking: but Washington also wanted to defeat the Japanese as quickly as possible and to 'bring the boys home'. It is a rational assumption that if Roosevelt, the Pentagon and the U.S. Navy had believed a total British commitment in the Pacific to be essential for this purpose they would have demanded it with at least the energy expended in their pressure for OVERLORD.

Their attitude was soon discerned. The deadlock in London at the beginning of March led to the old diplomatic device of seeking further facts, and possible American reactions came first on the list. On 10 March, therefore, Churchill informed Roosevelt of the two irreconcilable policies under discussion and asked him formally if 'there is any specific American operation in the Pacific (a) before the end of 1944 or (b) before the summer of 1945 which would be hindered or prevented by the absence of a British Fleet detachment'. Three days later the President replied:

(a) There will be no specific operation in the Pacific during 1944 that would be adversely affected by the absence of a British Fleet detachment.

(b) It is not at the present time possible to anticipate with sufficient accuracy future developments in the Pacific to be certain that a British Fleet detachment will not be needed there during the year 1945 but . . . it is my personal opinion that unless we have unexpected bad luck in the Pacific your naval force will be of more value to our common effort by remaining in the Indian Ocean. . . .

This cold douche merely made Churchill more stubborn. He now switched his line of attack and sent to each of the Chiefs of Staff, as the heads of their different Service departments and not as members of an indivisible Committee, a *diktat* in which he instructed them that the Far East need now be considered only from the viewpoint of British interests and that 'I, therefore, feel it my duty, as Prime Minister and Minister of Defence, to give the following rulings . . .': in effect, that his 'Indian Ocean' policy must be pursued. A note in Alanbrooke's diary summarises the immediate result:

March 21st. We discussed at the C.O.S. meeting how best to deal with Winston's last document. We cannot accept it as it stands, and it would be better if we all three resigned sooner than accept his solution.*

* In the spring of 1944 Alanbrooke, Portal and Cunningham, like Churchill, were fine-drawn by years of war and the immense pressures of OVERLORD. The mental states of all four must account, to some degree, for this unfortunate controversy. It is a matter for speculation as to which side would have first retreated—bearing in mind the appalling consequences for Britain of a resignation. No doubt the withdrawal would have been simultaneous.

Yet catastrophe was averted. The same day a statement arrived from the American Joint Chiefs of Staff that 'the requirements for a major amphibious operation in the South East Asia Theatre this year are not in sight': for them the opening up of north Burma and increased aid to the Chinese remained the outstanding objectives. This was a turning-point. The aims of both Churchill and his Chiefs were defeated in the short term, just as the course of history was to frustrate them in the long term. For as negotiations continued throughout 1944 the divergent but grandiose policies of the contestants in Whitehall were gradually whittled down, and for Britain the upshot was something intended by neither party—the brilliant destruction by General Slim of a Japanese army amid the jungles, plains and rivers of *central* Burma. The great debate over an 'Indian Ocean' or a 'Pacific' policy was a void parenthesis in the effective conduct of the war, and Slim's victory was parenthetical to the broad flow of military thinking in England. For Churchill the triumph of 14 Army was an uncovenanted blessing.

Amid all these tensions, however, an inner harmony persisted. The business of war continued to be prosecuted—and as D Day approached that business was urgent. Churchill never forgot that the function of a dynamo is to produce useful motion, not to spin in a vacuum: nor did he fail to retain the loyalty of a disputatious staff. Early in May, after the long haul of the Far Eastern debate, Alanbrooke took a midnight cup of soup with him, alone, at Chequers, in 'the little study where the secretaries work'. Churchill unburdened himself. Neither he nor Roosevelt, he said, were the men they had been: uncharacteristically, he would have been willing to spend the whole day in bed. He then told Alanbrooke how, in the view of the Defence Committee and the War Cabinet, they could not have had a better C.I.G.S. After the war Alanbrooke wrote a gloss on his diary entry for this night which summarises the point to perfection.

> I did not often get any form of appreciation of my work from him and therefore treasured it all the more on these rare occasions. He was an astounding mixture, could drive you to complete desperation and to the brink of despair for weeks on end, and then he would ask you to spend a couple of hours or so alone with him and would produce the most homely and attractive personality. All that unrelenting tension was temporarily relaxed, he ceased to work himself into one fury or another, and you left him with the feeling that you would do anything within your power to help him to carry the stupendous burden he had shouldered.

It was with a similar desire to provide reassurance after conflict that Churchill signalled:

Prime Minister to General Marshall (Washington)   *11.3.44*

 Since I got home from Marrekesh I have looked carefully into the following aspects of 'Overlord', namely:

(i) 'Mulberry' and all connected with it;

(ii) airborne assault lift, including method of glider attack;

(iii) inshore bombarding squadrons; and

(iv) Air Command arrangements.

I have presided at a series of meetings at which either Ike or Bedell has been present, and I am satisfied that everything is going on well. Ike and Bedell will probably tell you they are well pleased. I am hardening very much on this operation as the time approaches, *in the sense of wishing to strike if humanly possible, even if the limiting conditions we laid down at Moscow are not exactly fulfilled.** I hope a chance may come for us to have a talk before long. Every good wish.

This was not bombast. It was Churchill's great gift, once argument was over and a decision reached, to be able to forget the past and bring his energies to bear with an extreme concentration on what must next be done. The feature of the first six months of 1944 is that OVERLORD had passed the stage of summit conferences: it was now a matter of individual commanders, staff officers, technicians making ready within their special areas of responsibility. Indeed, if Churchill is to be criticised for boasting, it is for his statement in *The Second World War* that in January he set up an OVERLORD committee (to replace the Anti-U-boat Warfare Committee), as though this had provided some constructive mechanism for high-level control during the final months: in fact, the committee only met eight times during February, March and April. Where Churchill was invaluable was as a progress-chaser. As the preliminaries to the great venture advanced his restless but informed intelligence played over the whole field,

> *This way and that dividing the quick mind*

and with a dart here, a probe there, a minute, an objurgation, a nod of approval, he removed bottlenecks and hastened growth. In 1944, as in 1940, there was a debit side. His enthusiasm irritated, confused, impeded: he could be stupid, unjust, blind. But the price was small compared with the profit.

 His minutes before the Battle for France are as illuminating as those during the Battle of Britain. A glance through these written between

* Author's italics.

February and April, for example, reveals him asking: Why not shift three armoured divisions secretly into Morocco and throw them ashore at Bordeaux about D Day+20? What about an embassy for Cuba . . . 'great offence will be given if all the others have it and this large, rich, beautiful island, the home of the cigars, is denied'? There must be no national day of prayer for OVERLORD . . . 'we have to be very much on our guard against depressing the troops'. Why is the rubbish dump at Chalfont St Giles still there? What is the output of the new insecticide D.D.T.? Are U-boat prisoners now different in quality from earlier ones? Congratulations on new fog-dispersal equipment. We seem to have plenty of gas shells. And (to the Minister of Food), cut out silly prosecutions of little bakers 'by purging the regulations from petty, meticulous, arrogant officialism'. He could find time, too, for those acts which riveted a man to his side. On 2 February the only son of Harry Hopkins, a private in the U.S. Marines, was killed on Kwajalein Atoll in the Pacific. Shortly afterwards Hopkins, then in the Mayo Clinic, received *via* Roosevelt a beautifully lettered scroll, inscribed

> Stephen Peter Hopkins
> Age 18
> 'Your son, my lord, has paid a soldier's debt:
> He only lived but till he was a man;
> The which no sooner had his prowess confirm'd
> In the unshrinking station where he fought,
> But like a man he died.'
> To Harry Hopkins from Winston S. Churchill
> 13th February, 1944

The fear that thousands of other American and British soldiers might be similarly and perhaps vainly slaughtered on the beaches of Normandy, ever-present in Churchill's mind during these penultimate months, was multiplied by the menace of Hitler's secret weapons. How seriously these were treated may be estimated from the fact that in the Anglo-American CROSSBOW offensive against suspected installations in Northern France no less than 9,000 bomber sorties were flown between January and March —with good reason. On 1 March the directorate of the flying-bomb organisation met in Paris to play a 'war-game', in which bomber squadrons, rockets and flying-bombs were to be simultaneously launched against England at midnight in a sustained six-hours' attack. Colonel Wachtel, who commanded the flying-bomb Regiment, estimated that he would have released 672–840 bombs against London and 96–120 against Bristol. This was optimistic: when at last, at 4.18 a.m. on 13 June, the first 'incident' occurred at Gravesend, only 10 bombs were despatched in 24 hours—to be followed by 244 the next day. Still, the potential scale of assault was daunting, and there were other threats. At Mimoyecques, for example (only 95 miles from mid-London), 5,000 engineers under the Todt organisation were constructing an immense concrete structure containing 25 gun barrels each 416 feet long, capable at a maximum rate of landing one shell on London every 12 seconds.

Nobody in Whitehall could know that the Mimoyecques battery would be neutralised by the Germans themselves through bungling over the ballistics of the shell. No one could guess that German maladministration, as much as the Allied counter-efforts, would reduce the V1 (flying-bomb) and V2 (rocket) offensives to manageable proportions. Little could be done about the latter until the launching-sites were over-run: but the prolonged intelligence investigations and active measures against the flying-bomb, with which Churchill was intimately identified in all their stages, constitute one of the most remarkable British achievements in the whole course of the war. Under General Pile, C.-in-C. Anti-Aircraft Command, the elaborate DIVER plan for defeating the offensive was ready by April, and Eisenhower's appreciation of 28 March, never falsified in the actual battle, is Pile's accolade. The Supreme Commander reported:

1. That CROSSBOW attack would not preclude the launching of the OVERLORD assault from the south coast ports as now planned, and that the probable incidence of casualties does not make it necessary to move the assault-forces west of Southampton.
2. Although some interference with the loading of shipping and crafts must be expected, it is not sufficient to justify plans for the displacement of shipping and craft from these areas.

One instance will suffice to indicate Churchill's value as a progress-chaser. The flying-bomb was a robot, and the best answer seemed to be a robot defence. The Americans had evolved a special radar device, S.C.R. 584, which, properly linked with predictor and gun, meant that in an anti-aircraft battery instruments and guns could be aimed and fired by remote control, avoiding manual operation. 'Without this equipment', Pile has stated in his memoirs,* 'it would have been impossible to defeat the flying-bomb'. He describes a meeting of the Night Air Defence Committee at which he requested Churchill's support in obtaining supplies of S.C.R. 584. Cherwell was antipathetic, arguing that while heavy bombers

* General Sir Frederick Pile, *Ack-Ack*, p. 315.

were essential and should have priority in the technical field, A.A. was of minor importance. Churchill, however, insisted on hearing Pile's case. 'I want the General to tell us what equipment he wants.' The consequence was that the Prime Minister ordered the War Office to do everything possible to secure S.C.R. 584, an intervention of critical significance for the ultimate success of DIVER.*

Considering the stresses to which he was subjected, and the emotional nature of the occasion, it is not surprising that when Churchill attended the momentous meeting at St Paul's School on 7 April, Good Friday, at which Montgomery and the senior OVERLORD commanders outlined their plans, he looked, according to one eye-witness, 'puffy and dejected and his eyes were red'. His immediate reaction may be considered irrelevant or perceptive. 'The amount of paraphernalia sounded staggering, and reminded one of Admiral Andrew Cunningham's story of dental chairs being landed at Algiers in the first flight of operation TORCH.' Was he unreasonable to be staggered at the revelation that on D+20 there would be one vehicle (including guns, armoured cars and tanks) ashore for every 4.77 men? Churchill never grasped the necessary proportions of men and metal in modern technological warfare, nor, perhaps, could he or anyone else visualise how Allied air superiority over the Normandy beachhead would be so absolute that the vehicular ratio could safely have been doubled. What stuck in his mind was Anzio—the 'stranded whale'. He recalled the stockpiling ashore, the lethargic movement inland, the lightning German reaction—and the stalemate. Would this be repeated in France?

He insisted on a meeting with Montgomery at his headquarters on 19 May. 'This interview', he subsequently wrote, 'has been misrepresented'. Churchill denied either that Montgomery threatened to resign or that he himself demanded and was not allowed to address the General's staff. In 1969 Montgomery told the author during an interview that Churchill did indeed wish to address his staff on what he held to be the disproportions in the loading scales for the landings. 'I took him into my study', he said. 'I sat at my desk. That seemed the proper arrangement. I told him that he could not address my staff. He became tearful, and gave in.' Montgomery's aptitude for self-dramatisation is as developed as Churchill's for self-

* 'Only when in 1944 the much more accurate American 10 c.m. set came into operation and was linked with the new American electronic predictor was a really adequate radar A.A. system attained. This combination, together with the proximity fuse, came just in time to compete brilliantly with the V1 menace in the summer of 1944.' P. M. S. Blackett, *Studies of War*, p. 209. The proximity fuse of course, was a direct consequence of Churchill's decision to dispatch the Tizard Mission to the United States in September 1940.

justification: the truth, perhaps, lies midway. In any event, after dinner that evening Churchill wrote in Montgomery's autograph book

On the verge of the greatest adventure with which these pages have dealt, I record my confidence that all will be well, and that the organisation and equipment of the Army will be worthy of the valour of the soldiers and the genius of their chief.

He tried hard to share the adventure himself. Nothing except his King could have prevented Churchill from sailing in a cruiser with the assault forces on D Day, but he was out-manoeuvred. An appeal reached him from Buckingham Palace on 2 June. 'Please consider my own position. I am a younger man than you, I am a sailor, and as King I am head of all these Services. There is nothing I would like better than to go to sea, but I have agreed to stay at home; is it fair that you should then do exactly what I should have liked to do myself?' Still, a week later the Prime Minister himself went to sea, and had 'a jolly day on the beaches'.

Churchill's policies in regard to a Second Front had an inner consistency, even though expediency or wayward emotion made him seem Laodicean or reluctant. They were misunderstood at the time and have often been misrepresented since—particularly in the United States. It is appropriate, therefore, to end this chapter with some observations by one of the most distinguished of the American official historians.

Looking back one can now see that from the first the British had taken an impressive number of practical measures that paved the way to success for the invasion of France. If they refused SLEDGEHAMMER, they did not flinch from undertaking alone the bloody cross-channel raid on Dieppe as early as August, 1942. It was a failure. But the British diligently wrung from the experience lessons that were valuable in making OVERLORD successful. It was the British who invented and first engineered the instrument of war, the LST, that made a cross-Channel assault in force a feasible military operation. It was Mr. Churchill who dreamed up, and the bold ingenuity of his engineers that constructed, the indispensable offshore harbours by which the Allied expeditionary force was supplied over the beaches throughout the summer and fall of 1944. General Morgan (COSSAC) was a British officer, completely loyal to the concept of a cross-Channel invasion. ... From QUADRANT on it was Mr. Churchill and his military chiefs, and not the Americans, who urged the need for a stronger cross-Channel assault, and certainly they pulled their full weight in the provision of ocean shipping and other measures to insure a build-up for the invasion that would make it decisive. ... In short, it can be plausibly argued that it was the British (and Mr. Roosevelt) who are to be credited with the realistic approach to OVERLORD that insured its success.[*]

[*] Kent Roberts Greenfield, *American Strategy in World War II*, p. 41.

10

This Happy Conclusion 1944-1945

'In the present war indeed there were at first but small hopes that we should ever be able to bring things to this happy conclusion. Not that we were under any apprehensions about the Justness of our Cause; but from the mighty Powers we had to contend with there was some room to doubt that we should not be able to make the glorious figures which the Event has produced. But we see that the battle is not always to the strong, and that true valour, when exerted in a righteous cause, and properly supported by wise counsels, and unanimity of the subjects, which are the sinews of war, will face any dangers and flourish under the severest apprehensions.'

Sermon by the Reverend William Maugham in celebration of Wolfe's victory at Quebec, 1759

In his diary for 13 August 1944 Major-General Sir John Kennedy,* Director of Military Operations at the War Office from 1940 to 1944, noted:

Winston remarked the other day that the operations of June bear the stamp of a great design to anyone not acquainted with their inner history. The Anzio landing came in as a great aid to the capture of Rome, and the capture of Rome (on 4th June) fitted beautifully, in the end, into the June operations in Normandy, although it was meant to take place much earlier.

This was typically Churchillian. A profound believer in predestination for himself, he was always conscious of the rôle of contingency in military affairs: this, indeed, was why, as a general principle throughout the war, he was reluctant over committing his country to binding agreements about long-term strategies. Instinct impelled him to seek loopholes and *caveats*. And if the pattern of events preceding D Day had an apparent Grand Design which was spurious, so, too, the turn of affairs after the Normandy invasion followed no predictable course. Who on 6 June would have forecast, for example, that Bomber Command would soon be ranging almost freely *by day* over Germany or that Slim would destroy a Japanese army on the banks of the Irrawaddy? Who in the audience for Montgomery's confident exposition of his plans in St Paul's School on Good

* Sir John Kennedy, *The Business of War*, p. 338.

Friday could have imagined that the time would come when Eisenhower would sit in a headquarters in France studying his signal to Marshall which, if despatched, meant the removal of Montgomery from command? How few could have prophesied Hiroshima?

Once D Day was over and the Allied armies were firmly established in Normandy the critical question, so far as Churchill was concerned, was whether he would keep his nerve and trust his generals—particularly Montgomery. A *British* officer in charge of the climacteric battle: here was an immense temptation for a War Lord to intervene. Recollection of what happened to Wavell and Auchinleck—the misunderstandings, the badgering, the peremptory signals—is a reminder that if Churchill had been allowed to misread the method behind Montgomery's conduct of the Normandy campaign he might well have erupted. Possibilities and pressures abounded. Until the American avalanche was set free to roll forward under Patton there was every inducement for the Prime Minister to protest at an apparent stagnation of his own 21 Army Group around Caen. It was in his nature to demand offensives, advances, captured cities whose names he could proudly proclaim in the House of Commons. The savage denunciation in the American press of Montgomery's alleged lethargy: the doubting Thomases on Eisenhower's staff (including British officers like Tedder): Eisenhower's own deep incomprehension of Montgomery's purpose—these were powerful forces, liable to trigger off a Churchillian detonation. But nothing untoward occurred.

It is true that during the weeks between D Day and the retreat of the Germans beyond the Seine Churchill had much to distract him. He was anxious about Alexander's progress northwards from Rome: about the continuing debate with his Chiefs of Staff over policy in the Far East: about the actual flying-bomb and imminent rocket offensives. But many preoccupations in 1940 had not prevented him from seeking to impose his will on his Commander-in-Chief in France. The truth is that among Alanbrooke's finest achievements must be rated the fact that in the summer of 1944 he kept Churchill calm about Montgomery. His patient exposition to the Prime Minister of what the General was attempting from day to day, and his careful coaching of Montgomery himself in how to avert Churchill's anxieties by keeping him informed and encouraged, were masterpieces of military diplomacy. The danger-point came at the end of July—just before the American breakout at St Lô—when, as Eisenhower's Chief of Staff Bedell Smith noted, the Supreme Commander wanted 'an all-out coordinated attack by the entire Allied line, which would at last put our forces in decisive motion. He was up and down the line like a football coach, exhorting everyone to aggressive action'. Alanbrooke's diary reads:

> *July 26th*. At 4 p.m. I was sent for by Winston and kept for an hour. Eisenhower had been lunching with him and had again run down Montgomery and described his stickiness and the reaction in the American papers. The old story again: 'H.Q. was sparing British forces at the expense of the Americans, who were having all the casualties.'
>
> However, Winston was in a good mood and receptive to argument. He even said that on all military matters I was his *alter ego*! In the end I was asked to dine tomorrow night to meet Eisenhower and Bedell Smith.

It was not Montgomery but the Americans who caused Churchill to lose his head. Throughout June and July, with the Normandy battle unresolved and the Italian front paralysed, the feeling in London intensified that if ever ANVIL had a *rationale* this was no longer the case: that sustained pressure on the Germans in Italy would have a more immediate value for OVERLORD than the doubtful effect, inevitably delayed, of fresh landings in the South of France. The American Joint Chiefs of Staff remained adamant for ANVIL. Churchill tackled Roosevelt on 1 July with a long letter which mingled logic and emotion in his most skilful vein, but the President's reply next day was unyielding: 'I always think of my early geometry: "A straight line is the shortest distance between two points." ' After this classic summary of American strategic philosophy the view of the more powerful ally prevailed, and the Combined Chiefs of Staff sent General Wilson a plain statement: 'ANVIL will be launched at the earliest possible date. You will use every effort to meet a target date of 15 August. . . .' It seemed that no more could be done.

Churchill disagreed—allowing pique and frustration to lead him into one of his most impetuous and ill-considered propositions. He told his Chiefs of Staff that 'an intense impression must be made upon the Americans that we have been ill-treated and are furious'. The judgement of a War Lord should never be debauched by anger. But first he became confused. Alanbrooke wrote in his diary on 4 August:

> Today Eisenhower has asked for the famous South of France landing to be cancelled and that same force to be transferred to Brittany instead.

This was a Churchillian fantasy. On 5 August, in fact, the Prime Minister went down to Eisenhower's H.Q. at Portsmouth and spent six hours trying to make him agree that DRAGOON (as ANVIL had now been re-christened) should be finally abandoned and the assault shifted to the west coast of France around Brest and Lorient. 'Ike said No', his A.D.C. recalled, 'continued saying "No" all afternoon, and ended saying "No" in every form of the English language at his command'. On the 9th Churchill again attacked the Supreme Commander at 10 Downing Street, even declaring that if DRAGOON was launched 'I might have to go to the King and lay down the mantle of my high office'. But Roosevelt, now far away in the Pacific, stood firm, and on 15 August the landings took place, observed by a sardonic Churchill from the destroyer *Kimberley*.

> As far as I could see or hear not a shot was fired either at the approaching flotillas or on the beaches. . . . On the way back I found a lively novel, *Grand Hotel*, in the Captain's cabin, and this kept me in good temper till I got back to the Supreme Commander and the Naval Commander-in-chief, who had passed an equally dull day sitting in the stern cabin.

Here, however, was no laughing matter. Whatever the merits or demerits of DRAGOON, to propose on its eve that a modern amphibious operation, with its infinite complexities, should be shifted 1,600 miles against targets whose defences and future usefulness had not been properly evaluated was to abdicate responsibility. It is astonishing that the Chiefs of Staff should have supported Churchill in his folly. Wedded to incorrect suspicions in Washington that the British were striving to preserve armies in Italy for politically-determined ventures in the Balkans (whereas Alexander and Churchill intended to make for Vienna *via* the Julian Alps), the affair of DRAGOON and the Brittany ports only increased transatlantic doubts over the integrity of their allies. The fear that the British would always warp strategy to suit their self-interest was not dead, and events in North West Europe would continue to reveal its vitality. The Germans, indeed, had scarcely been pushed out of Normandy before another controversy began—limited in its scope at first, but ultimately expanding to dangerous and almost disastrous proportions. This was the famous issue of a Single Thrust or a Broad Front.

A distinct thread runs through the story of the campaign in North West Europe from the time of the Seine crossing right up to the final days in front of Berlin. Its origin may be found in a flaw in the COSSAC plan for OVERLORD and the consequences of the command arrangements for the operation. Inevitably, neither COSSAC nor those who subsequently refined his plan could look much further than the Normandy battlefield: the way was thus left open for dispute about what to do next. At the same time the reasonable provision whereby Montgomery commanded all the land forces, both British and American, for the effective period of the battle, and Eisenhower then assumed overall command (with Montgomery and Bradley under him as peers in charge of their respective army groups), made it only too possible for a man like Montgomery, self-sure, insensitive and ambitious, to feel a profound sense of rejection and a determination to re-establish himself in the top seat.

The argument therefore began with a technical disagreement between Montgomery and Eisenhower about the way the Allies should drive east. During August Montgomery started to press on the Supreme Commander his private proposal that all priorities of supply should be given to a compact body of 40 divisions, drawn from both his own 21 Army Group and Bradley's 12 Group, which should force its way in a single thrust past the left flank of the Ardennes, taking the Ruhr in its stride, and make for Berlin *via* the open country of northern Germany. The force should be under a single commander—preferably himself, though he was prepared to accept Bradley. But nothing would persuade Eisenhower to ground American forces on his right wing to facilitate a 40-divisional drive on his left. Instead, he insisted on a two-pronged advance, one prong to be driven along the line advocated by Montgomery and the other to be aimed due eastwards, to the south of the Ardennes, the object being to enter Germany *via* the Saar. On 29 August he sent Montgomery and Bradley a long letter in which he defined his intentions with uncompromising clarity. This was the core of a controversy which swayed back and forth during the coming months, reaching a peak of intensity when Hitler launched his Ardennes offensive and breaking out again during the last weeks of the European campaign. Moreover, what began as a genuine disagreement between commanders in the field about a correct strategy broadened into debates over the re-introduction of a single controller of the land armies, and in this way a battlefield dispute reached into areas of high policy and entered the most sensitive areas of Anglo–American accord.

Though Churchill and the Chiefs of Staff were naturally aware of what was happening, in its earlier stages they held aloof.

> The Combined Chiefs of Staff were not called on officially to take notice of the divergence of opinion. Despite the size and gravity of the issue, it was not indeed by its nature a matter for their intervention. The alternatives referred solely to a plan of campaign whose object and shape they had already approved, and involved faces already within the theatre, which no action of theirs could reinforce immediately. While both sets of Chiefs of Staff, and the Prime Minister, were informed personally of the discussion, and while they both followed it with keen interest, they were not therefore in any way implicated in the result. It is indeed a good illustration, on the largest scale,

of the type of circumstance dividing the responsibilities of a theatre from those of the central Command.*

As the months passed, however—with Arnhem a disappointment, Antwerp still unusable as a port, and the Allied army groups appearing, as a result of Eisenhower's Broad Front strategy, to be stretched in an impotent line along the German frontier—impatience in London inevitably increased. Montgomery's undiplomatic advocacy of his case steadily embittered his relations with Eisenhower. As the idea emerged of interposing a competent officer between the Supreme Commander and his armies London had to consider what practical action to take over a matter which immediately affected relations with Washington. And there were deeper issues. For Churchill and the British administration the apparently flagging advance in Europe was more menacing than for the Americans. Their country's economy was stretched to the limit, and its manpower reserves were nil— one infantry division, indeed, had to be broken up after Normandy to provide reinforcements for others. Moreover, they had a political as well as a military purpose in favouring a thrust to Berlin *via* northern Germany under, if possible, Montgomery. This would mean, for example, a speedy liberation of Holland (for whom Britain felt a large responsibility), and seizure of the V2 sites; a clearance of the German naval bases and harbours (of prime concern to Britain); and (of immense importance for Churchill), a British presence in the German capital before the Russians arrived.

Nevertheless, until the last phase of the war Churchill was temperate. He never went as far as Alanbrooke and Montgomery in their contemptuous (and unjust) dismissal of Eisenhower as militarily inept. He did not particularly favour the notion of an overall ground commander. He was ready, in view of his great partiality for Alexander, to ventilate the idea that Tedder should be brought back to the Air Staff in London and that Alexander should be called from the Mediterranean to replace him as Eisenhower's Deputy. But he never became militant. It was Hitler, indeed, who temporarily resolved the whole dispute in December by launching his secretly assembled Panzer Army through the Ardennes.

At dawn on 16 December the problem was instantly converted from how to advance into Germany to how to deal with advancing Germans. Churchill wrote to Smuts: 'I spoke to Eisenhower on the telephone during the afternoon of the 20th and suggested that he give to Montgomery the whole command north of the break-through, and to Omar Bradley everything south of the break-through, keeping control himself of the concerted

* Ehrman, *op. cit.*, p. 381.

operation. He replied that he had issued orders exactly on these lines in the morning.' Circumstances thus created the very conditions Montgomery and his masters desired: but in spite of his genuine contribution to victory in the Battle of the Bulge Montgomery threw the opportunity away. He had been warned by Alanbrooke.

> Events and enemy action have forced on Eisenhower the setting up of a more satisfactory system of command. I feel it is most important that you should not even in the slightest degree appear to rub this undoubted fact in to anyone at SHAEF or elsewhere. *Any remarks you may make are bound to come to Eisenhower's ears sooner or later and that may make it more difficult to ensure that this new set-up for Command remains even after the present emergency has passed.**

Montgomery unwisely went his own way. A letter to Eisenhower at the end of December, insubordinate in tone, re-iterated his conviction that *all* available offensive power should be assigned to the northern line of advance, under a single commander. He followed this with the notorious press conference at which he appeared to arrogate to himself the main credit for success in the Ardennes battle. The situation was swept out of Churchill's hand. Montgomery's Chief of Staff, de Guingand, described in 1964† how, sensing an emergency, he flew back to SHAEF in France to find Eisenhower checking a signal he was about to despatch to Marshall informing his chief that he could no longer work with Montgomery. 'I was stunned by what I read. In very direct language, it made it crystal-clear that a crisis of the first magnitude was indeed here.' De Guingand's diplomacy stopped the signal. Had it been sent Churchill would have had to face a crux. Only he and Roosevelt were competent to cope—and perhaps not even they. In any case Marshall was well aware of these tensions, and on 30 December he informed Eisenhower that to give a British general command of considerable American forces would be unacceptable: the President, he himself and the whole of America had complete confidence in Eisenhower's handling of the campaign. Thus it was that when, in the spring, Churchill and the British once again came into conflict with Eisenhower over his strategy in regard to Berlin, the Supreme Commander was in an unassailable position.

Nevertheless, the Battle of the Bulge had illustrated Churchill's possession of a War Lord's basic requirement, the gift of being right about essentials. It is against this that one must weigh such incidental lunacies as his attempt to shift DRAGOON more or less overnight from the

* Author's italics.
† Major-General Sir Francis de Guingand, *Generals at War*, p. 106 foll.

Riviera to Brittany. For in the autumn of 1944, indeed until the failure of the attempt to cross the Rhine at Arnhem, a mood of high optimism spread through the Allied command. The American Chiefs of Staff were affected. On 7 September Alanbrooke informed Churchill that though the British Chiefs 'had not ignored the possibility that German resistance would be prolonged into the winter', they were 'influenced by the optimistic Report which the Joint Intelligence Sub-Committee had just completed'.* But the Prime Minister's realism made him less credulous. His comments on the Report concluded with: '*It is at least as likely that Hitler will be fighting on January 1st as that he will collapse before then.*' Apart from Cherbourg and Arromanches, he pointed out, the Allies lacked harbours. The Scheldt was still to be cleared. Lorient, St Nazaire, Bordeaux were uncaptured. Will the Allies be able to advance through the Siegfried Line? Will the Germans withdraw from Italy? Will they pull back their mass of divisions from the Baltic States into the Reich? 'The fortifying and consolidated effect of a stand on the frontier of the native soil should not be underrated.' This view, he recalled in his memoirs, was unhappily to be justified.

The Report of the J.I.S. was received as Churchill and his advisers were sailing once again for Quebec. This mid-September meeting of the Prime Minister, the President and the Combined Chiefs of Staff, OCTAGON, was the last of the summit conferences primarily devoted to the conduct of the war. At Yalta military matters were peripheral; at Potsdam the problem was the war's aftermath—the consequences, as Churchill wrote to Truman in June 1945, of 'bringing Soviet power into the heart of Western Europe and the descent of an iron curtain between us and everything to the eastward'. Yet even before OCTAGON the shadow of the iron curtain was falling. The brutal refusal of the Russians to support the August rising of the Polish Home Army in Warsaw had struck a sinister note of warning for Churchill—far louder than for Roosevelt. On the night of 4 September (the eve of his departure for OCTAGON), a Cabinet meeting was held to discuss the implications of Stalin's attitude. 'I do not remember', Churchill observed, 'any occasion when such deep anger was shown by all our members, Tory, Labour, Liberal alike. I should have liked to say, "We are sending our aeroplanes to land in your territory, after delivering supplies to Warsaw. If you do not treat them properly all convoys will be stopped from this moment by us." ' But the war was still there. Russian offensives on the eastern front would be critical for the

---

* This Report, and Churchill's reply, are in Ehrman, *op. cit.*, p. 398 foll. Churchill quotes his reply in *The Second World War*, Vol. VI, p. 170.

success of Allied arms in the west, and Stalin's promise of intervention against Japan was on record. In the event, therefore, Anglo-American support for the Poles consisted of no more than vain protests to Moscow and the useless loss of aircraft on gallant supply-dropping missions over Warsaw.

But at Quebec, and thereafter, Churchill's attitude towards immediate military strategies was profoundly affected by his fears about Russian post-war policy. It was thus both a surprise and a satisfaction to discover during OCTAGON that the Americans—even Admiral King—far from requiring withdrawal of their forces from Italy were prepared to accept an advance into the Po valley and amphibious operations in Istria. For Churchill this meant Vienna. Without any difficulty, also, the direction of the strategic air forces was removed from Eisenhower (whose OVERLORD mission was now fulfilled), and restored to the Combined Chiefs of Staff with, as in the past, Portal and Spaatz acting as their executive agents. For Churchill this meant the restoration of a proper freedom of action to Bomber Command.

As was now usual, the campaigns against Japan caused most debate. By September Churchill and his Chiefs had composed their differences, to the point of agreeing a directive to Mountbatten (which laid down that his primary object was the recapture of Burma, subject to the safeguarding of the air and land communications with China), and a decision to send to the Pacific only a fleet and an air component. In Burma Operation CAPITAL, the conquest of the north with exploitation south towards Mandalay, and DRACULA, an amphibious assault on Rangoon, were to be completed by 15 March, before the 1945 monsoon, thus preparing the way for a possible move towards Malaya after the anticipated collapse of Germany. The Americans readily accepted the proposals about Burma, but, once again, were obstinately reluctant to allow the British to share in the Pacific the main final engagements with Japan. Admiral King and his colleagues thought these were their private preserve. Just as Churchill and Alanbrooke failed to understand, over ANVIL, that behind the American strategic arguments lay a passionate desire to get into Europe the divisions piled up in the United States, and just as Montgomery failed to grasp that Eisenhower's refusal to allow him full priority for a single thrust was predetermined by knowledge that American public opinion would never accept it, so the Joint Chiefs of Staff insufficiently recognised that for Britain a presence at the defeat of Japan was a matter of *amour propre*. It was Churchill who, by extracting from Roosevelt an admission that 'he would like to see the British fleet wherever and whenever possible', provided the lever which at last enabled Alanbrooke and his colleagues to secure a definite commitment, formally enunciated by the Combined Chiefs of Staff: 'Agreed that the British fleet should participate in the main operations against Japan in the Pacific.'

Once OCTAGON had set a seal on blueprints for the last phases of the Allied campaigns in the west and the east, Churchill's contribution to the higher direction of the war was virtually completed. The rest lay with the generals. After the Ardennes battle had brought to a head the Eisenhower/ Montgomery dissension the atmosphere improved. There was a final flurry when, to the Americans' annoyance, the Chiefs of Staff re-opened the question of command. The idea of an overall land forces commander was still unacceptable. Churchill intervened with Roosevelt, and a possible solution appeared to be the replacement of Tedder by Alexander—whom Eisenhower, like Churchill, would have welcomed. Even so, the Supreme Commander was definite that Alexander's rôle as Deputy would not give him a special responsibility for land operations. This prolonged controversy, however, suddenly terminated when Montgomery decided that the present structure of command was satisfactory, and preparations now went steadily forward for a spring crossing of the Rhine. In Italy Alexander was left with his multi-national army to fight the winter, the mountains, and the unyielding Germans. The matters abroad in which Churchill became personally involved—Tito and the future of Yugoslavia, the Christmas complications in Athens, Yalta in February—were all, in one way and other, about the cold war of the coming peace. But he was determined, even if it was for the last time, to share once again the heat of the battlefield.

Whatever may be said pejoratively about Churchill's romanticism there is much in favour of a War Lord whose imagination can contemplate, as a consummation of his life, death in the front line on the eve of victory. Some may consider this a childish whimsy: others as quintessential, the natural aspiration of a cavalier spirit. Alanbrooke knew what was involved. On 22 March he wrote in his diary: 'I start off with P.M. on this visit to see the Rhine crossing. I am not happy about the trip; he will be difficult to manage and has no business to be going. All he will do is to endanger his life unnecessarily. However, nothing on earth will stop him!' On the banks of the Rhine Churchill's party was observed by the Germans as they examined the remains of the shattered bridge at Wesel. They were on the front of the American General Simpson, who went up to Churchill and said: 'Prime Minister, there are snipers in front of you; they are shelling both sides of the bridge and now they have started shelling the road behind you. I cannot accept the responsibility for your being here and must ask you to come away.' At which, Alanbrooke recalled,

> the look on Winston's face was just like that of a small boy being called away from his sand-castles on the beach by his nurse! He put both his arms round one of the twisted girders of the bridge and looked over his shoulder at Simpson with pouting mouth and angry eyes. Thank heaven he came away quietly.

Unfortunately the crossing of the Rhine, like the crossing of the Seine, was a victory which fathered a controversy. On their way to the Yalta conference in January the Combined Chiefs of Staff held a preliminary meeting in Malta during which they agreed, among other matters, on a statement of Eisenhower's intentions which was accepted unhesitatingly by the Supreme Commander. The final paragraph read:

> To deploy east of the Rhine, on the axis Frankfurt-Kassel, such forces, if adequate, as may be available after providing 35 divisions for the North and essential security elsewhere. The task of this force will be to draw enemy forces away from the North by capturing Frankfurt and advancing on Kassel.

In London it was therefore taken for granted that with the Rhine behind him Eisenhower would make his main final effort a thrust through northern Germany with Berlin as its objective: an assumption which came the more readily because it conformed with British hopes. These hopes were quickened by a message from Montgomery on 27 March that he had ordered his armies to advance 'with utmost speed and drive' to the Elbe. Astonishment was therefore followed by consternation when it was discovered in London next evening that the Combined Chiefs of Staff in Washington had received '*for information*' a copy of a personal message to Stalin, which Eisenhower had despatched that afternoon on his own initiative. Irritation at this unorthodox procedure was magnified by alarm at its contents. Alanbrooke was scathing. 'To start with, Eisenhower has no business to address Stalin direct, his communications should be through the Combined Chiefs of Staff; secondly, he produced a telegram which was unintelligible; and finally, what was implied in it appeared to be adrift and a change from all that had been agreed on.'

This, at least, was certain: the Supreme Commander had changed his mind. Nor, indeed, was the telegram obscure. It informed Stalin that Eisenhower's immediate intentions were to encircle the Ruhr; then to proceed *via* Erfurt-Leipzig-Dresden ('it is along this axis that I propose to make my main effort'); and finally to effect a junction with the Russians in the area Regensburg-Linz, 'thereby preventing the consolidation of German resistance in Redoubt in Southern Germany'. There was no reference to Berlin. To assist his advance and to avoid the danger of confusion when the American and Russian armies drew together, he reasonably requested from Stalin some information about the Marshal's own intentions. Eisenhower's new plan, it is now clear—though it was certainly not obvious in London at the time—was based on three considerations. The Ruhr was doomed, and resistance in northern and central Germany was thus enfeebled: the Russians were 40 miles from Berlin with some 1,000,000 men, while the Anglo–American armies were still seaparated from the capital by 200 miles broken by many lakes and rivers: and Eisenhower, like Marshall himself,* was misled by erroneous intelligence estimates that the Germans were creating a 'National Redoubt' in the mountain fastnesses of Bavaria and Austria.

Analysis of Churchill's behaviour over this episode is instructive. The prevalent image, of a man whose permanent instability was more or less controlled by the prudence of his advisers, is once again dispelled. The situation was explosive, and disruption of Anglo–American unity in the last weeks of the German war would have been both damaging and absurd. It was not, however, the Chiefs of Staff but Churchill whose statesmanship and common sense closed and healed the wound.

Alanbrooke was over-heated about Eisenhower's procedure. This subsidiary issue was reduced in its proportions as the Supreme Commander logically defended his action and Marshall supported the case for direct communication between SHAEF and Moscow: all, in the end, accepted the principle that in future such exchanges should be with the Russian General Staff rather than with the Generalissimo. As to Eisenhower's strategy, the C.I.G.S. made a mistake. Without referring to Churchill, he allowed a Chiefs of Staff signal to be sent to Washington which criticised the Kassel-Leipzig-Dresden thrust on the grounds that it ignored the need to clear the hinterland of the North Sea and the Baltic, to free Holland and Denmark and to make a start on Norway. 'We are forced to doubt whether there has been sufficient appreciation of issues which have a wider import than the destruction of the main enemy forces in Germany.'

This was unwise, since Eisenhower was soon able to demonstrate that he had all these considerations in mind and that they were comprised

* A signal from Marshall of 27 March drew attention to the need to 'prevent the formation of any organised resistance areas. The mountainous country in the south is considered to be a possibility for one of these'.

within the scope of his plan. He was puzzled by the British reaction, and infuriated by its tone. To Marshall he wrote:

> The Prime Minister and his Chiefs of Staff opposed ANVIL; they opposed my idea that the German should be destroyed west of the Rhine before we made our major effort across that river; and they insisted that the route leading northwestward from Frankfurt would involve us merely in slow, rough-country fighting. Now they apparently want me to turn aside on operations in which would be involved many thousands of troops before the German forces are fully defeated. I submit that these things are studied daily and hourly by me and my advisers and that we are animated by one single thought which is the early winning of the war.*

'May I point out,' he added, 'that Berlin itself is no longer a particularly important objective'.

Churchill, fortunately, was alert to the dangers. He rebuked the Chiefs of Staff, in a minute which is a model.

> ... of course, it is a good thing for the military points to be placed before the Combined Chiefs of Staff Committee. I hope, however, we shall realise that we have only a quarter of the forces invading Germany and that the situation has changed remarkably from the days of June ...
> ... It must be remembered that Eisenhower's credit with the [Joint Chiefs of Staff] stands very high. He may claim to have correctly estimated so far the resisting strength of the enemy and to have established by deeds:
> (a) The 'closing' of the Rhine along its whole length:
> (b) The power to make the double advance instead of staking all on the northern advance.
> ... It seems to me that the ... sentence ... about 'issues which have a wider import than the destruction of the main forces in Germany' is a very odd phrase to be used in a Staff communication. I should have thought it laid itself open to a charge of extreme unorthodoxy. ...

Most of these words, incidentally, were omitted by Churchill when he selectively quoted from his minute in his memoirs.†

The Prime Minister's own misgivings had a different base. Eisenhower had informed Montgomery on 28 March that so far as Berlin was concerned 'that place has become nothing but a geographical location; I have never been interested in those'. But, as Churchill remarked in his minute, 'the idea of neglecting Berlin and leaving it to the Russians to take at a later stage does not appear to me correct. ... The fall of Berlin might cause nearly all Germans to despair'. On the 30th, therefore, he telephoned

---

* See Ambrose, *The Supreme Commander*, p. 634 foll. This protest appears neither in Churchill's *The Second World War* nor in the British *Official History*.
† See *The Second World War*, Vol. VI, pp. 403-404.

Eisenhower for fuller details, and on 1 April sent a long, good-tempered message to Roosevelt, arguing the case for Berlin but carefully pointing out that 'I wish to place on record the complete confidence felt by His Majesty's Government in General Eisenhower, our pleasure that our armies are serving under his command, and our admiration of the great and shining qualities of character and personality which he has proved himself to possess in all the difficulties of handling an Allied Command'. The storm now blew itself out. Roosevelt was at death's door, and Marshall held the reins. Following the Prime Minister's line, the Chiefs of Staff saw that they must compromise, and Eisenhower's policy was endorsed with the face-saving formula that there had been no change of plan. On 5 April Churchill informed Roosevelt that 'I regard the matter as closed, and to prove my sincerity I will use one of my very few Latin quotations: *Amantium irae amoris integratio est*'.*

In his heart, though, the matter was never closed. The man who once told Montgomery how Marlborough 'sat on his horse and directed by word of mouth a battle on a five- or six-mile front, which ended in a day and settled the fortunes of great nations, sometimes for years or generations to come', found it difficult to shed the conviction that the Supreme Commander of the Allied Expeditionary Force had it in his power, by entering the German capital, to make a similar momentous stroke. But this was unrealistic. Stalin was determined to capture the city. When the Marshal received Eisenhower's signal of 28 March he immediately summoned Zhukov and Koniev to Moscow and ordered them to produce instant plans for seizing Berlin at the earliest possible moment. And in any case the long-considered blueprint for the post-war carve-up of Germany, ECLIPSE, which had been ratified at Yalta, laid down that Berlin would be split into zones each occupied by one of the Allied powers, but that the city itself would lie within the area to be controlled and dominated by Russia. The Russians were going to enter the city: they had in their hands a contractual guarantee assuring their permanent presence: they had the will and the force to maintain that presence, whereas after Unconditional Surrender it was certain that a swift Anglo–American demobilisation must follow. The stakes for which Churchill was playing were visionary.

In any case the climax was near at hand. At 1830 hours on 4 May 1945, in a tent on Lüneburg Heath, Montgomery signed the Instrument of

---

* The classicists in the U.S. War Department made a translation: 'Lovers' quarrels are a part of love.' The phrase from Terence actually means a renewing or restoring of love. This was more apt.

Surrender of all German forces in Holland, in Northwest Germany including all islands, and in Denmark. All hostilities ceased at midnight on 8 May. On the morning of 2 May unopposed landings were made on the seaward approaches to Rangoon, and by the evening of the 6th, a few hours before the Germans capitulated, advanced troops from the amphibious assault made contact with Slim's triumphant 14 Army. There only remained Hiroshima—and peace. Churchill was mainly pre-occupied, during these weeks, with the General Election from which he assumed that he would receive a renewed mandate. But the War Lord who had got so much right had made a final miscalculation. Slim came back to England and visited Chequers, to be inspected by the Prime Minister he had never met. 'Well', he said, 'there's one thing. My army won't be voting for you'.* Whatever their political affiliations—and war had denied to most of them an acquaintance with the politics of parties—the returning servicemen sought instinctively for a Premier who could bring to them at home the new world they had fought for abroad. But Churchill, who under Asquith had served in one of the great reforming administrations of the century, was now detached from the realities of civil government. And he was very tired.

Long before, on 12 January 1916, while he was in France and about to serve as a battalion commander in the trenches of the Western Front, his wife had written to him with the Gallipoli disaster in mind. 'Try not to brood too much. I would be so unhappy if your naturally open and unsuspicious nature became embittered. Patience is the only grace you need. If you are not killed, as sure as day follows night you will come into your own again.' He had survived: and now he had fulfilled what he had always known to be his destiny.

* Private communication from the Viscountess Slim.

The Sunlit Garden

'It would be a sad pity to shuffle or scramble along through one's playtime with golf and bridge, pottering, loitering, shifting from one heel to another, wondering what on earth to do—as perhaps is the fate of some unhappy beings—when all the while, if you only knew, there is close at hand a wonderful new world of thought and craft, a sunlit garden gleaming with light and colour of which you have the key in your waistcoat-pocket.'

Winston Churchill, *Painting as a Pastime*

' . . . ce n'est pas l'armée carthaginoise qui faisait trembler l'armée républicaine aux portes de Rome, mais Annibal; ce n'est pas l'armée macédoine qui a été sur l'Indus, mais Alexandre; ce n'est pas l'armée française qui a porté la guerre sur le Wéser et sur l'Inn, mais Turenne; ce n'est pas l'armée prussienne qui a défendu sept ans la Prusse contre les trois plus grands puissances de l'Europe, mais Frédéric le Grand.'

Napoleon

On 24 March 1938 Churchill addressed the Commons on the fall of Austria. 'For five years I have talked to the House on these matters—not with very great success. I have watched this famous island descending incontinently, fecklessly, the stairway which leads to a dark gulf. It is a fine broad stairway at the beginning, but after a bit the carpet ends. A little further on there are only flagstones, and a little farther on still these break beneath your feet. . . .' Exactly six months later the crack occurred. On the day Chamberlain flew to Munich Churchill and the 'Focus' group met at the Savoy Hotel to draft a telegram to the Prime Minister warning him against further concessions over Czechoslovakia. It was to be signed by Eden, Attlee, and others: but, Lady Violet Bonham-Carter recalled, 'The telegram was not dispatched and one by one our friends went out—defeated. Winston remained, sitting in his chair immobile, frozen, like a man of stone. I saw tears in his eyes. I could feel the iron entering his soul. His last attempt to salvage what was left of honour and good faith had failed'. This was his nadir: an unhappy being locked out from power. Yet a wonderful new world was close at hand in which he would soon be able to exercise his thought and craft, and the key was in his waistcoat-pocket.

The salient feature of Churchill as a War Lord is that he unashamedly enjoyed power—and war. Long before Austria and Munich, in 1927, Lord Keynes remarked that 'Mr Churchill does not dissemble his own delight in the intense experience of conducting warfare on the grand scale which those can enjoy who make the decisions', and in the 'fifties, when it was all over, the old man asked Lord Moran, 'Don't you feel lonely without a war? I do.' These passions were not reprehensible—not in a man who had to function as Stalin's ally and Hitler's adversary. But the mere mention of this alliance and this confrontation identifies the particular manner in which Churchill exercised power: its purpose was to restore and retain, not to conquer. From the moment he entered his sunlit garden in May 1940 his aim was never predatory, since his three essential objectives were at first, survival: then the restoration of the *status quo ante*; and finally the establishment of protective devices which might prevent aggression in a post-war world. Stalin grasped the Baltic states long before BARBAROSSA and extended his empire after Potsdam: Hitler's ambitions were boundless. But Churchill was a War Lord whose casting was not in the traditional mould.

It is true that he was intermittently ruthless. This was a strong vein in his nature, and the astonishing aspect of his behaviour during the Second World War is not that he sometimes gave way to it but that he mainly kept it under control. Here was a man who during the Irish Troubles was dissatisfied because not enough people were being hanged—the man who, at the time of intervention against the Bolsheviks after 1918, can be found in the Cabinet records advocating the despatch from France of un-expended stocks of poison-gas shells even though it was pointed out to him that innocent Russian civilians must suffer. There was a devil within. But *sub specie aeternitatis*, or merely by comparison with Hitler's nihilistic relish of death, what does his 'ruthlessness' amount to between 1940 and 1945? His motives in supporting the policy of area bombing were more military than vengeful—though ideas of retribution played their part, and until 1944 the military results were often miscalculated. As to Hiroshima, 'it must be remembered that the atomic bombs dropped in 1945 were weapons that were not so obviously on a different plane from those already used in the war. They were regarded primarily as super-explosives, as an economical means of delivering the equivalent of a massive quantity of T.N.T.'* 103,000 people were killed at Hiroshima and Nagasaki: by 'ordinary' bombing 43,000 died in Hamburg during one week of 1943, and well over 100,000 in Dresden, while in March 1945 alone 83,000 were

---

* Gowing, *op. cit.*, p. 381.

killed and 102,000 injured by the Americans' conventional incendiary attacks on Tokyo. The post-war controversy about the genetic consequences of the atom bomb is virtually irrelevant so far as Churchill is concerned. Even the scientists involved had only an imprecise awareness of the general effects of radiation, and of those scientists only one, so far as can be ascertained*—Sir James Chadwick—drew the Prime Minister's attention to its possible consequences. (Cherwell may also have done so.) In any case, apart from the determination of the United States to drop the bomb, *all* those responsible in the British administration gave their approval without hesitation. Churchill was not lying when he wrote that 'the historic fact remains, and must be judged in the after-time, that the decision whether or not to use the atomic bomb to compel the surrender of Japan was never even an issue'.†

His ruthlessness had a more restricted field. He was firm in decision—sometimes in situations where others were wavering about the right but difficult course, sometimes when he was being merely obstinate about wrong or trivial policies. He was downright in his treatment of subordinates: often correctly, but on occasion unfairly or even with prejudice. A close analysis suggests that he was justified in his actions over both Wavell and Auchinleck, but in his handling of them, and in his attitude towards them, he displayed a modicum of magnanimity and a maximum of misunderstanding. 'Between 1939 and 1943 there was not one Admiral in an important sea command—Forbes (Home Fleet), Cunningham (Mediterranean), Somerville (Force H at Gibraltar), Tovey (Home Fleet) and Harwood (Mediterranean)—whom Churchill, sometimes with Pound's support, did not attempt to have relieved.'‡ His treatment of Admiral North after the Dakar affair is impossible to condone. All this was an excessive application of the doctrine enunciated by the Marquis of Halifax in his *Character of a Trimmer*: 'State business is a cruel trade. Good nature is a bungler in it.'

Yet good nature was rarely lacking. Churchill civilised the process of high command. His way of running a war at times seemed intolerable, but it was tolerated. The men most close to him, most subjected to his imperious pressures, were those who loved him most. Late nights at Chequers, wild demands for instant examination of unpractical strategies, the braggadocio of his interpositions in the debates of the Chiefs of Staff, the condemnations of his commanders in the field, the offensive signals

---

* Private communication.
† *The Second World War*, Vol. VI, p. 553.
‡ Captain S. W. Roskill, *R.U.S.I. Journal*, December 1972, p. 50.

which Ismay or Alanbrooke had to ameliorate, the sheer impossibility of the man ... all was sweetened and made digestible by his irrepressible humanity. The artist Walter Sickert once observed of Degas that 'he had the good nature and high spirits that attend a sense of great power exercised in the proper channels, and therefore profoundly satisfied'. Churchill, exercising great power, and profoundly satisfied by the exercise, rarely lost his high spirits and good nature, so that he not only remained sane himself under stress but also erected a canopy of sanity under which his staff could retain their individuality and, in truth, enjoy their servitude. This was an extraordinary achievement. All Churchill's idiosyncrasies, his reduction of the way of life of a Minister of Defence and a Prime Minister to that of an uninhibited eighteenth-century aristocrat, the grotesque dressing-gowns, the afternoon sleep and the mandatory baths, the cigars, the brandy, the best of everything provided an *ambience* which, for all its extravaganza, was actually efficient. How different was this gay, bustling but human world from the cold recesses of the Kremlin or the clinical severity of Hitler's retreats! There is no doubt that Churchill could make those close to him afraid, but the fear he inspired was not of a merciless autocrat whose whims meant death: he could forgive, if he could not always forget, and after his rage had thundered periods of sun and calm would usually supervene. Nobody, certainly, was suddenly dismissed to the executioner.

When he entered the garden of power, however, he was determined to stay gardener-in-chief. He once observed of Gallipoli: 'My one fatal mistake was trying to achieve a great enterprise without having the plenary authority which could so easily have caused it to succeed.' 1940 gave him authority; the executive system evolved by himself and Ismay then supplied an efficient, flexible machine which (like another war-winning weapon, the Spitfire), proved so right in its basic design that only modification was necessary to keep it in action until 1945. But did he misuse such plenary power? One thing is certain. During the critical debate in the House of Commons in July 1942 he said of his Commanders-in-Chief in the field that his duty was 'not to worry them but to leave them to do their job ... it is absolutely impossible to fight battles from Westminster or Whitehall. The less one interferes the better ...': he was talking nonsense, and he knew it. Of course he interfered: consistently, intentionally and sometimes outrageously. He claimed that he never *overruled* the Chiefs of Staff, but this is a matter of terminology. During the conflict about Far Eastern strategy in 1944 which brought his Chiefs to the verge of resignation the documents, as quoted by Churchill himself, show him in the very process of over-ruling—and there were other occasions. In any case, the line is thin between a direct order and the Machiavellian method Churchill constantly employed of wearing his advisers down by non-stop argument, admonishment, oratory, emotional appeals, subterfuge and even vicious allegations of cowardice. How much, in the end, did it matter?

This is the price his country paid for a man who, so far as can be judged, saved it—aided by German incompetence—in 1940: the man who could look Stalin in the eye and never flinched before Hitler. If he was imperious, the trait was an imperative necessity, for Britain needed a War Lord. 'It is in my character', he once said to General Pile, 'that the nearer I get to the event, the more resolute I become'. Chamberlain, Halifax, Attlee, Eden— who of the alternatives to Churchill had this backbone of tempered steel? It is well to remember how many of those who began with doubts ended by believing him irreplaceable—Ismay himself, Normanbrook, sardonic P. J. Grigg, caustic Cadogan at the Foreign Office who started by writing in his diary 'Winston is useless.' All the men most responsible for the conduct of the war recognised his unique value, and never more so than when he drove himself towards mortal illness. When pneumonia struck, the Cabinet, the Chiefs of Staff and indeed the whole country learned the truth of a comment made by Gibbon about the Emperor Bajazet after an attack of gout stopped him from marching into Europe: 'an acrimonious humour falling on a single fibre of one man may prevent or suspend the misery of nations.'

In casting a balance sheet one sees much in his achievements that cannot be quantified: the maintenance of British morale, the successful fostering of the American connection, the avoidance of a premature Second Front. His errors glare. But when all is said, what Baudelaire wrote of Hogarth remains true of Churchill: 'his name fills the memory like a proverb'.

Bibliography

As indicated in the text, I have consulted *passim* the six volumes of Winston Churchill's *The Second World War*, and the relevant volumes in the various series of the British *Official History*. Other works consulted include:

ALEXANDER, Field Marshal the Earl, *The Alexander Memoirs*, Cassell, 1962

AMBROSE, Stephen E., *The Supreme Commander : the War Years of General Dwight D. Eisenhower*, Cassell, 1971

ASPINALL-OGLANDER, C., *Roger Keyes*, The Hogarth Press, 1951

ASTLEY, Joan Bright, *The Inner Circle*, Hutchinson, 1971

BARNETT, Corelli, *The Desert Generals*, Kimber, 1960; *The Collapse of British Power*, Eyre Methuen, 1972

BATESON, Charles, *The War With Japan*, Barrie and Rockliff, 1968

BLACKETT, P. M. S., *Studies of War*, Oliver and Boyd, 1962

BETHELL, Nicholas, *The War Hitler Won*, Allen Lane, The Penguin Press, 1972

BIRKENHEAD, the Earl of, *The Prof. in Two Worlds*, Collins, 1961

BONHAM CARTER, Violet, *Churchill as I knew him*, Eyre and Spottiswoode, 1965

BOYLE, Andrew, *Trenchard*, Collins, 1962

BRADLEY, General Omar, N., *A Soldier's Story*, Eyre and Spottiswoode, 1951

BRIGGS, Asa, *The War of Words: The History of Broadcasting in the United Kingdom, Vol III*, O.U.P., 1970

BRYANT, Sir Arthur, *The Turn of the Tide* (1957) and *Triumph in the West* (1959), Collins

BULLOCK, Alan, *Hitler*, Odhams Press, 1952; *The Ribbentrop Memoirs* (Ed.), Weidenfeld and Nicolson, 1954

BUTLER, Lord, *The Art of the Possible*, Hamish Hamilton, 1971

CALVOCORESSI, Peter and Wint, Guy, *Total War*, Allen Lane, The Penguin Press, 1972

CARELL, Paul, *Hitler's War on Russia*, Harrap, 1964

CARVER, Michael, *El Alamein*, Batsford, 1962

CHANDOS, Lord, *Memoirs*, The Bodley Head, 1962

CHAPMAN, Guy, *Why France Collapsed*, Cassell, 1968

CHURCHILL, Randolph S., *Winston S. Churchill: Youth* (1966) and *Young Statesman* (1967), Heinemann

CHURCHILL, Winston, *My Early Life*, Odhams, 1930; *The World Crisis 1911–1918*, Thornton Butterworth; *The Second World War*, six vols., Cassell

CIANO, Count, *Diary, 1939–1943*, Heinemann, 1946

CLARK, Alan, *Barbarossa*, Hutchinson, 1965

CLARK, Ronald W., *Tizard*, Methuen, 1965

COLVILLE, J. R., *Man of Valour: Field Marshal Lord Gort*, Collins, 1972

COLVIN, Ian, *The Chamberlain Cabinet*, Gollancz, 1971

CONNELL, John, *Auchinleck*, Cassell, 1964; *Wavell: Soldier and States-man* (1964) and, edited by Michael Roberts, *Supreme Commander* (1969), Collins

CUNNINGHAM, Admiral Lord, *A Sailor's Odyssey*, Hutchinson, 1951

DEAKIN, F. W. D., *The Embattled Mountain*, O.U.P., 1971; *The Brutal Friendship: Mussolini, Hitler and the Fall of Italian Fascism*, Weidenfeld and Nicolson, 1962

DE GAULLE, Gen. Charles, *War Memoirs. Unity 1942–1944*, Weidenfeld and Nicolson, 1959

DE GUINGAND, Maj.-Gen. Sir Francis, *Operation Victory* (1947) and *Generals at War* (1964), Hodder and Stoughton

DEUTSCHER, Isaac, *Stalin*, O.U.P., 1949

DILKES, David (Ed.), *The Diaries of Sir Alexander Cadogan*, Cassell, 1971

DIVINE, David, *The Blunted Sword*, Hutchinson, 1964

DOENITZ, Admiral, *Memoirs*, Weidenfeld and Nicolson, 1959

DOUGLAS, Marshal of the R.A.F. Lord, *Years of Command*, Collins, 1966

EADE, Charles (Ed.), *Churchill by his contemporaries*, Hutchinson, 1953

EISENHOWER, Gen. Dwight D., *Crusade in Europe*, Heinemann, 1949; *The Papers of Dwight Eisenhower: The War Years*, Johns Hopkins Press, 1970

EISENHOWER FOUNDATION, *D-Day: The Normandy Invasion in Retrospect*, The University Press of Kansas, 1971

EISENHOWER, John, S. D., *The Bitter Woods*, Putnam, 1969

FEILING, Keith, *The Life of Neville Chamberlain*, Macmillan, 1946

FEIS, Herbert, *Churchill, Roosevelt, Stalin*, O.U.P., 1957

FERGUSSON, Brigadier Sir Bernard, *The Watery Maze*, Collins, 1961

FLEMING, Peter, *Invasion 1940*, Hart-Davis, 1957

GILBERT, Martin, *Winston S. Churchill, 1914–1916*, Heinemann, 1971

GOWING, Margaret, *Britain and Atomic Energy 1939–1945*, Macmillan, 1964

GREENFIELD, Kent Roberts, *American Strategy in World War II*, Johns Hopkins Press, 1963; *Command Decisions* (Ed.), Methuen, 1960

GRETTON, Vice-Admiral Sir Peter, *Former Naval Person: Winston Churchill and the Royal Navy*, Cassell, 1968

GRIGG, P. J., *Prejudice and Judgement*, Cape, 1948

GUDERIAN, Gen. Heinz, *Panzer Leader*, Michael Joseph, 1952

HARRIS, Marshal of the R.A.F. Sir Arthur, *Bomber Offensive*, Collins, 1947

HOBBS, Joseph P., *Dear General: Eisenhower's wartime letters to Marshall*, The Johns Hopkins Press, 1971

HINSLEY, F. H., *Hitler's Strategy*, C.U.P., 1951

HORNE, Alistair, *To Lose a Battle*, Macmillan, 1969

HOWARD, Michael, *The Mediterranean Strategy in The Second World War*, Wiedenfeld and Nicolson, 1968

HYDE, H. Montgomery, *The Quiet Canadian*, Hamish Hamilton, 1962

IRVING, David, *The Destruction of Dresden* (1963), *The Mare's Nest* (1964), *The Virus House* (1967), William Kimber; *The Destruction of Convoy P.Q.17*, Cassell, 1968

ISMAY, Lord, *Memoirs*, Heinemann, 1960.

JACKSON, Lieut.-Gen. Sir William, *The Battle for Italy* (1967) and *Alexander of Tunis* (1971), Batsford.

JACOBSON, H. A., and Rohwer, J., *Decisive Battles of World War II*, Andre Deutsch, 1965

JENKINS, Roy, *Asquith*, Collins, 1964

KAHN, David, *The Codebreakers*, Weidenfeld and Nicolson, 1966

KENNAN, George F., *Russia and the West under Lenin and Stalin*, Hutchinson, 1961

KENNEDY, Maj.-Gen. Sir John, *The Business of War*, Hutchinson, 1957

KESSELRING, Field Marshal, *Memoirs*, Kimber, 1963

KING, Admiral E. J. and Whitehall, W. M., *Fleet Admiral King*, Eyre and Spottiswoode, 1953

KIPPENBERGER, Maj.-Gen. Sir Howard, *Infantry Brigadier*, O.U.P., 1949

LEASOR, James, and Maj.-Gen. Sir Leslie Hollis, *War at the Top*, Michael Joseph, 1959.

LEE, Gen. Raymond E., *The London Observer*, Hutchinson, 1972

L'ETANG, Hugh, *The Pathology of Leadership*, Heinemann, 1969

LEWIN, Ronald, *Rommel as Military Commander* (1968) and *Montgomery as Military Commander* (1970), Batsford

LIDDELL HART, Sir Basil, *The Other Side of the Hill* (1951), *The Tanks* (1959), *Memoirs* (1965), *History of The Second World War* (1970), Cassell

MACDONALD, Charles B., *The Mighty Endeavour: American Armed Forces in the European Theater in World War II*, O.U.P., 1969

MACINTYRE, Donald, *The Naval War against Hitler*, Batsford, 1971

MACKSEY, Kenneth, *Armoured Crusader* (1967) and *Crucible of Power* (1969), Hutchinson

McLACHLAN, Donald, *Room 39. Naval Intelligence in Action 1939-1945*, Weidenfeld and Nicolson, 1968

MACMILLAN, Harold, *The Blast of War 1939-1945*, Macmillan, 1967

MAISKY, Ivan, *Memoirs of a Soviet Ambassador: The War 1939-1945*, Hutchinson, 1967

MALLABY, Sir George, *From My Level*, Hutchinson, 1965

MARDER, Arthur, *Winston is back: Churchill at the Admiralty*, Longman, 1972

MARTEL, Lieut.-Gen. Sir Giffard, *An Outspoken Soldier*, Sifton Praed, 1949

MASTERMAN, J. M., *The Double-Cross System*, Yale University Press, 1972

MENZIES, Sir Robert, *Afternoon Light*, Cassell Australia Ltd., 1967

MELLENTHIN, Maj.-Gen. von, *Panzer Battles 1939-1945*, Cassell, 1955

MONTGOMERY, Field Marshal The Viscount, *Normandy to the Baltic* (1946) and *El Alamein to the River Sangro* (1948), Hutchinson; *Memoirs*, Collins, 1948

MORAN, Lord, *The Struggle for Survival*, Constable, 1966

MORGAN, Lieut.-Gen. Sir Frederick, *Overture to Overlord* (1950) and *Peace and War* (1961), Hodder and Stoughton

NICOLSON, Sir Harold, *Diaries and Letters*, 1930-1939 and 1939-1945, Collins

NICOLSON, Nigel, *Alex*, Weidenfeld and Nicolson, 1973

NOBECOURT, Jacques, *Hitler's Last Gamble*, Chatto and Windus, 1967

PATTON, Gen. George S., *War as I saw It*, W. H. Allen, 1950

PILE, Gen. Sir Frederick, *Ack-Ack*, Harrap, 1949

POGUE, Forrest C., *George Marshall. Ordeal and Hope 1939-1942*, Mac-Gibbon & Kee, 1968

PRICE, Alfred, *Instruments of Darkness*, Kimber, 1967

RHODES JAMES, Robert, *Gallipoli*, Batsford, 1965; *Chips: The diaries of Sir Henry Channon* (Ed.), Weidenfeld and Nicolson, 1967; *Churchill: a study in failure*, Weidenfeld and Nicolson, 1970

ROMMEL, Erwin, *The Rommel Papers* (Ed., B. H. Liddell Hart), Collins, 1953

ROSKILL, S. W., *Hankey, Man of Secrets 1919–1931*, Collins, 1972

RYAN, Cornelius, *The Last Battle*, Collins, 1966

SEATON, Albert, *The Russo–German War 1941–1945*, Arthur Barker, 1971

SHEPPERD, G. A., *The Italian Campaign, 1943–45*, Arthur Barker, 1968

SHERWOOD, Robert, *The White House Papers of Harry L. Hopkins*, Eyre and Spottiswoode, 1948

SIXSMITH, E. K. G., *Eisenhower as Military Commander*, Batsford, 1973

SLIM, Field Marshal the Viscount, *Defeat into Victory*, Cassell, 1956

SLESSOR, Marshal of the R.A.F. Sir John, *The Central Blue*, Cassell, 1956

SPEARS, Maj.-Gen. Sir Edward, *Assignment to Catastrophe*, Heinemann, 1954

SPEER, Albert, *Inside the Third Reich*, Weidenfeld and Nicolson, 1970

STRAWSON, Maj.-Gen. John, *Hitler as Military Commander* (1971) and *The Battle for the Ardennes* (1972), Batsford.

STRONG, Maj.-Gen. Sir Kenneth, *Intelligence at the Top* (1966) and *Men of Intelligence* (1970), Cassel-Giniger

SWEET-ESCOTT, Bickham, *Baker Street Irregular*, Methuen, 1965

SYKES, Christopher, *Orde Wingate*, Collins, 1959

TAYLOR, A. J. P., *The Origins of the Second World War*, Hamish Hamilton, 1963; *English History, 1914–1945*, O.U.P., 1965; *Beaverbrook*, Hamish Hamilton, 1972

TEDDER, Marshal of the R.A.F. Lord, *With Prejudice*, Cassell, 1966

THOMPSON, R. W., *The Yankee Marlborough*, Allen & Unwin, 1963

TREVOR-ROPER, H. R. (Ed.), *Hitler's Table Talk*, Weidenfeld and Nicolson, 1953

VERRIER, Anthony, *The Bomber Offensive*, Batsford, 1968

WARNER, Oliver, *Admiral of the Fleet: The Life of Sir Charles Lambe*, Sidgwick & Jackson, 1969

WATSON-WATT, Sir Robert, *Three Steps to Victory*, Odhams, 1957

WESTPHAL, Gen. Siegfried, *The German Army in the West*, Cassell, 1951

WHEELER-BENNETT, Sir John, *The Nemesis of Power*, Macmillan, 1953; *The Semblance of Peace* (with Antony Nicholls), Macmillan, 1972; *Action this day: Working with Churchill* (Ed.), Macmillan, 1968

WILMOT, Chester, *The Struggle for Europe*, Collins, 1952

WINGATE, Sir Ronald, *Lord Ismay*, Hutchinson, 1970

WOOD, Derek and Dempster, Derek, *The Narrow Margin: The Battle of Britain and the rise of Air Power, 1930–1940*, Hutchinson, 1961

WRIGHT, Robert, *Dowding and the Battle of Britain*, Macdonald, 1969

Index